WEAVING POLITICAL TIME IN MOROCCO

/ AFRICAN
/ ARGUMENTS

African Arguments is a series of short books about contemporary Africa and the critical issues and debates surrounding the continent. The books are scholarly and engaged, substantive and topical. They focus on questions of justice, rights and citizenship; politics, protests and revolutions; the environment, land, oil and other resources; health and disease; economy, growth, aid, taxation, debt and capital flight; and both Africa's international relations and country case studies.

Managing Editor, Stephanie Kitchen

Series editors

Adam Branch
Eyob Balcha Gebremariam
Ebenezer Obadare
Portia Roelofs
Jon Schubert
Nicholas Westcott
Nanjala Nyabola

BÉATRICE HIBOU & MOHAMED TOZY
(*Translated by* Katharine Throssell)

Weaving Political Time in Morocco

The Imaginary of the State in the Neoliberal Age

OXFORD
UNIVERSITY PRESS

IAI International African Institute

OXFORD
UNIVERSITY PRESS

Oxford University Press is a department of the
University of Oxford. It furthers the University's objective
of excellence in research, scholarship, and education
by publishing worldwide.

Oxford   New York

Auckland   Cape Town   Dar es Salaam   Hong Kong   Karachi
Kuala Lumpur   Madrid   Melbourne   Mexico City   Nairobi
New Delhi   Shanghai   Taipei   Toronto

With offices in

Argentina   Austria   Brazil   Chile   Czech Republic   France   Greece
Guatemala   Hungary   Italy   Japan   Poland   Portugal   Singapore
South Korea   Switzerland   Thailand   Turkey   Ukraine   Vietnam

Oxford is a registered trade mark of Oxford University Press
in the UK and certain other countries.

Published in the United States of America by
Oxford University Press
198 Madison Avenue, New York, NY 10016

Copyright © Béatrice Hibou & Mohamed Tozy 2025

All rights reserved. No part of this publication may be reproduced,
stored in a retrieval system, or transmitted, in any form or by any means,
without the prior permission in writing of Oxford University Press,
or as expressly permitted by law, by license, or under terms agreed with
the appropriate reproduction rights organization. Inquiries concerning
reproduction outside the scope of the above should be sent to the
Rights Department, Oxford University Press, at the address above.

You must not circulate this work in any other form
and you must impose this same condition on any acquirer.

Library of Congress Cataloging-in-Publication Data is available
Béatrice Hibou & Mohamed Tozy
Weaving Political Time in Morocco: The Imaginary of the State in the
Neoliberal Age.
ISBN: 9780197816684

Printed in the United Kingdom on acid-free paper

To Latifa

CONTENTS

Acknowledgements	ix
List of Acronyms	xi
Preface to the English Edition	xv
Introduction	1
Prolegomenon: The Moroccan State over Time	21

PART ONE
THE FOUNDATIONS OF POWER

1. Representation	61
2. Violence	87

PART TWO
GOVERNING THE NATION

3. Shifting Spaces of Territorialisation	119
4. Administrating by Consensus (*Einverständnis*)	139

PART THREE
THE NEOLIBERAL ART OF GOVERNING
AFFINITIES WITH IMPERIALISM

5. Indirect Government	169
6. The Bearers of Neoliberalism	191

CONTENTS

Conclusion	219
Glossary	235
Notes	241
References	281
Index	305

ACKNOWLEDGEMENTS

The impossible is impossible. The impossible would be to thank all those without whom the writing of this book would not have been possible at the end of some 30 years of field research, including numerous interviews with unknown or very well-known people, perhaps too well-known to want to be quoted. The weaving of time in a book is like that of a kingdom. The moments of research intermingle and sometimes blur, but the memory and gratitude towards all those who helped us remain vivid and precise. They may or may not recognise themselves in the pages that follow, but we can't express our gratitude enough: 304 pages of smiles and winks ...

But our debt to some of them is too great to remain silent: Fariba Adelkhah, Jean-François Bayart, Mounia Ben Brahim, Ahmed Bendella, Ikram Benmadani, Irene Bono, Ayşe Buğra, Massimo Cuono, Abdeslam Dahman Saidi, Jean-Pierre Grossein, Nadia Hachimi Alaoui, Saïd Hanchane, Aziz Iraki, Martine Jouneau, Adriana Kemp, Abderrahman Lakhsassi, Jean Leca, Mohamed Mahdi, Badiha Nahhass, Dorian Ryser, Boris Samuel, Abdelahad Sebti, Mohamed Souafi, Mohamed Tamim and Latifa Wahbi, in a variety of ways, are the real inspiration behind this book, which has escaped them and for which they cannot be held responsible. Our analyses and errors are our own responsibility.

This long-term research was supported by our institutions: the Ceri at Sciences Po Paris, the CM2S at Hassan II University in Casablanca, the Cherpa at Sciences Po Aix-en-Provence, the Cresc

ACKNOWLEDGEMENTS

at the School of Governance and Economics in Rabat and two research associations: Targa and Fasopo. We are honoured by their patience and support.

Finally, our work would have been in vain if Judith Burko and Sylvie Tailland had not held our hand and if the Recherches Internationales collection and Éditions Karthala had not agreed to accept our extensive manuscript. We are all the more grateful to Xavier Audrain because, over the last few years, his publishing house has published several works on Morocco based on research carried out by Fasopo and Cresc and has produced a reference catalogue for people interested in the area.

For the English version, we would like to thank Stephanie Kitchen of the IAI for her constant support. We are also extremely grateful to Katharine Throssell, our translator, for her competence, her rigour and her acute analytical skills, which made a very Franco-Moroccan way of thinking perfectly clear in English.

LIST OF ACRONYMS

ANHI: Agence nationale de lutte contre l'habitat insalubre—National Agency for fighting against insalubrious housing

BNPJ: Brigade nationale de la police judiciaire—National Brigade of Judicial Police

CCDH: Conseil consultatif des droits de l'Homme—Consultative Council on Human Rights

CDG: Caisse de dépôt et de gestion—Deposit and Management Fund

CGEM: Confédération générale des entreprises du Maroc—General Confederation of Moroccan Enterprises

CGI: Compagnie générale immobilière—General Real Estate Company

CGT: Confédération générale du travail (France)—General Confederation of Labour (France)

CIFIE: Commission indépendante pour la finance islamique en Europe—Independent Committee for Islamic Finance in Europe

CNSS: Caisse nationale de sécurité sociale—National Social Security Fund

COS: Conseil des œuvres sociales—Social Works Council

xi

LIST OF ACRONYMS

COSEF: Commission spéciale éducation-formation—Special Commission on Education and Training

ERAC: Établissements régionaux d'aménagement et de construction—Regional bodies for planning and construction

EU: European Union

FAO: Food and Agriculture Organization

ICJ: International Court of Justice

ICRC: International Committee of the Red Cross

IER: Instance équité et réconciliation—Equity and Reconciliation Commission

IFAD: International Fund for Agricultural Development

IGAT: Inspection générale de l'aménagement du territoire—General Inspector of Territorial Planning

IGF: Inspection générale des finances—General Inspector of Finances

INDH: Initiative nationale pour le développement humain—National Initiative for Human Development

MASEN: Moroccan Agency for Sustainable Energy

MP: Mouvement populaire—Popular Movement

NDM: New Development Model

NPM: New Public Management

OAU: Organisation of African Unity

OCE: Office de commercialisation des exportations—Board for Commercialising Exports

OCP: Office chérifien des phosphates—Sharifian Phosphate Office

OECD: Organisation for Economic Co-operation and Development

OGD: Observatoire géopolitique des drogues—Geopolitical Observatory on Drugs

LIST OF ACRONYMS

ONCF: Office national des chemins de fer—National Railways Office

ONE: Office national de l'électricité—National Electricity Board

ONEE: Office national de l'électricité et de l'eau potable—National Electricity and Drinking Water Board

PAGER: Programme d'approvisionnement groupé en eau potable des populations rurales—Collective Rural Drinking Water Supply Programme

PCM: Parti communiste marocain—Moroccan Communist Party

PDI: Parti démocratique de l'indépendance—Democratic Independence Party

PERG: Programme d'électrification rurale global—Global Rural Electrification Programme

PJD: Parti de la justice et du développement—Justice and Development Party

PLS: Parti de la libération et socialisme (ex-PCM)—Party of Liberation and Socialism (ex-PCM)

PNCRR: Programme national de construction des routes rurales—National Programme for Rural Roads

PPS: Parti du progrès et socialisme (ex-PLS, ex-PCM)—Party of Progress and Socialism (ex-PLS, ex-PCM)

RNI: Rassemblement national des indépendants—National Rally of Independents

SCET: Société centrale pour l'équipement du territoire—Central Company for Regional Amenities

SNESUP: Syndicat national de l'enseignement supérieur—National Union of Higher Education

SONADAC: Société nationale d'aménagement communal—National Municipal Development Company

TMSA: Tanger Med Special Agency

LIST OF ACRONYMS

UGTM: Union générale des travailleurs du Maroc—General Union of Moroccan Workers

UMT: Union marocaine du travail—Moroccan Labour Union

UNFP: Union nationale des forces populaires—National Union of Popular Forces

USFP: Union socialiste des forces populaires—Socialist Union of Popular Forces

WHO: World Health Organization

PREFACE TO THE ENGLISH EDITION

This book was originally published in 2020 in French, with the title *Tisser le temps politique: Imaginaire de l'Etat à l'ère néolibérale*. Unfortunately, due to editorial constraints, the English version has been abridged, and readers are encouraged to consult the French version for a full presentation of our analysis.[1] However, the English translation has also provided the opportunity, four years after the original publication, to incorporate comments made by the two reviewers solicited by the International African Institute and to respond to questions or misunderstandings the book encountered when it was originally launched in France, Italy and Morocco, and to take on board the most relevant remarks. On a fundamental level, the English book is the same as the French, but we hope to have clarified aspects that some may have seen as ambiguities or lacunae, or considered frustrating.

This book is born from an intellectual collaboration over more than 20 years. Writing a book *à deux* is not the same as writing one alone. That might seem obvious, but it is a genuine choice, a conscious position we have adopted, fuelled by an epistemological goal. It involves preparing the "field", commenting on and interpreting it, mutually proposing new problem questions, debating the choice of concepts, reading key texts together that are important for our reflection and so forth. All of this collaborative work has had a profound impact on our intellectual trajectory and is part of what makes this work so original in comparison with our previous studies. Conducting this research together has allowed us to

xv

PREFACE TO THE ENGLISH EDITION

satisfy a dual objective that has always driven both of us: a search for discomfort and a refusal of easy explanations. This has helped us to remain vigilant and neutralise both the effect of naivety, resulting from exteriority and distance, and the effect of false evidence that is a result of over-familiarity. As a result, we have not merely shared the fieldwork. We have created something original from the intersection of two different intellectual trajectories, resulting from our different training but also our prior socialisation and experiences.

This fieldwork draws on a plurality of ways of "observing". Given that we have focused on following the transformations of actors in situ, interviews were an integral part of our approach. They took place over the long term, were repeated and were reiterated several times, sometimes over a period of 20 years. They were not simply moments of listening, but a perpetual and rigorous exchange. Although we both conducted the fieldwork, we only rarely conducted interviews together. Instead, conscious of our respective positions as *insider* and *outsider* and our different competences, we conducted the interviews separately, sometimes with the same people, more often with different ones. Indeed, certain respondents are impossible for a foreigner to interview; others are inaccessible to a local. However, for each interview, both the preparation and transcription were done together, and each interview was accompanied with a description of the research situation and the subjective impressions of the interviewer. This strategy allowed us to overcome these constraints and increase the number of interviews, but above all to have as broad a panel as possible of justifications, reasonings and motivations, to understand the postures, behaviour and self-presentations in all their diversity, to avoid the pitfalls of self-censorship, self-evidence or—inversely—exoticism.

However, this observation, and socialising with interviewees, helped to enrich different forms of understanding, as discussed by Weber.[2] Concrete participation occurred in the realisation of different projects (such as ethno-lineage cooperatives, *coopératives ethno-lignagères*), in the conceptualisation of frameworks (such as the local development plans) in assessment operations (such as the

xvi

PREFACE TO THE ENGLISH EDITION

ONE rural electricity project) and presence in commissions (Commission for the Revision of the Constitution and the Special Commission on a New Development Model). But this participation was not always formalised as such. Sometimes it took the form of socialising with interviewees, always maintaining a distance, which allowed us to present our research questions differently, either explicitly or, more often, implicitly. Nor was this the responsibility of the "recognised local" researcher, who had experienced a process of distancing through his experience as a university professor in France. Indeed, Morocco seemed not quite so exceptional in light of his observations of the functioning of French society and imperial modes of government in France. Conversely, after a certain number of years, the "foreigner" progressively integrated into Moroccan social circles and even into the Moroccan university system, where she had a challenging professional experience that provided an intimate grasp of such intangible elements as the different apprehension of time, the weight of structuration based on orders, the importance of codes, postures and what goes unsaid in power relations, or the contained violence of authority. These experiences were not only a means of personally experiencing what the actors studied here also live through, but of grasping the ways of reasoning, the categories mobilised and the values behind both arguments and practices. Working on "meaning", which is always evasive by nature, also means observing everyday experiences that are not necessarily expressed verbally, but which can be perceived in attitudes, gazes, postures, physical interactions and so forth.[3] Whether we were prepared for this or not, we integrated these informal situations, of life, of moments of socialisation, in order to see our reflections progress—festivities and funerals, haggling in the *souk*, purchases at the grocer, chats with neighbours, exchanges between colleagues and reunions among old friends. In these moments of participation, observation and socialising, the fact that there were two of us allowed us to take a systematic approach to the objectification of lived experience, which is essential for interpretative sociology.

Similarly, archival research like the "exegesis" of texts, whether scientific, journalistic or even from social media, was less a means

xvii

PREFACE TO THE ENGLISH EDITION

of "reconstructing" phenomena for us than it was a "clue-based paradigm"[4] that fed into our interviews and helped us understand the complexity of the facts we were studying. It helped us to understand that these facts only acquired meaning in the interaction with our interviewees—and in the interaction among ourselves, in a small group of friends, or in dialoguing with studies exploring similar questions in different fieldwork, or conversely exploring different issues that were inspiring for our own research.

INTRODUCTION

On 2 March 2020, a Moroccan national on his way back from Italy tested positive for Covid-19 three months after China announced the first confirmed case of the virus in Wuhan. In the week between 9 and 15 March, Morocco implemented drastic and unexpected measures to contain the spread of the virus. Maritime connections with Spain and France were cut; flights to numerous countries were suspended; crèches, primary schools, high schools and universities, as well as cafés, restaurants and sports fields were all closed indefinitely. On 12 March, the Minister for Habous and Islamic Affairs issued a statement outlining the protective measures for mosques, encouraging those at risk and those with low immunity to pray at home, reducing the duration of sermons and classes, closing toilets and removing articles used for ablutions, removing prayer garments ordinarily available for women to borrow and asking attendees to greet each other without touching. Eventually, on 16 March, the decision was made to close all places of worship. This was a delicate and unprecedented decision, which required a certain number of precautions—the King, the "Commander of the Faithful" and the only person competent on this question, had to bring the question before the High Council of the Ulema. On 19 March, the Interior Minister declared a state of health emergency and brought in measures to limit movement within Morocco, to be applied from 20 March at 6pm until further notice. On 22 March, a decree-law was passed by the government formalising the regulations in place since 9 March.

1

WEAVING POLITICAL TIME IN MOROCCO

These rapidly implemented measures were widely applauded at the international level. They may be interpreted as the mark of a state that is quick to react, well organised, efficient and responsible for its population, and which has strong decisive leaders operating in coherence with the principles of the modern state. Yet things are not quite that simple. This capacity to efficiently manage a health emergency and cope with an unpredictable situation is accompanied by very limited performance in the application of public policies, particularly in health and education, as can be seen in the country's poor human development indicators. This is a paradox that needs clarification, as could be seen in the Interior Minister's statement announcing the health emergency. Indeed, the ministry offloaded responsibility for the implementation of the most important decisions regarding the situation—the control of citizens' movements and the collection of information needed for quarantining the sick—onto the *muqaddam*, a figure straight from the Sharifian empire. The first part of the minister's statement was similar to those made by other states on the frontline of the pandemic, specifying that "the state health emergency does not mean the economy comes to a halt, but rather the implementation of exceptional measures that require limiting movement of citizens". However, the application of these measures was somewhat different because it introduced a new temporality. The declaration stated that "any travel outside of one's home is permitted only after obtaining an official document from the agents and auxiliaries of authority", and the authority in question here is the *muqaddam*. This subaltern figure is the public official closest to the population, the lowest-level incarnation of the state structure. The *muqaddam* is an ambivalent figure in political imaginary and in everyday practices, representing both local everyday services and the arbitrary nature of power. Its role and responsibilities are vague, but the *muqaddam* is required to know everything that happens on the local level and ensure order and security there. This figure is omnipresent but operates at the limits of informality. In fact, the *muqaddam* is not officially integrated into public service like other officials are.

To understand the specificity of these figures and their role in the management of the health crisis, we shadowed one of them

INTRODUCTION

over the first days of the health emergency. Youssef was responsible for a constituency of several tens of thousands of people, all of whom, on 20 March, needed the attestation that he was supposed to provide. But on this first day of confinement, the *muqaddam* had not received his instructions, he had not received the forms to be filled out for the attestation and he had to print them off himself and distribute them to "his" population. Armed only with his official stamp and his red Peugeot 103 scooter, he was so swamped by demands in one working-class neighbourhood of his constituency that he panicked and shut off his telephone (one of his main work tools) while he tried to find a solution. He disappeared that Saturday. By Sunday, the ministry had provided printed authorisations, and from then on, he worked from dawn until dusk on the main square, sitting at a little desk under a parasol lent by some locals, with the residents filing past to obtain this golden ticket that would allow them freedom of movement. Those who knew how to read and write filled out the forms for those who could not (there being many illiterate residents in these working-class neighbourhoods) and the *muqaddam* stamped them. He worked 16 hours a day for three whole days without stopping, except to have a quick meal provided by the residents of the neighbourhood. And eventually, everyone had their attestation.

What should we make of this configuration in which the state delegates such an essential role (the freedom or restriction of movement and lockdown conditions for millions of people) to a subaltern figure that is not really part of the administration? How can we characterise a state that appears efficient, quick to react, organised and yet can be described as "old-fashioned" in its everyday management of the pandemic? What should we make of the fact that it is ready to take necessary risks such as closing borders, that its decisions are in line with WHO recommendations and careful to respect legal frameworks, but on the ground, it seems almost "archaic"? How should we understand the fact that technocrats, trained in the most modern governmental techniques, often at the best European or American universities (promoting new public management, sophisticated financial planning and, in these pandemic-driven times, distance learning, children's educational television, and so forth) are those who entrust the regulation of the movement of the population to this figure from a bygone age? How is it that the Moroccan people find this "normal" and "naturally" take it upon themselves to provide the organisation it requires (the table, the chair, the parasol and even the *muqaddam*'s meals)?

Thinking differently about the state

Analyses of the Moroccan state have often been mired in exoticism or exceptionalism, with a vision of the system as archaic and dysfunctional. To move away from such an approach, it is important to think about the state in non-normative terms, without any preconceived judgements as to what a modern state ought to be. To do this, it seemed best to use a notion that goes beyond the state as a simple institution or system of institutions, beyond an entity whose key claim is to the monopoly on the legitimate use of force as canonically defined in political science textbooks. Unfortunately, this definition is often presented as being simply the "legitimate use of force", overlooking the essential nuance that lies in the idea of the *claim* to the legitimate use of force. Worse still, it is systematically presented as being Max Weber's key definition, as though it were a general theory and not an expression linked to a specific geographical and historical situation. Yet Weber proposed other, more complex definitions, such as this one:

> ... an infinite number of diffuse and discrete human actions and acts of acquiescence, and of relationships regulated in practice and legally, of which some are unique, while others recur regularly; and all [this] is held together by an idea, namely, the belief in norms and relations of authority of some human beings over others, which are actually or should be valid. This belief is found in manifold nuances in the mind of each individual, partly intellectually well thought-out, partly vaguely felt, [and] partly passively accepted. (If these individuals themselves actually had a clear *conception* of this "idea" as such, they would have no need of the "general theory of the state" which sets itself the task of articulating it.)[1]

Over the course of these pages, we will revisit certain aspects of this definition, but it immediately introduces what will be one of

INTRODUCTION

the originalities of this book, taking into account both the diversity of forms of action—including in terms of non-action or a laissez-faire approach—and a belief in norms that, through constant adjustment of different kinds, enable domination.

Taking the state as the starting point for a reflection on power and domination in Morocco means coming up against two well-established traditions. It also means tracing a path for analysis away from some of the major concepts that underline these traditions, which we consider less relevant in capturing the subtleties, incoherencies and variabilities in the different political configurations of the kingdom.

The first of these traditions considers the state from an evolutionist perspective, focusing on the type of political regime, according to the level of differentiation and complexification of institutions and predispositions for adopting transition scenarios. Moving away from this means thinking outside of the concept of authoritarianism without necessarily denying the authoritarian aspects of power,[2] or thinking outside the concept of democracy without neglecting the dynamics driven by subaltern groups or the more or less institutionalised modalities for seeking compromise.[3] It also means taking changes seriously, without making assumptions about their direction or their meaning; without falling into the trap that Peter Brown calls the "ideology of change".[4] This is why this research draws primarily on Weber, who provides a magnificent critique of the idea of a linear and irreversible development of capitalism or of political systems.

The second tradition, which extends the heritage of orientalism while also criticising it, and which some have called "orientalism in reverse,"[5] produces other ways of essentialising an ideal Muslim state. Moving away from this means thinking outside theories of the patriarchy[6] without neglecting the importance of marriage strategies or how tribes[7] are used in elections or in development strategies and participation practices. It means thinking outside theorisations of servility due to relations between master and disciples in the brotherhood tradition[8] without obscuring the marginal presence of these positions of servility on both a domestic and a political level. Finally, it means thinking outside the Islamic theory

WEAVING POLITICAL TIME IN MOROCCO

of power,[9] again without denying the role religion plays in how it is exercised and legitimised. Thus, we refer to the principle of usurped power in Islamic political theory to renew approaches to obedience and disobedience. This idea of usurpation stems from the monotheistic logic of the sovereign deity who saturates the space of power, but it also stems from the idealised narrative of the shift from the experience of the four "well-guided" Caliphs to the hereditary royalty established by the founder of the Umayyad dynasty. Man may only aspire to the status of a curate, suspected by his very nature of being tempted to usurp the place of God.

Distancing itself from these traditional approaches, this research is driven by three conscious choices: a decision to reason in terms of ideal types; to take an alternative approach to contemporary scholarship on empire; and to make the imaginary central and consider it the matrix in which the violence of domination is naturalised and legitimised.

Thinking with ideal types

Using ideal types as a basis for analysis does not mean attempting to identify a figure that would reflect reality as a whole at a given moment of time—in this case, in the contemporary period we frequently refer to as neoliberal. Rather, it highlights the distinctive traits of social practices in their "sharpest" and most "consistent" features based on "the concretely given" components such as "historical reality presents them to us".[10] In other words, the ideal-type method is a useful intellectual construct for analysis, which contributes to the complexification of the description of government practices, helping to distance ourselves from often implicit normative appraisals.

If we follow Weber, the ideal-type method does not mean forcing the infinite variety of historical reality into schemas[11] just as it does not allow us to grasp a hypothetical essence of a particular form of the state. An ideal type is neither a representation nor a schematisation of reality; it is an intellectual construct that enables thought. It applies to all kinds of concrete reality but also, and above all, to any kind of intellectual problem.[12] The one that con-

INTRODUCTION

cerns us here—understanding the transformations of the state and forms of government—has led us to construct two ideal types that are specific to our analysis. We call these two types "Empire" and "Nation-state". The former ideal type combines the following elements: a lack of aspiration to control society as a whole and the whole of a territory and a propensity to prioritise adaptation and compromise; an ignorance of any connection between legitimacy and having the monopoly on power, including on violence; itinerancy; a desire to govern at least cost by increasing the forms of intervention by intermediation and translation; an adaptation to the pluralism of legal regimes, ethnic groups, nations and religious groups and an ability to manage discontinuities, including temporal and territorial; large-scale investment in the production and control of certain kinds of information and a gamble on people rather than institutions or structures. By contrast, the second ideal type, the Nation-state, is based on: principles of unity and continuity; voluntarism and domestication; uniformisation and abstract equality; investment in systematic and homogenising information; and a preference for averages and the law of large numbers and the valorisation of transformative action.

These two types were not pre-constructed; they emerged little by little over the course of our undoubtedly very personal reading of historical experiences in Morocco and thus through the study of archives, correspondence, chronicles and biographies. These are historical narratives as much, if not more, than work by historians, and they will all be discussed in the Prolegomenon. These ethnographic texts provided access to concrete facts and situations that allowed us to develop the ideal types and begin to interpret the diversity of forms of government, particularly from the eighteenth and especially nineteenth centuries. These two types were also constructed in response to our particular desire to understand the transformations in ways of governing. In other words, we not only take into account institutions and ideologies, formal procedures and explicit protocols, but also the constant inventing and staging of everyday practices as well as the subjectifying of public servants and politicians, including the most subaltern among them, along with all the other actors who contribute to the social order and to

7

WEAVING POLITICAL TIME IN MOROCCO

the government of people, goods and territories. This explains why we do not use the ideal types Weber proposed (which are often employed to describe the use of power in Morocco): patrimonialism, sultanism or charisma.[13] These emphasise "features" such as clientelism and allegiance, confusion between public and private or the arbitrary and personal power of the prince.[14] These "features", although they may exist, do not appear sufficient, nor indeed the most relevant, in characterising government in Morocco. This also explains why our Empire type awards little importance to certain characteristics valued by empires that have existed historically (such as the propensity for expansion or cosmopolitanism), while our Nation-state type is undoubtedly very French.[15] Perhaps this is because we are ourselves deeply imbued with this culture, but it is probably also because the colonisation of Morocco was primarily French, and the French model of the nation-state was hegemonic when the modern Moroccan state was formed, and this influence continued after independence, perpetuated by elites that are often educated in France.

The research therefore consciously adopts this deductive approach in the tradition of Weber. Of course, we could have also mobilised concepts of sovereignty and biopolitics proposed by Michel Foucault,[16] an author who inspired our work in other ways. Moreover, Foucault—unlike many of his exegetes—did not consider these two modes of government to be stages in a linear evolution, but possibilities and techniques through which individuals are guided and with which their bodies are invested and their behaviour shaped. However, it seemed more important to us to begin with the concrete reality provided by the archives and interviews, as well as the density of the appropriation of these techniques by the actual actors, out of respect for our fieldwork in which the conception of power in the empire did not necessarily resonate with Foucauldian sovereignty.

Consequently, the Weberian ideal-type method is considered the most appropriate here. According to Weber, an ideal type never exists in its pure form, and in reality, there are only ever intermediary cases and mixed forms combined into different types in the most varied ways.[17] An ideal type is "not real".[18] It does not aim to

INTRODUCTION

describe reality but rather to help in understanding it by way of an intellectual construct. Thus, the Sharifian empire (from the Battle of the Three Kings in 1578 to the establishment of the Protectorate in 1912) is not the model for the Empire ideal type, as we can see in the coexistence of various modes of government in pre-colonial Morocco, integrating direct and legal-rational interventions characteristic of the Nation-state ideal type.[19] Likewise, contemporary Morocco is also not the model for the Nation-state type, as seen in the sophisticated staging of ceremonies of allegiance or the persistence of *dahir*[20] as a tool for legislating. These ideal types allow us to shed light on the simultaneous coexistence of a wide range of power relations, visions of authority, sovereignty, responsibility and representation, modalities for action and the role of the state, as well as ways of understanding its legitimacy.

In an approach based on interpretative sociology (*verstehende Sociologie*),[21] which grants a fundamental place to representations and meanings, our understanding of the ideal-type approach not only takes into account facts but also, and above all, their different levels of representation and the plural meanings attributed to them. Therefore, the mobilisation of the *muqaddam* must not be considered merely in terms of facts, as an everyday administration that is not solely based in legal-rational bureaucratisation, but which also considers territorial administration through the itinerant and quasi-personal proximity of the representative of authority with "his" population. It must also be studied in light of what it represents, the way it is understood, through technocrats who, in pursuit of their goal to reduce movement, opted for a formal document awarded by the authorities rather than a sworn statement, or even no authorisation at all, and who "naturally" turned to the *muqaddam* for its implementation, the most lowly public servant and probably the most removed from the doxa they promote of what a representative of a sovereign state should be. It should also be considered through the figure of the *muqaddam* himself, who also considers it "natural" to be personally responsible for this, and through the population that considers it "natural" to turn to the *muqaddam* for an authorisation and also to contribute to the organisation of his "offices". As we can see, the elaboration of this con-

WEAVING POLITICAL TIME IN MOROCCO

ceptual framework is fuelled by factual elements drawn from an anthropological study of everyday life, which only an ongoing close connection to the fieldwork can provide.

Enriching the studies on empire

To build these two ideal types, we have drawn extensively upon historical chronicles and narratives not to write a history of Morocco but rather a historical sociology of Morocco. We have brought to life the texts that historians on Morocco use but without conducting the work of a historian. Moreover, and this may seem paradoxical, we ultimately did not draw much on the work of our historian colleagues studying Morocco because most of them are overly focused on the construction of the nation-state, with reform and reformism and in fact overlook these "other" forms of government that we specifically wish to explore. Of course, there are some exceptions. Abderrahmane Moudden has conducted a remarkable study of the relations between the tribes and the *Makhzen* in a very in-depth monograph that allows us to rethink the idea of epistolary art as an art of government. His description of the ethos of rural clerks and their expertise in correspondence, the art of well-worded letters and appropriate calligraphy allow us to consider another aspect of the structural function of a state assumed to be absent or weak, acting only sporadically and with violence. Similarly, our work on the realm of power was only possible with the help of Abdelahad Sebti. Reading his research and discussing these questions with him helped identify the main auxiliaries in a political economy of control and consider dissidence a moment in negotiation. His description of *ztata* (the go-between), the figure who weaves the empire's web and fills in the holes of insecurity, allowing the movement of people and goods, was the condition for conceiving the distinction between administration and government and for exploring the world of invisible mediators. Research by Bezzaz or Rosenberger on the management of famines and epidemics was central to our reflection on the empire as a state capable of conceiving and managing risk.[22] Bezzaz's argument in particular allows us to take a new perspective on the responsibilities of the

INTRODUCTION

state in disaster management. We can talk about an emerging political responsibility that is only tenuously linked to questions of charity and assistance drawn from the Islamic tradition. However, what enables us to understand the plurality of forms of government and registers of the state are the correspondence and chronicles from Ibn Zaidane, Nasiri or Mokhtar Soussi, among others. These ethnographic texts gave us access to concrete facts and situations that allowed us to develop our ideal types and grasp the diversity of modalities of government, particularly in the eighteenth and above all in the nineteenth century. The letters bring to life figures and exchanges without regard for overall coherence or the production of a national history. They were our guides in elaborating the plurality of ways of governing and the diversity of conceptions of power, representation and responsibility.

Paradoxically, it is work by historians with nothing to do with Morocco, that is fundamental to our demonstration. In particular, this includes all the existing research on empire, which has undergone a veritable revival in recent years. We have long been attentive to the plurality of registers of legitimacy and articulation of the state, and the broad diversity in its possible forms, but we interpreted them in the general context of the state, although we never adopted the "legal-rational" and "bureaucratic" definitions and always remained attentive to its transformations.[23] In the case of Morocco, we have used the concepts of *Makhzen*, as a bureaucratic structure,[24] and also *dar-al-Makhzen*, as a place where knowledge, behaviour, values and the art of governing are formed.[25] It was these studies on the history of empire that led us to conceptualise them in terms of the "imperial dimension of the state", precisely because the general teachings of these studies[26] echoed what we were reading in the chronicles and narratives of the pre-colonial period. They also echoed certain characteristics of contemporary Moroccan government. These include the role of brokers and mediators in the exercise of power, the forms of indirect government more generally based on the principle of government at least cost and the use of more or less official intermediaries, or the way in which power was reinforced under both Hassan II and Mohammed VI through the interplay of differences and pluralism.

11

WEAVING POLITICAL TIME IN MOROCCO

However, having said that, we distanced ourselves from these studies[27] on two fundamental points, once again characteristic of our approach based in historical sociology rather than history. Firstly, it was important to distinguish the empire as a form of the state from the empire as an expression of domination in colonised territories. This latter is in fact merely an adaptation of the nation-state to the constraints of colonial management, whereas the former is a mode of organisation and expression of government in a particular state. First and foremost, we do not consider Empire an outdated form of government characteristic of some past era prior to the nation-state but as a register different from that of the Nation-state, which allows us to consider the contemporary state in all its complexity. Not only do we not consider that Empire shaped the nation-state, a point we will come back to throughout this book, but we do not consider Empire and the Nation-state to be two kinds of state that are different and distinct over time. On the contrary, they are two simultaneous registers that both help us conceptualise the Moroccan state in all its complexity.[28] We therefore consider that Empire as a concept is still present and fundamentally important in the practice of domination. The naturalisation of logics of action, the art of governing[29] and ways of doing and thinking induced by neoliberal ideology are more often supported by the imperial register than by that of the Nation-state. The pages that follow will demonstrate how this imperial presence is incarnated and takes shape in concrete terms, obviously differing according to circumstances and periods, actors and issues. These studies have provided a greater understanding of contemporary Morocco, but this is nevertheless a country that can only be understood by taking into account the depth of its history, which does not mean it is eternal or unchanging. In fact, one of the objectives of this book is to grasp the transformations in the state and the art of governing and to reveal the fundamental changes at work in power and society in Morocco.

Putting the imaginary at the heart of political analysis

The hypothesis of the continued relevance of the imperial register has nothing to do with its potential political instrumentalisation.

INTRODUCTION

Empire is not the veneer of the "Mamounia decor" that is omni-present in the Moroccan landscape and the discourses of those in power. It is also not merely a tradition held up as ideology. We consider Empire to be an aspect of the imaginary of the state. The concept of the imaginary is central to this analysis. It allows us to encompass very distinct aspects of social life within a single per-spective: language, passions and bodily communication; strategies for appropriation and interpretation, as well as manners and every-day ways of being and doing; strategies for reinventing the tech-nologies and frameworks[30] of power; concepts, categories and modalities for understanding time, space and social relations.[31] Reality cannot be grasped independently of the imaginary (or what Paul Veyne called "constitutive imagination")[32] beyond the catego-ries, frameworks and principles that order the tangible world. This grey zone between true and false, between "real and unreal"[33] is "what holds society together".[34] The imperial frame of reference and that of the Nation-state do not have the same meanings and do not allow the same interpretations of reality, and it is the range of coexisting repertoires that we are interested in revealing here. In this respect we are particularly attentive to two aspects of the imaginary. The first sees it as creating, "it is what frames the struc-turing of individual and interactive experiences, their significations and corresponding values."[35] The other considers it as "interaction" and "continuous dialogue" between heritage and innovation,[36] and more broadly between the different conceptions of authority, power and society. From this perspective, the imaginary is not society's subconscious; it is something deeply material and con-scious for actors,[37] embedded in the everyday, although this aspect cannot be reduced to instrumentalisation. The latter exists, of course, but it does not explain why people support it, believe in it and refer to it.[38] This last point is crucial for us and introduces one of the structural themes of our demonstration, the importance of "meaning" and significations. The "fact that 'external' signs serve as 'symbols' is one of the constitutive presuppositions of all 'social' relations", according to Weber.[39] The imaginary is thus an all-encompassing concept that allows us to reproduce the guiding line of meaning in both its social and historical depth, to the extent that

13

WEAVING POLITICAL TIME IN MOROCCO

"individual action is not understood as a first beginning, unfolding from a social starting point, but is situated from the outset in a historical world that is always structured by pre-existing orders."[40]

The use of the concept of the imaginary is not a sophisticated way of conceptualising permanence or continuity. Quite the opposite. If we consider it in its ideal, even dreamlike, dimension as well as in its everyday material form, the imaginary helps conceptualise change. We could have chosen the concept of legacy, as Michael Meeker did, understood not as the expression of nostalgia or the persistence of elements of the old regime in the new, but as the immediacy and performance of key elements of the imperial system in the nation-state.[41] This perspective is interesting in that it emphasises the importance of "intangible heritage" and the "kinship front"[42] (much like Giovanni Levi, but without referring to his work). In particular it shows how in the Trabzon province, families with Ottoman origins maintained their notability throughout the twentieth century through their ability to create an informal hierarchy to shadow that of the state bureaucracy. However, our decision to reason in terms of imaginary seems both more relevant, more all-encompassing and better able to avoid the problems associated with searching for "traces" and "prefigurations," and not being limited to the reconversion of capital acquired under empire into the nation-state. Drawing on the imaginary seemed more able to reveal the dynamism and creativity at work in power relations and governmental practices, specifically because it does not reify historical experience and because it can only be understood in the encounter between registers that enables the creation of new ones.

The imaginary therefore emerges as an intermediary; the link that confers meaning on practices but also on change. It is a medium that enables the assembly of disparate situations into a coherent whole.

Weaving time

The ideal-type method and the use of the imaginary constitute the foundation of another aspect of the core problem this book explores: accounting for the interpenetration of durations.

INTRODUCTION

However, the question of time, or the interconnectedness of different kinds of time, was not only the result of an intellectual construction. Above all, it was imposed upon us by the nature of the field. This was not intended, as such, but stems from our desire to move beyond commonplace sentiments on the omnipresence of the past or the continual invention of tradition. We also wanted to move beyond our own dissatisfaction with considering the diversity of behaviour and representations, both of elites and ordinary citizens, in their relationship with the state, through the sole perspective of the duality between tradition and modernity. Our fieldwork took us away from existing analyses that oppose different "modes of production,"[43] or are focused on duplicity or even schizophrenia. But the idea of woven time was not simply an abstract construction, albeit stemming from fieldwork, in response to the theoretical questions we were exploring. It emanated from the actors themselves and their understanding of their actions, as well as our ethnographic observations of situations that appear contradictory, in which actors perform comfortably and naturally. How can we take into account the demands of actors who express the need—or the art—of connecting different temporalities? How can we characterise attitudes, behaviours and actions that appear to be in tension or even contradictory? Our intuition, from the very outset, was that this was not a confusion of temporalities, nor even a "fragmentation" of time between heterochronous instances or levels of sociability.[44] Rather, it is important to understand the distinction and simultaneity of these different times in the eyes of the actors themselves, who are primarily responsible for maintaining these differences and their cohabitation. The distant past does not merely impact memory, it is also present through a repertoire of meaning and the technologies of power that are considered normal and understandable.

This can be seen in the case of one senior public servant, a Franco-Moroccan graduate from an elite French institution, who was both proud of and comfortable with the fact that he oversaw the most sophisticated management reforms in the public companies he managed (particularly the airline, RAM). Yet he simultaneously found it completely normal to behave like a *khadim* (servant

15

of the prince), even accompanying the King on his tour around Africa, keeping an aircraft on standby for him and accepting to behave like the "*caid rwa*".[45] This is also the case for the current constant reference to expansionism, that typical characteristic of empire. From a historical perspective, this expansionism existed only in the very distant past, in the Morocco of the Almoravids, the Almohads and the Marinids. With the Reconquista and the push back from the Iberian Peninsula, it rose up again with the Saadians,[46] who responded to the challenge of insularity by spreading south. It is striking to see the ease with which this expansionist heritage, assumed to be a thing of the past, was brought back to life, firstly by the territorial aspirations and reconfigurations that followed the abolition of the Protectorate and then through the accompaniment of the Moroccan diaspora, whether Jewish or Christian, through perpetual allegiance, to the point where the "thirteenth constituency" was recently created by business leaders to cover "global Moroccans". Even more recently, it has emerged in Morocco's ambitious African policy, playing on the African "foundation" of society, much like the old families from Fez who discretely but distinctively make it a point of honour to serve the Senegalese dish *thieboudien*,[47] as a reminder of their properties in Senegal or Guinea. This example suggests that this long term is that of the population as well as the state. The history of a state is quasi-geological; it has strata, sedimentations, erosions and so forth. This is an important idea that will come back throughout the book. It explains the singularity of the Moroccan case without making it unique. This is a singularity that is historically constructed but ultimately, in itself, is banal. Morocco is a state like any other, with its own necessarily specific historical trajectory.

Finally, another example can be found in the cohabitation between claims of citizenship and the ritual of *baisemain* (hand-kissing), which is completely incomprehensible for many outside observers. The general acceptance of *baisemain* is part of a heritage that is legitimised and recognised by the historical depth of the royal family (and its descendance from the prophet), by Moroccan culture, which is marked by the worship of saints (an important marker both in the face of Islamism and secularism) and by family

INTRODUCTION

ethos (as a gesture of respect for the father, whose hands are kissed in greeting). This practice is both traditional and contemporary and is comfortably connected to the idea of "deactivated citizenship",[48] i.e. a form of citizenship that is expressed indirectly but is nevertheless the expression of political issues.

The coexistence of these two registers, these two temporalities, reveals a new meaning of *baisemain*, from which politics has not been evinced. Kissing the King's hand, shows the diversity of social statuses. In order to understand this, it is important to pay close attention and conduct a genuine ethnography of the moment. The kiss may be a simple brush of lips or chin, it may be wet, or it may be that the shoulder is touched or the hand is kissed on both sides. Equally, the King may either leave or withdraw his hand. All of this is part of a very subtle language drawing on not only levels of proximity but also perspectives of the appropriate temporal register. It is not a question of submission or unconditional renunciation of citizenship, but the expression of respect and authenticity that by no means erases the reality of power relations or the possibility of regicide.

Indeed, as we will show over the course of this book, people are continually setting thresholds, with temporalitiesthat have beginnings and endings, which allow them to have the "right" attitude, the "right" information and the "right" social interactions, whether in their social, economic and political activities or in the intimacy of the domestic sphere. There is no shortage of examples of instances when access to meaning and community are lost when an individual get the appropriate temporality "wrong". In seeking to document governmental practices and technologies of power as closely as possible, we are not merely shedding light on the importance of "structural durations" specific to each institution or type of actor.[49] We will show that the repertoires of representation, of staging, of action, of rationality and of understanding are not only manifold, but they may also refer to different durations and sometimes to the extremely distant past.

These temporalities are complex. As we have seen, they refer to the long term (even the very long term) of history and to the short term of connexions to the contemporary world. However,

17

WEAVING POLITICAL TIME IN MOROCCO

they also refer to the difference between social time and secular time, between economic time and cultural time, between types of lived experience, between social, institutional and individual time. These considerations echo the classical discussions on the way the social sciences take time into account, particularly different times. They are perhaps less focused on the recent questions to do with regimes of historicity[50] than those—typical in philosophy—that articulate apparently conflictual temporalities (or heterogenous levels of temporality).[51] Following Marc Bloch, it seems to us that time is indeed a space in which phenomena become intelligible, which provide markers that are shared but also multiple.[52] Following Husserl or Bergson, it seems that duration also reflects an intimate consciousness and as such is an action, specific to each of us, or an elaboration that is specific to a society, which recreates the past to live the present.[53] From Hobsbawm and Ranger we draw on the idea that the invention of tradition is an active principle in state-building.[54] This research also resonates with work done by Jean-François Bayart, whose development of the notion of "imbrication" of durations,[55] stemming from a re-reading of Bergson's interpenetration of durations,[56] allows us to understand the invention of modernity not as new rationality or the domination of one time over another[57] but as the overlapping of often new internal logics and different durations.

This interpenetration or imbrication is what Michel de Certeau called layers of time;[58] overlapping temporalities. Times, places and social levels are discontinuous and the relations between these different "layers" are complex, fluctuating and enigmatical. In this book, rather than "layers" of time, we prefer to think of time as "woven". It is woven through genealogy, through *isnad* (the chain of those who vouch for information connected to the Prophet) and *silslat* (the chain of transmission), which works to link the Commander of the Faithful to his ancestor, the Prophet. For believers, it is also woven through the path of *hadith* and the vulgarised *sira* (prophetic practice) as they consciously or unconsciously reproduce the inaugural prophetic gesture and consequently transcend duration.[59]

Woven time is not the simple cohabitation of two times, the time of Empire and the time of the Nation-state. What we have

18

INTRODUCTION

sought to show through this expression is the production of constantly novel configurations that associate the registers of different times, that articulate them without combining or mixing them. The image of the rug is a powerful one here. The weaving of a rug is not simply the coexistence of the threads. Weaving creates a fabric with specific patterns; through weaving, the threads are more than merely juxtaposed. This state-rug is constructed through the temporalities that are interwoven. But it is more than that. What we emphasise here is that the actors consider this weaving of registers, repertoires or protocols completely normal, and they master its syntax. This articulation-weaving constitutes a contemporary political language that provides renewed meaning to gestures, attitudes or behaviours that appear outdated, even archaic, but which are well and truly contemporary. On this point, we can draw on Weber's conceptualisation of the notion of *übergreifend* (overflow, overlap). Temporality does not refer to time past, but on the contrary, to the embeddedness of social logics in the present. Although distinct, these may interpenetrate each other and give rise to mutual reinterpretation and thus new registers of meaning.[60]

PROLEGOMENON

THE MOROCCAN STATE OVER TIME

The case that Morocco constructed to assert its claim over Western Sahara is a paradigmatic example of the power of the imaginary, allowing the coexistence of arguments belonging to different and apparently incompatible logics and frames of reference. When King Hassan II requested an opinion on the matter from the International Court of Justice (ICJ) in 1975, he had very limited possibilities of "recovering" the territories in the Western Sahara. The mental world of the time, dominated by principles of the rights of people to self-determination and the intangibility of colonial era borders, made it impossible to conceive of a notion of power based on the theory of the Caliphate, let alone to evoke any kind of imperial paradigm. In the context of decolonisation, claims to Western Sahara were the result of the evolutionist position of the state imposed by the public law doctrine of the time. The idea of empire is not only lacking in this context—it is inconceivable. Morocco's submission to the court makes no reference to empire, even though the official seals of the Sharifian empire were on all the treaties set up by the parties involved in the conflict. Morocco's appeal, via the "positivist" lawyers representing it, argued that it was "the only independent state ... in north-west Africa"[1] and emphasised "the geographical contiguity of Western Sahara to Morocco and the desert character of the territory". Given this, it affirmed that the historical documents are sufficient to establish

WEAVING POLITICAL TIME IN MOROCCO

Morocco's claim to the land based on "the continued display of authority."[2] However, the Moroccan argument also discretely introduced the idea that "where sovereignty over territory is claimed, the particular structure of a state may be a relevant element in appreciating the reality or otherwise of a display of state activity adduced as evidence of that sovereignty."[3] But this plea did not go any further in explaining the meaning that should be given to this "particular structure". It merely adopted the colonial theory of *Bled Siba/Bled Makhzen* to counter the objection that it had no effective authority over the territories it claimed.

The ICJ was sceptical. It was no easy task to convince judges who had been trained on the theories of Kelsen and Carré de Malberg that Morocco was a special kind of nation-state, consisting:

> partly of what was called the *Bled Makhzen*, areas actually subject to the sultan, and partly of what was called the *Bled Siba*, areas in which the tribes were de facto not submissive to the sultan ... the two expressions, *Bled Makhzen* and *Bled Siba*, merely described two types of relationship between the Moroccan local authorities and the central power, not a territorial separation, and the existence of these different types did not affect the unity of Morocco. Because of a common cultural heritage, the spiritual authority of the sultan was always accepted. ... Thus, the difference between the *Bled Makhzen* and the *Bled Siba*, Morocco maintains, did not reflect a wish to challenge the existence of the central power so much as the conditions for the exercise of that power; the *Bled Siba*, was, in practice, a way of affecting an administrative decentralisation of authority.[4]

The judges were not convinced. They did not recognise Morocco's sovereignty over these territories. However, they did accept a more exotic argument drawn from the paradigm of the Caliphate, and they handed down an opinion that was deliberately ambiguous, attesting to the historic connections between Morocco and some of the Saharan tribes.[5] For those defending the Moroccan argument, the initial statement in the opinion is what matters: the recognition of historical ties of allegiance equates to a recognition of the "Moroccaness" of the Sahara. For those supporting the Polisario, it was of course the second finding that mattered; the lack of legal ties

PROLEGOMENON

between Morocco and Western Sahara was proof of independence and recalling these ties of allegiance was merely an instrumentalisation of history to legitimise the "occupation" of the territory.

Morocco did not manage to benefit from the breach opened up by international law and validated by the ICJ doctrine, enabling the association of a "particular structure" (i.e. a state with specific structures) with particular modalities of government and the expression of sovereignty. Morocco's reaction to the ICJ opinion is less suggestive of the political instrumentalisation of a particular conception of sovereignty, artificially reactivated to serve a national cause, than it is the reflection of the simultaneous coexistence of different, even incompatible, approaches to sovereignty and territory. The ambivalence that enables this coexistence can be seen firstly in Morocco's arguments to the ICJ and those mobilised on the international stage more generally in support of its claim.[6] Although it emphasised the continuity of acts of allegiance, appointment of *caids* (authority figures) and *cadis* (judges) by the *Makhzen*, the frequent *harka* (military campaigns) and *mehalla* (movements of the court), the Moroccan perspective was steeped in the vocabulary and themes of the nation-state: territorial integrity, national unity, international treaties and negotiations on the question of the border with Algeria.

As the ICJ episode shows, it is essential to problematise the trajectory of the state if we are to understand contemporary Morocco. The ideal-type perspective paves the way for a reading that distances itself from the idea of the archaic or failed state, breaking away from the reformist paradigm—whether these reforms were the work of the late nineteenth-century *Makhzen*, the colonial power, or a nationalist elite opposed to the monarchy after independence.[7] At the same time, it encourages us to distance ourselves from a standpoint that relies on a linearity in which the nation-state replaced the Sharifian empire through a negation of "woven time" constituted of different intertwining "durations".

The Sharifian empire and its regions

The period we are interested in here ranges from Morocco's defeat in the Tétouan War in 1860 and the Sharifian empire's challenge

WEAVING POLITICAL TIME IN MOROCCO

from nation-states, to the early 1900s and its confrontation with competing European colonial ambitions. We have chosen to explore the modes of government in Morocco during this period from two almost opposite examples. The first is that of the Tétouan region and its status as a *Taghr*.[8] In this northern area of the empire, accustomed to stand-offs with Europe, the idea of the border is embodied by the surrounding sea but also the presence of another unalterable alterity—the Christian community. The corpus of letters analysed in the following pages shows a way of governing that is specific to the centralised Nation-state. It involves a vision of public action as both territorialised and direct, with state power that is far from symbolic. Indeed, the state here is concerned with temporal and spatial continuity and its own constant and effective presence in all areas. Here we see a state that develops and imposes policy[9] on a range of aspects of life, all sharing a vision of public order similar to that imposed by the Protectorate in 1912. The state is omnipresent here. It is in the everyday work of public servants and the issues they are responsible for; it regulates and enacts the procedures for the procurement of contracts or the manufacture of weapons. Here, "public policy" targets communities, like in the most remote regions of the empire, but also individuals. The only thing required of them is obedience.

The second example we explore is the Sous region, which is the site of a very different conception of power, in which indirect government dominates. Here, it is not obedience that is required but loyalty. This approach to governing requires a large number of intermediaries and does not assume that hierarchy will be systematically respected. Power is negotiated here more than it is in the north, and policies are produced through collaboration.

Sous, governing at a distance

This form of governing, laid out in discontinuities, ruptures, absences and vacancies, reflects the conception of imperial power at a distance as part of a regime operating with minimal resources. Most contemporary historians have trouble characterising this "extreme Sous region" and its relationship to the Sharifian state. It is variously described as an "independent principality" led by a local

PROLEGOMENON

"Sharif"[10] and as a "Siba" space that only recognises the symbolic authority of the sultan.[11] From the late nineteenth century, however, both of these perspectives saw this region as a space where a new kind of government was being tested, as a result of international conjuncture as much as the transformations within the Moroccan state.[12] This was known as the period of reforms, which aimed to bring the region to heel through violence. During this period, the nature of the ties to the central power was strained through confrontation with European countries, bearers of a different conception of the state, ordinarily described as Westphalian. These tensions did not undermine the primary founding paradigms of political legitimacy, the idea that God is the source of all norms and the belief that Islam is the solution to all things. Hassan I—of whom it is said that his throne was his saddle—sought to reinstate the territorial continuity of his kingdom by ordering four costly military campaigns toward Sous, reorganising the army and the postal service. But he was not thinking of sovereignty, law, people, territory, borders or responsibility in the same terms as the theorists of the nation-state, or even in the terms of the negotiators that his representatives would have to confront during the Madrid conference (1880).[13] For Hassan I, like for the Moroccan elites as a whole, this was a matter of unwillingly facing pressure and not a way of thinking about or questioning reforms. Nor was it a sign of the emergence of the nation-state, as certain contemporary historians suggest.[14]

The *harka* led by Hassan I in 1882 on the borders of the Sous was spectacular. It was intended to create an impression rather than provoke combat, but the submission of the region was the result of countless negotiations, which the sultan called *syassa*, in the equine sense of the word.[15] There were many intermediaries, both frontline protagonists and those working in the wings. Moulay Larbi Adouzi, who is referred to in the following letters by his position as *taleb*,[16] is one among many of them.

In less than a week, between 8 and 17 July 1882, the *taleb* Adouzi received six letters. In the first, the sultan who was camped along the symbolic border of the Sous, asked him to intercede on his behalf with the Maader tribes, so that they would join the *harka*

25

WEAVING POLITICAL TIME IN MOROCCO

near the Oued Oulghass river. On 11 July, the *taleb* received two more letters. The first, sent by a prominent court official, Mohammed Ben Mekki Jam'i, asked for his blessing in the form of a talisman and mentioned two emissaries who he wished to introduce to the sultan. The second letter, sent by an agent of the *Makhzen*, informed him that his letter had been received and given to the sultan and that the response was attached. It was long and highly structured, much like an official missive. In it, the sultan addresses the rural clerk as a "friend" (*mouhib*), as he does the eminent figures who choose to be in his service.

The letter is made up of two parts. The first revisits the elements in the letter received previously and the second provides answers point by point. The sultan begins by noting that the *taleb* indeed announced the nomination of Ahmed Abllagh and Moussa Ben Bakass as *caids*, that he conveyed his blessing and his *amane* (guarantee of security) to the tribe and appreciated their joy and submission in keeping with the precepts of the Qur'an and the Sunna. The sultan added that he now knew the two Sheikhs were preparing to meet his convoy in Tiznit. He concluded with the most important point and the most problematic—the head of the Illigh house, Husayn. The sultan noted with satisfaction that the *taleb* had written to the *mourabit* reassuring him of his good intentions and reminding him to "be in the community and not stray from it." He notes that Husayn of Illigh responded that "he has no other refuges than the *taleb*" and that the latter solicited the sultan's affection on his behalf, erasing any bad news he may have heard about him.

In the second part of the letter, the sultan responded to each point, in no particular order. He began with Husayn, the Chief of Illigh. The sultan said he would accept to "integrate this dissident" in the company of the *taleb* "both him and those with him". He then said he blessed the two notables recommended and appointed *caids* of their respective tribes, before again returning to the issue of Husayn of Illigh, to which he dedicated several long passages full of undertones conveying his disapproval as to the latter's apparent mistrust toward him. Without explicitly mentioning the veiled duels with him back when he had been *khalifa* (Viceroy), he nev-

26

PROLEGOMENON

ertheless did not fail to restate that Husayn had served the interests of the *Makhzen*, even from a distance.[17] The letter then went on in this same subtle undertone, and it is an example of the sophisticated art of *syassa* as the sultan understood it. He writes, "How can we bring him down from this pedestal, or allow him to be slighted, whether we accept or not to convey upon him our attention … God preserve us from any intention of extinguishing this light … we seek only to reform."

On 17 July 1882, an agent of the *Makhzen* advised the *taleb* that he had received and conveyed the letter addressed to the sultan and that his response was attached. In the letter, dated that same day, Hassan I notes that the *taleb* went to Illigh to convey orders to Husayn and his intention to mobilise the mountain tribes and incite the *Semlala* notables (those of his tribe) to join the sultan, as well as noting the meeting planned for the Monday. In fact, Husayn did not attend that meeting in Tiznit but sent a delegation (including a close family member or his son), moved his most precious assets to the *hurm* (sacred space) of the saint and took refuge in the mountain.[18] Aside from a clandestine encounter described by Paul Pascon, from the time when the sultan was still *khalifa*,[19] the face-to-face meeting between the sultan and Husayn never took place.

The second series of letters followed four years later. This time it was the *taleb* who took the initiative. He was now considered an important notable,[20] officially endorsed by the sultan, and could allow himself to behave in ways that might be considered an abuse of power today. Even as his usefulness declined, he tended to combine his affairs with those of the state. In the first letter, dated 24 January 1886, the sultan commented on a letter he had received informing him of the degradation of a bridge over the Oued Oulghass river and asking him to advise the nearby tribes to repair it. The letter he mentioned also told him about the unpleasant behaviour of the chief of the Zawiya Timakdicht, about which complaints had been made. The sultan responded that "on the question of the bridge, orders have been given to the tribes' governors", but he did not agree in the denunciation of the chief of the Zawiya. In another letter dated 4 May of the same year, the sultan reacted to a request by the *taleb*, in connection with this task as the *'adel*

27

WEAVING POLITICAL TIME IN MOROCCO

(traditional notary).[21] The latter had previously written regarding an inheritance case that had been resolved by a colleague, one Benbrahim, whom he accused of having forged his signature. The sultan said he was sure the *taleb* was not at fault. In a letter dated the same day, he announced to the *taleb* that he had intervened to send another individual, one Mohammed Ben Hassan Guelouli, a *dahir* on respectability (*tawqir wa al-ihtiram*).

In the last group of letters, the style is different. Although the *taleb* is still referred to as "our blessed friend", and although he has an important place as an intermediary liable to obtain favours for his friends, the responses are shorter and he is sometimes refused. The last letter we have is dated 23 November 1898, under the reign of Sultan Abdelaziz. Many things have changed. The state has now tightened its control over the kingdom. This time, the *taleb* does not have direct access to the sultan. It is simply an agent of the *Makhzen* who acknowledges receipt of his letter informing the sultan that the dues normally paid by the Maadar people have not been sent, the *Makhzen* having sent an agent to collect them for the Treasury. The agent responds that the sultan has been informed and that he has asked how much money is owed. The exchange suggests that the *taleb* is no longer particularly useful, but the authorities maintain his status without awarding him tax-free benefits. The sultan did not wish to humiliate his servant, nor permanently relegate him to the fringes of the *Makhzen*.

Tétouan, governing and administering of the city

A few years earlier, in May 1862, the sultan had celebrated the evacuation of the Spanish from Tétouan and announced a project for direct administration of the Northern region. This was completely different from the government "at a distance" in the Sous. The previous month, on 14 April, he had appointed Haj Abdelkader Aachaach governor of Tétouan.[22] This series of events reveals an entirely different approach to governing, which we will explore in detail, beginning with the nomination of the first regional governor only a few days before the evacuation of the Spanish from the area.

The context is singular. In the space of just a few years, Morocco had lost its status as a feared and mysterious empire after a defeat

28

PROLEGOMENON

against the French—established in Algiers since 1830—and another against Spanish, which was particularly painful as it led to the occupation of the Tétouan. These losses brought the ruin of the public treasury and paved the way for colonisation. The new governor, Abdelkader Aachaach, received hundreds of letters between his nomination in April 1862 and his dismissal on 28 May 1864. Mohammed Daoud, Tétouan's historiographer, has published 104 of these letters. All but six of them are from the sultan (the others being from the high commissioners of the *Makhzen*). Of course, it would be impossible to discuss all these letters here, but the first series of them (twenty-nine letters) is sufficient to illustrate the specific approach to governing that operated in this region. The first letter is addressed to the "people" (*ahl*) of Tétouan, via their new governor, who was soon to receive the keys to the city from the Spanish. In it, the sultan rejoices in the enemy army's evacuation of the town, lists the damages incurred and exhorts the people of Tétouan to rise up and return the city to its former glory. To this end, he announces the nomination of an experienced man who knows the city and its residents as governor.[23]

The first letters, which take the form of a *dahir* of nomination, provide the outline of the territory under the new governor's command. The five tribes of the Tétouan region are carefully listed, even the most insignificant of them.[24] The sultan states his intention to develop a close administration over this territory, as an interface of relations with the Spanish. The territory was also to be extended to Chefchaouen, a town in the mountains inland from Tétouan. This town is important because of its geographical situation and above all because of its population, made up of Andalusians and *chorfa* from Jbel Alem.[25] In addition to those dealing with the issue of the evacuation of Spanish troops, the letters from this first year of new Sharifian control meticulously cover ordinary administrative themes, such as taxes on merchandise sold tax-free by the Spanish to Muslim traders during the occupation, the distribution of two quintals of gunpowder and a thousand rifles to the people of Tétouan,[26] the appointment of a weapons expert to buy canons,[27] the sultan expressing his concerns as to their calibre[28] and the equipment for the city guard, for which he provided fifty horses.[29]

29

WEAVING POLITICAL TIME IN MOROCCO

A particular letter may cover several subjects of course. In one, dated 18 May 1862, the sultan acknowledges receipt of a load of wood left by the Spanish, which the Queen of Spain proposes to offer as a gift to the people of Tétouan, the appointment of two public servants (the *cadi* and the *mohtasseb*),[30] the attribution of the wood beams given by the Queen to *waqf* assets and the refusal to use them to repair mosques. On 26 June 1862, the sultan expressed his concern about the wages of the 150 soldiers of the city guard and replied—in a separate letter dated the same day—to the Spanish consul's request that his wages be aligned with that of the French and English consuls. On 8 July 1862, in response to a rural *caid* who had asked the sovereign to appoint a deputy in Tétouan to collect local payments from the members of his tribe, the sultan ordered the governor of the city to accept this request for extra-territoriality, under certain formal conditions, specifically a written record of each and every operation.

From 10 July 1862, the sultan was responsible for the supply of wheat to the region and was faced with rising prices due to the shortages following the years of war. He asked an intendent to supply Tétouan's market with wheat at cost price, obtained from El Jadida. On 4 August 1862, he allowed a merchant to charter a ship full of grain, on the condition that the latter accepted minimal profits and that this charter occurred within a period of two months, so as not to compete with the Tétouan merchants who had chartered ships of wheat from Safi. Finally, on 30 August 1862, he sent 7,000 measures of wheat to Tétouan, via the intermediary of his clerk in Safi, Tayeb Benhima.[31] The wheat bought by the *Makhzen* was sold at market for cost price. Religious policy was not left behind. In a letter dated 12 September 1862, the sultan mentioned the request from the *cadi* Azziman[32] to put an end to the principle of freedom in proclaiming *fatwas* and limit them to only four Ulema who had been accredited to pronounce rulings on religious matters, as these contradictory opinions were considered necessary for the operation of justice. In keeping with this, he advised his governor that he had asked a Sufi scholar, who had been in exile during the occupation, to return, emphasising the importance of his presence for the spiritual balance of the city.[33]

30

PROLEGOMENON

On 24 September 1862, the sultan granted the merchants of Tétouan a loan of 100,000 mithqal in gold (the mithqal is a unit of mass equal to 4.25 grams), with a six-month term for reimbursement. Twenty merchants would benefit.[34] Their debts were recorded before an 'adel. The money had been transferred to Tétouan by the intendants at the ports of Rabat, Larache and Tangier, so the sultan asked that the records not be noted twice on the ledgers of both the mandators and the recipients. Instead, he insisted that the governor send a copy of the Tétouan ledger so that the mandators could annul their records and demanded he himself review the terms to allow for accommodations with merchants who may have difficulties repaying their debts.

These letters and the following ones show a sultan who is directly involved in the city administration and supplies, in maintaining public order (whether by negotiation or using force with the border tribes), in arms policy (even looking into the prototypes of muskets best suited to the habits of recruits) and in maintaining the stables and the horses for the cavalry. He was also involved in financial policy connected to tax collecting, organising its delegation by awarding a rationalised tender. The sultan was thinking like a statesman, both concerned with taking care of his subjects and providing them with security. He was clearly concerned with the details on the ground but also with the more abstract construction of norms. Behind the archaic formulations used by his scribes we can see new ideas that stem from a logic of administration and sometimes even a logic of public service (maslaha). These traits that are so characteristic of the nation-state were undeniably present in the empire at the "time of the Mehalla".[35]

Multiple levels of government: the art of the imperial state

These two examples, the dissident Sous and the Makhzen North, both illustrate the extent of the state's actions, enforced by either conviction or constraint, according to different (even opposing) modes of government that were nevertheless adapted to each situation. The exceptional nature of this historic moment is not in question. These same traits of multifaceted imperial government

WEAVING POLITICAL TIME IN MOROCCO

can be observed in the times of Moulay Ismail and the Saadi Sultan Al-Mansur.[36] This state was clearly different from the model of the Nation-state, but it was nevertheless a state conscious of its own existence, the limits of its territory, its human components and its responsibility and defined by constant references to Muslim laws and traditions. This reference should not only be seen as a discourse of legitimation but also as a sign of a legalistic mode of operation. This state was neither a proto-nation-state nor a nation-state in the making. Its modes of governing were either closer to or more removed from this idea depending on circumstances, contexts and power relations. The state fully accepted the discontinuity of its authority—and sometimes its genuine absence. The plurality of standards of measurement, currencies and legal regimes, even when that meant the pre-eminence of local customs over Islamic law, all reflect a unique conception of sovereignty rather than a renunciation of it. This discontinuous and intermittent form of government was not seen as a weakness or as a sign of dysfunction; the territory was considered an indivisible whole that could be identified by its edges. Sometimes these edges were objectified in the form of borders, like a nation-state confronted with a kind of embedded otherness in a space where identity is not limited to religion. Sometimes edges were the confines of the space where the sovereignty of the imperial state covered people or communities rather than territories.

This art of governing, along with these practices, ways of understanding and social and political relations, were all made possible by specific skills, of which only letter writing is explicitly explored in our analysis of this correspondence and in the imperial state archives more generally, whether private or national. For a time, these were obscured by the organisational and administrative power of the Protectorate, but their specificity and results were revealed in the 1930s by Ibn Zaidane, during his lectures on the Alawite state.[37] This correspondence reveals the particularities of pre-colonial Sharifian government. The letters shed light on particular artforms that transmit "other" conceptions of the state (which we call the imperial register) within the political imaginary. We have chosen to use the concept of artform for clarity. It denotes

32

PROLEGOMENON

both elements of mastery, expertise (*handassa*) and engineering, but also an artistic dimension (reflecting the Arabic *fann*) in the exercise of power. Based on a foundation of skills defined by objectives, the Arabic incorporates both improvisation and uncertainty into this notion. When we talk about the art of governing here, we therefore include three dimensions: specific competencies and skills linked to modes of governing; technical content implying knowledge and expertise; and everything that makes up the material culture of power through its usages that have been codified and incorporated (in the primary sense of the word) to the point they become 'second nature'. These artforms are shared and not only characteristic of the *Makhzen*, but also of the tribes, large families, clerks of all levels and ordinary people; everyone has an element of this knowledge and expertise.

The art of letter writing

In his second chapter, dedicated to the sultan's diary and organisation, Ibn Zaidane sheds light on the importance of letters, missives and other administrative correspondence in "matters of state"; they constitute a cog in the machinery by which the whole empire is governed.[38] The analysis of these corpuses of letters between the sultan and various correspondents—governors, eminent figures, or ordinary subjects—confirms the central role of this epistolatory artform. The sultan is an "epistolary prince" who largely rules "by correspondence."[39] A single letter can cover both important state issues and banal private matters, which are thus, in the space of a missive, put on equal footing.[40] There are thousands of examples of this kind of letter in Morocco under Mohammed ben Abd al-Rahman (Mohammed IV) and Moulay al-Hassan bin Mohammed bin Yusef al-Alawi (Hassan I). The protagonists may be brotherhood leaders, governors, low-level *caids* of marginal tribes, *cadis* and Ulema of varying importance from the towns or the country. Today all major families and communities have private archives that document the intensity of this relationship. Historians have used this material extensively but have never managed to provide an overview of the volume of these exchanges, probably because only a very small proportion of them are in national archives.

33

WEAVING POLITICAL TIME IN MOROCCO

The sultan's correspondence suggests the "social efficacy of letter writing ... creating strong bonds between individuals."[41] This is social efficacy, but it is also political. As we have seen, this correspondence is a tool for administration, evaluation, taking into account local power relations, exchanging information and understanding societies, mobilisation, negotiation, recommendations, reprimands, rewards and the expression of power and sovereignty.[42] As we saw above with the *taleb* Adouzi in Sous, these letters contribute to the construction of a certain status, because through them the recipients are granted a fortuitous opportunity to fulfil an advantageous political position within their group. The sultan's correspondence thus contributes to processes of legitimation. It operates both as an instrument for the exercise of power and a tool for the knowledge of society, through a very detailed understanding of all the regions of the empire. As such, this constitutes a central modality of government at a distance.

The art of letter writing is highly codified. The conditions in which each form of address, each formal salutation or expression of etiquette, levels of language, content or official seals are used are all strictly defined.[43] Much like any kind of royal etiquette, it is clear when harsh language should be used, when literary Arabic or dialects are most appropriate, when the seal should be large or small and so forth. Although many of these formalities are preconstructed, epistolary expression enables infinite variation and leaves room for individual performance and thus ingenuity and virtuosity. The ceremonial proclamations, plays on language or certain characters and signs clearly reveal the tone of the messages. Expressions of greeting and closing were perfectly codified,[44] and beginning a letter with "our dear friend" or "our servant" does not convey the same information. This epistolary language was also a form of established knowledge, it played on what was left unspoken and implicit with consummate skill,[45] and supposed the recipient could read between the lines. Thus, when the sultan refuses a demand, he never makes this refusal explicit; he annotates the missive with the letter *saad*, which in the nomenclature of the *Makhzen* means "noted". By contrast, the annotation *sanaraa* or *sanandhor* means "we will see" which was a way of defer-

34

PROLEGOMENON

ring the decision.[46] The ruler could also use set expressions to reprimand his subjects, playing on the ingenuity of the language and its nuances to convey power relations, social status or a political climate.

This epistolary artform, which is also found in the art of today's royal speeches, is by no means limited to the state. In this respect, it is not state knowledge as such, even though it is central to the art of governing, particularly in situations of itinerance where a letter always accompanies the sultan in his movements. This is a kind of knowledge that is shared and diffuse; it is an attribute of and required by power at all levels of society. Tribes had to possess this same knowledge, as much as the central power and they all called on the services of specialist scribes, even though the *Makhzen* attracted the best of them. Abderrahmane Moudden is one of the first historians to have traced the paths of these distinguished scribes, so highly sought-after for their mastery of the mysteries of *Makhzen* writing in their travels with the tribes.[47] This mastery was not only a product of centralised bureaucracy, it also sheds light on the plurality of channels by which a social or political practice is spread throughout society, reflecting the non-hierarchical, non-centralised and non-unified nature of power.

The logistics of mobility

The sultan's itinerant court is a well-known phenomenon that has been studied by many historians in recent years.[48] It ensured a presence in places where the *Makhzen*'s reach was weak and was in this sense an expression of power itself, as it was in other empires.[49] The logistics of this itinerant government have been less widely studied, however. In his chapters dedicated to the sultan's movements and the geography of travel Ibn Zaidane provided a detailed description of the demands of a mobile court.[50]

Before moving the whole court, surveyors had to be sent to identify roads and choose the itinerary according to security requirements. They had to outline stages, ensure the local populations were not hostile, organise supplies by commissioning boats and preparing the storage of necessary goods and organise the progress of the court and the army. Then at each stage they had to set up camp respecting a pre-defined structure, with the tents situ-

35

WEAVING POLITICAL TIME IN MOROCCO

ated in concentric circles reflecting the social hierarchy and status of different groups, with the royal tent (where the royal family slept, as well as their mosque) in the centre. They also had to distribute the garments, horses and weapons, plan the arrival and departure of the sultan, coordinate the movements of his retinue and the sending and receiving of post while on the move. The government also had to be organised, that is the holding of court, arbitrations, rewards and reprimands, the reception of tribes, the respect of protocols and how administration could be managed from camp. Everyone had to be given an occupation, the arrival at the final destination had to be carefully orchestrated, which meant organising the way people were foretold of the arrival. Reproducing an identical court in an entirely different location (and it is indeed the fact that it was identical that attests to the permanence of the state) requires sophisticated logistics that are delegated to specialist professions. Some were given the task of counting the number of camels, horses, donkeys, mules or tents required; others were charged with overseeing the preparation of the tents, the freighting of boats or the managing of food supplies; still others were responsible for organising the King's affairs, depending on the ceremonies, events and contexts; others had to requisition armies within the tribes or organise entertainment (music, storytelling etc.) in a specific order and so on and so forth.

All of these logistics reflect bureaucracy in action: they show an organisation into corporations; standardisation of ordering, making and distributing tents; definition of normative frameworks for the organisation of the logistics of feeding animals and people, according to a process of delegation (or "having something done"—*faire faire*) that determines who gives what and when; the use of quantification both in the logistics of feeding and in providing tents, through the art of counting and surveying required for the distribution of the cost of the *harka* between the different tribes.[51]

The art of reception

The art of reception is something that is shared by society as a whole, as an expression of the centrality of the value of hospitality, and an art of governing by example and staging, and which is also

PROLEGOMENON

a moment of sublimation of power and its representation. From the mid-nineteenth century, *dar-al-Makhzen* became the site of identification and diffusion of these arts of reception and celebration. But it was not the source of their production. Several historical narratives testify to the authority's lack of imagination in this matter, while also emphasising its ability to capture and absorb the knowledge spread across the territory. The fact that they were comfortable with this indigence reflects the previously mentioned principles of frugality and government at least cost. In 1860, Mohammed Ben Abderhamane decided to send women to Tétouan to learn to make paella and chocolate[52] and to send gardeners to learn the basics of Andalusian gardens.[53] The art of reception had a very important role in the exercise of power here. The sultan had to be above reproach and the key reference in all things, in clothing fashions, cooking fashions, arts of fine dining and reception. Although he could choose to seek advice, send his daughters away for their education or have his servants trained elsewhere, he was the one who set the tone.

Although this artform involved the mastery and appropriation of specific knowledge, it also involved other roles that contributed to the sultan's exemplary status, like that of organising celebrations or religious ceremonies or establishing norms. By bestowing gifts, particularly in territories outside his direct control, the sultan exercised his power by generalising the consumption of goods that define the social order. This was the case for tea,[54] for example, or clothing made from imported cloth, essentially from England, used to make djellabas.[55]

The production of status

Much of the historiographical documentation is made up of texts that provide information about tax exonerations, the biography of local notables, the presence or absence of the state and so forth. Many are official documents recognising specific statuses, mobilised by actors as part of political competitions or rivalries. Both their content and the figures they mention are varied, ranging from the low-level *taleb*, to the eminent *Sharif* families and native lineages that owe their survival to just this kind of distinction, as well

37

WEAVING POLITICAL TIME IN MOROCCO

as chiefs of the Zawiya or distinguished artisans.[56] Although these documents are underused, even in Moroccan historiography, they represent a source of documentation that is particularly interesting because they demonstrate a performance, a sophisticated and intimate knowledge of the social fabric and its key figures, as well as possible alliances. As a result, they also reveal the ability to recognise and above all produce new status groups. They therefore render the sultan's recognition highly effective, even though in the sociology of sainthood and eminence it has always been recognition by the group that has been most important.[57]

This correspondence hints at the modalities by which this status was created—tax exemptions, gifts and donations, treatment at court, placement in the *harka* or the *mehalla*. All kinds of privilege contributed to status, and the *dahirs* recorded and renewed this regularly. In the context of a Nation-state type organisation, the creation of hierarchical statuses is the result of a "legal-rationalist" mode of governing. But in an imperial context, it constitutes a central and independent modality of government through the simultaneous coexistence of multiple different statuses (rather than in a nation-state where the status hierarchy is relatively stable).

Two situations coexisted here. Firstly, there was the status that granted rights and privileges to different groups, such as corporations, religious communities or brotherhoods, that were subject to specific regulatory regimes and for which the sultan's power was limited to recognition and accommodation of power relations. And secondly there were the statuses that relied on personal distinction, the work of the sultan through edicts of respectability, a whole range of statuses creating tax benefits or possibilities to claim tax privileges in certain situations.

Whether pre-existing or created, these "men of status" were at the heart of the strategy of indirect government and least cost administration, because they constituted an intermediary instance between the sultan and local populations. For the former, the compromises created, awarded or reinforced by privileges that he handed out enabled him not only to reduce the expenses of public servants and administrative organisation. By playing on competition between local notables, they also made it possible to limit their power and bring them to perform "liturgical roles" which

38

PROLEGOMENON

would be today described as public services. But in the long term, this frugal government via the reinforcement or creation of status proved risky and onerous—the processes of autonomy and accumulation led to *harka*, and the circulation of privileges, gifts or donations came at greater and greater cost. It all began to get complicated when, subject to pressure from Europeans, the sultans saw their responsibilities extend over the entire territory and thus had to increase their pressure for taxes.

Mastery over time

Although he did not master space, the sultan did master time, reflecting the valorisation of people and social relationships rather than goods, capitals or territories. This correspondence suggests that his power was built through waiting (for nominations for example), but also through accelerations (the *harka* is a perfect example here), stretching time (references to past events for example) or latent time (the sultan's disposition to "sleep" or "close one's eyelids").[58] This elasticity allowed the *Makhzen* to play on surprise and improvisation, in short, on uncertainty, and in that it is a powerful form of government.

But this mastery of time was never absolute. Ibn Zaidane introduces us once more to the complexity of this artform. In his chapter dedicated to "matters of state", he reminds us that the sultan had a specific programme for each day of the week: Friday and any holidays were dedicated to receptions at court, Tuesday and Sunday were reserved for hearing grievances of the people (*chikayas*), Saturday was for hunting, Monday for military exercises, Wednesday for the review of the army, and Thursday was the day of rest.

Mastery over time is also ambiguous. The sultan was of course a master of time, but he was also a slave to religious time. The latter is so highly codified that he could not miss the call to prayer for Eid—even though he could cancel a trip overseas, decide on a last-minute action or resolution or even suspend time until conditions were better for a given appointment, submission or reward.[59] The arbitrary power of the sultan was not absolute; there were signs that told his entourage what he would do and when. He was also affected by the plurality of time, particularly the superposition

WEAVING POLITICAL TIME IN MOROCCO

of religious, agrarian and lunar times with the time of the *Makhzen*. But this multiplicity and overlapping times also gives the sultan room to maximise them.

These artforms would eventually be challenged, however. The authorities of the Protectorate would come to adopt them, even reinvent them and superimpose them over other artforms, specific to their understanding of colonisation. This process is often analysed as the beginning of a dualism that is often assumed to be a characteristic of Morocco today.

The Protectorate and the invention of dualism

During the Protectorate, the lines clearly shifted, and changes took place. But these were not linear, nor directly attributable to identifiable causes. Above all, these transformations cannot be reduced to the emergence and then development of a dualism between the modern sector and the traditional sector, a dualism perpetuated by convenience, conviction and choice—and attributed to Lyautey, perceived as a visionary figure.[60] The complexity of the state in Morocco cannot be reduced to a juxtaposition between a burgeoning nation-state and the vestiges of an archaic *Makhzen* state. However, this image has the advantage of not obscuring certain incongruities of history: a sultan with merely religious and symbolic power, grand *caids* with the power of suzerains over half the territory, a Grand Vizier confined to his office (*béniqa*), tribes granted the status of moral entities under public law via the creation of the legal category of "collective lands" and so forth. It is far from easy to characterise the transformation of the Moroccan state over the 50 years of the Protectorate, given that this is such an old empire, colonised ("protected") by a Jacobin nation-state that had itself experienced revolution, empire, restoration, a second empire, the Commune and then a second and third republic. Above all, this was merely one colonial empire competing among others.

What kind of dualism is this?

When Morocco was colonised, the French political and administrative staff responsible for implementing colonial policy covered

PROLEGOMENON

a very broad ideological spectrum, ranging from Maurrassians to Saint-Simonians.[61] Morocco's policies were dependent on these fragile equilibriums that must be taken into account on an ideological level, but also on a socio-political and human one. The "poor whites" from colonial Algeria or the southern side of the Mediterranean did not share the same visions, interests or behaviours as the engineers from the prestigious *Ponts et Chaussées* school in Paris, the veterans of the "pacification" of Algeria, the public servants working for French interests or the industrialists working in nascent French capitalist interests, specifically those of family groups or financial conglomerates.[62]

The actions of the Protectorate—which were the result of this complex constellation of interests, logics and beliefs—played out in two directions according to different rationales. The first was ideological, conveyed by a humanist orientalising legacy that saw itself as an alternative to the aggressive colonial experience in Algeria. The second was political, guided by a logic of traditionalisation driven by Lyautey, who embellished some of the most ordinary actions of colonial domination and political control with a glossy veneer.[63] This choice, which has often been analysed as one of the only French examples of British-style indirect rule,[64] resulted from the first Resident-General of Morocco's penchant for the monarchy and fascination with orientalism,[65] and a desire to avoid repeating previous experiences in North Africa.[66] But it also stemmed from ardent opposition from segments of the Moroccan population that the colonial authorities were forced to contain, through negotiations and the mobilisation of pre-existing tribal oppositions. This clear choice of restoration to lend credibility to their action was limited to discourse and the scrupulous respect of form, appearance and symbols. The reality was completely different. The Protectorate took control and replaced the traditional administration, which found itself relegated to a ceremonial role, a simple replica. Direct administration was in fact established as part of the organisation of the Protectorate, based on a tendentious interpretation of article 4 of the 1912 treaty.

From this perspective, the *Makhzen*'s power was reduced, and the rigorously organised French administration took control of

41

WEAVING POLITICAL TIME IN MOROCCO

governing the country. This "reform of the *Makhzen*" was interpreted as the creation of a new structure alongside the old, which was to be preserved from any change in the name of respect for tradition. But this discourse of preservation was merely a façade; the traditional order was in fact undermined by a policy of museumisation and archaisation. The removal of the previous protections against arbitrariness ran counter to traditional order and gave rise to a more developed form of authoritarianism. Over and above the limitations to internal and external sovereignty included in the treaty of 1912 the colonial Protectorate relegated the sultan to a role of merely approving decisions made without him and reducing his administrative structure to a handful of viziers, disconnected from the realities of the country despite their numerous theoretical responsibilities.

The colonial authorities therefore used the instruments of the empire they controlled. This can be seen in the preservation of the exotic customs and expressions of the Sharifian empire, such as the codifications of what was supposed to be a specific protocol, in a highly museological vision that froze traditional practices and encouraged a return to those that had been abandoned.[67] We can also see this in public law which made the tribe a legal entity, while preserving the language of ethnicity; or in the process of modernisation based on spatial organisation (civil zones, military zones, zones run by grand *caids*) and statistical categories (indigenous peoples vs. Europeans, Sharia law vs. modern law vs. customary law) to promote modern colonial order. All this conferred reinvigorated government practices at least cost, as well as legal pluralism and the use of intermediaries for indirect administration.[68]

The new configuration that emerged cannot be summarised as the promotion of a clearly defined nation-state; it relied on the Resident-General's collaboration with the sultan, whose power and role were largely reinvented through classical reification (of tribes), selection (with an emphasis on the central role of religion to the detriment of customs), reinterpretation and naturalisation. The sultan's power and status were expressly defined in the Treaty of Fez, he was "confirmed" in his role as imam, the source of all indigenous power due to the supremacy of Qur'anic law. This is a clear illustration of how much colonial ideology idealised the religious

42

PROLEGOMENON

origins of the monarchy and over-valued their holy status. This interpretation betrays a false understanding of theological tradition but also the reality of the *Makhzen* where customs have always played an important role, even sometimes counteracting the application of Qur'anic law. It stems from an essentialising orientalist perspective that considers socio-historical reality as malfunction.[69]

Rationalisation of archaisms, or legal exoticism

This equivocal position of the Protectorate with regards to the modernisation project was confirmed by what is often called the "policy of grand *caids*". From the first years of the Protectorate, Lyautey envisaged using the *caid* system,[70] a strategy led by the officers of indigenous affairs. Primarily this was a way to limit military operations, rally notables by entrusting them with the command of their tribes and encourage the recruitment of partisans for "pacification". It was also a way to give the Protectorate the opportunity to reaffirm its policy of conservation and respect for traditional structures. The valorisation of *caids* overlooked an essential aspect of the system, however, the institutions of tribal deliberation and representation that progressively disappeared or were transformed into simple cogs within the administration, which encouraged the emergence of "*caid* authoritarianism."[71]

Reinforcing the authority of the *caids* thus gave rise to administrative delegations that were not subject to the rules of the state of law advocated in France. Exactions and arbitrariness were commonplace and were no longer tempered by local counter powers, nor by the sultan, proof that the "traditional system" was no longer operating.[72] This localised despotic power was extended to all areas of the country, including those that enjoyed a relative degree of autonomy.

The turning point came not so much from the Treaty of the Protectorate, as from the Manifesto of Independence, written by a young urban elite combining graduates from prestigious European schools and the university of al-Qarawiyyin. It was this movement, modern in the content of its demands but traditional in its approach and particularly in its reference to religion, that heralded the vision of the nation-state using the same elements as the authority of the Protectorate but adding lexical devices drawn from the Arab

43

WEAVING POLITICAL TIME IN MOROCCO

nationalism fashionable at the time. These included referring to *sha'b* (the people) rather than "tribes", *al-watan* (nation) rather than *ummah* (community of the faithful) and "king" rather than "sultan". Through this unprecedented movement, the monarch and the Crown Prince became the symbols of national unity. Nationalism had made this exile unbearable, although the French were relying on a dated reading of Moroccan history according to which monarchs were interchangeable. They had not seen the shift from sultan to king coming, and paradoxically, it was this colonial intervention that concretised the advent of the king.

Morocco under the Protectorate was neither a modern state nor a modernising state; nor was it a nation-state, nor even the prefiguration of one. Naturally, the idea of establishing a nation-state was voiced in certain circles, particularly within the Protectorate's administration. But this was a sector undergoing a process of modernisation, as can be seen in the impact of interest groups in mining, financial and industrial sectors, as well as the remoteness of decision-making from metropolitan France where the Ministry of Foreign Affairs was bogged down in matters of the Fourth Republic, along with the fact that the colonial administration was unable to exercise direct rule over the territory as a whole. Although the Protectorate provided the tools and technical efficiency of territorialised state presence, paradoxically the ideas of the nation-state were born within the "traditional state", as a reaction to the colonial policy of cultivating archaisms. The exile of Mohammed V on 20 August 1953, saw the monarchy gain a kind of precedence within the nationalist movement. It enabled them to optimise the timid clandestine connections between Prince Hassan, future King of Morocco and several members of the first nationalist networks. The two years between exile and the return of the King in 1955 were also those in which Mohammed V took on the status of a hero and became the object of very particular devotion.[73]

The woven time of independent Morocco

Breakthroughs, shortcuts or regressions are all terms that are often used in describing the trajectory of the Moroccan state. Many his-

PROLEGOMENON

torians and political scientists consider this trajectory as a straight line extending from a proto-state, i.e. one with patrimonial authority and low levels of differentiation, to a developed state, i.e. one that is legal-rational, authoritarian and for the most optimistic observers moving towards democracy. This comfortable and simplistic vision is not supported by the facts, however. In reality, different configurations have been observed since independence, which all associate—in different ways—the traits of the Nation-state and the traits of Empire.

The first of these configurations corresponds to the first years of independence, marked by the illusion of the construction of a nation-state in its ideal form, with a young elite breaking away from older generations and drawing its ideals from political liberalism, from Arab nationalism and from socialism.[74] Their credo was simple: fight against archaism and take the path of modernity. This choice seemed all the more self-evident in that the misguided actions of emblematic figures of the old regime—particularly *caids* and members of the brotherhoods—meant the monarchy could be absolved of any wrongdoing, along with the nationalist bourgeoisie due to their involvement in the economy and education rather than in armed resistance. In this configuration, resorting to imperial artforms seemed to be either a slip up, an oversight or a kneejerk reaction. In this way it was rendered almost clandestine or at least unconscious, given that the imperial register is so outdated; it was made invisible, unspeakable, treated as an archaism within a developmentalist reading of the state. The ICJ episode discussed at the beginning of the Prolegomenon, was a challenge to this modernising voluntarism. The orientation towards the nation-state prevented the Moroccan argument from taking full advantage of the opportunity the court statutes provided, other than through the instrumentalisation of *bay'ah*, the allegiance ceremony presented as a simple superficial backdrop.

The second configuration was characterised by a strategy of traditionalisation that could be described as ideological, and which borrowed from theological arguments and the promotion of the Caliphate. It paved the way for the reactivation of certain imperial practices. This option emerged towards the end of the 1970s, at a

WEAVING POLITICAL TIME IN MOROCCO

time when religion was becoming hegemonic in the expression of political divides. Competition around this resource was so intense that the Moroccan authorities, in order to assert their singularity and ensure their monopoly on symbolic production, chose to reinvent certain registers of the Sharifian empire. The *bay'ah*, the Commander of the Faithful *Amir al-Mu'minin*, Malikism, Sharifism and Sufism, traditional ways of living, dressing, cooking and eating, the entrepreneurial ethos of traders in imperial cities, or the virtuosity of artisans, all made it possible to refashion imperial traits and integrate them into the modernity of the nation-state.

The third configuration shows a situation where rules governing the nation-state are no longer considered to be in contradiction with the imperial regime (whose traits have become naturalised and spread throughout all spheres of society), including by former left-wing militants and Islamists. Although the conflicts and political violence in the 1980s could have meant the end of the monarchy, it was saved by its new "offer" of government, which was both intentional and spontaneous. Seizing upon the resources of neoliberalism, the monarchy took the initiative and contributed to setting up a new configuration in which imperial dynamics reinvented the art of governing based on methods that were historically rooted in Moroccan practices.

In reviewing this series of recent transformations of the state and its art of governing, our goal is not to rewrite a history of contemporary Morocco, nor to propose an alternative approach that would be paradoxically just as linear as previous ones and in which the guiding line would be the progressive rediscovery of the imperial aspect of the Moroccan state. Instead, we seek to shed light on the key moments and political expressions of voluntaristic nation-state building while emphasising, even implicitly, the traits of Empire that are sometimes so clearly marked they become important—or even dominant—characteristics in these forms of governing.

The illusion of the all-powerful nation-state

The conditions under which independence was negotiated established the colonial power as the dominant player. The dissolution

PROLEGOMENON

of the Treaty of Fez in 1956 created a new regime, straight out of the imagination of Edgar Faure who was then President of the Counsil of Ministers, "independence through interdependence". This was not merely a play on words or an attempt to perpetuate colonial power. It reflects the entanglement of two ways of perceiving the state. Beyond its colonial interests, France defended the idea of an eternal Morocco, the same celebrated in the lyricism of figures like Lyautey. The geopolitical context of the era (marked by the Suez crisis and Nasser's activism) exacerbated the French position against Arab nationalism. The spectre of pan-Arabism—whether republican or militarist—facilitated the enrolment of the palace, as well as of certain francophone nationalists close to the liberals, in a compromise project that provided the best defence for French interests. This compromise had the advantage of consolidating the role of the monarchy by protecting the imperial resources required to curb the Istiqlal party's pretentions to hegemony. This is why Mohammed V, once he was King, returned to the pluralism that was essential to his survival and worked (possibly unknowingly) towards attenuating the now dominant choice of the nation-state. Following this, Hassan II, who had been socialised in a context of nationalism and debates around the struggling Fourth Republic and the promises of Gaullism, set out resolutely on a path to the construction of a modern authoritarian nation-state in the interests of efficiency.

This configuration reflects a panorama dominated by uncertainty but rich in intertwining cultures and political projects. The "cast" of the Aix-les-Bains delegation,[75] or of the first government presided over by Mbarek Lahbil Bekkay,[76] the pardon of Thami Glaoui, the all-powerful Pasha of Marrakech,[77] and later that of Addi u Bihi,[78] all illustrate this intertwining and contrast with the unitarian dynamic of the nationalists that would lead to the systematic liquidation of opponents in the name of a single unified nation.

The ways in which the two periods of dissidence that Morocco experienced in the first years of its independence have been approached and later analysed reinforce the idea of an entanglement of repertoires and artforms of power, despite the hegemony of nationalism. The pre-eminence of the nation-state was undeni-

47

WEAVING POLITICAL TIME IN MOROCCO

able, but the imperial register enabled certain "arrangements" to be made. Thus, the state reacted differently to these two periods of dissidence; the revolt in the High Atlas and then that in the Rif were interpreted differently in view of the construction of the state and the legitimacy of the resistance.

The rebellion in the western High Atlas Mountains, in the region of Errachidia, was launched in 1957 by Addi u Bihi, against the Istiqlal, but not necessarily in defence of the monarchy. Addi u Bihi had been a *caid* under the Protectorate but had not signed the deposition of the Sultan Moulay Youssef and had been enrolled in the national struggle. Nationalist historiography attributes the repression of this revolt to a pro-monarchy plot aiming to weaken the victorious Istiqlal party.[79] Although we cannot completely discredit this hypothesis, we cannot entirely accept it either. That would mean overlooking both the numerous pre-existing divisions within the "national movement"[80] and the impact of local dynamics, which are all the more important as similar incidents took place in other parts of the country, although they were not documented by historians.[81] Ernest Gellner saw this High Atlas revolt by the former *caids* of the Protectorate as a demand for more state.[82] Although he did not spell out the nature of the desired state, it is clear that the dissidents did not share the vision of the nation-state promoted by the Istiqlal. The revolt by Addi u Bihi was not violently supressed, however. Several attempts at negotiation preceded the sending of troops under the command of the Crown Prince, and although Addi u Bihi was arrested, he was not executed. He died in prison in 1961 and was pardoned the same year. Hassan II paid homage to Addi u Bihi later saying, "he rebelled so that royal power would be respected."[83] Our analytic framework encourages us to see the sultan's clemency as much as a deliberate strategy to fight against the hegemony of the Istiqlal party as the extension of an imperial attitude to dissidence. In this context, the latter is considered the expression of local interests and a particularism that did not threaten state unity, through a conception of power that allowed for the existence of different levels of government.[84]

By contrast, the Rif revolt in 1958–9 was brutally repressed. Yet it was also an anti-Istiqlal movement, driven by the same

PROLEGOMENON

resentment against the appointment of urbanites to the region, condescension toward Berber peoples, compulsory Arabic and religious orthodoxy. Several factors may explain the violent repression of this second expression of dissidence. It is clear that the local memory of past events had an important impact; Abdelkrim Khattabi, who was then exiled, had previously attempted to organise a state within a state, and his behaviour at the time of independence appeared to stem from a "republican" position.[85] The Crown Prince's control over the events in Rif did the rest; the future Hassan II was then a proponent of nationalist ideology and imbued with Jacobin culture that (beyond the Fourth Republic that was scorned by his masters) valued above all else the heritage of Napoleon. He saw this rebellion as the continuation of the Rif war of 1921 and the entirely symbolic presence of the region's Emir, in voluntary exile in Cairo, was the link to a new generation of republican and nationalist Arab states. As a result, in the purest paradigm of the Nation-state, the terrible repression was proportional to the challenge (real or imagined) to national unity.[86]

The 1971 and 1972 coup attempts would shake Hassan II's regime. However, his miraculous survival gave him the possibility of reconnecting with a culture he had previously renounced. In addition to evoking the *baraka*, the sultan returned to the imperial techniques of negotiation and useful mediation and turning around dissidences. An initial rapprochement with elements of the national movement took place. The King openly displayed his desire to change the way of governing, and it was in these conditions that in March 1972 a new constitution was promulgated with a view to timidly rehabilitating parliament. Above all, the processes of producing statuses were reactivated in the form of the creation of a new party, the RNI (*Rassemblement national des indépendants*), which became the country's primary political movement in the space of one election. This party was supposed to respond to new needs resulting from the extension of public services to serve the needs of territorial administration, the creation of new categories of entrepreneurs beyond the traditional families of the urban bourgeoisie with close ties to the planned economy and ostracism by traditional activist parties leading to the rise of "independents".

49

WEAVING POLITICAL TIME IN MOROCCO

This new group, approved by a monarchy in search of new power relations with the Koutla,[87] rapidly became a political party and pushed older formations to change. The Socialist Union of Popular Forces (USFP) broke away from the National Union of Popular Forces (UNFP), the Moroccan Communist Party became the Party of Liberation and Socialism (PLS) and the Party of Progress and Socialism (PPS). The culmination of this project involved the reinvention of a "new Morocco", made possible by the 1975 "recuperation" of the Sahara.

We will not revisit this episode, already discussed in the introduction to this chapter, other than to outline a paradox. Morocco's argument to the international court, which was intended to defend a nation-state inspired idea of territorial integrity, ultimately resulted in the reactivation of the imperial frame of reference, through the instrumentalisation of traditional ties of allegiance. The opinion of the ICJ, which was deliberately ambiguous, was nevertheless sufficient for Hassan II. In 1976, he revived the *bay'ah* of the notables in the traditional assembly formed by the Spanish, and then three years later organised the *bay'ah* of Dakhla in great pomp and ceremony.

Redesigning the imperial register, between religious doctrine and theatralisation

In his speech the day before the Green March, on 6 November 1975, Hassan II called on nationalist sentiment[88] (invoking the flag, territorial integrity and the notion of borders), but he also drew on religious and symbolic dimensions, painting the March as the expression of sovereignty and the exercise of power. The Green March itself can be considered the most nationalist and "western focused" (to use the terms of the debate at the time) response possible, because it involved the physical occupation of a territory Morocco considered its own, with its control symbolised by the presence of its administration, its army, its population and its flag. The March was a symbol of newfound national unity focused on the figure of the King and his "united" people, to the point where it remains "even today a founding symbol of royal Moroccan nationalism."[89] But the Green March was also imagined and imple-

PROLEGOMENON

mented in the name of an imperial vision of the territory. Vows of allegiance were the expression of this form of governing of a territory that could be indirectly controlled through the connections between the sultan and local figures and through the mobilisation of Islam. The March was made possible through an art of organisation involving techniques specific to the Nation-state—the use of state administration to enrol and oversee the 350,000 marchers, preparations for monitoring these marchers according to territorial divisions of the nation-state into provinces and regions, training leaders from the national movement to supervise the masses. But this art also drew on techniques specific to Empire. The art of mobility and its specific logics of movement enabled the control of the territory, with its encampments, transport, logistics, food and health supplies. As for the art of representation, it claimed to shape the people marching to this reclaimed land into the image of the community in all its diversity. The marchers were carefully enrolled to ensure all areas, all ethnic groups and all social categories were present.[90] The success of this "crazy" gamble[91] on the part of Hassan II can only be explained by this combination of arguments, representations, references and techniques that work together in unconscious and unexpected ways. The Green March marked a turning point. Up until that date, the Nation-state paradigm was hegemonic, and the references to the imperial regime were little more than folklore. But the Dakhla *bay'ah* in 1979 was the opportunity for a spectacular staging of the pomp of Empire.

This *bay'ah* was emblematic in two respects. Firstly, in its staging and in the content of the text that accompanied it. This text established the emerging doctrinal framework that was the foundation of the political connexion, by considering the *bay'ah* as a kind of founding social contract. This was clearly visible in the way the allegiance was staged, both as a way of ordering society as a political community and as the expression of imperial performance. This was to be the first in this series of itinerant *bay'ah*; after Dakhla would come Casablanca, Fez, Tangier and Tétouan. It highlighted the art of itinerance that has been analysed above, involving thousands of people, all dressed in white, laying down thousands of rugs in an improvised "camp" in the middle of the desert, facing the ocean, all

51

The naturalisation of imperial traits

The return to the imperial register occurred at a very specific political moment; the status of the monarchy was henceforth unchallenged and unchallengeable. The question of the Sahara renewed discourses on the nation, power relations within the political field now operated to the benefit of the monarchy alone, and the "leftist danger" was reduced to nothing. Moreover, Hassan II had managed to impose the religious frame of reference as the foundation of the legitimacy of power, to the detriment of national struggle. Society was transformed by this nation-building, new elites appeared, while the limits of economic nationalism in the form of a powerful public sector and the pursuit of "Moroccanisation" were beginning to be felt. This further opened the doors to reforms and the transformations of institutions because the monarchy was directly confronted with society, without the filter of parties or intermediary bodies, which proved to be potentially dangerous (as the riots in the early 1980s show). These transformations took place in an international context where now-hegemonic neoliberal ideology was the only matrix in which economic and political reforms could unfold.

The premises of the neoliberal turning point can be identified in 1978, when the government sought to introduce its own austerity policy and to clear up state finances—an attempt that would be rapidly abandoned due to social tensions.[93] This first neoliberal period was marked by the restoration of public finances and an attempt to resolve the debt problem. It officially ended in 1992 when the country, considered stabilised, emerged from structural adjustment. During this period, in Morocco like almost everywhere else, the Washington consensus would spread and legitimise another vision of the economy and the role of the state and facilitate the transfer of new norms. This spread was not limited to macroeconomics but also developed in particular sectors, notably in agriculture. Agricultural structural adjustment programmes

PROLEGOMENON

began in 1985 and led to a reduction in the state's financial commitments, the liberalisation of structures of production and sales and the removal of most state offices, such as those for commercialising exports (OCE) of tea or sugar. But they also led to a dramatic reduction in state subsidies, with the exception of a handful of goods considered staples and politically sensitive such as flour, oil, sugar and gas. They were also associated with the first programmes for monitoring-evaluation around irrigation perimeters, such as that of Loukkos in the region around Tangier between 1982–8.

These first reforms suggest that new criteria and norms for intervention were rapidly adopted and led to a new concern for efficiency, transparency and responsibility. Although they presented a challenge to the way in which the state had functioned during the 1960s and 1970s, these policies nevertheless revived certain fundamental traits of imperial government, such as minimising costs via the use of intermediaries and soliciting the private sector in public management. This first period was also one that allowed the expression of a range of opinions and relatively strong opposition, as can be seen in the bread riots (in 1981 in Casablanca, in 1984 in the north of the country and in Marrakech). But there was also reticence, avoidance and scheming on the part of Moroccan authorities.[94] This shift came as a shock, given the nation-state interventionism that had been hegemonic in Morocco. However, and this is perhaps unusual, from this first period many Moroccan institutions and actors adopted and spread these new norms very easily. Some even saw them as a way to protest against or evade authoritarian power,[95] others saw it as a possibility to bypass institutions or mechanisms that were no longer useful,[96] still others as the ability to reactivate declining legitimacy.[97]

The period that followed and which continued up until 2005 could be described as the "hallalisation" of neoliberalism. It was inaugurated by the famous opening speech of the 1995 parliamentary session, known as the "heart attack" speech, in reference to the metaphor used by Hassan II to describe the crisis and announce the shift towards austerity and neoliberalism, a shift that was acknowledged but not explicit.[98] This movement paved the way for

53

WEAVING POLITICAL TIME IN MOROCCO

approval from organisations like the World Bank and very rapidly from foreign consulting groups, which became national actors in their own right, once they had the support from the palace and thus managed to neutralise resistance from traditional administration. This period was characterised by two paradigms. Firstly, there was that of openness, liberalisation and free trade, concretised in the signature of crucial trade agreements for the Moroccan economy such as that with the young World Trade Organization (born in Marrakech in April 1994) or the free trade agreement that Morocco and the EU signed in November 1995, just as the Euromed partnership came into effect. On the other hand, there was the paradigm of the spread of neoliberal norms and those of privatisation, public-private partnerships and participation and good governance in public policies and programmes. There was a genuine process of "customisation" that drew on the imperial vocabulary: *touiza* (collective mutual assistance), *kulfa* (trials), *jma'a* (deliberative assembly) and so forth. Although they took the path of international funding and expertise, these new paradigms ran through many institutions and administrations and were given new meaning by a shared political imaginary. Foreign consulting firms were only able to influence policy because these paradigms were appropriated in a "Moroccan" way.

Fifteen years later, in spite of the deep transformations that have taken place, the characteristics of the political system seem to be the same, which goes some way to explaining the extent of the often very aggressive criticism levelled at the regime by Moroccan or international actors or organisations. This tension between the affirmation of change and a feeling of being trapped (or at least subject to constraints that prevent the stated change) is not unrelated to the protests, social conflicts, political tensions and the ineffectiveness of relays and mediations. Understanding this situation requires us to situate this neoliberal moment—which was in fact not really very liberal politically—in the *long durée* of the Moroccan state. The imaginary alone enables the naturalisation of assemblages of logics, behaviour and understandings drawn from temporalities that are as different as they are remote from each other. Indeed, it is only if we take into account the imaginary of the state that we can understand that the engineers who graduated

54

PROLEGOMENON

from the most prestigious international schools claim the title *khadim*.[99] Moreover, it is only through this imaginary that we can understand how the CEO of Royal Air Maroc, who otherwise is extremely attentive to applying management rules to stabilise the company's finances, considers it normal to personally accompany the aeroplanes mobilised by the King and recognises himself (even jokingly) in the figure of the "*haras caid*" described by Ibn Zaidane.[100]

It is important to recall this trajectory in order to specify our understanding of the affinity between neoliberalism and the "traits" that are associated with Empire. Firstly, it evokes the weight of unexpected effects, paradoxes, the causal meanders of any kind of social action and the fragility of ideological and teleological visions of history. Even though the years 1956–61 were central in the sequence that explicitly mobilised the frameworks of the nation-state, configurations were established (pluralism, intangibility of property laws, diversification of forms of government through the use of private actors) that would allow—just a few years later—for the emergence of frameworks that were characteristically imperial. Secondly, it reveals the inanity of all intentional interpretations—imperial government techniques were not reactivated according to a pre-conceived government strategy but through constant trial and error and adjustments, practices that were progressively institutionalised and implemented, intellectualised and rationalised, before being established as a legitimate repertoire of government.[101] Finally, recalling Morocco's trajectory in this way outlines an apparent paradox: the ease and speed with which Morocco adopted neoliberalism by no means prevented tensions, confrontations and conflicts that were sometimes violent. In this way, these struggles, competitions and divergences, these adjustments between different positions and complex relations, the reconfigurations and margins for manoeuvre that they enable and the uncertainties they imply are all conditions for the art of governing and contribute to the naturalisation of neoliberalism. The latter can only be understood as a form of absolute domination of governmental ideology. In both the most humble and the most profound ways, it pushed the Moroccan state in all its complexity into the spirit of the time.

* * *

WEAVING POLITICAL TIME IN MOROCCO

Aside from serving as a homage to the author of the *Prolegomena*,[102] these introductory pages are intended to lay out the necessary analytic tools and construct two ideal-type figures of the state: Empire and the Nation-state. Empire combines a lack of pretention to controlling society as a whole with a propensity to prioritise adaptation and accommodation. It also claims ignorance of any association between legitimacy and the monopoly of power, including that of violence; as well as a desire to govern at least cost by drawing on forms of intervention, mediation and interposition. Empire also involves accommodating pluralist legal regimes, ethnic groups, nations and religious groups and successfully managing discontinuities, including temporal and territorial ones. It supposes intense investment in production and control of certain kinds of information and investment in people rather than institutions or structures. As for the other ideal-typical figure, the Nation-state, it is based on the principle of unity and continuity, voluntarism and domestication, uniformisation and abstract equality. It prioritises investments in systematic and homogenising information, with an emphasis on averages and laws of large numbers and valuing transformative action.

Our Prolegomenon has allowed us to provide a long-term perspective without depicting the trajectory as linear, as an unavoidable passage from Empire to Nation-state or as the return of Empire as part of a deliberate strategy for inventing tradition and still less as a status quo. On the contrary, this book presents unprecedented forms of government, new actors, artforms and issues, different ways of perceiving and understanding the world and a society that is continually changing. Yet all of this occurs within its own historicity, which combines elements from both the registers we have developed.

PART ONE

THE FOUNDATIONS OF POWER

In June 2018, millions of Moroccans decided to boycott three major consumer goods: milk from the *Central Laitière*, belonging to Danone; Sidi Ali water owned by the Ben Salah family (whose eldest daughter Meriem was president of the Moroccan business confederation up until May 2018); and petrol from Afriquia, of the Akwa group managed by Aziz Akhannouch (who was then Minister for Agriculture, Marine Fisheries and Rural Development, as well as Water and Forests, but who was also president of the RNI, an influential party in the government majority and perceived as being close to the King). The economic implications were significant for the actors targeted, as suggested by their press statements at the time. But the consequences were also political. In addition to the minister targeted directly, the Islamist party in power lost one other standing minister, at least symbolically, Lahcen Daoudi[1] along with his reputation. The former Prime Minister Abdelilah Benkirane who had resigned in favour of Saadeddine Othmani did not escape this tidal wave either. Even as he tried to stay afloat in order to capsize Aziz Akhannouch, whom he considered responsible for his disgrace, he was accused of helping the multinational by inciting people to break the milk boycott.

This unprecedented phenomenon gave rise to numerous and contradictory comments. Initially underestimated and sneered at,

WEAVING POLITICAL TIME IN MOROCCO

as though it were a marginal example of the kind of irrational movements that proliferate on the internet, the boycott eventually attracted the attention of analysts by its sheer size. Some attempted to identify the instigators at any price. Others minimised the phenomenon, seeing it as a consequence of the crisis of the middle class or simply as herd mentality. Still others saw in it the premises of a political revolution or an electoral campaign before its time, or they interpreted it as a form of cyber riot with firm, but vague, political goals. The boycott probably combined a little of all these things along with many others.

The objective here is not to explore explanations for this phenomenon, but what the boycott shows is the importance and political aspect of the signifying action. Of course, it involved isolated individuals, but these people considered themselves as "belonging to a community", they "felt connected" or had the "impression of being one."[2] They did not share the same objectives or the same motivations, but they found themselves sharing the same modalities for action. Thus, on 18 June 2018 in Ounagha, a small Chiadma town situated at an intersection of the routes between Agadir-Casablanca and Essaouira-Marrakech, our negotiations over the price of a watermelon progressively became a political discussion on the boycott. The seller was asking for 2.50 dirhams per kilo and in keeping with the rules of bargaining, we proposed two dirhams. "Impossible," he replied, "I only make ten centimes in every kilo because I buy them for two dirhams, and Akhannouch takes 40 centimes!" Surprised, we asked "But why Akhannouch?" To which he answered, "that's the cost of petrol." Somewhat provocatively we asked, "So you're not part of the boycott"? On the verge of anger, he replied, "But of course I'm boycotting, I'm buying it elsewhere." And when, with our implacable logic, we objected that the prices "elsewhere" were higher in the region, he replied, "in any case, I'm boycotting those people up there!"

This anecdote encourages us to envisage the boycott from a different angle. As a form of protest, it challenges the foundations of power itself, specifically representation, responsibility and the use of violence. It reveals the emergence of actors engaged in the *polis*, pursuing their objectives with a certain sense of self-awareness.

PART ONE: THE FOUNDATIONS OF POWER

These individuals do not feel represented but ostentatiously manifest their presence on the public stage directly through their actions. To a certain extent they accept the widespread idea that traditional political actors are no longer credible and that mediation mechanisms no longer function smoothly. The boycott means that representation is not necessary; it expresses—better than the vote—both a personal perspective and the belief that each individual can have a political impact. Boycotters also name those they believe responsible. They are not waging general war against "the cost of living", but instead focus on one dominant figure or another. Of course, this imputation of responsibility is akin to scapegoating and it is easy to mock its incoherencies—why Akhannouch rather than Total? Why Sidi Ali water and not Aïn Sais, which is produced by Danone? And why boycott Danone yoghurts but not those of the Domaines Agricoles, which is part of the royal holding company? What matters here is not how relevant the underlying analysis of the boycott is, but what it says about the need for responsibilisation and the spread of the question of "accountability" in society. Finally, although the community of boycotters was not structured, it was a movement in the sense that the individuals who participated came together around a particular action. Yet the foundation of originality and efficiency of this action lies in the fact that it invents a mode of action that avoids violence while managing the element of violence within itself. We can understand this as an "after-*hirak*" (after revolt). It avoids confrontation with the violence of the authorities, while controlling the destructive impulses provoked by feelings of injustice.

These questions of representation, of responsibility, of using or avoiding violence all challenge the foundations of power and the social order. They help to understand the tensions at work in the process of legitimation and the changes in the way a particular order is accepted, reproduced or challenged. Moreover, they encourage us to accept the diversity of orders and modalities of legitimation, which may all be in competition with each other. The boycott forces us to broaden our observation lens, to take in not only institutional spaces but also everyday lives. The following chapters deal with these changes in a non-linear and multivocal perspective. At a time when electoral representation dominates, co-optation appears central; when accountability is the leitmotiv, confusions between irresponsibility and impossibility of responsibility create disorder and weaknesses; when physical violence is framed by institutional mechanisms, symbolic violence becomes visible and frequent, while simultaneously appearing less and less acceptable. These changes give rise to tensions and conflicts often minimised by a perspective that, overly focused on the pomp and staging of power, sees only immobilism.

1

REPRESENTATION

After the legislative elections of September 2016, one concept became key for both supposed specialists of Morocco and for journalists: "blockage". For eight months following his nomination, the leader of the Justice and Development Party (PJD), Abdelilah Benkirane, was unable to form a coalition government. This period of latency did not contravene the dispositions of the 2011 constitution, either in form or in content. Having come first in the vote, the PJD was immediately given the prime ministership by the King.[1] But very rapidly, the new head of government's ways of conducting negotiations led straight to a dead end. Benkirane had an interpretation of his victory that displeased his future partners. He offered them a membership contract (according to civil law) rather than discussions on a coalition platform. Negotiations also suffered from his way of communicating. As an experienced "political animal," the head of government thought that the "Deep State" did not want him and that his partners negotiating a role in the coalition were puppets manipulated into inflicting humiliating conditions on him. But he never questioned the King. On the contrary he constantly reiterated his status as a servant. However, at the same time he did not hesitate to remind his party activists that he was beholden to his voters and expressed their will—to fight against corruption (*fassad*). This dual discourse was quite normal.

WEAVING POLITICAL TIME IN MOROCCO

Benkirane was the head of a party that owed its support to anti-politically correct discourse, and this was even more the case now that he had made his way into the system. But he was also the underdog who knew that his ideology, inspired by the Muslim Brotherhood's frame of reference, would not sit well with the King, who would have preferred the ballots to bring him a party closer to his own "projects for society". But this did not prevent Benkirane being convinced that "Monarchy is the only possible regime in Morocco", nor putting his popularity and the energy of his party "at its service".[2]

For a little more than eight months, the "blockage" was considered a battle of wills: one resulting from the election, the other historical but inscribed in the constitution. The King eventually removed Benkirane from his position, as the constitution allowed, to name another PJD leader in his place. The latter was just as legitimate but considered more accommodating and less charismatic by the youth of the PJD and a good part of the party sympathisers. This tends to lend support to the idea of a conflict between the King and the party leader, even though it is less intense and personal today than it was between Hassan II and Ben Barka. But above all, it illustrates the difficult cohabitation between "popular" will expressed through the vote and royal will consecrated by both history and the 2011 constitution. This gives the impression that the "victory of the PJD" went against the will of the King, who is seen as having resigned himself to appointing an Islamist Prime Minister out of respect for the constitution. This is a metaphorical equivalent of a defeat, in terms of the popularised image of an omniscient and omnipotent King. But this turnaround had no impact on the popularity and status of the King, who was still the source of salvation, even though his entourage had been targeted directly.

There is nothing surprising in this, however. Whether defeated on the battlefield and held prisoner (Moulay Slimane), sent into exile (Mohammed V) or subject to repeated coup attempts (Hassan II), no Moroccan sultan has seen his status as adored and honoured King genuinely challenged. This allows us to raise the following question—why is the status of the King maintained, even strength-

REPRESENTATION

ened, when he is defeated or his will is overturned? Is it, as many anthropologists suggest, to do with his status as a saint? Or is it that, in the context of the contemporary crises many countries are facing, the King is simply considered the only fortress against chaos?

Back to history: representation in the face of defeat

In volume 9 of *Al- Istiqsa*, an-Nasiri[3] tells of the defeats suffered by Moulay Slimane in 1819 against the Zayane and then a few years later against the Zawiya Cherradia.[4] This second defeat is the most eloquent because this was a conflict between two holy lineages that began with a scandal involving a governor of Marrakech. The latter, jealous of the spectacular development of the Zawiya Cherradia, only a few kilometres away from the ochre city, convinced the sultan to send an expedition to punish them, with disastrous results. The 200 horsemen were defeated and had to return to Marrakech on foot. Nasiri's tales are surprising enough that colonial literature, and later certain anthropologists, seized on them to promote the idea of a holy sultan.[5] Essentially, even if the king is defeated, the saint remains. Yet these narratives allow for alternative interpretations. Indeed, in both of these unfortunate episodes, Nasiri describes the warm welcome of the victors, while also specifying that the manifestations of devotion to the holy king were more commonly expressed by women. And despite his reservations, he noted an important fact that illustrates the status of Moulay Slimane among the Cherradia. He participated in Friday prayers as the vanquished host, behind an imam who pronounced the prayer in his name. The pact was therefore intact.

Was Moulay Slimane honoured as the holy recipient of the *baraka*, or as the head of the community of communities, of which the victors remained members? The hypothesis of sainthood is attractive, but it comes up against at least two obstacles. The first of these is that in his fight against the Zayane, the sultan lost his son, Moulay Brahim, who was also a descendant of the saint and had also completed his pilgrimage. Moreover, the second was a fight between two holy lineages—one royal and the other a brotherhood—the latter having proved itself to the point of establishing

WEAVING POLITICAL TIME IN MOROCCO

a flourishing household. The war of a saint against another holy family and the death in battle of a saint from the royal line both raise questions.

We can therefore not content ourselves with the hypothesis of sainthood, even though it is convenient for emphasising the singularity of the Moroccan regime. Colonial literature made it the key to the system, which meant Morocco could be described as a Sharifian kingdom, and the king could be confined to a symbolic role.[6]

In his final book dedicated to Morocco,[7] the anthropologist Raymond Jamous continued and updated a well-established tradition based on reasoning that brings together the distinction between *Bled Siba* and *Bled Makhzen* and segmentary lineage theory. Jamous summarises all this in decisive terms,[8] although he also (rightly) emphasises the role of the representative of the sultan's (or king's) unity. The problem is that he reduces "religious legitimacy" to sainthood and descendance from the Prophet. In so doing, he minimises, like many others,[9] the theory of power in Islam, which introduces an extreme tension between the theoretical potential of radical monotheism—according to which the site of sovereign power can never be occupied by a human whoever they may be—and the need for the physical and symbolic presence of he who holds an aspect of this power by procuration.[10] God is power; men are merely ephemeral expressions of the divine, in the form of "*autoritas*".

This philosophical background does not mean the "end of history". Islamic societies have continued to study the need for power to organise the community of believers and make religious practice possible.[11] The holder of authority emerges firstly from social power relations; religious figures, or more specifically those tradition calls "men who connect and disconnect", and behind them all Muslims, merely accept a *fait accompli*. In Morocco, a popular saying reflects the prudence of the Ulema. In moments of uncertainty, during invocations that conclude Friday's prayer, the accepted saying is "God's blessings and support on he who lives to see another day."

Returning to these defeated sultans allows us to reflect on the exercise of power and in so doing, the question of representation.

64

REPRESENTATION

As we have seen, the sultan faced constant challenges, but these did not undermine his status. The power relations that historically brought him into being had no impact as long as the exercise of his power did not lead to a loss of territory, subjects or still less, religion. The sultan was the core of a consensus—in this respect he represented the community of communities in all their conflictualities—because in a world of violence and shifting power relations, he was the only bulwark against chaos.

From the early twentieth century, Muslim societies experienced a deep movement of secularisation, yet held back from necessarily following those minority voices contesting the Qur'an and the Sunnah as the source of power.[12] Nevertheless, the breech was opened and provided a glimpse of numerous variations, such as those recorded in the latest Moroccan and Tunisian constitutions. Without undermining the principle of Islam as the state religion, the nation had been established as the site of "derived"[13] sovereignty, entirely distinct from any reference to the theory of the Caliphate.

The new constitution: between the centrality of elections and practices of co-optation

In the formal evolutions brought about by the 2011 constitution, the question of the site of sovereignty appears to have been unequivocally resolved. By contrast, article 41, which "ostentatiously" dissociates the religious status of the King from that of the head of state, or the abandonment of the mention of the sacredness of the royal personage, introduced by French constitutional experts during the writing of the first 1962 constitution, is less so. Article 2, which comes after the definition of the type of Moroccan state and before the mention of its religion, stipulates that "sovereignty belongs to the nation which exercises it directly, by way [*voie*] of referendum, and indirectly, by the intermediary of its representatives." (subparagraph 1) and that "The Nation chooses its representatives from among the institutions elected by way of free, honest [*sincère*] and regular suffrage" (subparagraph 2). This affirmation seeks to ground the Moroccan monarchy in political modernity by emphasising the fundamental role of elections, which according to

65

WEAVING POLITICAL TIME IN MOROCCO

article 11, subparagraph 1, must be "free, sincere, and transparent", stipulating that they are "the foundation of the legitimacy of democratic representation."

However, in spite of the strength of these two articles, which pave the way for new modalities of government and new mechanisms for the production of legitimacy, a careful reading of the constitution reveals grey areas. One such area is the status of the Commander of the Faithful, which has uncertain legislative implications in a society that universally believes in the supremacy of religion over the law. This ambiguity is still more explicit in certain formulations, such as the "kingdom's constants," in article 19 on the equality of men and women. It essentially voids the article of its content, makes the connection between state law and international law obscure and opens up the possibility for very restrictive interpretations, particularly in terms of women's rights.[14] It also allows for multiple and paradoxical usages of certain principles, such as the right to life, which may be mobilised both by anti-abortion activists and by proponents of the abolition of the death penalty. Above all, it shows that the massive presence of an international frame of reference inspired by the Third Wave constitutions, particularly in terms of economic and social rights, direct democracy, participation and accountability (Article 1) did not erase the traces of an imaginary fuelled with the idea of Morocco's specific trajectory. It was in fact this imaginary that outlined the forms of appropriation by political actors, sometimes giving the impression the constitution was "ill fitting" or "overly ambitious" for the current political culture.

At first glance, in this new constitution elections seem even more central because the King is bound by their results, as part of the exercise of his functions. He is charged with designating a head of government from the party that wins the majority (Article 47) and cannot end his mandate without running the risk of provoking new elections and dissolving parliament (Articles 51 and 96 to 98) and seeing the outgoing majority strengthened. As we can see in the vigour of the electoral competition and the royal nominations after the vote, all these dispositions in favour of electoral representation are taken very seriously and determine the shape of the media por-

REPRESENTATION

trayal of political life. But this reading, which is essentially literal, obscures another conception of representation which is even more important, and which can be seen less in the organisation of elections than in co-optation practices. From a doctrinal perspective, this comes from a reflection on the return of representation based on historical legitimacy and "Moroccan *durée*",[15] but also from a desire to ensure Morocco is "in phase with" what is "best" in modern constitution building; it accompanies a new distribution of power. The constitution actually implicitly evokes spaces where *intuitu personae* nomination and co-optation appear to be appropriate modalities for functioning. By stipulating that "the public powers work to the creation of instances of dialogue [*concertation*], with a view to associate the different social actors with the enactment, the implementation, the execution and the evaluation of the public policies." (Article 13), by establishing "participative democracy" and bodies that promote human rights, good governance and human development (Articles 161 and 170), it opens up the possibility for the expression of other forms of representation that echo recent debates in Western democracies on the "crisis of representation" that has marked the neoliberal moment. The organic laws that define the make-up of these bodies, however, do not prevent the salience of an organisation into orders, within Moroccan society.[16] Although these orders may evolve over time, they continue to structure the process of nomination by the King. They ensure room for professionals living overseas, technocrats, professors with various sensibilities, representatives of civil society, on the left and on the right, feminists, independent businessmen, human rights activists or iconoclastic atheist philosophers. Of course, they do not overlook "traditional" categories such as Jews, palace attendants, Berbers, Sahrawis, Rifians, peoples of the central plains and so forth. Royal power is deeply imbued with this understanding of representation as an image of the nation in all its diversity, a vision which even influences the innermost spheres of power, beyond political processes.

But co-optation is not an exclusively royal practice. It is also frequent among other political and social actors, although it may take other forms. The ten structures created by the new constitution[17] were not the result of efforts by isolated experts, but from the pressure generated by the consultation processes that governed its writing. The leitmotiv of almost all those auditioned as part of this dialogue (associations, unions, political parties, representatives of social movements) was the "constitutionalisation" of such commissions or councils.[18] These suggestions reveal a demand for democratisation and, simultaneously, an attachment to historically established corporatism. We can also read these suggestions as the coexistence of an explicit desire to avoid electoral risks, a rejection of politics incarnated by political parties and a fear of "majority dictatorship", in the perspective of transparent elections and in keeping with criticisms expressed against democracies in which the principle of representation had lost its way.

The paradox lies in the fact that frameworks that are philosophically attached to an authoritarian conception of power are promoted in the name of democratisation. This paradox is by no means specific to Morocco. It is characteristic of the contemporary period and its reflections on the waning of democracy and the "crisis" of representation and on their corollary, the need to develop new forms of legitimation.[19] In the case of Morocco, it tends to give new meaning to these corporatist structures, closer to Empire than to Nation-state. It has sought to update them, integrating them into a new international doxa and giving them a veneer of "good governance".

These different understandings of representation converge around the reinvention of the pivotal role of the King, not only as the adjudicator overseeing the equilibrium, but also as producing a snapshot of the nation in all its diversity. In other words, he is the expression of a type of representation that is different from electoral representation. What was openly accepted but not constitutionalised under Hassan II[20] has become implicit but constitutionalised under Mohammed VI. This evolution was directly linked to the modernisation of imperial performances and in particular the widely shared hypothesis that the *Makhzen* possesses this specific knowledge of the community—which is today expressed each time controversial reforms make it necessary to invent instances that can be substituted for electoral representation.[21] This hypothesis is sometimes confirmed, as we can see in the casting of the Commission

REPRESENTATION

for the Revision of the Constitution.[22] But it may also be invalidated because of the loss of this typically imperial knowledge when it becomes entangled in other forms of knowledge from the nation-state repertoire. The replacement of the *nisba*[23] by the CV, as the tool for recruitment, for example, increased the possibilities of "poor casting" and led to dead-ends or even to situations being aggravated instead of resolved.

Nearly ten years after it was promulgated, the democratic dynamics of the constitution are still limited. The radical changes introduced in 2011 have not been activated, as though the political actors did not believe in their effectiveness. This was the case for the Senior Security Council (Article 54), that was to have brought together elected officials and been presided over by the head of government, even though security and the army are the exclusive domain of the King: it was never created. Should we take this to mean that, in reality, historical representation has overtaken electoral representation? Although any such claim would be premature, it is clear that there has been a process of naturalisation of practices that were previously seen as not conforming to the canon of democratic representation. This is also true for the Court of Accounts, the Council of the Economy, Society and the Environment, the Senior Magistrature Council, the Senior Education Council and the Constitutional Court. All of these are instances in which the King has clear powers of co-optation.

This process is ambivalent by nature. It draws on the most contemporary and varied legal, political and philosophical reflections. It affirms the central importance of elections as an expression of national sovereignty, but also takes into account the "crisis" of the political party system, linked in particular to the "imperfections" of electoral representation and popular disaffection with it. By contrast, it values expertise and professionalisation, frameworks for deliberation and participation and the idea of community. In terms of principles it prioritises equality, impartiality and neutrality and the need for disintermediation—and all of this based on a differentiation between the citizen and the voter. At the same time, the Moroccan context is significant, particularly through its long history of conservative reformism which considers that the

69

elites—ahead of the rest of society—are best placed to promote democratic principles, the only ones able to counter the excesses or shortcomings of democracy and outline any remedies. The meeting of these two dynamics, global and national, leads to a revaluing of co-optation. The imperial register recasts this as a skill, a framework providing a knowledge of society in all its complexity and an unmediated incarnation of society through its men. This is because the legitimacy of co-optation as a framework, reactivated by fashionable political theories, enables it to be spread through all political spheres—even though the royal entourage remains the key example. In the name of taking other aspects of representation into account, co-optation is now accepted by political parties and by the head of government or the President of the Parliament. It appears all the more natural because it lies at the intersection of three forms of legitimacy: historical legitimacy, constitutional legitimacy and operational legitimacy, linked to skills and knowledge.

Images of political community: staging and theatrics

The experience of power, defeat or the new additions of the 2011 constitution meant representation could be considered as an attempt to make what was absent present and to depict society as it is, with all its diversity and power relations, with the tension between the obligation of loyalty (as a mirror of society) and the obligation of efficiency (as a rationalised presentation depending on objectives). But as Louis Marin has argued, representation also implies exhibition and exposure, and representation is always a "reflection" on power itself, power that is presented as representing something, and which is constituted as its own legitimate subject through the exhibition of qualifications, justifications and status.[24] Representation therefore consists just as much of staging as it does distancing. It is this aspect of exhibition and play, in other words theatrics, that we wish to explore here by showing how the intertwining of national and imperial registers runs through the forms in which the nation reveals itself and how power becomes representation.

REPRESENTATION

The House of Representatives and the House of Councillors, which are brought together in the annual opening ceremony of the parliamentary session, provide the staging for a sparse and monochrome image of national representation. This image incorporates the King who fosters a hierarchical conciliation between the two bodies in a ritualised moment. This is constructed through the dress code, white, considered the national dress. Variations on this dress code (djellaba, burnous, babouches, with red chechia hats) are marginal and more to do with the quality of the fabric or the mark of the dressmaker. Differences are barely noticeable. Young or old, rural or urban, intellectuals or illiterate, from one region or another, everything is red and white. The women, of whom there are many due to the quota system, also wear white djellabas (which is a traditionally male garment they have appropriated, like the caftan in the public space). In fact, here the costume embodies the link with Empire, essentially through the chechia hat, of which the shape (like the fez) and colour (red) evoke proximity to the sultan. The nationalists had invented a different head covering, the tarbouch *watani* (national) which was adopted by Mohammed V as the incarnation of the nation. But in the parliament during official ceremonies, it is the red chechia that dominates.

The *bay'ah* annual allegiance ceremony that comes at the closing of the celebrations of the throne festival is another way of staging the political body. It contributes to the ceremonial framework, on a level that above all emphasises the imperial aspect of representation through an interplay of images and symbols, even though the ceremony itself expresses a discursive register more linked to the Nation-state. The connection with Empire can be found in itinerancy (the *bay'ah* ceremony is held in imperial cities), the physical proximity of the palace (it takes place in the *mechouar* that faces the palace itself), the costumes (which as well as being national are reminiscent of imperial times) and in the ritual itself. In the latter, the King, preceded by the *caid* of the *mechouar*, temporarily takes on the traditional attributes of the sultan, seated on horseback and sheltered by the parasol immortalised by Delacroix,[25] exactly as Ibn Zaidane described him a century ago. The imperial aspect is symbolised by the gestures—kneeling, an expression of submission—

71

WEAVING POLITICAL TIME IN MOROCCO

and the speech, the expression "May God bless our master" repeated after the master of ceremonies. Everything else depicts a political body and a social body combined into a single entity, unified by the dress code, which is in keeping with the (also aesthetical) demands of the Nation-state. The social bodies recognised under the Sharifian empire (corporations, tribes etc.) are now standardised as a reflection of the territorial divisions of the country. At the annual *bay'ah* there are representatives of the territorial authorities (towns and regions), who fall into line behind the standards bearing the insignia of their provinces, with the *walis* in front, before the governors and the *caid*, who are all public servants of the Ministry of the Interior.

The sites of this staging of society, with its diversity recalling a fragmented political body or an assembly of several communities, are today patrimonialised and associated with the private sphere of marriage. For example, the *hdya*, the presentation of blessings and gifts during religious celebrations that had disappeared after Ibn Zaidane's most recent exhaustive description, made a surprising return for the marriage of King Mohammed VI's brother, Prince Moulay Rachid. This was possibly a reminder that its vulgarised form was none other than the marriage ceremony—whether lower class or bourgeois—staged and produced by the figure of the caterer, a veritable institution in Morocco. Indeed, society is reflected in all its diversity in this ceremony, through the different costumes the bride wears over the course of the evening and the title given to the groom for the bridal evening, Moulay Sultan.

The *hdya* appears as the stage on which, via an exchange of gifts, the link between dissident groups and the sultan's power is performed, even though in terms of accounting the balance is clearly in the hands of the court. Those involved or who aspire to be vie for prominent positions through the quality and value of their official gifts—they express their singularity and investment in the court through their costly gifts.

The other function of the *hdya*, the one that interests us here, is the ritual of representation (in the theatrical sense) of an "imagined community" as an entity that is both hierarchical and diverse, with its classes and ranks. It is a moment that allows competition between

REPRESENTATION

groups and the updating of an expression of unity through diversity.[26] Up until independence, the *hdya* regulated political life. Whether in Rabat, Fez or Marrakech, the sultan received representatives from the tribes, corporations and brotherhoods and major families of the Ulema or *chorfa*. The order of presentation depended on the location, with the locals taking pride of place. But aside from this characteristic, the hierarchy remained stable, reflecting a strict hierarchy and differentiation in the power positions of communities. The *hdya* was also an opportunity for emulation, with those present having to honour their position and their ambitions. As a result, its staging was highly codified and meticulous.

As part of the project to affirm the eternal grandeur of the Moroccan state in the face of the condescension of the Protectorate, Ibn Zaidane considered the *hdya* as a major argument. Luckily for us, he laid out the details, which are valuable in understanding the salience of the imperial reference in the current context. The *hdya* is a snapshot in a chronicle seeking to depict the Moroccan state in all its splendour, with its order and grandeur. It is one of the most rich and colourful expressions of this. In his narrative, Ibn Zaidane emphasises its immutability and its meticulous organisation; in his eyes they symbolise the stability of the state that runs through the ability of actors to eternally reproduce a ceremonial staging in an identical form.

The document that is the foundation for this reflection takes into account Ibn Zaidane's text as well as the annotations by Abdelwahab Ben Mansour, who was the royal historiographer between 1961 and 2008. It describes five scenes: the celebration prayer, the distribution of gifts, the movements of the King between the exterior and interior doors, the reception of friends and family and the private moment where the sultan receives those who have asked to see him. These five scenes demonstrate the way in which the political community is conceived through its empirical contents. The Sharifian empire considers itself a community of communities, but its concern with representativity should clearly not be understood in the democratic sense of the term but rather as the updating of pluralism and diversity as constitutive principles. The protocol as a whole is a stylised representation of the political community,

73

WEAVING POLITICAL TIME IN MOROCCO

presented aesthetically and symbolically—or even stereotypically because it is reproduced in identical terms. And this community is diverse, divided and hierarchical. Its staging is codified. It is not an exhaustive inventory, like tax records or military registers that serve to mobilise resources and distribute contributions between groups. Instead, it is stylised, a way of moving from the population seen as a black hole, chaos, to an ordered political community. Moreover, this community is understood as being much larger and broader than just the minority who "connect and disconnect, "[27] evoked in the classics of Muslim political doctrine and seen as involving the Islamic *ummah*. This stylisation is a depiction of the order at the time, which governs power relations and hierarchy. The matrix of this staging is always the same; although there might be variations on different occasions, the events and spaces are codified in themselves.

The first two scenes described in the document reveal a territorial representation of community; the imperial territory is present in the celebrations in its extreme diversity and division, with the heads of the tribes, representatives of groups and cities and particularly the governors who "represent" them by delegation or proxy. Several levels and variations are juxtaposed here—tribes and tribal confederations, towns and territories—which Zaidane's historiography describes precisely by listing all the tribes they cover. The sizes of the tribes themselves are variable; very small tribes are quoted directly; much larger tribes are incorporated into broader groups. This apparent heterogeneity is in fact unsurprising. In this representative system it is not the size of the groups (how many members, or the scope of their financial or military resources) that is noted, but the importance of their connection to the sultan and to power. This, in turn, depends on their strategic geographical situation on the roads of the *harka* or in ports, or their functional utility (whether they are warriors or not). This order thus depicts a territory. The official ceremony is a metaphor, an abstract image of the community that constitutes the territory. But it also reveals the criteria of representation which is constructed around the importance of the group in relation to control over the territory, through barriers, passages, meeting places or the historicity of the

74

REPRESENTATION

state. This helps us understand the priority and eminence of the Idrisids,[28] or the Tlemcenians[29] who incarnate the country's independence. The arrival of these groups as exiled migrants helped mark the country's borders, consolidated sovereignty and thus marked Morocco's autonomy from the Ottoman empire.

The third scene depicts a different kind of representation. This is the functional representation of corporations, with their notables, *chorfa*, Ulemas, *cadis* or viziers, who are not mandated by their group but whose diversity also offers a vision of the orders that structure society and in particular the key figures in the process of intermediation and intercession. This is a stylised representation of the community that demonstrates the place of different actors in the mechanisms of power, whether the goal is controlling territory or intermediation. The permanence of the state and its continuity are expressed through the miraculous identical reconstruction of the court, whatever the site may be. Each morning, hundreds of tents are taken down, stacked in the same order, then put back up again a few kilometres down the road when night comes, and the sultan arrives. The *hdya* follows this same staging of an unshakeable order that seeks to incarnate the permanence of the state.

Today both the *hdya* and the *harka* are far-off memories, obliterated in practice but nevertheless preserved at least in the lexicon. *Harka* is used from time to time to refer to violence, whether a cleansing campaign or the repression of a demonstration. The nation, united and purified, much like power, needs to showcase this diversity outside of agricultural fairs and museums of traditional arts, which are mostly still in the project stage. The reason for the monarchy itself is only relevant when the political and social space is fragmented. Alongside this there are also the ongoing changes that emphasise questions about regionalisation, multiple identities, etc. But diversity, even when it is constitutionalised in the form of a lyrical preamble linking identity with multiple sources,[30] even when inscribed in the organic law on regionalisation, can only be represented as folklore or heritage. The spread and naturalisation of diversity and pluralisation of identity in society can only play out on the margins of domestic spaces, during marriage ceremonies for example, even though their meaning is political.

75

WEAVING POLITICAL TIME IN MOROCCO

In November 2014 during Moulay Rachid's marriage ceremony, the *hdya* was mobilised in a form reminiscent of—but not identical to—Ibn Zaidane's stylised description, presented above. This form has been reinvented, couched in folklore and heritage, apparently without any political connotation, but nevertheless portraying a vision of society and the political community.[31] It no longer involves tribes and corporations but rather a parade of particular identities and regional ties expressed through traditional dress and songs, reflecting the major regional denominations that the new administrative divisions have produced. Indeed, the spaces and frameworks of political representation are now elsewhere. They must be sought in the new constitution. In a compromise that reflects the power relations and interpenetration of registers and temporalities, this constitution—from its very preamble—presents the national community as a broad and varied spectrum of identity. It presents the nation as the site of national sovereignty and the Commander of the Faithful as the key religious figure.

Representation in the Nation-state and the Empire

Beyond the picturesque images of traditional costumes and exotic languages, what do these ceremonies actually say about representation or rather about the way in which representation operates in the empirical reality of the contemporary Moroccan political system, and what does it say about their diffusion in society?

As we saw above, in Morocco like in all countries with a Muslim tradition, the theory of the Sunni Caliphate or the Shia Imamate still permeates imaginaries,[32] even though it has little impact on constitutional texts. The theory of the vicariate makes the mirror and the stage indissociable.[33] The mirror is of course altered because it is impossible to represent the community; it instead represents the different communities that constitute it, which are reflected in all their contradictions and conflicts, without searching for averages or sublimations. In these momentary instances of theatralisation, with their stylisation and aesthetics, the representation-staging takes on the ephemeral nature of power, the result of the necessarily shifting power relations that are constantly being

REPRESENTATION

reconfigured. The representativity of the representation of society—which is at the heart of the tension between electoral representation and historical representation—can only be understood in light of these power relations.

This is where our ideal-type reading can enrich the understanding of these multiple interlocking facets of representation. Given that representation itself is by definition a distancing, it is important to understand what kind of distances dominate in these two ideal-type repertoires. In our Empire ideal type, Muslim theology means the sultan is dispensed from any kind of representation because he is the Vicar of God on earth. The ideology of the Caliphate excludes the idea of incarnation. As he is the "shadow of God on earth" the sultan cannot possibly be the mirror of society. But in the pragmatics and struggles of earthly power, representation occasionally arises in moments of scriptural theatralisation (hence the importance of the letters, the royal seal and its contents) or symbolic theatralisation (hence the importance of the standards, the two riderless horses,[34] the parasols). But above all, this representation is present in the scrupulous staging of the *hdya* or the *bay'ah* where the sultan appears to be the expression of what constitutes community, through the recognition of diverse and often conflictual groups.

However, governing requires a mirror, an image of the power relations between the groups and communities that constitute society at any given time. Guiding society without using force demands the ability to represent that society in its diversity. Not to change it, uniformise it or create a homogenous whole or build a united and indivisible nation, but on the contrary to govern with society as it is, made up of diverse communities that are constantly reorganising and changing shape. Representation is a way of ordering different communities in respect of this pluralism. It is not an ongoing fiction, like "the people" or "the nation" characteristic of the Nation-state ideal type. Rather it is necessarily temporary, intermittent and must constantly be reactivated. Knowledge of this complexity is an advantage for the sultan, who gains efficiency in his choice of mediators, the "right" people (those who are efficient) through whom he can effectively reign. Taking into account rep-

77

resentation at the level of the court—in other words the representativity of the court, which includes the elite as well as the lowest levels of society in the form of slaves or artisans—is what enables him to govern. Co-optation is the tool of this representativity.

By comparison, in our Nation-state ideal type, the imaginary of the nation creates an obligation of symbolic representation. It is not the diversity of communities that is represented here but the nation—a fiction discursively defined by language, religion, history, territory etc. This representation requires the creation of order, a process that takes concrete form through the reinvention of categories. There is a shift from populations to the voting public. Tribes, statuses or corporations have all been replaced by men and women, young and old, urban or rural dwellers, who all share the same belonging. It is now they who must be represented. The supreme representative is the King, who is the incarnation of the nation. And in this context, the *bay'ah* in its new version, in which the uncertainty of succession is erased, is not seen as theatralisation but as the expression of a contract between the supreme representative and the nation. From the very beginning, however, the King is not alone in this. Elected MPs are also representatives of the nation. This narrative of the nation paves the way for an authoritarianism of the nation-state and opens the door to the idea of representation as the incarnation of national sovereignty. The key tool of this representativity is the election.

The spread of co-optation

As we have seen, the 2011 constitution was a turning point for the meaning of elections in Morocco. Henceforth elections represent a dual constraint. On one hand, they constrain the King, who is bound by the results, and on the other, they constrain politicians who can only access resources and spheres of power via election. In this respect, elections have become the reference model that has spread through all political bodies. Yet co-optation has not disappeared; in fact, it has been strengthened by being constitutionalised. As a result, this makes it important to understand how the electoral system is redeployed in a context where co-optation is

REPRESENTATION

reconfigured and what that has changed for the meaning of elections themselves, for their narrativisation and their staging.

The current situation teaches us that elections are not antithetical to co-optation. As a result, it is important to understand how these two frameworks interconnect in contemporary Morocco. Our hypothesis here is that elections operate, among other things, as a moment that facilitates the rationalisation of co-optation. This idea evokes the limits of this traditional tool of the representation of power, which does not seem either as efficient or as functional in contemporary Morocco. Of course, co-optation never killed politics; it excludes neither negotiation, nor risk-taking, nor competition, nor transactions. As a political activity in its own right, it provides substance to the representation of communities, in other words, it allows for integration. But it also has other functions. For example, it facilitates the management of dissent, the expression of choices, visions and preferences. However, it is characteristic of a specific political context that is "defused"[35] in a certain sense, which does not deny politics but shifts its significations and the places through which it is expressed, and in which there are only skills that the central power can decide to have at its disposal or not. Co-optation is an instrument of this form of government *par excellence*. This does not mean that it is the only instrument of representation. Like any authoritarian context, elections have always been the subject of scrutiny, but for other reasons; they play on a permanent misunderstanding between representation and intercession.

When Morocco became independent, the only form of representation was co-optation. This was all the more legitimate because it was regularly updated in response to contestation by the figures supposed to carry it out or because of tensions between segments of society. During the first years of independence, elections were rapidly appropriated by the populations, not so much for their "theoretical" logic as because of their relation to co-optation. This was for two main reasons: firstly, because political competition (between the national movement and the monarchy and then between the different political parties) took place through notables; and secondly, above all, because co-optation no longer functioned as efficiently as it had in the past. Elections laid

79

WEAVING POLITICAL TIME IN MOROCCO

the groundwork for co-optation, contributing to knowledge of local people and situations and to the emergence of notabilities. They thus appeared as the first stage in a central framework.

As they have been progressively more institutionalised, elections have become a powerful tool for rationalising co-optation, replacing or complementing certain instruments of leverage that have become obsolete or less efficient. In this period of nation-state building, itinerance was marginal and inoperative in any case. Local contacts, or mediators, proved to be both too numerous and also less effective, due to the combined effects of demographic growth and challenges to certain statuses and traditional orders. Marriage relations were transformed by the mixing of populations, and genealogical knowledge lost its relevance after the demographic boom and population movements. Elections came to be a substitute, or at least a powerful complement, to the *nisba*, which was the basis of all co-optation. Electoral competition was a test for the credibility of those who claimed to be "chosen", in both an electoral and religious sense. It was a way of choosing who would be the representative of the constituency, but it also facilitated the process of integration into the system—in other words, co-optation.

This aspect of elections explains the professionalisation of elected representatives-notables and the narrowness of the political class. It is reflected in the banality of the political "transhumance" process. Electoral trajectories were personal, dissociated from belonging to a political party. The loyalty of elected representatives found its justification in long electoral careers, and joining the partisan system was a decisive step. Between the 1980s and 2000s, control of elections—by group voting, vote buying, transactions and clientelism, gerrymandering and simple fraud—only served to continue this understanding of the electoral process as a kind of preamble to co-optation. It was only with the new regime and its aspiration to democratisation (accentuated by the new constitution) that the meaning of elections radically changed as they were appropriated by the population.

The political context, the arrival of new actors and in particular the Islamists of the PJD, but also the changes in forms of government resulting from discourses on participation, transparency or

REPRESENTATION

the new concept of authority, all undermined the traditional tools for controlling elections. Henceforth elections would be won or lost on the ground, on issues to do with the availability of resources for local development. Traditional forms of mediation had lost their effectiveness[36] due to having fewer connections within administration and a lack of specific skills needed to prepare submissions on concrete issues (road repair, water supply, infrastructures, etc.). Yet co-optation had not disappeared. On the contrary, it had spread into political parties, in associations and commissions. We cannot see this as the rhetoric of "change without change."[37] Indeed, although co-optation has not disappeared, elections have become important in their own right. Even the way they are understood is different; the search for fair and precise representation of the state of society has moved beyond discourse and into people's minds. The "truth of the elections" is now a major concern. In addition to the power of its electoral machine, the PJD managed to impose a new way of doing things. Because it never entirely trusted ideology, it guaranteed a daily presence in the constituencies through the provision of services. "Work your constituency if you want to be re-elected" is a leitmotiv that expresses the existence of genuine competition.[38] The now-central role of elections in political life and in forms of government must be interpreted on three levels.

The first is the level of democracy. Electoral processes are considered the best indicators—or in any case the clearest indicators—of the process of political liberalisation or democratisation. There can be no doubt that the reign of Mohammed VI fully engaged with this reading of elections, given the authorities' zeal in demonstrating their credibility. This is based on a very banal understanding, stemming from the most traditional studies in political science, which see elections as the number one criterion determining whether a situation can be described as democratic. Generally, any reflection on forms of non-electoral representation is evacuated, and the question of co-optation is addressed only on the margins, considered a malfunction or archaism stemming directly from authoritarian and/or patrimonial domination. Debates on the transparency or truth of results permeate the analyses of electoral deadlines, in the same way as for discussions on the size and mate-

81

WEAVING POLITICAL TIME IN MOROCCO

rials used for the ballot boxes, electoral boundary divisions or differing kinds of voting. In keeping with "transitology," elections that are now "free, sincere, and transparent" according to the terms of the constitution have become a decisive element in the contract between the elites and the population. They cover both the question of party pluralism as the foundation of the political order and freedom and the question of credibility in accountability. For the Moroccan elites, it is no less true (once again according to a very consensual reading of debates in political science) that the imperfections of this form of representation require the development of "corrections". The latter should be able to ensure the efficiency of public policies, in the form of civil society participation and calls for technocratic expertise.

Public discourses present elections as a modality of representation rather than as a tool for co-optation. However, although the idea of representative democracy is spreading, its practice has remained ambiguous. The "planning" of elections still occurs and is obtained by various methods, including by "legitimate" fraud (extra voting stations, indirect pressure on candidates, revelations of scandals, biased media campaigns), as an attempt at rationalisation in response to the arbitrariness of chance. But this planning is above all obtained by electoral divisions and the voting system. The issue at stake in the elections is therefore representativity (of different segments of society) rather than representation. The creation of electoral lists specifically for women and young people is a good illustration of this. We now know in advance who will be elected through a close examination of the order of those on the lists and by gauging the electoral weight of the different parties. The same is true of the arrival of private sector leaders in the upper house, who, along with union representatives, have managed to transform the House of Councillors, which was initially intended to only represent territories (according to a first version of the Constitutional project).

The second level at which the role of elections must be examined is in their connection to local political life, and thus, the type of relationship between the political world and the population. Even though conviction and persuasion are involved too, this rela-

REPRESENTATION

tionship implicitly and systematically reflects the question of clientelism and transactions. Elections are the moment of truth in this form of politics that sees different candidates for the role of the mediator face off in competition that breaks away from the idealised, rose-coloured image of political life. These practices cannot be (solely) seen as malfunctions. They reveal a certain conception of representation that, among all political actors, reconciles with co-optation. This reconciliation is often justified by the need to correct injustices of electoral sanctions, even when they are transparent. The argument is then that corruption and vote buying (by other parties of course) must be faced up to, along with intrusions from the Minister of the Interior, the effects of redrawing electoral boundaries and interference from "shadow figures". Sometimes royal benevolence is invoked in order to "correct" representation.

Often, the resources that political actors are able to deploy determine their position. Some focus on campaign resources (finances, voting machines, communication, media etc.) above all, not without suspicions of vote buying (real or potential) from their competitors. But maintaining this kind of political machine is costly, even if only in terms of representatives in voting stations, and it is a path that only the largest political parties can pursue, after an initial electoral breakthrough and once they have access to public funding. Other actors simply rely on the sincerity of their commitments, the righteousness of their beliefs and their trust in the intrinsic legitimacy of rational discourse and knowledge. Above all, it is left-wing candidates who make this choice, although they may pair it with an organisational aspect. Finally, others may emphasise their representativity through everyday networking—essentially using ethical and financial resources— and the provision of services. For these actors, electoral success is a modality of political integration that can force co-optation, in which the latter must be earned. It is therefore important for them to show that they are the most integrated in their constituency, in the best position to serve as intermediaries and thus interest those in power.

Finally, the third level is that of representation. What kind of understanding do politicians have of this concept once they are

83

elected? The tension between the emergence of the idea of representation (particularly in light of the new constitution) and the older understandings of elections as a tool of co-optation, mean answers to this question are variable or even contingent. In the PJD or the RNI or the Istiqlal, representation does not mean the representation of categorical interests or the representation of a project for society. It is understood above all as "representation of services" (*maslaha*) bringing together aspects of both charity and politics. From this extends a sort of "charity politics" (*goufa/couffin*) in which the party spills over into charitable associations at the neighbourhood level, thus creating and maintaining a loyal clientele.

Thus, it seems good that the most frequent interpretation of representation is that of intercession rather than mandate. This should not be overdramatised, nor interpreted as the expression of Moroccan, Arab or non-democratic specificities, even though in the lexicon of Moroccan imaginary the practice of intercession has a specific name—*chfa'a*. This also happens in democracies, although it is most often implicit, such as in the case of the French senators who, as representatives of their constituency rather than the fiction that is the nation, constantly intervene with public authorities on behalf of their fief. In contemporary Morocco, there is another dynamic that is in keeping with the imperial register: the "government at a distance", remote, delegated or decentralised government. Intercession is also a modality of indirect government that operates through the intervention of notables, servants and now elected figures.

* * *

At the conclusion of this chapter, it is striking to note how central co-optation remains in Morocco after the 2011 Arab Spring. This revitalisation of a technique that was long considered arbitrary, and which we have conceptualised as imperial, is paradoxically valued by new neoliberal artforms of participative democracy. In this new configuration, co-optation seeks to reconnect to representation as a mirror, while correcting the limits of the voting method, attenuating the risks of majority dictatorship, ensuring the survival of endangered minorities and increasing the visibility of emerging groups and

REPRESENTATION

sensitivities by opting for a specific formulation of positive discrimination. It is worth noting that the current situation of co-optation draws on theories of representation as incarnation even though the latter stems from a deeply authoritarian, and widely criticised, reading of Islamic philosophy, which is removed from the very idea of the vicariate. The naturalisation of co-optation does not prevent the emergence of very strong tensions on the political stage, between elective legitimacy and historical legitimacy.

2

VIOLENCE

Published in 2011 by the Royal Institute of Historical Research, the book *History of Morocco: A Work of Synthesis and Update*,[1] provides valuable insight into today's consensual discourse on state violence. This historic synthesis completes one of the recommendations of the IER (Equity and Reconciliation Commission), to integrate the study of the present into the field of history as a discipline. The implementation of this recommendation resulted in the controversial regime of Hassan II being integrated into the history of the construction of the modern Moroccan state, moving away from the exclusively memorial treatment it had begun to attract. This distancing was all the more necessary because YouTube has helped to keep the former sovereign alive on the internet; with every minor crisis he comes back into the spotlight. This collective book, in its section on the contemporary period, reveals one of the expressions of this "right to inventory" that is now characteristic of the new regime, and which is interesting to take into account because this synthesis is not the result of official historiography. It reflects a vision that is not consensual and conclusive but rather an attempt to create coherence in a context of appeasing political relations and avoiding any shocks or antagonisms.

The violence of the Moroccan nation-state

Chapter 10 in *History of Morocco* bluntly and explicitly describes the connexions between violence and the building of the nation-state.

WEAVING POLITICAL TIME IN MOROCCO

From its opening paragraphs, the paradigm of state violence is clear and unreserved, reflecting the general and widespread acceptance of this interpretation. The spread of this paradigm was made possible by the work of the reconciliation commission and the 50 Years of Human Development report, which had freed up the space for discussion on these issues a few years earlier. It also benefited from the complicity of other key actors, such as Abderrahmane Youssoufi, who provided a critical perspective on the years of the struggle for independence, without making their participation conditional on regime change.

Nation-building: open and pervasive violence

Much of the reign of Hassan II is publicly recognised as a period of despotism. The consensual narrative proposed in *History of Morocco* recognises the violence of the nation-state but treats it as a widely shared form of political violence. In so doing, it confers responsibility onto all protagonists; it does not clear the monarchy of blame, but nor does it name it solely responsible.

Based on this recognition, which is today uncontested, we wish to go further and interrogate the forms of violence that took place during this period of nation-building. How can we characterise its place within the forms of government that have changed over time? In all the narratives on the history of independent Morocco, Moulay Hassan has a central role, whether as Crown Prince or King. The fact that the consensual figure of Mohammed V is overlooked, corresponds at least partly to reality, but it is also suggestive of a change in era marked by the affirmation of the nation-state. The monarchy as an institution was not conceptualised as such by Mohammed V, unlike Hassan II who was directly involved in the national movement and raised on a typically French reading of the state and confronted with a biting criticism of the practices of the Fourth Republic.[2] On this point it is interesting to recall a passage in which Hassan II recounted a discussion with his father, in his famous speech of 19 January 1984 following the "events of Nador and Marrakech" (quoted in his interview with the journalist Éric Laurent, *La Mémoire d'un roi*):

> One day I said to His Majesty Mohammed V, "tell me Sidi, imagine that you decided to pray in one of the mosques in the Medina and

88

VIOLENCE

that out of a million people there to welcome you, 800,000 cheered and applauded you, and 200,000 booed and whistled— what would you do? Would you go down to confront them and explain to them that they are wrong?" His majesty remained silent before saying, "I would not go down." I replied, "well I, Majesty, I would go down, and I would beat them all, and destroy their fathers' houses."[3]

Violence and the struggle for power

This narrative reveals two different visions of how to manage contestation. This is not an opposition between styles of government, between a harsh evil king and a kind benevolent sultan but rather two different understandings of the royal function or indeed the legitimacy of power. Mohammed V, who is immensely prestigious among Moroccans, represented the old regime. The fact that he agreed to exchange the title of sultan for that of *malik* (king) and to be enthroned as the first leader of the national movement did not produce a profound change, and he remained the sultan of the Sharifian empire. Within this paradigm, the power incarnated by the leader is external to society. It is an overarching power, not because it is divine in origin, as Hassan II set out to show, but because it is fragile and neutral. It is a power that does not make decisions for or in the place of those it governs,[4] but rather implements consensus, mediated through the elites and led by the Ulema. The legitimacy of the sultan does not stem from the people, but his existence and his access to power nevertheless depend on them. His reign was thus the result of a struggle for power on the ground, which involved particular government practices and the management of violence. Where it was used, violence was extremely brutal, because it was this very brutality that meant it could be used punctually and parsimoniously. To survive, the sultan had to avoid being challenged, including in situations where he was sure to emerge victorious. He had to preserve himself from the gaze of commoners, except in highly ritualised and codified situations, swathed in mystery and veiled by the *hajeb*. He protected himself, but in so doing also protected his subjects from himself.

89

WEAVING POLITICAL TIME IN MOROCCO

However, the reign of Hassan II was indeed within the register of the Nation-state, which would remain dominant for some time to come. Once King, he became the incarnation of the nation's victory over colonialism. During his long fight to monopolise power resources (including violence), he proved himself harsh and pitiless. This struggle began while he was still the Crown Prince (a new status that allowed him to avoid any initiation tests along the path to power) but also already the Major General of a fledgling army. The future Hassan II, however, succeeded in blocking the Liberation Army in its path towards the Sahara at the cost of a compromise with colonial powers and then integrating the more malleable elements of that army while pushing the others into armed struggle or exile.[5] The image that remains of him, broadly relayed in many narratives, is of a young man flying an old helicopter and showering the rebels in the Rif with machine-gun bullets.

Moulay Hassan was not the only protagonist in this sequence (1955–60) that the historical synthesis quoted above cautiously describes as a "violent struggle for power",[6] in a monochrome vision of the nation. Although it was not written by historians, the IER report revealed other actors to public opinion and shed light on conspiracies, physical liquidations, abductions, arbitrary imprisonments, clandestine detention centres and mass graves that hint at the direct or indirect responsibility of the King, nationalist leaders of the Istiqlal party (Allal El Fassi and Ben Barka), Liberation Army leaders (in the North and the South) and resistance organised in secret groups in major cities (such as the Black Crescent).[7]

This initial and foundational violence was not the only characteristic of the nation-building period. There were other kinds of violence, more systematic, which seemed justified at the time, and which took on an aura of legitimacy in the name of "progress for all" and the "fight against archaism and heresy." This was the case of the Istiqlal's attempt to create a single party, adopted by a monarchy that sought to be the exclusive incarnation of this unity.

The Years of Lead paradigm

But state violence can take on more brutal forms specific to despotism, and which were characteristic of the period from 1965 to the

90

VIOLENCE

very early 1990s. This is illustrated by the Ben Barka affair and the secret prisons of Tazmamart and Keelat M'gouna.

The research conducted by the IER has provided rich and valuable documentary resources. The international framework and vocabulary of human rights adopted by the commission has revealed this extreme violence in very crude terms. Moreover, this has contributed to ensuring that its existence and formal qualification are now accepted.[8] Indeed, the commission relied on highly specific categorisations and periods, which do not seem favourable to an exhaustive account of the exactions perpetrated during this era. How is it possible to talk about innumerable instances of violence that are still painful and difficult to document or which are still controversial or taboo? It is in this context that we must understand the dual register behind the work of the commission. The first level concerns the adoption of international norms and categories, and the second, the search for material signs that are locally embedded and thus impossible to disprove, the result of meticulous field work and interactions with victims and their descendants.[9]

Working with international norms and categories had the advantage of not presenting this violence as singular or exclusive to the Moroccan situation. As a result, it made it easier to condemn. By adopting a neutral tone and near-bureaucratic language, moderated by formal denominations of different types of violence, the IER was paradoxically able to give consistency to what can only be described as horrors: "forced disappearances" and "people whose fate is unknown"; "arbitrary detention" in legal centres used for illegal actions or in illegal centres; "torture and poor treatment"; or "excessive and disproportionate use of public force". In addition, it was able to clearly and precisely describe, once again using internationally recommended methodologies, episodes that are today no longer in dispute. These include the violence of the first years of independence, now associated with a moment of civil war in which exactions and deaths were not only the result of state actors, but often also clashes between different factions within the armed nationalist movement,[10] political violence towards opponents characteristic of the Years of Lead,[11] and the violence of the urban riots in Casablanca in 1965 and 1981, in northern towns and in Marrakech in 1984 and in Fez in 1990.[12]

91

WEAVING POLITICAL TIME IN MOROCCO

However, these international norms and categories were largely unable to address the chapters in Moroccan history that remain in the shadows, specifically moments or practices that are still controversial or taboo. The IER therefore set out to track the material traces of acts of violence, primarily through the recognition of sites of detention or burial. The general and indeterminate nature of international categories was echoed by a very specific—and macabre—identification of victims in these sites, including not only the dates of death and incarceration but also a very detailed characterisation of types of violence, specifically types of torture and methods of execution, the conditions and circumstances of imprisonment and death, the type and condition of burial and so forth. The secret prison in Tazamamart, for example, revealed evidence of the inhumane repression of the alleged authors of the attempted coups in Skhirat (1971) and the attack against the royal aeroplane (1972), victims of an illegitimate action that was impossible to situate within a legitimate chronology of dissidence. The Tagounit centre provided accounts of the forgotten victims of the roundups in Casablanca, during the preparation for the Islamic Summit Conference in March 1972, which targeted not only combatants but also all the villages that had housed them.[13] Similarly, the detention centres in Gourrama, Agdez and Kelaat M'gouna revealed traces of the violence used during the Sahara conflict. Finally, the documentation of the prisons of Dar Bricha, Ghafsay (in Casablanca), Bouizakrane and Tafendilet, all help understand the violence of the first years of independence, from all protagonists—the Istiqlal and the PDI on the side of political parties, the Liberation Army, the resistance and the national security organs (then only recently created) on the side of the armed forces. The documentation of burial sites completed this macabre inventory while also providing a voice for other groups of victims, of events that are difficult to classify, such as the "Sidi Moktar Seven", former Liberation Army soldiers who refused to lay down their weapons at independence and were killed in 1960 as part of score settling between former resistance members.

A close reading of the IER reports also encourage a broad understanding of the meaning of extreme political violence. This includes

VIOLENCE

forms of violence that might be unfairly described as "gratuitous", but which in fact reveal an understanding of politics that does not only target open opponents of the regime but concerns the most marginal aspects of public order. This was the case of the treatment inflicted on the "Casablanca group." Between December 1971 and March 1972, beggars and homeless people were rounded up and imprisoned in order to "clean-up" the city for the Islamic Summit Conference. This example is particularly revealing of the mood of the time, which encouraged people to almost naturally "forget" the victims in detention centres, regardless of their "faults," including the simple fact of living on the margins of society. Perhaps more than anything, this reflects the reality of despotism.

The format of the IER final report reveals sophisticated and skilful writing that illustrates the particularity of a moment in time marked by uncertainties about the reactions sparked by the revelations of these horrors and the challenging of a "taboo"—that of the Sahara conflict, which is still impossible to describe and incorporate into the accepted political chronology.[14] The category of "disappeared people", "prisoners of war and people entrusted to the ICRC", along with the inventory of these detention centres, implicitly allow the Sahara conflict to be discussed covertly, even if only partially. This suggests the powerful influence of the desire for international credibility. It also reflects the extreme sensitivity of this ongoing conflict, which prevents the process of distancing that has begun for the Years of Lead, and which explains, for example, why it is impossible to talk about "a war with the Polisario" or with "Algerian brothers," in spite of the existence of battlefields and the presence of the ICRC.

Updating imperial violence, between brutality and avoidance strategies

During these first decades of independence, however, state violence was not limited to violence by the nation-state. It also included what, from our ideal-type perspective, we call "imperial violence." Before analysing the forms of this kind of violence under the reign of Hassan II, we must rapidly revisit its characteristics, which have been raised in passing in the discussions above.

93

Violence in the Sharifian empire

As the introductory narratives in the Prolegomenon reminded us, the expression of imperial violence is extremely brutal, both in discourse and in action. Unlike the Nation-state that euphemises its violence in the name of modernisation, progress or national unity, imperial violence has no qualms about its cruelty. It does not balk at cutting off heads, salting them and posting them at the entrance to cities or displaying some notable or pretender in a cage.[15] But although this violence is spectacular, it is sporadic and necessarily limited in time.[16] Once again this is an obvious difference with the violence of the Nation-state, which seeks invisibility and aims to blur the boundaries between legality and legitimacy while also being exhaustive and continuous. Imperial violence above all serves an exemplary function. Although this characteristic is not specific to Empire—as Foucault's "*stratégie du pourtour*" in the Nation-state shows,[17] and as the examples cited here illustrate—it is nevertheless central to it. Its role is not to re-educate and integrate people into an indivisible whole, but to absolve and re-establish loyalty without demanding either submission or a denial of difference. It also serves to negotiate for the purposes of restoring order.[18] Opposition and dissidence are part of the "normality" of the imperial order.

It is not the acts of rebellion in themselves that are problematic and result in the use of violence but rather their excessive nature. Under Empire there is no idea of a systematic and established public order. The imperial state is not threatened by any unrest, contestation or rebellion unless the throne itself is coveted by another. There are to a certain extent, sliding scales of order, just as there are scales of government. The tales of defiance from southern tribes in response to the sultan's demands, or the signing of treaties with Europeans in spite of their prohibition by sultan Hassan I, show that minor disorders rarely incur violence.[19] Violence seems to be an ultimate form of negotiation.

If the exercise of power is less linked to the reason of the state than it is to the reason of God, this must be reflected in the power relations on the ground. Violence in accessing power is brutal (between members of the same lineage aspiring to the throne)

VIOLENCE

specifically because God recognises his own and supports the victor. By contrast, where there is negotiation, even intermittently and in the perpetuation of opposing positions, violence is not useful because imperial power does not feel threatened. Violence is thus overseen by the theory of necessity, which makes preventing *fitna*[20] a religious obligation and absolute imperative. Brutal, sporadic and unlimited violence by the Empire is also a direct result of the principle of government at least cost and the use of intermediation.[21]

The avoidance of imperial violence

Although it is intermittent and short-lived, imperial violence is so brutal that it demands the development of avoidance strategies. The first is that of the *haiba*. Rather than "symbolic" violence, we might refer here to "restrained" violence. This is potential violence, which aims to achieve submission through subjugation and terror. As a result, it is inseparable from exemplary violence while also being its counterpoint. Indeed, in a context where aspiration to domination involves avoiding violence, which is costly, the *haiba* constitutes the foundation of government at least cost. Yet *haiba* cannot avoid spectacular and exemplary violence if it is to continue to act. Violence must be brutal to be able to update itself and give form to the *haiba* as the personal and magical quality of the sultan. The sultan must be able to contain this violence linked to his own personage. He protects those around him from the natural violence that results from his *haiba* by veiling his body, which must be hidden from view, just as the subject's gaze must be hidden from him, which explains the need for both the *hijab* and the *hajeb*.[22] But when that violence is unleashed, it must be as terrible, as unimaginable, as the violence of God.[23]

Of course, the population must also avoid violence. Modes of imperial government that award an important role to intermediation and intervention allow for the organisation of time and space when violence is suspended. These are the spaces and months of *hôrm*.[24] Historically, the months of *hôrm* are those during which war is suspended, except in situations of legitimate defence.[25] The *hôrm* spaces, on the other hand, are the three mosques in Jerusalem, Medina and Mecca, and by extension and in principle all mosques.

95

WEAVING POLITICAL TIME IN MOROCCO

In the Moroccan tradition, these spaces include mausoleums and holy cities, and the most important are the *hôrm* of Moulay Idriss in Fez[26] and that of Dar Damana in Ouazzane. The idea of a holy space that is a refuge against violence has deeply impacted society to the point that universities are considered *hôrm* spaces—although they are regularly violated. In the sanctuary of Moulay Bouchaib, patron saint of the town of Azzemour, up until the 1980s there was a space dedicated to women fleeing domestic violence, who lived there under the protection of the saint, fed by pilgrims.

The tragic dimension of power, which is explicit, visible and openly expressed, explains the deep belief held in Moroccan society that in power relations, face-to-face oppositions are always dangerous. This belief is demonstrated and not imagined: face-to-face encounters end in struggles for power in which there is always a winner and a loser. The risks of frequenting power are well-known, and a distancing occurs, including in situations of proximity, by the cultivation of difference. Several popular sayings reflect this violence in face-to-face encounters. For example, the "Makhzen is like a dromedary, it treads on those under its feet and always looks at the horizon", or "there are three things that you cannot trust, a horse that rears, a calm river and the Makhzen", or "when the Makhzen gives you a horse, don't ever ride it, content yourself to lead it by the bridle."

But as we saw with Mohammed V's response to Hassan II, this avoidance strategy is also due to power that knows this face-to-face encounter can be dangerous, or at least a potential challenge. Hence the importance of government at a distance. On the one hand, intermediation reduces the risk associated with being exposed to the sultan's power by allowing a distancing from violence; but on the other hand, the use of intermediaries, such as the veil (and thus mystery, uncertainty, questions on the nature of power, what it hides, how to interpret it and so forth) all accentuate this feeling of risk and risk-taking.

The current salience of imperial violence under Hassan II

This conception and these characteristics of violence remain salient today, particularly in the social imaginary. Language undoubtedly

VIOLENCE

constitutes the primary contemporary expression of this imperial violence. The violence of words, of speech, of specifically chosen language was particularly strong under Hassan II. The speech he made the day after the 1984 riots around the country, particularly in Marrakech and Nador, illustrates this. YouTube has enabled this speech to be widely diffused.[27] The comments of internet viewers say much about the conditions in which it is received today, attracting as many nostalgic comments lauding his authority and iron fist, as comments from viewers who are scandalised.

In simple *darija* (Moroccan Arabic), with a slight Marrakchi accent, which further emphasised the popular aspect, Hassan II addressed protestors directly, calling them *awbach*, worse than nothing, dregs of society. His eyes fixed on the camera, his finger brandished like a sword, he harangued the demonstrators in stigmatising and condescending tones, barely distinguishing between the "unemployed and *awbach*", "trainee lawyers", "street children (*drari*)" and "students pushed by irresponsible teachers" whom he insulted directly with "we know who you are, we will apply the law to you, that law[28] we knew under the Protectorate and that we confirmed after independence, that says any disturbance to public order will be severely punished."[29] The speech concludes with a direct threat in imperial tones addressed to very specific communities: "the people of the Rif, who knew the Crown Prince, it would be better for them if they do not know the king. As for the people of Marrakech [to them I say] I thought I would come on holidays, but I will not come until they see the error (*ghay*) of their ways." A few days later, a delegation of notables from Marrakech visited the royal palace in Rabat to solemnly ask for his forgiveness.

A second contemporary expression of this imperial violence is violence within the royal court. Under Hassan II, this was above all a kind of domestic violence, only made public through rumour, which renewed the reference to Empire. It essentially took the form of grace or pardon (thus reflecting the violence of the gift) and above all of disgrace (which meant political or social death for the victims).

Exemplary violence, both brutal and extreme, was not limited to the Nation-state version described above in relation to the Years

97

of Lead. It also took on an imperial form as some of those found "guilty" were considered personal prisoners of the King. Moreover, this guilt was not solely attributed to the individuals but to all of their families, as we can see in the treatment inflicted on the members of General Oufkir's family, forced into exile or social exclusion.[30] This violence also took the form of the punishment extended to the whole of the collective or community to which the "enemies" belonged.[31] It is therefore not anodyne that the IER identified whole territories that were the object of the sultan's curse or forgetting as punishment for political events or rebellions that were the responsibility of isolated individuals.

The *haiba* is not restricted to the political sphere. Under Hassan II, it was a daily event; a concern bordering on fear that was highly salient in the 1980s. It could be seen in the eyes of a mother waiting for her son to come home from the film club, an activity considered very risky, or in those of a father who, terrified by his son's basic criticisms of the functioning of the state, constantly repeated this saying to him, "put your head among the others, and call the executioner." This fear of the *Makhzen* has nothing to do with the fear of a police state, it is closer to the feeling of being close to something sacred. There is a deep-seated awareness of risk, even without knowing exactly what that risk consists of. This spread of violence in the form of shared *haiba* was based on Hassan II's belief that he could substitute himself for the collective itself because, in his own words, it was within himself. He did not need to consult the collective because he knew it all instinctively. There is no shortage of examples here. For example, Hassan II was convinced that he held the truth about the rhythm of music and choreography, a belief that earned the dancer Lahcen Zinoun a fall from grace.[32] This conviction that he knew everything often gave rise to tragicomic situations because of these overlapping registers; although the essence of this violence lay in the Nation-state register, its staging and reception were imperial.

This was the case, for example, in architecture and decorative arts.[33] In this instance, violence was not directly enforced on the architects themselves, nor on society as such, but ran through appointed intermediaries who reinterpreted and sanctified the

VIOLENCE

King's word, reducing it to a norm. Thus, in the famous speech of 14 January 1986, in which a genuine aesthetic sensibility can be seen, Hassan II declared he was deeply concerned about the ugliness of Moroccan cities. Explaining to the architects he had assembled in a conclave that they were responsible for being attentive to the history of Moroccan architecture and the sophistication of the aesthetic repertoire of artisans, he encouraged them not to impose an architectural model in their private contracts but to bring their clients to take into account the importance of heritage through pedagogy and innovation. This discourse, which became emblematic, was reduced by the then Minister for the Interior Driss Basri (also responsible for urbanism and urban agencies) to the single demand to incorporate green tiles from Fez and Meknes in development projects and public buildings, as a marker of authentic Moroccan architecture. At the same time, around fifty professors from the law faculty at the University of Casablanca had organised into a housing cooperative and were in the process of constructing a collective housing project, designed by the very avant-gardist architect Abderrahim Sijilmassi, on land the state had given them at a reasonable price. The Garden City that Sijilmassi had imagined was modernist and far removed from the Moroccan style, incorporating neither green tiles nor traditional mosaics. However, the new urban doctrine did not fail to spark debate within the cooperative—launched by Driss Basri himself, who was a member of it— about the need to bring the project into line with the national aesthetic norm by adding green tiles to the houses' roofs. In addition to the reluctance of the architect, who considered this an adulteration of his project, the cost was also problematic. Adding a layer of tiles onto the villas would have increased their total cost by 10%, making them inaccessible to the teachers the project was aimed at. All parties were convinced that this was an incongruous, even ridiculous, demand, but that it was necessary to submit. The idea that the King might pass by here on his way to the airport and ask why there were no green tiles, was improbable but not impossible. This is an example of the *haiba* at work in society, including within a supposedly enlightened elite. It was impossible to think of taking such a risk! Therefore, after much debate, a crafty solution

WEAVING POLITICAL TIME IN MOROCCO

was found, which managed the risk by tiling only a few houses visible to the road and leaving the others as they were. A lottery was organised to decide which teachers would get the tiles.

This diffuse *haiba* that runs through the social body as a whole can still be seen today in the relationship Moroccans have to certain administrations, such as those who depend on the Minister for the Interior. The architecture of its sites and this administration's continuation of the titles of pasha and *caid* and the presence of *mokhazni*[34] in their buildings, an imperial legacy dating back to the Protectorate, gave these buildings an aura of an imposing, even frightening, *dar-al-Makhzen*.

The imperial staging of nation-state violence: institutionalised haiba

Resorting to the register of theology, centred around the notion of the Commander of the Faithful, is the first "imperial" ingredient that is used. Excommunication and the royal curse are mobilised as part of a violence that, although symbolic, is also very much social and political. The imprisonment of Abderrahim Bouabid and other members of the left-wing USFP in 1981 must be understood in light of this.

After obtaining a compromise on the Sahara with the Organisation of African Unity (OAU), Hassan II decided to organise a referendum on the subject. The bureau of the USFP declared themselves against this project not because they did not consider the Sahara as Moroccan, rather because they considered it so Moroccan that the referendum was incongruous—or even invalid. Bouabid explained this in the French newspaper *Le Monde*[35] and Hassan II had him immediately imprisoned, at the same time as Mohammed Mansour.[36] Even before the justice system had formally accused him, the King had pronounced his sentence: the royal curse and excommunication. For Hassan II, the crime was not so much in the refusal of the referendum as in breaking with the consensus around the Commander of the Faithful. It is in that respect that this violence is nation-state style violence; any expression of difference was impossible. But the way it was articulated and staged were imperial because it was religion rather than the law that was used

100

VIOLENCE

as punishment. This combination of genres resulted in the fact that the sentence of the royal curse took on legal effects thanks to the invention of the crime of "inciting disorder and undermining the attachment of citizens to the personage of the king."[37]

In this respect, the principle of the Commander of the Faithful has become a particularly violent political invention. But although this violence is anchored in the Nation-state in its mobilisation of the idea of a unity of the nation-state itself, it has two clear imperial dimensions: the clash with judicial power in the name of Islamic tradition, specifically the primacy of the Commander's interpretation and the recourse to intervention by the saints.

Being able to dispose of others and their time is another form of violence that is ostentatiously staged in this overlapping of registers. It can be seen in the way the royal servants are treated, in the fact that, depending on the sovereign's moods, events, constraints or opportunities, political configurations or simply court rumours, they are appointed or dismissed, reappointed or redismissed, without any possibility for refusal, appeal or redress. This configuration was frequent in the Sharifian empire and the accounts by the historiographer Abou al-Qacem Zayani, a member of a *Makhzen* Berber family, are emblematic of this requirement for ineluctable availability, to be at the disposal of the sovereign.[38] All the crises that he related, including five disgraces, testify to the fear and irresistible attraction of working for the sultan, even though his father warned him, with a quote from Lahcen Lyoussi,[39] a seventeenth-century Ulema and contemporary of Moulay Ismail Ibn Sharif, saying "Do not approach a king or entrust yourself to his protection, even if he grants you riches and power; he will use you as he wills, and your life will fly away, you will have no rewards in this life, nor in the afterlife."[40] This form of violence remained standard in Hassan II's Morocco, as seen in the case of the five ministers condemned for corruption in 1971. These ministers, including Mohammed Jaïdi, the only one to have provided an account of this episode more than 40 years later, were accused of having blackmailed the American company Pan Am.[41] Summoned before Hassan II, they were struck down by the sentence, which they did not immediately understand, with the sultan saying, "Henceforth you are born for

101

WEAVING POLITICAL TIME IN MOROCCO

a second time."[42] They remained a few more months in office before being arrested during the Skhirat attempted coup. They were never questioned but immediately sentenced to a prison term of between 4 and 12 years. Jaïdi, who was sentenced to 8 years, received early release in the context of the Green March which ushered in a new political moment. He was rapidly integrated into the cabinet of the Prime Minister Karim Lamrani at the request of Hassan II himself. We can clearly see the arbitrariness of this prerogative, of a head of state who can dispose of individuals as he sees fit according to circumstance and without any need for explanation or justification. This practise is by no means exceptional but is characteristic of Hassan II's attitude towards those he considered his servants.[43]

A change in reign: from the framing of violence to its naturalisation

The late 1990s marked the preparation for the arrival of the opposition in power as part of the *gouvernement d'alternance* and the first timid but genuine steps in this experience of political openness. This involved a significant decline in the use of violence, the systematic mobilisation of the principle of political renewal through the absorption of dissidence and the establishment or reactivation of institutions for the pacification of socio-political relations, such as the Consultative Council on Human Rights (CCDH). But it was the change in monarch, in July 1999, that marked the turning point. Not only had time inexorably changed things, but only a new king could distance himself from the heritage of the Years of Lead and a systematic interplay of the multiple forms of state violence. Once Mohammed VI was crowned, one of his first initiatives was to inventory these coercive practices.

This inventory was Mohammed VI's main and undoubtedly most direct step towards distancing himself from his father's reign. His advisers at the time encouraged him to mark his ascension to the throne by a sort of honourable gesture. The IER was a spectacular agreement, foundational even, much like the INDH (National Initiative for Human Development, *Initiative nationale du développement humain*) was in the social sector, or the major eco-

VIOLENCE

nomic projects. The IER sketched out a new shape for power relations in Morocco. Even before the 2011 constitution, the commission enabled progress through its research, debates and discourses, as well as the taboos that it overcame, the fears that it addressed and the principles it laid down, all of which established limits to the use of violence. By proposing a whole series of recommendations, the IER undertook an unprecedented process of framing the use of violence and paved the way for institutional change. In 2011, the constitution provided new strength to this dynamic by institutionalising some of its recommendations, particularly concerning a series of safeguards against the use of violence, including the right to life (article 20), criminalisation of violence against individuals (articles 22 and 23), the independent justice system (articles 107–109); constitutionalisation of the National Council of the Rights of Man and the role of the Mediator (articles 161 and 162). The abolition of the death penalty on the other hand was not included, in spite of a significant mobilisation by civil society. Although these reforms and this "sincerity" did not signify any renunciation of absolute power, the new reign introduced a remarkable difference in the way power was exercised. The aspiration to total domination was neither affirmed nor claimed, but left to the imaginary, playing more on cultural and political hegemony than on the use of extreme and brutal violence.

Political earthquakes, rationalisation and the naturalisation of the curse

Since October 2017, earthquakes have become a political concept used to interpret royal actions and events, evoking terrible and unpredictable imperial violence. As an idea, it is meaningful for the population because it reflects the unpredictability of power as well as the idea of equality in treatment among those upon whom this catastrophe is unleashed. It conveys a sense of justice, in the fact that the elites are also affected by it, for example political leaders like Nabil Bendabdallah, Al Houcine Louardi or Larbi Bencheik, or public servants known to be close to the palace, such as Mohammed Hassad or Mohammed Boussaïd. Other earthquakes may therefore be expected or even demanded.

WEAVING POLITICAL TIME IN MOROCCO

Yet any earthquake is far from banal. Royal curses represent more than just symbolic violence. They destroy careers in politics or administration; at worst they bring political death, at best a difficult period (a metaphorical "trip across the desert") that is not without consequences. They erase the limits of legality, because these upheavals, these royal earthquakes, take on the status of law. This is an important difference from the pre-colonial period where the sultan's curse only held weight within the seraglio, as it had no legal status. Therefore, when it was unleashed against tribes who did not pay their taxes it did not have any real effect on them. Political earthquakes have an impact precisely because they are incorporated within the nation-state. Consequently, they appear as a specifically nation-state form of rationalisation and an institutionalisation of imperial violence. Indeed, they are the expression of a strange legal order in which the cohabitation of two kinds of decisions, with totally different statuses, is never questioned. On the one hand, there is a decision that is based on an institutional, although perhaps not political, foundation. Indeed, article 47 of the constitution authorises the King to dismiss members of government. The application of this decision was in every respect in keeping with the constitution. Following a report by the Court of Accounts and the presentation of the conclusions of that report and after consultation with the head of government, a royal statement was published announcing the dismissal of serving members of government. On the other hand, there is a decision that is difficult to qualify in legal terms, although it has considerable impact on the lives of individuals; these royal curses are not merely words, they are words that herald political and often social death and "banishment".[44] Surprisingly, the legitimacy and legality of this decision were not questioned either in the media or in political comments. Malediction pronounced against leaders was subject to the same treatment as any institutionally founded decision, as though it was of the same status and based on the same mechanism as a simple resignation. Some astute commentators mentioned the—totally improbably but nevertheless heuristic—hypothesis that one of these "banished" party leaders, might run for election and win. Would the King then be obliged to appoint them?

VIOLENCE

Political earthquakes however are subject to a process of normalisation and naturalisation, as the episode of the boycott analysed above shows. Henceforth, it appears to be a political and institutional solution like any other. This normalisation plays on the confusion between a law and an arbitrary act, on the confusion between these two registers of action. The royal curse, an arbitrary act *par excellence*, legitimately acts as a constitutional or legal text because it produces the same effects. Naturalisation also operates through an invention of historical continuity, once again as a gauge of legitimacy. Although historical background may be scant, the invention of genealogy by journalists and public actors serves to consolidate the validity of the decision.

Above all, naturalisation occurs through the mobilisation of the imaginary. In order to understand the power of the latter, it is interesting to analyse the arguments of those who rationalise, theorise and give meaning to a situation by identifying continuities but also judging the legality of this decision. Naturalisation is made possible by the use of the imperial metaphor of severed heads, set on pikes, which is presented as banal and natural and never questioned.[45] This reference to past imperial practices comes from commentators not from royal statements but clearly conveys the salience of the imperial register in society. These commentators are journalists[46] but also activists and even political scientists. For example, Zefzafi,[47] who applauded the earthquake from his prison cell, interpreted it as proof of the validity of his own struggle. Even more surprising is the fact that this professor of political science from Tanger University proposed three scenarios for the outcome of the crisis in the Benkirane II government, putting government responses (increase in wages), parliamentary responses (voting a no-confidence motion and the resignation of the government) and the royal response all on the same level: an earthquake indeed, as though these curses were legal and constitutional.[48] This professor was not alone; a few days later, the media published a long exchange between three other professors of political science, debating the possibility of this decision and its consequences, a sign that the political earthquake had now permeated ways of thinking and become normal in politics.[49] Moreover, naturalisation is fuelled

105

by institutions and not the most marginal ones. The Court of Accounts for example, in its report on financial jurisdictions in the media, assembled everything that had been published on the political earthquake, thus contributing to its normalisation.[50] But first among these institutions is of course the royal cabinet. Its statement on 24 October 2017, institutionalised the royal curse, even constitutionalised it, by referring to accountability when it said:

> In view of the constitutional prerogatives of His Majesty the King, as the guarantor of citizens' rights and protector of their interests; in application of the dispositions of Article 1 of the Constitution, specifically subparagraph 2, relating to the correlation between responsibility and accountability; His Majesty the King has decided to terminate the functions of several ministerial officials. ... As concerns other members of the previous government, equally responsible and concerned with this dysfunction, His Majesty the King, May God Keep him, has decided to declare his dissatisfaction with the fact they were not worthy of the trust placed in them by their Sovereign and for the fact that they have not taken responsibility for their actions, declaring that no official positions will be granted to them in the future.[51]

This collective participation in the normalisation of arbitrariness and the naturalisation of the use of spectacular and exemplary violence says much about the confusion of political markers and democratic principles. It also reflects the violence in society itself. It may be reasonable to fear that henceforth political earthquakes become a form of government in their own right. This would intensify violence in terms of frequency (or at least the frequency of this kind of reasoning) and in the process of legitimisation and lawfulness that would result from it.

Anger, or the banality of disgrace

The second example of the tourism project "Madinat Badis", also in Al Hoceima, suggests the progressive banality of disgrace. A key means of imperial violence, disgrace is now considered an acceptable or even legitimate and effective means of governing, in the name of accountability and a certain understanding of justice. This example is important because the primary protagonists are the

VIOLENCE

general real estate development company, the CGI (*Compagnie générale immobilière*) which is a subsidiary of the state-owned financial institution *Caisse de dépôt et de gestion* (CDG), known for its integrity, rigour and honesty, and Ali Ghannam, the archetypal senior civil servant.

During one of his visits to the north of the country on 23 August 2014, the King was solicited by Moroccans living overseas who had invested (sight unseen) in the apartments built by the CGI as part of the tourism development project at Al Hoceima, but which did not meet the promises of the project. Mohammed VI immediately launched an administrative investigation that was entrusted to a combined commission involving the Minister of Finances and the Minister of the Interior. After documenting the failings in the project (defects and poor workmanship), the case was transferred to the General Inspector of Finances (IGF), the General Inspector of Territorial Planning (IGAT) and surprisingly to the powerful National Brigade of Judicial Police (BNPJ based in Casablanca. Just a few months later, in October of the same year, the investigation led to a formal charge—the attorney general described the events as "the misuse of public funds and fraud, forgery and falsification, criminal organisation." The trial, involving twenty-seven accused and fourteen witnesses eventually began on 3 April 2018.[52]

The arguments exchanged during the investigation and the two first sessions of the trial shed light on a whole range of confusions, slippages and reasonings that foster the banality or the invisibility of violence. Thus, at the origin of the trial was not an accusation but a grievance; the trial was not driven by a referral from victims of the defective workmanship in the project but by royal anger. This gave rise to an administrative request, with the King asking for a joint commission to verify any abnormalities.[53] This was then submitted to the supervising institutions without any clarity as to the procedure followed, particularly as concerns the National Brigade of Judicial Police (which has been the main arm of the authoritarian state since the fight against terrorism became a priority). This brigade represents the defence of public order, shaped by the fight against terrorism, legitimising brutality and excessive means but also progressively spilling over into social order. The

WEAVING POLITICAL TIME IN MOROCCO

involvement of the National Brigade of Judicial Police) shifts this case about real estate from a question of simple mismanagement to a question of state security.

The arguments exchanged between the defence and the prosecution are also highly instructive.[54] The defence rejected the jurisdiction of the appeals court in Fez and argued that it could not be a question of misuse of public money because the CGI is a private company funded by individuals and all the transactions involved commercial contracts. The report by the IGF was therefore not valid or legal,[55] as the employees of the CGI were private sector employees and not public servants. All these arguments justified the request for annulment and the transfer of the case to a commercial court. For the prosecutor, however, although this was not a question of the protection of public money, the accusation was justified in the name of "trust bestowed on those responsible", with everyone understanding that this trust was that of the King. As for the staff's employment status, his understanding was broader, considering each individual linked to a public institution or public utility company in which the state has a degree of power as a "public servant". Given these conditions, the judge, Abdelaziz El Bakkali, rejected the defence's arguments, and mentioning articles 241, 260, 261, 333 and 334 of the Criminal Code covering financial offences, he confirmed that this case fell under his jurisdiction stating that the "Criminal Chamber of Financial Offences is also responsible for public order, abuse of power, and protection of trust."[56]

These arguments may seem absurd, presenting trust as a characteristic of the public aspect of an offence, or the link to a public utility company as the definition of a public servant. However, they demonstrate a certain knowledge of Moroccan political economy and of the profound nature of the argumentation: both the CGI and the CDG are financial arms of the state, the employees in the highest levels of the hierarchy of these institutions are state officials, even *khadim*, and the plaintiff is the King. The apparent absurdity reveals the invisible structure of the connections between the sovereign and his civil servants. The head of the CDG is appointed by the King and it is worth noting that Anas Alami, then in service, emphasised its belonging to the public sphere when, in response to

108

VIOLENCE

the prosecutor's question about his actual involvement in the projects he responded that he could not have been party to these details but that the CDG contributed to developing laws on finance and retirement[57]—thus confirming that the CDG is indeed the financial arm of the state. This formal absurdity reveals the confusions and crossovers specific to both Moroccan modes of government and to the neoliberal moment: the private sector does public sector work and private entities behave like public enterprises and not only because of their leaders but because public authorities consider them as such. Governing elites bask in a promiscuity that facilitates perpetual transfers between public and private and the private sector benefits from the advantages of public power. In other words, the arguments of the prosecutor are totally founded in political terms, but they are not legal.

These confusions are not only the sign of a political economy that is somewhat insensitive to the distinctions between public and private, between economics and politics, they also produce and indeed reveal violence. Violence is primarily inherent in the combination of registers leading to the charge of "criminal groups" for example. The one-upmanship of the public ministry is not limited to this specific episode[58] and can be explained by the desire of this institution to protect itself within a system that is arbitrary, even towards itself. Judges must not consider facts in light of the Penal Code or any other legal text, they must gauge royal will expressed in the form of anger. They reflect the empathy of courtiers; their careers are conditioned on the integrity of this evaluation and their efficiency in interpreting royal will. They must therefore be pseudo "virtuosos" to be able to make the accusation into charges and justify royal demands. This virtuosity is not a matter of professionalism but of the royal court; diligence cannot be measured against the law but instead in terms of loyalty. The goal here is to cover one's bases with respect to the sovereign, to ensure no mistakes are made and there is no risk of being considered lax or incompetent.

This violence is also linked to the timeframe. From the moment they are accused, to the end of the trial, even if they are free, the accused are considered pariahs.[59] For Ali Ghannam, who was a recognised *wali*, this was a sort of social and political death. He will

WEAVING POLITICAL TIME IN MOROCCO

probably come through it, but the timeframe is nevertheless essential. It is the violence of the intermediary period that is of interest to us here, a violence of marginalisation and exclusion, of uncertainty, of the questioning of integrity and everything that is the ethos of a senior civil servant. Being assumed to be guilty is a situation of extreme violence. Exemplary punishment no longer involves severed heads on pikes outside the city; today those heads are thrown to the mercy of the media. Ali Ghannam unquestionably embodies the figure of the expiatory victim.

Finally, violence is directly linked to attribution of responsibility. Who is responsible? When the prosecutor asked Ali Ghannam to explain the defective workmanship, he presented himself as a "manager" who only focused on the business plans; when he was asked why water towers were not installed, he replied "El Omrane [a public enterprise] was to do it"; and when he was asked what had justified the shift from the sale of apartments to the sale of blocks of land, he did not refer to a change in economic and financial policy but rather blamed "the intervention of the *wali* of Al Hoceima". In so doing, Ghannam placed himself within this confusion. As a former *wali*, he described himself as the manager whose main role was to maximise profits, but equally he did not accept responsibility for the change in economic and financial strategy of the company and blamed it on politics. *L'Economiste*, empathising with Ghannam, ran the title "Ghannam blames the *wali*"![60] The scapegoating that he was himself a victim of also enabled him to cover his bases. This is a standard strategy but none the less efficient.

This process is symptomatic of the black hole of the justice system. The latter is undeniably the institution that has most escaped the current transformations, and which has shown an inability to regulate imperial violence. The 2011 constitution nevertheless solemnly inscribed the principles of an independent judiciary (articles 107 to 110). And this principle was endorsed by the King, who had almost renounced this "Ministry of Sovereignty"[61] after the "*alternance*" government because the ministry was successively headed by politicians from the USFP, PJD and the RNI. This insistence was limited however by the judiciary's understanding of the question of its responsibility as an independent power, in view of

110

VIOLENCE

the 2011 constitution. Indeed, its independence from the legislative and executive branches is the fundamental condition for any attribution of responsibility within the rule of law.

The independence of the judiciary was consecrated by the High Judicial Council, in which civil society is represented by laymen who sit alongside judges, elected by their peers. It can also be seen in the autonomy of the attorney general, who was removed from the Minister for Justice (article 113). Yet the legal world's reticence regarding the question of independence, which was already made clear during debates on the constitution, was confirmed from the beginning of the High Council's activities and the implementation of organic laws laying down the modalities of the attorney general's autonomy. The attorney general displayed a troubling understanding of independence during his audition by the Special Commission for a New Development Model (NDM) in 2020, when both the President delegate of the Senior Council on Judicial Powers, as well as the Royal Prosecutor for the Court of Cassation, stated that they were only accountable before the King.[62] This led those writing the NDM to match English title above report to their grim observations on the state of the justice system.

The ambiguity of the text of the constitution which makes the King not only the president of the High Council (article 115) but specifies that rulings are "made and executed in the name of the king and by virtue of the law" (article 124), is exacerbated by the very specific conception that the Royal Prosecutor has of his independence. For him, like for most judges, the King is not considered part of the executive (despite article 42) or the legislatiure (despite article 41). His reading of independence concerns only power resulting from elections, in a very limited vision of politics. This representation that the judges have of their relationship with the monarchy stems from a traditional interpretation that can be traced back to the work of Al-Mawardi who, in a very specific context of the weakening of the Caliphate, developed a theory running counter to the traditional theory of the independence of the judiciary, considering it a delegated power of the Caliph. This perspective, which was adopted by the authorities of the Protectorate, remains influential among judges even though the 2011 constitution clearly changed things in this respect. Indeed, it does not refer to the judiciary as a delegate power and restricts the role of the King to that of a guarantor.

This vision of the justice system as accountable only to the King and the difficulty in achieving reform mean that the judiciary is in fact a vector of violence rather than a tool for regulating it. Firstly, as we have said, it is incapable of tackling imperial violence. Secondly, in order to accommodate the "independence" that makes judges accountable, the latter seek above all to protect themselves from rules that are sometimes obscure and from political instructions that may be difficult to interpret. As a result, this self-protection against uncertainty results in a dynamic of bureaucratisation—mindlessly applying the rules in a configuration where a substantial portion of the legal body impinging on freedoms makes the justice system blind, even more so given that the law has long been considered not as an instrument to be applied but as a weapon to avoid deviant behaviour. Thirdly, the justice system is particularly vulnerable to corruption and incapable of producing ethical and deontological rules that could prevent it being compromised.

* * *

At the conclusion of this chapter, it is clear that one of the foundations of this violence lies in the difficulty in attributing responsibility for it, which the institutional means established following the IER and the 2011 constitution appears unable to regulate. The figure of a severe and judgemental God who is accountable only to himself and to the scapegoat, with the expiatory victim as the crystallisation of divine punishment, reflect this articulation between violence and responsibility. The dilution of responsibility and the search for scapegoats that results from this, act as a catalyst for fear and uncertainty and enable order to be redefined as simple, understandable and controllable.[63] Much like the witches' sabbath in sixteenth-century Italy,[64] the identification of a scapegoat operates as an ideological mechanism for the transfer of responsibility. The individualisation of responsibility in the form of recognisable figures who can be condemned allows for a shift from a complex model with multiple causes to a causal relationship that is unique

VIOLENCE

and gives the illusion of highly efficient power.[65] The emphasis on accountability reporting in the context of the search for a scapegoat and the resolution of this dilemma seems logical, but this logic is also found in the 2011 constitution, which very redundantly associates responsibility and accountability and proposes mechanisms to enforce that responsibilisation. The constitution considers the government responsible before the parliament and the parliament responsible before the people, just as the torturer is responsible before the victim (Article 22 on the prevention of torture). Except that no one acts accordingly. Violence in the form of banishment, disgrace or symbolic death has consequently become a modus operandi. This type of violence is now considered one of the conditions for the survival of society, as though it was necessary to rid the body of an impurity to keep it healthy. The inability to name those responsible unleashes violence.

The functioning of society according to a consensus model erases all forms of recognition of difference, pluralities of truth, including ways of regulating violence. Consensus is generally used as an argument in decision-making, but here it is empowered and becomes a sort of paradigm. It creates an equivalence between the results of the electoral processes and the production of consensus by elections. But it is also inhibitive, and all competing actors find themselves trapped by this consensual representation that prevents any rupture or reform. Thus, on the question of gender equality for example—which is formally established in the constitution—the confrontation between the law and consensus is crystallised around heritage. All the political actors—even the most "progressive" among them—refuse to think in terms of a contradiction between the two orders (legal order and the ideology of consensus) and content themselves with proposing avoidance strategies on the one hand,[66] and prolonging the consensus by consulting the population on the other.[67] As a result, these consensual truths enable and empower all kinds of violence. This means empathy for those who stone homosexuals; it means lenience for traders in Inezgane (Sous) who lynched a girl for wearing a mini skirt. This is not state violence or even really morality policing—it is the expression of the violence of a consensus that refuses difference within it. This is the

WEAVING POLITICAL TIME IN MOROCCO

violence of a time consolidated by the arrival of Islamists in power, who consider electoral competition as a battle between good and evil, between the consensus of the communities they represent and the "Westernised elites" and who accentuate the conservatism of Moroccan society. This bigotry produces a society that can no longer bear difference or uniqueness in the public space. It transforms disapproving looks into violent weapons that prevent women wearing bikinis on the beach, stop girls wearing skirts above the knee and even make the simple purchase of a bottle of wine in a supermarket a veritable ordeal for men.

PART TWO

GOVERNING THE NATION

Transformations in the exercise of power and the acceptance of the political order create significant conflicts and tensions. These make the future uncertain, despite the strength of the imaginary, which consolidates the expression of an "us" and contributes (often unbeknownst to the actors) to the naturalisation of the changes at work. As a result, we must ask how the unity that enables reference to "the Moroccan state", or "Moroccan public policy", or "Moroccan exercise of power", or "Moroccan modes of government" is conceptualised—if indeed it is. Most researchers and authors who work on Morocco consider this unity only in the form of the nation and posit that the latter only emerged in the wake of colonisation. They argue that the Protectorate enabled the emergence of the idea of nationalism which paved the way for the construction of the nation-state;[1] although some affirm that it emerged slightly earlier, during the years of confrontation with European powers.[2] Official historical doctrine, which seeks to demonstrate the continuity of Morocco since Idriss I (788–91), considers this in the context of a religious paradigm. Although this is an attempt to rationalise a certain uneasiness in the face of this insular mentality, and even though the withdrawal and closedness of the Sharifian empire is seen as a moment of disfunction, this historiography remains marked by the nation-state paradigm.

115

WEAVING POLITICAL TIME IN MOROCCO

The analyses that restrict this unity to its religious dimension appear problematic; they are unable to explain the distinction— salient in Sharifian society—between Muslims of the Sharifian empire and Muslims of the Ottoman empire, or the existence of clear but shifting and constantly fraught limits with the Regency of Algiers.[3] Interpreting the speeches on *dar al-Islam* as proof that this unity is exclusively understood as the Muslim *ummah* would simply be taking ideology at face value. In our approach to the historical sociology of politics, which looks at practices to understand this unity, *dar al-Islam* lacks substance. It is not the space in which the statuses of insiders and outsiders, the Muslim and the *dhimmi*, are defined, or where notabilities and social differences are created, or where power is exercised (at least from the fifteenth century and the withdrawal of the Ottoman empire from Andalusia and the central Maghreb). The Sharifian empire distinguished itself significantly from the Caliphate, and this differentiation has been made explicit ever since the Saadis.[4] Of course there are affinities between the two empires, but they are considered a continuity, of which the strongest expression is the pilgrimage. In other respects, the Sharifian empire has demonstrated a certain independence from *dar al-Islam*.

But how is this unity fulfilled outside the religious framework? And how can this connectedness be achieved in a context other than that of the nation-state? In fact, the idea of the nation was undeniably present in the Sharifian empire. In other words, we argue that the idea of a single unified entity existed before the Protectorate, independence or even encounters with Europeans in the nineteenth century. This cannot be considered proto-nationalism, however, as that notion implies an altered or immature version of the nation. On the contrary, our reading of history encourages a different conception of the nation, one that is specific to Empire.[5] This hypothesis is not only the result of the clear shortcomings of the religious paradigm. It emerged with the analysis of the *Makhzen* and its relations with the regions. The historical material that we draw on reveals symbolic actions, such as the *bay'ah* or the *hdya* but also highly concrete actions like letter writing, the art of status or a close knowledge of communities and individuals, which all suggest the idea of

116

PART TWO: GOVERNING THE NATION

unity even if it is not expressed continuously or uniformly throughout the Sharifian empire as a whole. Such actions transcend diversity. Although the discourse and language that frame them are religious, they reveal something else. They provide a glimpse of a territory that has borders and limits, a language that is not always classical Arabic (as we can see in the fact that historians working on this era need to provide a glossary for their research) but rather a local form of Arabic that is accepted in correspondence and finally, the complex administration of the *Makhzen*.

In this second part of the book, we set out to understand how the nation is conceived in different ways, over time of course, but also at a given moment depending on actors, circumstances and power relations. To grasp this broad range of understandings we have chosen to focus on the specific trajectory of Morocco and its transition from organisation as an empire, to organisation as a nation-state, while intentionally (and perhaps this is its specificity) not abandoning the imperial register. Therefore, we set out to follow the traces of the imperial understanding of the nation in the political imaginary and the mechanisms that enable this togetherness in diversity and confrontation. In other words, we have tried to untangle the interconnectedness of different conceptions of the nation that stem from this specific history, but which are now lived through the framework of the nation-state. This has been achieved through two modes of intervention that are characteristic of the state today. The first, which we call the "royal treatment", is based on the near-miraculous "success" resulting from the involvement of the prince, explicitly associated with different registers of administration. By contrast, the second is banal, non-exceptional and involves all the everyday management of the state.

The processes of territorialisation and administration constitute the two main "scenes" in which the nation has been shaped through direct and unifying interventionism specific to the nation-state. But although the process of territorialisation shows a head-on opposition between two visions of sovereignty and the exercise of power, the administrative process emphasises the diversity of possible trajectories and interactions between the imperial register and the nation-state register depending on changing contexts and situations. Using a quasi-archaeological approach, these two scenes allow us to shed light on the different but simultaneous ways in which the nation is understood in contemporary Morocco. They help us to understand how authority and domination operate in this context based on extremely varied understandings of the nation.

3

SHIFTING SPACES OF TERRITORIALISATION

Governing means firstly constituting a territory. But what is a territory, if we abandon our substantialist and naturalist perceptions of it, if we do not consider it as a space that is objectively delimited and qualified by its topography, geology or natural and even human characteristics? The definition of a territory depends above all on the ways in which it is understood, occupied and administered,[1] and the way it is incorporated into the social imaginary that it institutionalises.[2] It is the power relations built over the course of history that shape the boundaries of this territory, boundaries that are more or less stable and precise. In this context, the process that accompanies and enables territorialisation expresses a perspective on sovereignty and on the exercise of power and indeed on the very conception of power itself.

However, the objective here is not to write the history of the processes of territorialisation in Morocco but rather to revisit certain elements that allow us to emphasise its complexity and particularly to present the different visions of the territory and relations to it, which seek to dominate and become hegemonic. These are particularly salient in moments of crisis, which have historically also been moments of violent confrontation.

WEAVING POLITICAL TIME IN MOROCCO

Conquering territory: historical markers

The letters and correspondence of the nineteenth-century *Makhzen* have given us a glimpse of the plural modalities of territorial administration, in the form of arguments but sometimes reforms and other actions designed to resist incursions by European powers. Although the diverse visions of the territory and the responsibilities that stemmed from it were the expression of a conflict of interest in which colonisation was the key issue, they revealed elaborate but incompatible understandings of territorialisation and beyond that of the state. These conceptions gave rise to trickery, negotiations, tactical delays, compromises or takeovers, in an asymmetrical relationship between Morocco and European powers, which were then in a phase of aggressive colonisation. Faced with this pressure, and after the battles of Isly (1844) and Tétouan (1860) that opened up Morocco (with commercial, but also diplomatic, legal and judicial consequences), the country found itself forced to control its territories even if the means for this control relied on traditional practices. Indeed, the *harka* was not merely a theatrical staging of power, it was also a bureaucratic mechanism, a condensation of state structures that delimited the territory and administration in a very specific context. Territorialisation was not seen as geographical knowledge of the territory but as a knowledge of the people within it.

Learning borders

The time of colonial expansion and the competition between European powers for the control of the Sharifian empire was a moment where Morocco had to "learn territory and borders" and move from limits and fringes to formal borders.[3] Moroccan leaders had to learn to deal with states that had a different conception of territory, one that was clear and mappable, delimited by national borders and marked by internal limits defined by uniform administrative law. These leaders saw Morocco as the juxtaposition of various territories, some of which were subject to direct patrimonial administration by the *Makhzen*, while others were more remote and autonomous, indirectly controlled through the intermediary

120

SHIFTING SPACES OF TERRITORIALISATION

of local figures. Still others were even more remote and only nominally dependant, which only paid their tithes under constraint. The Mackenzie case is an example of this.

Donald Mackenzie was a Scottish merchant and adventurer, like so many others in this era, and he meant to increase his business by controlling trans-Saharan trade. To do so, he aimed to create a port around Cape Juby (today Tarfaya), on land ceded to him by Beyrouk in an agreement signed in April 1879.[4] The sultan, concerned, acted rapidly; he simultaneously launched several expeditions into the Sous region. These can be interpreted as training for a new conception of territory. The *harka* was also a way of expressing the new desire to concretise the *Makhzen's* sovereignty in the Sous region and its direct control over the territory, by limiting the autonomy of the tribes and in particular their ability to trade with foreigners.[5]

In the north-east of the empire, during the same period, between 1880 and 1906, the European presence was concretised through the military occupation of the oases by the French from Algeria.[6] The Moroccans considered these oases their own,[7] and the French considered they belonged to no one.[8] Historically, in this region the Sharifian empire included the "nomadic territories"[9] which were included although they were not covered by the same rules. The limits of the empire were vague, varied and also shifting, because they were incarnated by nomadic tribes. But this did not prevent a process of delimitation. The limits of the empire could be subject to disputes with the Muslim powers supposed to be part of *dar-al-Islam*, such as the Ottoman empire.[10] But during the nineteenth century, France considered that all territory had to be limited by stable borders that were recognised by international regulations. This different understanding led to tensions and incidents between Bedouins from these regions and French authorities, incidents which provided colonial France with a pretext for activity in Morocco, even more so given the exercise of power in these territories prevented the *Makhzen* from directly intervening.[11] For the first time, Morocco felt the need to define clear set limits on the ground so these opposing forces (in this instance the Bedouin population and the French army) could be separated.[12] This was the empire's first attempt to trace a border.

WEAVING POLITICAL TIME IN MOROCCO

From the second half of the nineteenth century, the diversity in forms of territorialisation enabled struggles for power, which partly explains the resistance of the Sharifian empire to colonisation and its survival through successive conflicts and adjustments. However, European states also simultaneously increased the sites of pressure and incursions, having successfully imposed their way of understanding territory and how it should be controlled. This asymmetrical confrontation led to an eventual alignment with the European understanding of the state. Contrary to popular wisdom, this European hegemony did not take place under colonisation but over the course of the century that preceded it.

Territorial diversity and diversity of relations to politics

In their description of the relationship between the *Makhzen* and the tribes, European chronicles and accounts of the court from the nineteenth century[13] and most contemporary western historians[14] have emphasised the juxtaposition of different conceptions of territory. They note that no two tribes or regional spaces have the same relations with the *Makhzen*. These relations range from total recognition of the tribe's allegiance to the sultan, to a simple exchange of correspondence; from the periodic sending of delegations to the court, to a single contribution to the war effort by sending troops; from regular contributions by the *Makhzen* for religious celebrations and gifts, to the simple tolerance of one man's demands for sainthood and the acceptance of his initiatives for local mediation and conflict resolution etc. These differences were not only expressed between tribes and regions but also evolved over time and in response to power relations. However, these descriptions do not define the modes of government associated with this differentiated territorialisation. Recent studies by Moroccan historians,[15] much like our ideal-type reading of Sharifian letter writing,[16] encourage us to refine our understanding of these diverse relations to territory. At the time, diversity was the norm and it lay at the heart of relations to politics. All of these differences were founded on history, or more specifically on the types of political and social relations inscribed in history.

On one hand, the nature of these relations varied according to the distance between the territory and the *Makhzen*, a distance that

122

SHIFTING SPACES OF TERRITORIALISATION

could be physical (particularly in terms of topography with strong contrasts between mountains and plains) but was above all political. Territories that were "closer" were subject to patrimonial direct administration by the *Makhzen*, entrusted to the public servants of the court. Provinces that were more "remote" were more autonomous, but justice remained in the hands of the sultan who appointed the *cadis*.[17] Finally, on the very fringes were zones that only nominally depended on the sultan, particularly because the cost of submission would have been too high both in terms of means and men.

The borders between these territories were blurry, however, because they were embodied not in the land or physical spaces but in people and tribes. The relationship between tribes and the *Makhzen* were therefore shifting and intermittent, fluctuating according to circumstances and power relations. Harassment by the tribes was considered one type of relationship among others, not constituting a challenge to the authority or sovereignty of the *Makhzen* which remained tolerant of insubordination. It was only with the pressure from European powers that this conception of territory as independent of the physical presence of power, was seen as a "weakness", which was the first step towards adopting a different—unified—conception of territory and its control. This understanding of territory can be seen today in Moroccan historiography, which stems more from a juxtaposition of local histories—"a careful inventory of little homelands", to paraphrase Chartier's description of eighteenth-century France[18] or "an inventory of differences" according to Veyne's expression[19]—than an attempt to write national history.[20]

Governing by mobility

Itinerancy is the other specificity of these modes of administration and government of territories. Whether in person or through his army, the sultan spent more than half his time on the move. For the Alawite empire, and among their predecessors, the Marinids and Saadians, it was movement that created territory by ensuring a presence in places where the *Makhzen* was weak.[21] This was the main role of the *harka* (which in Arabic firstly means action and

WEAVING POLITICAL TIME IN MOROCCO

movement);[22] itinerancy is the expression of the exercise of power, revealing the state of power relations between the central power and local powers. The mobility of the court is the expression of the sovereign's independence both in his action and in the choice of the stages, because it affirms his lack of dependence on his residence and his hosts. It is also the reflection of the extent of his empire because the *harka*, which has a military aspect, only has an impact internally, within the limits of the sultan's reach. When it goes beyond these limits, it is *jhazwa* or *jihad*.[23]

This is why the *harka*, and mobility more generally, are not a way of breaking free of territory[24] but rather a process of territorialisation. This practice does enable the collection of taxes and reduces resistance against payment, but it is also a form of inclusion; it enables the incorporation of submissive populations. It has four primary functions,[24] the first of which is pedagogical in a certain respect. The *harka* contributes to the spread of a model of authority and behaviour; it demonstrates exemplary behaviour while also dispensing *baraka* (blessings), happiness and the promise of salvation. The second function is managerial: the *harka* allows for inspection and investigation, management of everyday affairs of the country, decision-making, constituting inventories of tribal groups for the next military expeditions, updating records of their debts, appointing and sanctioning local figures, ensuring the protection of towns, proper functioning of provincial administration and the handing down of judgements—the sultan operating as the final level of appeal against injustice. In this respect, it also enables war, the undertaking of military operations against bandits or predation and the repression of rebellions. The third function of the *harka* is symbolic: it is to leave a trace of central power through euergetism, commemoration of the sacred or simply the sultan's presence[26]—as the passage of the sultan contributes to building sites of memory and in so doing marking the symbolic appropriation of the territory. This is not only mobile government but government by mobility. Finally, the fourth function of the *harka* is linked to the political order; it perpetuates frugality without renouncing splendour in conditions of extreme discomfort. This property, which combines agility and endurance, is supposed to

124

SHIFTING SPACES OF TERRITORIALISATION

feed group cohesion (*asabiyyah*). Ibn Khaldun focused a lot on the loss of this ability, inherited from Bedouinism and nomadism, to explain the waning of empires.[27]

Transit points and mediator

This logic of movement leads to a particular understanding of the art of governing. What is important here is not so much the spaces but the transit points, the mountain passes, the rivers crossings, the souks and the caravanserai. These were tightly controlled. Power over men was not enforced through physical appropriation of the territory as a whole but through control of distances via a monopoly of instruments of mobility. Hence the importance of stages and itineraries of the *harka*.[28] One of the reasons Abdelahad Sebti's work is interesting is this detailed description of the stages of the "*Makhzen*'s route" and in the close analysis of this particular form of the exercise of power.[29] The shift from space to territory apparently occurred in response to a need to guarantee safe roads. From the Marinid dynasty up until confrontation with European powers, territory remained a matter of paths, stations, waypoints, river crossings, mountain passes and lookouts, knowledge of the state of the roads, their accessibility ... and the road police. The "*Makhzen* route" was strictly laid out on each tour, which creates rights and responsibilities.[30] It was marked by caravanserai, which were built on the sultan's orders and maintained and regulated by the *Makhzen*.[31] Power was therefore discontinuous, between one stage of the *harka* and the next. For the *Makhzen* this was more a question of managing discontinuities than administering a territory and the caravanserai were a central element in this configuration, just as the control of passes and river crossings were. It was fundamental to be able to secure roads so that power had a strong foundation, that orders could be sent, links could be consolidated with the agents of the *Makhzen* or official intermediaries to ensure that the army could continue on its way. For Abderrahmane Moudden, the security of the route was one of the necessary conditions for the *bay'ah*.[32]

Territory was not only considered through transit points but through people, and thus it was ultimately controlled indirectly. Territorialisation varied according to the type of connection

WEAVING POLITICAL TIME IN MOROCCO

between these people and the local and central power, which explained the diversity of types of territorialisation in the empire as a whole. The relationship between tribes and the *Makhzen* was permanent—*siba*, as we saw, was not anarchy or even dissidence. Territory was managed locally in different ways, either independently from the central power, in association with it or through direct delegation. The *Makhzen*'s presence was intermittent, as is its control of the territory, but continuity was ensured by relations with important local figures or by the mere possibility of these relations. Tribal management was not contradictory with the presence of the *Makhzen*. The permanence of tensions suggested the permanence of these relations; it reflected both the autonomy of the tribes and the incessant negotiations between them and the central power. In this type of relationship, the "passers" (*ztata*) played a major role.[33] They provided information both about the physical conditions of the routes and passages and the efficient and effective mobility of the *harka*, as well as on the political condition of possible relations with the tribes and local powers more generally. On the "*Makhzen* route", negotiations and payments were necessary to pass from one place to another. In this context, the management of the territory and its discontinuity also involved unpredictability.[34] Knowing how to use surprise or expectation, how to appear unexpectedly—in other words a mastery of time— was of fundamental importance for the *Makhzen*.

As Stuart Elden shows, inspired by Foucault, the meaning of a territory or a population is transformed over time and according to circumstances.[35] What we see here is that colonisation led to a new and very specific configuration, which made room for this imperial vision of territoriality, while also transforming it. In the name of a respect for traditions and the profound incompatibility of French and Sharifian modes of government, a number of dichotomies were institutionalised through law and administrative practices. Dichotomies between dominated and dominators, those under military or civilian administration, ethnic or territorial communities, positive or customary law, direct or indirect government and so forth.[36] It was thus the Protectorate that concretised these discontinuities by establishing them as hierarchical dualities.

SHIFTING SPACES OF TERRITORIALISATION

Ethnic groups and territorial communities

The process of territorialisation that the Protectorate began in 1912 took the form of armed "pacification" which lasted until 1934. However, the territory was not organised with a view to promoting the nation-state. On the contrary, once again the politics of the Protectorate took the path of an authoritarian rationalisation of traditional structures, managing populations and mapping territory.[37] The distinction between military and civilian zones and the sanctification of orders of major *caids* went hand in hand with attempts to organise ethnic groups, into administrative *jma'a*, alongside legal *jma'a* and others responsible for the trustee management of "collective goods".[38]

From ethnic group to territory

The *dahir* of 1916[39] was the first text to organise the representation of tribes and fractions of tribes into a system of co-optation of notables. It was modified on the eve of independence, on 28 June 1954, although its essential philosophy remained the same. With independence, Morocco inherited an organised administrative system, which was centrally structured into directorates (the Directorate for the Interior, responsible for central and local administration, the Directorate for Services and Public Safety or the Directorate for Sharifian Affairs) and technical services (finance, agriculture, public works) and at the local level municipalities for urban areas and constituencies and local centres for the countryside. These entities had limited power. The country also inherited a division into seven regions in the former French Protectorate zone, themselves divided into territories or circles. The northern zone of the ex-Spanish Protectorate was divided into five regions.[40] From 1956, the map of the Moroccan provinces drew on this division in order to provide a foundation for the state authority. In 1960, the country was divided into fifteen provinces plus the prefecture of Casablanca. In the same year, the map of newly created towns partly replaced the map of the tribes to establish the framework of the first local elections in independent Morocco. Another legacy of the Protectorate was the network of authority agents crisscrossing the territory, combining traditional representatives (pashas,

WEAVING POLITICAL TIME IN MOROCCO

caids, sheiks and *muqaddam*), officers of indigenous affairs and civilian controllers holding all kinds of power, including legal power. These different authority bodies were then combined into a single hybrid one. *Caids* became public servants, while sheiks and *muqaddam* were kept in an obscure status as auxiliaries. The project to break away from ethnicity can be attributed to Mehdi Ben Barka. For him, this was not a matter of tackling the tribes directly, but instead of following the French model of decentralisation, so the tribe and the municipality were parallel and that the *caids* became prefects or sub-prefects working as public servants and thus accelerated national integration by repressing—at least institutionally—demands for consideration of local specificities. Certain managers wanted to go further, moving from management of people to management of territory, with 800 towns replacing a little more than 700 tribes. Hassan Zemmouri, responsible for divisions within the Ministry of the Interior had a specific mandate, with Rémy Leveau later explaining: "The tribal order had to be broken to lay the foundation for a new administration ... elections meant the destruction of the old order to substitute it with a system based on supervision by the parties."[41]

Yet this project came up against resistance from the monarchy, at least in part, as it was considered radical. But King Hassan II knew that his most solid support came from the rural segments of society. Thus, his main objective was not so much to replace ethnic groups with territorial communities as to maintain his control over the techniques and design of municipal and territorial divisions to continue to manage loyalties, breakdown oppositions and draw on leverage to weigh in on electoral results.

In 1960, at the time of the first municipal consultation, the confrontation between the Istiqlal and the UNFP on the one hand, and between these parties and the monarchy on the other, reflected electoral issues rather than questions of territorialisation and decentralisation. The municipalities were primarily a site for the production of the Council electors who were to participate in the designation of Councillors in the Upper House, which is reputed to be more conservative and more rural and also more likely to follow royal opinion. Under his different pseudonyms, Rémy

SHIFTING SPACES OF TERRITORIALISATION

Leveau (Marais, Chambergeat)—and in full knowledge of the facts because he was then expert adviser to the Minister of the Interior—mentioned the hesitations between territorialisation and continuation of the tribes, noting that municipalities had been artificially constructed in most cases against tribal reality, which was still an important dynamic at the time.[42] The powers of the municipality were less important than its optimum size, given its loyalty or dissidence. The most important factor was not redefining territory in accordance with the paradigm of the Nation-state but rather the electoral results in the fiefdoms of the notables loyal to the monarchy. The abandonment of attachment to ethnicity and tribalism thus appeared marginal. This conservative compromise lasted more than 50 years and only changed in 2011 with the new constitution and the introduction of the term "territorial communities." Up until then, decentralised communities had been referred to as simple local communities, with this term covering both municipalities and regions. Resistance against recognition of decentralised territorial entities stemmed from politicians and technicians who defended a Jacobin vision of territory. But this resistance was also couched in an imperial reference and in that of the tribes themselves—or at least what was left of them. Everywhere these tribes remained, where they were left to administer heritage or to act as leverage for mobilisation in border zones like in the east or in the Sahara, they constantly challenged the divisions imagined by the engineers of the nation-state (in this instance the Ministry of the Interior) or chose the public servant appointed to manage their affairs as their *caid*, forcing him to defend the local community and represent them against the administration or other tribes.

Impossible decentralisation

The debate around regionalisation, which led to a Royal Commission in January 2010 and eventually to a law, only after the promulgation of the 2011 constitution,[43] says much about the lines of action that run through the Moroccan political body. During this period, in a context of urgency, royal encouragements toward greater decentralisation and deconcentration[44] led to only partial results, even though the international credibility of the kingdom

WEAVING POLITICAL TIME IN MOROCCO

was at stake in the issues of regionalisation relating to the Sahara. This royal "goal" was effectively neutralised through the combined effects of the interests of central administrations reluctant to transfer their prerogatives to decentralised services, doctrines driven by the creators of territorial planning who were very close to those of French geography and the Datar,[45] and also the security arguments put forward by members of the Ministry for the Interior, the police and probably the army. Rumours of the debates within the court, between palace councillors and technicians, reveal a competition between those who, fed on the imperial framework, accommodate these independent communities and those who, faithful to the nation-state framework of the Ministry of the Interior and those close to the Koutla parties (Istiqlal, USFP, PPS), are wary of them. The arrival of the PJD in power in 2011 did not fundamentally change this situation. Thus, on 25 October 2018, the head of government communicated broadly about a decree on the "decentralisation charter". Yet this text consolidated the pre-eminence of the *walis* and the governors (i.e. representatives of the state and especially the King) even though it was in this party's interest to promote greater independence for elected bodies.

The decentralisation the technocrats propose is ultimately quite centralised. It has led to a sort of indirect government without autonomy for populations, far removed from any idea of local democracy. Even as they draw on history these technocrats have not understood that from an imperial perspective territorialisation integrates the discontinuities and pluralities of relationships with the central state. Yet the technical artforms promoted by the agencies responsible for regional and local development reactivate this characteristic by reinventing its contours.

The administration of the new fringes

Since the late 1990s, Moroccan authorities have developed a new territorial framework in the form of agencies. Dedicated to particular territories, these structures do not concern the country as a whole but rather what we might call the new fringes. This vision of territory is not new, a certain number of authors talk about

SHIFTING SPACES OF TERRITORIALISATION

peripheral spaces,[46] margins[47] or marginalised areas that share a low level of development and especially the fact that they are sites for contraband or illegal activities. Without throwing into doubt this geographic and economic data, it is important to emphasise not the similarity but the "marquetry of differences"[48] of these territories, which are born out of history but also the contemporary issues that they contain, shedding light on the way in which each space invents individual and specific ways of being governed. These "agency spaces" do not overlap with a specific province or tribe, nor a specific administrative geographic zone but trace a new territoriality based on particular ways of exercising authority, redistributing resources and ensuring local embeddedness. The fringes reflect this uncertainty—the uncertainty of statuses, types of beneficiaries, territorial limits and above all, the limits to the common law regime.

These agencies are characterised by a derogation from ordinary rules of territorial planning and local management. However, unlike the agencies that manage royal projects (such as Tanger Med or the development of the Bouregreg Valley or MASEN[49]), they depend on the government and are part of the inter-ministerial framework for infrastructure. In this respect, they do not have the exceptional or prestigious resources that, for example, Tanger Med benefited from, even though they do have considerable financial means that are more rapidly mobilisable than is normal for traditional administration. However even more than their ways of functioning, it is the presence of these agencies that reveals the status of these territories and the ways in which they are governed which interests us here. Two examples illustrate this particular way of governing that resonates with the imperial register.

The North, the cannabis fringe

The first territorial agency to emerge was the Agency for the North.[50] Initially focused on its political mission which was to show that the Moroccan state was finally taking care of a neglected territory, from 2003, the Agency of the North, with the nomination of Driss Benhima as its leader, focused on the economic and social development of the region.[51] The territory in question included the

WEAVING POLITICAL TIME IN MOROCCO

regions of Tanger-Tétouan and Taza-Al Hoceima-Taounate, in other words covered the "cannabis fringe", an area of illegal activities more generally. Behind the official rhetoric—contributing to a "coordinated and integrated" vision of development through a "participative approach"—in order to facilitate the region's "modernisation" and establish it as a "model for integrated regional development"—the Agency for the North aimed to use leverage in public action in its fight against the scourge of a region suffering from "corruption, mafia of all kinds, smuggling—which is the livelihood of thousands of families—and of course, the cannabis industry."[52]

The experience of the Agency for the North revealed a very specific process of territorialisation in the area of cannabis production (which, it is important to specify, did not cover all of the zone). It used a very specific form of government based on the administration of a territory without an attempt to control it. This somewhat abrupt formulation emphasises two characteristics that are specific to modes of government of the fringe today. On the one hand, the administration incorporates the illegal activities that proliferate in the area (cannabis, smuggling) by making them invisible, the *caid* does not have to see the production and commercialisation of cannabis, just as the customs officer does not have to see illegal trade. They only "see" these practices at specific moments, when an adjustment is necessary, and they are forced to show that the state can act if it wishes to. This is the case when the *caid* receives a letter denouncing the activities of a cannabis producer or trafficker,[53] or when smuggling impinges on extremely protected activities that are considered more important, such as the free circulation of foreign currencies,[54] or the arrival of expatriate Moroccans for the holidays.[55] The action of the state is therefore discontinuous, sporadic. Moreover, the state is only present in the cannabis territory intermittently. If we use the vocabulary of the imperial period, we might say that the administration defines the "watchtowers" as the places and moments of government. And today, these "watchtowers" are the *souks*, or more specifically the market day at the *souk* in a given village. Therefore, when the police have to arrest someone for growing or selling cannabis, they

SHIFTING SPACES OF TERRITORIALISATION

do not arrest him at home (even though they invariably know him and know where he lives) but instead at the "watchtower";[56] if the individual, who knows he is being followed, goes to the souk that day then he wants to be arrested, because if he stays at home, goes elsewhere or even goes to the village another day than market day, he will avoid arrest. This is not powerlessness but rather a differentiated use of power that plays more on social relations than on constraints, in a context where international pressure and image are important. Indeed, in situations where cannabis constitutes a major risk for the stability of the country (like during the 1992 elections)[57] the state is able to demonstrate the full weight of its power, for example, by burning plants and arresting traffickers.

The general regime is thus relatively laissez-faire, which in no instance suggests the state is side-lined, overwhelmed or overtaken but rather that it responds to an existing situation (involving the extent of illegal activities, their role in maintaining a delicate balance and social order) with which it tries to interact in accordance with the circumstances. The laissez-faire approach is a very well-known and powerful form of government.[58] It does not constitute the abandonment of any idea of government—in other words, "anything goes"—but instead reveals an ability to adapt politics to a complex and unpredicted or uncontrollable situation. Thus, it is well-known in the region (through rumour, collective understandings and experience) that in a situation of drought there are no criminal charges for growing and selling cannabis. Inversely, it is also known that when criminal networks of traffickers become too visible, too large or threaten the social order, the fight against them will be activated. In other words, the fact that the state acts or does not act, that it sees or does not see, is not defined by set rules or their violation but rather by intuitions, situations and circumstances that are interpreted as revealing moments that are "delicate" or "dangerous."

The South or the fringes of the Sahara

The South provides a vision of a region that is both controlled and administrated, but in a very specific way, combining an administrative policy that is purely Nation-state in style and deeply

WEAVING POLITICAL TIME IN MOROCCO

imbued with imperial references. The international recognition of Morocco as an "administrating power" is not only a description that is euphemised, neutral or acceptable to all parties in the conflict. It reflects genuine administrative involvement beyond the control of territory.

Very roughly speaking, the chronology of the Moroccan administration of the Sahara can be divided into three periods. The Green March was the concretisation of the process of territorialisation through physical occupation of space, in keeping with a classical nation-state vision of territory, even though the modalities to bring about this "recuperation," and the shift to obtain "national integrity", stem from deeply imperial ways of operating. The 1980s and 1990s were characterised by an extremely centralised administrative management of the territory with a Ministry of the Interior that was omnipresent and the direct involvement of the nation-state via generous public policies and the massive presence of the army. The 2000s were marked by the acceptance of independentist activities by elements of the internal Polisario and the return of Sahrawi activists from camps in Tindouf,[59] as well as the creation of the Agency for the South in 2002. Since then, public authorities seem to call more often on the register of Empire than on that of the Nation-state by personalising clientelism particularly around development programmes. Although this rapid chronological presentation reflects the general tendencies, it is clearly too brief. The administrative practices of territorialisation are infinitely more diverse, combining the different logics of the Nation-state and Empire in ever more original ways.

The administration of this territory is primarily based on a very close knowledge of people, via the networks and notables whose loyalty is constantly staged, as well as personalised intermediation.[60] Personal connections constitute the foundation for political practices (such as the co-optation of Saharan notables by tribes, factions, lineages and family)[61] as well as social practices, particularly the representation of society, in a process of reinvesting in the historic links between these notables and the *Makhzen* in the construction of loyalties.[62] The principle of allegiance that began in 1979 with the *bay'ah* in Dakhla, as we have seen, at the time of the

SHIFTING SPACES OF TERRITORIALISATION

withdrawal of Mauritania, has been constantly renewed ever since. Delegation in this area is thus based on personalised incarnation, but ethnic separatism and particularism are reinforced by reference to territory to take into account new situations that go beyond simple tribal references. Territorialisation therefore takes place through personal ties but also through representations—for example, of an empire that not only stretches to Timbuktu[63] but which has always drawn on resources from the South.[64] This has often been interpreted overseas as being pure instrumentalisation, but it is a powerful frame of reference that is constantly updated by official historiography and the ostentatious celebration of the historic depth of the Hassani culture.[65] According to this representation, the Sahara is depicted as the place for the regeneration of the monarchy. The new dynasties that had taken power and reinvigorated politics always came from the southern fringes.[66] It is also in this respect that the fringes are not marginal, instead they reflect a territory that is symbolically central if we consider it not from a geographical or even economic perspective but rather in terms of history and political or even sociological signification.[67] Indeed the movements of population and even the displacements have left a lasting mark, feeding significant interpenetrations of populations of various origins, to the extent that the Sahrawi people are not seen as foreign or even as marginal. The phosphate plateaus between Marrakech and Essaouira are still populated by Sahrawi people today (the Rhamna, the Ouled Dlim, the Mejjat, the Ouled Bousbaa, etc.) who proudly display their origins, with the women wearing the Sahrawi costume, the *mlahfa*, in Sidi Mokhtar, or the camel hair tents scattered along the road to Essaouira.

The administration of this territory is also based on the generalisation of exceptional frameworks, but this exceptionalism is expressed in the same terms as the nation-state and its bureaucracy. The Agency for the South is an incarnation of that Nation-state and its official presence. It finances many interventions and actions (which do not benefit from such support elsewhere in the territory) particularly in the airport, in agriculture, tourism or the organisation of cultural and sporting events.[68] But the agency is not a substitute for the central administration which remains very pres-

WEAVING POLITICAL TIME IN MOROCCO

ent in the Sahara. All the ministries, offices and independent national agencies are more visible here than in the rest of the territory because there is a need to affirm the state's direct and physical presence to signify its control. This control clearly concerns security; the region is highly militarised, and the army is very visible, which is not the case in the rest of the country. But the control is also civilian, through the extent of public interventions in social and economic areas.

In the Sahara these interventions share two characteristics. On one hand they are based on the differentiation of political relations, a differentiation that is not ethnic (Sahrawi vs non-Sahrawi) but territorial (all inhabitants of the Sahara combined) and which aims to favour a region with the objective of integrating it into the nation. On the other hand, these interventions are often large-scale and direct. The policy conducted over the last 40 years in the Sahara is striking in terms of the enormity of the investments, which also explains why it is impossible for Moroccan leaders to envisage a withdrawal from the region—quite independent of the salience of the imperial reference and the political signification of the territory. These investments take numerous forms: infrastructure, subsidies, public services, local implementations of major development policies, tax breaks and subsidy incentives and massive job creation.[69] According to the Economic and Social Council, the Sahara receives 4.6 billion dirhams per year in direct and indirect assistance to fight against poverty and absorbs 50% of the National Promotion budget[70] (which reaches 34,000 people and represents the primary employer in the region with 7,000 jobs). Compared to the number of inhabitants—3% of the total population of the kingdom—the portion of the special treasury account intended for equipment and fighting unemployment is disproportionately high (33% of the total). This is also true for the budget for investment (31% higher than the national average) particularly for infrastructure, whether in housing, road access or water and electricity, which have reached levels above the national average. Similarly, 10% of INDH projects go to the Sahara alone, where public servants benefit from a salary bonus of 25% to 75%, and investors are eligible for tax exemptions (partial in certain parts

136

SHIFTING SPACES OF TERRITORIALISATION

of the region and total in others) both as concerns VAT (especially for construction companies and companies domiciled in the province that trade with the rest of the kingdom) and corporate, income and domestic consumption taxes. Moreover, control of fishing in the area is also more "flexible" and this flexibility is a way of appeasing tensions and drawing support from certain segments of the local population.[71] The extent of this implicit "positive discrimination" is such that today some are beginning to denounce the "burden" it constitutes.[72]

Moreover, some of these measures are exclusively directed at Sahrawis, whether explicitly or implicitly. Rentier policy is generalised across this territory, targeting specific groups in the form of fishing licences, exemptions for public works companies and subsidies for camel-raising structures. It is essentially managed through the Agency for the South which has the advantage of increasing resources to be distributed to notables, because the agency does not depend on the Ministry of the Interior. Subsidies from the Agency for the South thus enable the funding of infrastructure (and bits on the side) in territories where inhabitants, who are recorded as residing and voting there but have in fact chosen to live in major cities such as Laayoune, Smara or Dakhla. This policy stretches beyond the Sahara, to Sahrawi notables living in Rabat, Tangier, Agadir or Casablanca. The Joumani, Derham, Ould Er-Rachid, Reguibi and Bouahida families are not only important local entrepreneurs (in the fishing industry as shipowners or owners of freezing units, in sand quarries, in land ownership, in military supply transport). Thanks to their connections or their role in recognising the Moroccan identity of the region they also have a national impact (in real estate, in oil distribution, in merchandise transport and public transport in major cities).[73] This other way of governing the fringes sheds light on the importance of imperial modalities of government that are more invested in people than in territory.

As we can see, the reason of the state, statistical logic, administration by abstraction and by norms—which are all characteristics of the Nation-state—are undeniably and massively present in the administration of the South, sometimes even to a caricatural degree. But the modalities of intervention that stem from the

137

WEAVING POLITICAL TIME IN MOROCCO

Empire ideal type are equally so, including government from a distance, which is based on ties of allegiance, intermediation and intervention that Sahrawi notables are supposed to bear. Indeed, they are even at the heart of politics in this territory, although they are implemented in an extremely centralised way.

* * *

The process of territorialisation at work in Morocco reveals significant tensions between the different ways of conceiving and governing a territory. This coexistence of a plurality of perspectives and understandings explains why the territorialisation of sovereignty and public policies inspired by the Nation-state occurs through modalities that borrow from the logics, techniques and operating strategies of Empire. Control of the space through the dynamics of economic development, equipment and infrastructure that are specific to a nation-state approach to territorialisation, all take place without abandoning the plurality of government levels that is characteristic of the imperial perspective. Similarly, the reinvention of these fringes goes hand in hand with an increasingly rigid understanding of borders. In this context, decentralisation takes on a very specific political meaning. In Empire, the independence and autonomy of local populations and areas does not challenge ways of governing and relations between state and society, whereas in the Nation-state its implementation is only meaningful in a democratic framework. However, in contemporary Morocco, decentralisation, which has become a categorical imperative of neoliberal globalisation, can only occur by likening it to indirect government, which is far from democratic.

138

4

ADMINISTRATING BY CONSENSUS
(*EINVERSTÄNDNIS*)

An approach via marginal figures rather than key players—the *muqaddam* or the *amghar*[1] rather than the *caid*, the *naib* rather than the governor—provides a perspective on how the administration operates on an everyday basis, closest to those who are in direct contact with the population. In some respects, subaltern figures constitute the foot soldiers of the administration, Lipsky's "street-level bureaucrats,"[2] even though they are not part of the adminis-trative hierarchy. These figures have an odd status, working for the administration but without being dependent on it, more on the ground (or street) than in offices. Looking at administration through them reveals a bureaucracy based on arrangements, made up of equal parts civil society and state apparatus. These hybrid figures act as go-betweens for the population and the administration; they are intermediaries in ideology, representa-tion, production and access to information. They are essential for gaining access to resources, whether symbolic or property, or in the form of information on citizens or in concrete situations. Simply put, they are at the heart of everything that allows us to take the measure of society with all its tensions and frictions, although they are not part of the police system or the mainte-nance of public order more generally.

139

WEAVING POLITICAL TIME IN MOROCCO

These figures of the administration combine characteristics from the imperial frame of reference and its technologies (cost minimisation, delegation, intermediaries, itinerancy) with capacities for adaptation that are specific to the nation-state framework. They provide an understanding of what, following Max Weber, we call "administration by consensus (*Einverständnis*)".[3] It is important to note that although we use the accepted English translation for this concept here, "consensus" does not reflect the sociological meaning of the German, particularly because for Weber this "agreement" or "mutual understanding" comes about through discord, conflict and struggles for power. We can therefore see that state power is also exerted through society. Applying this concept to Morocco, we can see how the two figures focused on in this chapter operate at the interface between state and civil society. They make connections, share information and have administrative powers. This position makes them particularly able to incorporate historical evolutions and reveal the distinctive characteristics of each era and in particular the always singular compositions between the imperial and nation-state registers. Indeed, it is never possible to generalise from a trend observed in a particular domain. An approach via these two figures allows us to reveal different tendencies, both over time but also at a particular moment.

The administrative grid constitutes the perfect example of legal-rational bureaucracy. It is incarnated at the local level by the figures of the *muqaddam*, the *caid* and the *wali*, who simultaneously stem from the Nation-state and from Empire. The case of the *muqaddam* is particularly interesting because it is the most remote from the image conveyed in political science textbooks of what constitutes a representative of the state in its regalian dimension. It is the illustration of the salience of the imperial register but also how it functions in the nation-state.

As for the figure of the *naib*, it illustrates the tensions resulting from the mobilisation of skills at the intersection of the registers of the Nation-state and Empire. The status of the collective land—created circumstantially by the Protectorate and reappropriated individually by peri-urban populations as an object of competition in a changing rural world—sheds light on a permanent void of

ADMINISTRATING BY CONSENSUS (*EINVERSTÄNDNIS*)

political vision. The inability to resolve conflict and outline a trajectory for population growth, urbanisation or pressure on property only made these problems more complicated. The figure of the *naib* never lost its centrality in formal procedures relating to the availability of property and gained new vitality from its method of appointment, through ever more democratic elections, in a context marked by the increasing importance of property in the application of public policy and by the institutional weakness of this figure under the tutelage of the state.

The muqaddam*: a reasonable wager on information*

It is interesting to approach bureaucracy through its simplest primary form, which is also its least straightforward: the *muqaddam*. This subaltern figure is responsible for security and public order, yet in reality he plays a central role that is well-known to all national administrations and all citizens. The *muqaddam* is the figure of authority that is the closest to the population; the lowest level auxiliary in the hierarchy of those embodying the state. This is an ambivalent figure both in the political imaginary and in everyday practice, representing the arbitrary nature of power and everyday services.

This figure can be traced back to the pre-colonial era and was paradoxically consolidated under the Protectorate, despite the latter's concerns with modernising Moroccan administration. Decolonisation could have meant its demise, yet it was reinforced; at independence there were only 20,000 *muqaddam* in the kingdom, today there are around 46,000.[4] Their responsibilities are vague, but they are expected to know everything that happens at the local level and maintain order and security. The *muqaddam* is omnipresent but operates on the fringes of informality. Officially he is not a member of the public service, unlike other agents of authority now organised into four professional bodies (*walis*, governors, *caids* and *khalifa*),[5] with each body divided into ranks.[6] A rapid ethnographic overview of a *muqaddam's* average day reveals a specific application of imperial artforms, the implementation of government by delegation based on an economy of resources and the externalisation of regalian functions by a minimisation of costs. It

141

WEAVING POLITICAL TIME IN MOROCCO

also shows the *muqaddam* as an agent of the Nation-state, a typical representative of the continuity of the state and its presence throughout the territory.

Si Raji, country *muqaddam*[7]

Si Raji, *muqaddam* and sheikh in Ouneine, a small town nestled in the High Atlas Mountains, is just like anyone else, he is ordinary. He wears no uniform and rides around on his Honda motorbike, which has extra suspension to allow him to navigate the rocky paths of the mountains. This auxiliary authority figure is a farmer in the local area, originally from a *douar* (village) in Tameslouht. He is not the most popular person in the valley, but he is the only representative of authority here. Si Raji always carries a pouch with him, whether he is at the town hall where he does not have an office or on the roads winding between Tamterga and Tiguicht. As well as being the representative of the administration, he is also the representative of his tribe, a position previously the responsibility of the *muqaddam*. Back in 1992 he saw the rural municipality set up in his territory and with it the political representatives and its registry office—but not the *caid*, who remained in Tafingoult, a "lookout"-town that surveys the southern pass of the High Atlas and the path that links Taroudant by the Sidi Ouaziz road to Marrakech. The *caid* was therefore some three hours away by mountain paths to the south, or one and a half hours by the new asphalt road inaugurated in 2017. Raji participates in local life; he is not impartial in the conflicts that create tension in the villages and takes a clear stance in the disputes over the water courses and rights to use them. He is only neutral during the electoral campaigns, although of course he has his own preferences. However, in recent times the rigour of the Ministry of the Interior has made his public stances very risky.

The pouch that he carries is the symbol of the link between the state and the citizen. It holds everything: letters from migrants to their parents who have remained back home, which he must distribute for want of a postal service; official summons before the courts or the police for formal demands or court hearings; fines for forestry workers; information records for the Minister for National

ADMINISTRATING BY CONSENSUS (*EINVERSTÄNDNIS*)

Education, to count young people of school age; but no tax records, because there are no taxes here in the rural world. Raji also brings news; he announces the new vaccination campaigns or the arrival of subsidised flour in the souk. Sometimes he distributes contraceptive pills, stepping in for the nurse who remained behind in the dispensary at the centre of the municipality. He must also collect declarations of births and deaths that the civil registrar will later copy into the municipal registries. Above all, he must know things; he must know about forest fires; about conflicts between villagers; epidemics; trekking trails; and other local events and anecdotes. He is the one who decides whether or not to pass on this information and to whom, to the *caid* or *gendarme*. Raji does not need to know how to read or write (but in this case he can, having attended Qur'anic school). His interactions are mostly oral, even though he always has his official stamp with him, one of the few signs he is part of the administration.

Youssef, town *muqaddam*[8]

In Casablanca, the situation is similar, with the exception that— winter or summer—Youssef always wears his Ray Bans. Although he spends his time differently, he fulfils the same functions, even though urban space is saturated with administration of every kind. Like Raji, he is immersed in the community. As a *muqaddam*, Youssef is responsible for the administration of a territory of several thousand people. He sees his immediate superior every day because the *caid* is established in his district, and he also has an office that he shares with other *muqaddam*. He is only there for barely an hour per day (half an hour in the morning and half an hour in the afternoon). Youssef does not have a pouch—the citizens in his administration come to see him during one of his office hours to obtain the documents they need. He validates and provides living certificates, celibacy certificates, residency certificates and attestations as to the poverty level of those in his area. His testimony is necessary for the Ramed system to operate.[9] Youssef is a jovial character, around 50 years old, and he is always where you least expect—standing on a street corner, in a café, outside the school or simply where he should be: at the headquarters of the

WEAVING POLITICAL TIME IN MOROCCO

caidat and the constituency of the town, known as Zenith (which brings together several residential "relocation"[10] neighbourhoods, around fifty high-density housing projects and the Zenith business district, which houses the largest companies in Casablanca).

Youssef begins his day at 6am with the dawn prayer, which he regularly attends at the mosque. He is not necessarily pious, at least he does not seem to be, with his jeans, baseball cap and Ray Bans. He attends one of the mosques in his constituency to maintain a connection with the believers and servants of the mosque and particularly the imam. His work here is not so much about monitoring or surveillance as it is about collecting knowledge and providing advice and warnings depending on his perception of the danger of "radicalism". The Grand Mosque is one of the strategic sites in this constituency because it is one of the most important and one of the few to be controlled by a very dynamic association, with one of the star imams in Casablanca, Imam Goraani, who attracts thousands of attendees during Ramadan.

After a quick breakfast, he sets out on his first rounds in his Peugeot 103. The administration only provides him with a mobile phone. He goes to meet grocers and watchmen around the neighbourhood, whether in prestigious villas or in social housing projects. Frequently his round begins with the projects (100 buildings each with twenty-two apartments) and then moves on to public and private schools, residential and gated communities and then the business district. These watchmen are therefore indirectly his employees; they are paid for by the population, who recruit and pay them informally with the prior approval of the *muqaddam*, who has a record of their age, ethnic background, level of education and copies of their identity cards and anthropometric files, along with a request signed by the inhabitants of the street. At any moment the *muqaddam* can advise his employers (the residents) to revoke them. In the Zenith constituency, there are around thirty watchmen who are constantly called on, day and night. Youssef prefers to talk with the night watchmen. The exchanges are quick, if they tell him all is *"hania"* ("peaceful"), he continues on his way. Anything that is not *hania* will be signalled and conveyed to his superiors, in this instance the *caid*. These might include suspicious

ADMINISTRATING BY CONSENSUS (*EINVERSTÄNDNIS*)

deaths, fights and brawls (he is the one who decides if any action must be taken), abandoned new-borns, illegal constructions, accidents involving injuries, strikes, protest movements and demonstrations. Contact with the nightwatchmen allows him to cultivate connections but also to collect reports on the events of the night and happenings in the neighbourhood. There are no specific instructions, everything depends on individual reactions and they depend on the circumstances (alerts after terrorist attacks, electoral campaigns and elections, royal visits and so forth). At 7.30am, Youssef stops for 10 minutes outside the high school to observe the students going into class and the hawkers and peddlers in front of the building. At around 8am he can be found on the roundabout that regulates access to the business district, discreetly observing the flow of cars moving into the headquarters of the major companies of the Technopark. A little later he is at the intersection outside the Marjane supermarket. Along the way there might be a strike, a meeting, a fight or an accident that requires his attention. What he dreads most of all is not knowing, something happening behind his back. In his territory, he must be the first to know when things happen, before the police and above all, before those he reports to (who are not necessarily his hierarchical superiors).

On a normal day when no incidents are reported, he has time to go home to have breakfast with his children and send them off to school. If not, he is welcome in any café or tavern in his sector. Often the cafés in the area provide him with free coffee or breakfast; they do not see this as racketeering, simply a way of maintaining good relations with someone who can make local life easier and facilitate administrative services. Around 9.30 am, sometimes 10 am, he goes to the place that functions as his office at the town hall. He is now something like a public servant, while providing administrative papers and documents that need to be stamped—residence certificates, poverty certificates, living certificates, celibacy certificates, passport applications. He also has to go and see the *caid* to account for all this, the challenge for the *caid* being to extract all the information the *muqaddam* has collected and have exclusive access to it. This is generally difficult even though the *caid* tries to set up his own network of informers when he has been in the constituency

145

WEAVING POLITICAL TIME IN MOROCCO

for a while. Alongside the demands from citizens, the *muqaddam* must take care of other tasks, such as filling in forms for the Ramed card or for members of the community associations' board.

Between 10 am and midday, Youssef walks around the neighbourhood, chats to residents, helps out local notables, particularly those who cannot attend his office to obtain birth extracts or residence certificates. At midday his second round begins, following the same itinerary as in the morning but backwards, first the schools, then the houses, then the mosque and the business district. Possible incidents of note are slightly different in the afternoon, essentially things like accidents and injuries, violent theft, food poisoning in restaurants and so forth. If everything is okay, if it is *"hania"*, he has lunch at home, if not, he eats in one of the local cafés. At 2pm, he returns to the town hall to deal with everyday matters and provides an oral account of his activities to the *caid*. Sometimes he has to provide more sophisticated information such as a census of unemployed graduates, hawkers and peddlers or individuals affiliated with unions and political parties. From time to time, the *caid* may accompany him on his rounds to mark his presence and authority. These rounds essentially target hawkers and often end with the seizure of goods, particularly fruit and vegetables, that are weighed and recorded in an official report and then distributed to the local orphanage. The *muqaddam* may also participate in the mobile commissions for price control, construction sites or sometimes the destruction of illegal buildings. At 4pm he begins the "after work" round, where he spends more time at the school, the offices and the mosque. His final round begins at 7 pm when the neighbourhood is at its most busy. Youssef's biggest fear is that his mobile phone runs out of battery—being uncontactable is akin to professional negligence. His day is essentially never finished because he can be contacted at any moment.

The eclectic responsibilities of the *muqaddam*

The heart of the *muqaddam*'s mission is collecting information. In English, this role could be translated as "being in front" or "being put in front"; the *muqaddam* must be aware of everything happening in his area.[11] In this respect, he works as a kind of surveillance

146

ADMINISTRATING BY CONSENSUS (*EINVERSTÄNDNIS*)

police, and he also conducts local investigations as part of his administrative role. He is not only the auxiliary to the *caid* but also an assistant to the police and *gendarmerie*. He is thus a street-level bureaucrat. His role also involves signing forms, constituting an essential link in the chain establishing all kinds of documents and administrative attestations, such as building permits, drivers' licences, passports, national identity cards or legalisation of migrants who need identification—indeed records need to be lodged with him for any kind of registration.[12]

The *muqaddam* is the administrative assistant of the Ministry of the Interior, for which he conducts extensive groundwork: distributing voting cards; identifying and recording the population, including illegal migrants; conducting security surveys, particularly for the members of associations and for people liable to be appointed to positions of responsibility. But he is also effectively the administrative assistant of many other ministries or administrative entities because he is involved in the commissions responsible for hygiene, public safety or urbanism, for example.[13] He also acts as the postman in areas where there is no postal service, an essential cog in operations preparing for the census or conveying notices of enforcement of rulings in the countryside, in place of the court clerk. The *muqaddam* is therefore an essential administrative go-between. He conveys the decisions of the administrative services everywhere, publicises circulars and *dahirs* and conveys messages. Finally, the *muqaddam* has to be able to mobilise the population. During official events (royal visits, hosting foreign dignitaries, etc.) he is responsible for organising the transport of people from his neighbourhood or *douar*. Once he had to mobilise people for the *touiza*,[14] but today he calls on them in support of official projects.[15] He is also personally involved with the INDH or the creation of associations, in the name of appropriation by civil society.[16] In the 1960s, he promoted development projects such as Operation Labour, as well as those by the *Promotion Nationale*.[17]

Given all these attributions, the omnipresence of the *muqaddam* and his control over local society are striking. Moreover, this is what seems to corroborate the contemporary discourses on the usefulness of this territorial grid and particularly the role of the *muqaddam* in the fight against terrorism. The day after the terrorist attacks in Paris on 13 November 2015, the munitions supplier of the group behind the attacks was eliminated, revealing the "efficiency" of the BNPJ—a sort of Moroccan FBI—who were seen as having localised the hideout of Abdelhamid Abaaoud thanks to information from a small village in the Sous region where his parents lived. When questioned, the Ministry of the Interior praised the Moroccan system of information, with the *muqaddam* as its keystone, a legacy of the imperial era that coexists alongside satellite technologies, surveillance cameras and big data.

The apparent paradoxes of the *muqaddam*

The *muqaddam* encapsulates a certain number of paradoxes that can only be understood through historically grounded sociological and political specificities. Thus, he is both close to the population because he is a member of it, and he is distant because he represents the state. He is often the only incarnation of the state in the territory. So, he is a member of the group but also separate from it. He is dependent on his superior, the *caid*, and subject to his instructions, which are sometimes illegal, but he has a broad freedom of action including in relation to that superior. He is paid by the state but taken care of by the population. He is required to be apolitical, particularly during the elections, but his functions are also extremely political, which may raise issues in an environment that is familiar to him. This is the case for Islam, for example. His role monitoring Islamists is all the more difficult, because as a Muslim, he may be sympathetic to their cause or share their views. The *muqaddam* has a close knowledge of people but is ignorant of the general overview of situations; he cannot anticipate crises nor gauge the extent of what is informal or illegal. In truth, he does not have the distance necessary to see them because they are too familiar, as he himself operates on the fringes of informality and even sometimes illegality.

These paradoxes can be seen in the population's ambivalent and fluctuating appreciations of this figure. Although he is sometimes presented as a police informant,[18] a representative of a repressive and predatory order,[19] the *muqaddam* is most often also seen as an intermediary, a mediator who helps to improve everyday life and

ADMINISTRATING BY CONSENSUS (*EINVERSTÄNDNIS*)

particularly relations with the administration.[20] The *muqaddam* themselves relay this ambivalent perception of their role.[21]

For example, in 2011 they organised a protest movement to denounce their lack of public service status but also the fact that they are presented as "scapegoats in case of corruption and depravity." They said they "refused to 'execute oral instructions that lead to violations resulting in retribution and sanctions' as they [stood against] what they described as pauperisation, marginalisation and the threat of being barred from the body of auxiliaries of authority."[22]

These paradoxes can be understood by returning to a closer examination of the status and function of this subaltern figure within Moroccan bureaucracy. The *muqaddam* is undoubtedly an essential part of the nation-state bureaucracy. He is the incarnation of the desire and practice of creating territorial grids, a territory that is unified and governed through figures found all over the country. The *muqaddam* is present at the lowest level of the territorial division in towns and in the countryside, in the Sahara and in the Rif, in the Sous, in the east or in the Chaouia. Moreover, the *muqaddam*'s tasks have been rationalised; reforms, set rules and standardised procedures are all at the heart of his administrative work and he must systematically report on his observations, his discussions and his rounds. In the neighbourhoods and in the *douars*, his life is regulated like clockwork, marked by the same rounds every day, the same movements. He is the last and lowest echelon of agents representing the authority of the Ministry of the Interior.

However, the *muqaddam* also, and perhaps above all, shares many traits with patrimonial imperial bureaucracy. Firstly—like the *naib* or the *'adel*—he is not a public servant; he is not paid a wage by the Ministry of the Interior but rather an allowance.[23] This allowance, which was particularly low up until the 2000s (around 700 dirhams a month), has been progressively increased in recent years and is now around 2000 dirhams on average. Up until 2011, the *muqaddam* was not entitled to retirement or social security, he was not registered with the department of remuneration and pension payments and was therefore clearly on the fringes of the public service staff. Moreover, he can be sacked without warning or compensation and has to work seven days a week 24 hours a day. Since

149

2011, town *muqaddam* have benefited from the same advantages as public servants; they receive expenses for transport, sick pay and have the right to medical coverage, retirement and a certain career progression.[24] Their income is not specified, but in practice it is limited to between 2,400 and 3,020 dirhams for town *muqaddam*, all payments combined, and between 1,400 and 1,800 for those in rural areas.[25] Country *muqaddam* may have other professional activities (which implicitly justifies the fact that they are not public servants), and they are not subject to age restrictions.

Moreover, there is no text (*dahir* or regulation) that defines the role of the *muqaddam*. They are sometimes mentioned in decrees, such as the *dahir* of 1960 on the election of communal councils[26] or that of 1963 on the organisation of prefectures and provinces.[27] But they are not mentioned with a view to defining their attributes, responsibilities or status but rather to specify that as representatives of the state administration they are not eligible to run for council positions.[28]

The *muqaddam* are not recruited via competitive exams but are rather co-opted with minimal requirements, according to criteria in which trust is key. Most often he is hired via a network of contacts within the Ministry for the Interior. The *muqaddam* is forced to fund his expenses himself for an activity that can be seen not as a salaried position (or even a paid one) but rather as an "office" that must be paid for.

Another trait of patrimonial bureaucracy that characterises the *muqaddam*'s work is the non-rational way in which information is collected and reported on, relying above all on personal knowledge and intuition. Information is not required to be exhaustive, and subjectivity has an important role in gauging its relevance. The ultimate performance of the *muqaddam* is anticipation. This leads him to establish hypotheses, to let himself be guided by clues, signs and impressions but also to cross-check, to multiply sources of information and informers, both within the population and the state, even though he remains linked to the Ministry of the Interior. Unlike the public servants of the legal-rational state, his responsibilities require generalist rather than specialist knowledge, based on interpersonal knowledge and familiarity, both a broad knowledge of people and

ADMINISTRATING BY CONSENSUS (*EINVERSTÄNDNIS*)

society on the one hand and of public order and security on the other. He does not receive any specific prior training and, unlike the *caid*, does not attend the school for agents of authority.

The *muqaddam* must be a man on the ground, rather than a man in an office. This does not mean that he does not understand bureaucracy. The art of itinerancy and mobility is also, as we have seen, a bureaucracy. It includes the organisation of the official pouch (in which the stamp, pens, stamps, paper and forms are carried) but also the organisation of the rounds, which are extremely closely regulated and repetitive. Mobility and movement are fundamental not only for the collection of information—because the *muqaddam* is according to the common expression "the eyes and ears of the *Makhzen*"—but also for the completion of administrative work.

Last but not least, there is another element that is specific to these subaltern authority agents. Even though they constitute a specialised administrative body, they are also fully immersed in society. The *muqaddam* comes from the population; in rural areas he generally belongs to the ranks of the lower notability, and in urban areas he will have grown up in the neighbourhood.[29] To a certain extent, he must represent the population that he is supposed to know and be an active part in both their conflicts and their resolutions. His role as a mediator leads him to conduct negotiations, to find solutions in neighbourhood disputes or administrative problems. In the latter case, he is expected to help resolve problems with the local administration over health, teaching, water or electricity, for example.[30]

To a certain extent, the *muqaddam* is the incarnation of a cohabitation between the Nation-state (as the continuity and omnipresence of the state over the territory as a whole) and Empire (itinerancy, mobility, delegation and intermediation as a central way of exercising power). The *muqaddam* embodies the idea of control and comprehensive knowledge, national unity and public service. At the same time, however, he gives life to the performance of imperial engineering, that of least-cost government through intercession and mediation and temporal and spatial discontinuity in the exercise of power. Although this figure seemed destined to fade into obsolescence, it has lost none of its importance. Moreover, the *muqaddam*

WEAVING POLITICAL TIME IN MOROCCO

is increasingly aware of the fact that he must make up for the short-comings of the administrative bodies of nation-state bureaucrats.

The *muqaddam* and the heteroclite production of order

What we can see in the figure of the *muqaddam* is that security and public order are not only produced and maintained by actions that are deliberately programmed and planned from above. This figure often operates outside his area of jurisdiction, such as when he participates in the demolition of illegal houses,[31] or intervenes in the control of prices in place of inspectors from the Ministries of the Interior or Trade and Finance.[32] This intervention in the production of public order is not planned but occurs out of convenience because often he is the only public actor to have a sufficiently close knowledge of what is happening on the ground. This is important for the government even though it is not anticipated or conceived in these terms. But other actors may contribute to shaping public order by moving beyond their functions—like the *semsar*, an informal courtier who works in conflict management and intermediation between different social worlds and who not only collaborates with the *muqaddam* or the police but also participates in the production of norms, such as those relating to "good" servants and "good" behaviour in household staff or the definition of honesty.[33]

The *muqaddam*'s work collecting information is based on the connections he builds with a whole series of actors; day and (especially) night watchmen in buildings and joint tenancy housing in his zone, as well as parking attendants, grocers, newspaper sellers and café owners, who make up a genuine chain of delegation. The information he selects is largely dependent on the way in which these actors understand what is "*hania*" and above all what is not. These intermediaries are not public actors. On the one hand, they are not paid by the *muqaddam* (or by his superiors) but by the population (residents in the buildings, owners of the cars, clients at the grocers, in short, the users of these intermediaries). On the other hand, they have their own objectives and constraints, their own worldviews, their own lifestyles and obsessions, their own understandings of a particular phenomenon and so forth. But between them and the *muqaddam* there is an alignment of interests and alli-

152

ADMINISTRATING BY CONSENSUS (*EINVERSTÄNDNIS*)

ances. The *muqaddam* acts as guarantor for the caretaker with the population and in so doing enables the market and transaction to take place. In return, the caretaker of a building provides information (even if he may not say everything) and reports to the *muqaddam* on his profession—the latter thus objectively appears to be his superior even if he is not formally or legally. By contrast, the relationship between the *muqaddam* and the grocer or the café owner is of an entirely different nature; here there is no exchange of services but a situation of compromise. In this situation, the collaboration "only" allows them to buy peace and quiet. But this encounter with other interests may be much broader. This is the case for example with all those who provide information and arguments to the *muqaddam* (to obtain advantages, benefits or shortcuts but also because they think it is their duty to contribute to a public order that also serves their own interests) and thus to define what constitutes public order through the social order.

In all these situations, the *muqaddam* appears to be an actor among many others.[34] However, by creeping into the cracks in the normative systems of power, by strategically using social rules and their ambiguities, adjusting his position in response to power relations on the field, he is playing an essential role, not in imposing a vision but in overcoming conflict. His mediation does not erase oppositions or divergent points of view, or tensions, but it does allow cohabitation. It is in this respect that the *muqaddam* is an important element in the definition of order. He incarnates the leeway of local society and subaltern actors in the exercise of power and domination. The same is true of the *naib*, the representative of populations belonging to an ethnic community.

The naib, *a risky wager on the power of representation*

One incident in particular illustrates the fundamental role of the *naib* today. It took place in March 2006 in the suburbs of Beni Mellal, on the site of the future extension of the Sultan Moulay Slimane University. A key site for the province, the region and the town (which had a vocation to become a metropolitan area), this was a former waypoint on the sultan's route between Fez and

WEAVING POLITICAL TIME IN MOROCCO

Marrakech. At the junction between the Middle and High Atlas, around 15 kilometres from the biggest hydraulic plant in the country, upriver from the Bin El Ouidane dam, it dominated the Tadla plain. In the last years of the Protectorate, this plain had seen the emergence of a miracle, the first modern irrigation perimeter, perfectly laid out to form an A, on land belonging to the Beni Moussa and Beni Amir tribes. A discussion was launched on the subject of land collectively belonging to the tribe of one of the retired police commissioners. This person had recently been appointed *naib*, the delegate of his lineage responsible for negotiating the price of the land on which the university extension was to be built. As the procedure for expropriation in the public interest was not required, in this case it was up to the governor of the province to negotiate on behalf of the university but also for the tribes. The governor is both a provincial tutor for the tribes who own the land but also responsible for provincial development, i.e. responsible for the completion of the project under the auspices of the Minister for Higher Education. He often "sells off" the interests of these vaguely defined ethnic groups in the name of the "general interest". The *naib* is there to redress this, by attempting to obtain a price in keeping with market prices.

This is not a one-off example. In 2018, the Directorate of Rural Affairs within the Ministry of the Interior documented around 500 ethnic groups theoretically represented by several thousand *nouab* (the plural of *naib*). These groups are supposed to be the collective owners of property and to have an account open at the Directorate of Rural Affairs dedicated to recording income resulting from rent, sales or the exploitation of marble, sand, gypsum or rhassoul quarries[35] on these properties. This collective land ownership covered extremely large areas—nearly 15 million hectares, or some 40% of all useful land in Morocco, according to recent evaluations—and some 2.5 million beneficiaries. For the most part it is taken up with paths but also arable land (1.2 to 1.5 million hectares), forests and zones for the defence and restoration of the soil (nearly 100,000 hectares), as well as quarries and fields on the outskirts of imperial cities. Before 1912 these lands were occupied by the Guich tribes.[36] This was not land granted to them by the sultan but was in fact

ADMINISTRATING BY CONSENSUS (*EINVERSTÄNDNIS*)

exempt from the appropriation of the commons by vivification[37] to grant the tribes the right to use the land. Following independence, these lands of the Guich tribes were incorporated into collective lands.

Governing through collective lands

The amount of land involved here is astronomical. This demonstrates the extent of the issues at stake and the importance of the powers associated with ownership of such assets. It also explains why the authorities of the Protectorate went against Muslim law[38] and innovated by producing a "rationalisation of archaisms" through a text able to respond both to the needs of colonisation and those of civil peace, when faced with tribes that had a reputation for being turbulent. All of this occurred at a time when real estate was not yet under pressure, for demographic and economic reasons.

There are many actors in this long history, running from 1919 to today. There is the *naib*, the ethnic group, the beneficiaries, the tutelary council, the land registry and preservation, the major economic players—whether public like the OCP,[39] the Moroccan freeways, the ONCF, the CDG, El Omrane or private operators of major irrigation perimeters in the Sous or Gharb, benefiting from long-term holdings at minimal prices. They reveal the interconnection between government logics in a centralised Nation-state and, for once, the imperial frame of reference limited to the simple lexical borrowings from former times (tribe, *naib*, Guich) and a few traces of low-cost government by intermediaries and delegation.

The legal status of collective land has all the characteristics of an exotic legacy from the early days of Islam, of the Morocco of brotherhoods and tribes depicted in pre-colonial literature by travellers and adventurers. And yet it is an invention of the French Protectorate. The *dahir* of 1919 that drew up its boundaries still essentially applies today, although it has been modified dozens of times and even saw the promulgation of a new law in August 2019. These modifications have not altered its substance, however:[40] it still considers ethnic groups as entities that have no legal capacity, and yet which own around 40% of the property in the kingdom today,[41] under the fatherly gaze of the Ministry for the Interior, which presides over the tutelary council that manages these assets. The discussions and deliberations of this council are kept secret, as are its decisions, against which there is no possible appeal and no need for justification[42]—which is totally illegal in view of the most recent constitution.

The shift from a de facto collective status to a de jure status enshrined in the *dahir* of 1919 is a scientific curiosity in itself. The legal reasoning behind this is characterised by ambiguous language, shrouded in polysemous concepts whose materiality evokes other equally volatile realities—"collective lands", "indigenous groups", "beneficiaries", "uses" and "practices". Originally, this *dahir* aimed to emphasise conservative measures and hamper the dynamic of land colonisation, with the tribes representing a genuinely central military issue in the context of armed resistance. In the 1940s, it was used to accompany the dynamic of colonisation and large capitalist farms. Later, the first governments of independent Morocco used it to support the vision of the development of a socialising welfare state (Operation Labour in the 1960s).[43] Part of these collective lands was subsequently transferred into "colonisation lands" or "reclaimed land", driving the emergence of notable entrepreneurs operating according to liberal ideology. This eclectic pragmatism has never been driven by a coherent vision but is guided either by an understanding of the general interest prioritising public order or sometimes by an upheaval in traditional structures in the name of modernisation (such as the code for agricultural investment in 1969).[44]

In 1919 the legislation established a draconian and archaic legal framework that moved public authority—incarnated by the Protectorate and its Director of Political Affairs and then by the Ministry for the Interior after independence—away from the controls and regulations of binding positive law. The rules governing the functioning of ethnic groups including the organisation of the transmission and sharing of usage rights are defined by the customs and traditional uses of each of these groups. Although these "customs" have a specific legal definition and are described and operate as a source of law, the notion of "uses" is vague and opens up a whole range of possibilities and interpretations. The invisible hand

ADMINISTRATING BY CONSENSUS (*EINVERSTÄNDNIS*)

here is the "spirit of Lyautey", which we described in the Prolego-menon as the "rationalisation of archaisms", and which meant that until 2019 women were still excluded from the status of benefi-ciary despite the rules of Muslim law and the 2011 constitution.[45] It was only in 2019 that the new law on collective lands was passed, in response to unprecedented pressure from women.

The *naib*, downward mobility?

The *naib* is the metaphorical spanner liable to disrupt the smooth workings of this machine for governing via collective lands. His initial role as a decoy has evolved, as have the issues associated with the group. The value of property has shot up and the sociological profile of the *naib* himself, along with the populations he is sup-posed to represent, has been radically altered. This fieldwork took us to Tanger (to the town of Berich), to Khouribga and Tadla, Errachidia, to the Chorfa Mdaghra, the tribe of Ait Zdeg and to the Arabs Oulad Sebbah, in the outskirts of Casablanca to the Oulad Hriz and to the Gharb on the site of the large Sidi Taybi slums around Kenitra, among the cattle farmers of Beni Guil and Oulad Sidi Ali Bouchnafa and in the Eastern plains. In all these places, the key figure, the one who in theory connects and disconnects the ethnic group and gives it consistency by constituting a list of its members, was the *naib*. The governor, as all-powerful as he was, needed his approval to launch projects on collective land.

The *naib* has no equivalent among the plethora of traditional statuses. The concept of a person who is supposed to represent the collective group is not familiar in the local lexicon. The literal translation of *naib* is "representative," or "mandated". His role, even more than his status, is founded on the 1919 *dahir*. It was invented by the Protectorate and had few links to the history of the tribes. As long as it was assured by notables who dominated over the group, it retained its prestige, but once the traditional notable system became fragile in the 1990s, its prestige waned. This was initially because of the new abilities the *naib* had to have to repre-sent the group. Later, it was a consequence of the fact that the knowledge and expertise of the position became outdated, and the public servants representing authority became omnipresent. The arrival of topographers and engineers downgraded it still further.

WEAVING POLITICAL TIME IN MOROCCO

The increased weight of elections and the beginnings of a certain deconcentration meant that the *naib*'s presence in meetings with the governor was progressively more discreet. Even though he continued to represent ethnic groups, due to the importance of the 1919 *dahir*, he no longer has the monopoly he once did. His weakened position within the tribes is in stark contrast to his continued connection to the Ministry of the Interior and the formal and nevertheless real power he still has today, particularly the power conferred by the permit he must grant for all important administrative acts relating to collective lands. This proximity with his tutelary ministry predisposes him to intervene on the side of the authorities or for his own interests. Moreover, tensions in the property market mean he is exposed to pressure from the population every time there is a question of property transfers (inheritance, transfer by sale or donation) or the redefinition of cultural areas. In the collective lands close to towns, these issues are beyond his control, and the knowledge he is supposed to have is of no use in valuing heritage sites—except for his role as genealogist, which is increasingly controversial although necessary. His downgrading is accentuated still further by the emergence of other statuses that are more in keeping with contemporary demands. For example, communal councillors, community association activists or auxiliaries of authority have much more power than he does, except for in transactions on collective land.

The controversial return of the *naib*

The subaltern position of the *naib* is merely superficial, however, although his sociological downgrading is undeniable. This explains why notables have abandoned this role, which is costly in terms of transport and expenses, in a context where returns on investment are appropriated by other actors because of the presence of the administrative network and particularly the *caid*, and in which the governor can decide which direction to take the collective in and where beneficiaries have become increasingly demanding. But this downgrading is in tension with the legal status of the *naib* who remains the only figure able to undertake action on behalf of an ethnic community. Yet this legal dimension is increasingly impor-

ADMINISTRATING BY CONSENSUS (*EINVERSTÄNDNIS*)

tant whenever the state prioritises the respect of rules according to the principles of the rule of law.

The ever-increasing pressure on the property market reinforces the strategic position of the *naib*. They are essential auxiliaries of the governors and the *caids*. Their knowledge of local cultural areas, geography and toponymy of collective lands is essential and makes them influential informers, particularly in this context of social movements and demands. The *naib* has an undeniable power in reconstituting the memories of the group and the recognition of its rights and in establishing the list of beneficiaries of cultivation or the distribution of dues from land ceded to property developers or the OCP. In peri-urban areas where group identity is diluted in a population with mixed and uncertain origins, the explosion in property prices may link a family's fate with the *naib*'s interpretation of customary law. If he decrees, for example that this right should be extended to all post-pubescent family members, male and female, then the portion for each family will be increased relative to the number of family members. In major property projects, it is thus still the *naib* who influences the lists of beneficiaries of the transfers and the beneficiaries of "equalisation".[46] In the latter case, he is in direct competition with elected communal representatives and the *muqaddam*.

The year 2011 also marked a turning point in the area of collective lands. Figures of authority no longer had such easy access to this resource, the use of which was increasingly politicised by political parties particularly during electoral periods and by associations who made it a key point in the construction of counter powers. In this context, the *naib* once more became a central figure. However, he was now more a representative of beneficiaries then he was an auxiliary of local authorities, due to the opening of the field of possible demands. Accelerated economic and political changes brought about by major projects (the new towns of Tamsna near Rabat, Tamansourt near Marrakech, and Zenata in the suburbs around Casablanca, as well as the Tanger Med port and its various extensions, the solar power station Noor and so forth), the spectacular development of social networks amplifying the resonance of associative activities and whistle-blowers threw the *naib* into the

159

spotlight. This was accentuated by the fact that the pace of social change also increased. Group cohesion had been undermined by rural exodus and the subsequent mixing of populations—aspirations became more individual and led to private appropriations of collective assets, which led to increased conflict. The value of rural and peri-urban property and the increase in its different uses intensified competition between public and private operators.

The *naib* may seem more powerless than before, in comparison with the omnipotence of these authority officials and the extent of the financial stakes. But the changes in his sociological profile—he is more and more well educated and politicised—and the support that is given by the beneficiaries who are now organised into associations (which are not covered by the 1919 text), make it more difficult to outmanoeuvre him. Even though the beneficiaries cannot be directly involved legally they can support him as citizens invested in the public good and the use of heritage, which is now considered more a national resource than a tribal one. These beneficiaries may also mobilise public attention or file a civil case, strengthened by the prerogatives the constitution grants them. Thus, one of the most active associations in this area, the association Akal[47] (which means "land" in Amazigh), brought together several thousand people in Casablanca on 25 November 2018 to protest against the ongoing reforms particularly against the privatisation of collective land. Beneficiaries may also challenge the selection of a *naib* by the authorities. The Minister of the Interior, who faced questions in parliament on this subject, began by minimising the extent of the phenomenon, claiming that between 2010 and 2014 only 165 *nouab* out of 7,800 had been dismissed, before conceding that there were 600 cases brought before the courts by groups of beneficiaries.[48]

All these "problems" led the administration to bureaucratise the role of the *naib* still further. The ministry created a website (www.terrescollectives.com) to deal with the avalanche of demands and information (whether true or false) that were being spread by hundreds of websites focusing on the question[49] and to provide guides for the appropriate procedures. All of these measures did not prevent judicialisation developing at the behest of

ADMINISTRATING BY CONSENSUS (*EINVERSTÄNDNIS*)

the associations, because legal procedures do not avoid obscurity and do not deprive local authorities of their power to subjectively interpret concrete situations. Not a day goes by without websites or newspapers referring to *nouab* caught red-handed in the illegal sale of collective land.[50]

This analysis has been recently confirmed by the new law revoking the 1919 *dahir*. A speech made by the King had recently called for the creation of a new land strategy and the need to enable the development of a new rural middle class by transferring one million hectares to former beneficiaries but above all to the private sector in the form of urban or even international investors. Thus, the Ministry of the Interior embarked upon what it presented as the great reform to the hundred-year-old *dahir*. Although it confirmed its role as the dominant tutelary body, law 62–17 of 9 August 2019, changed nothing in the traditional lexicon; it maintained the ethnic group as the landowner and the *naib* as its representative. But the power of the latter was diluted in an assembly that was entirely controlled by the governor. Henceforth, the *naib* had much less margin for action. When he found himself in the minority, he could no longer oppose the decisions made by the assembly of *nouab*, and he risked prison time if he took the head of a group of rebellious beneficiaries. However, nothing prevented him from becoming their hero if such an association were to be formed independently with the help of social networks.

Administration by consensus (Einverständnis)

Beyond these two exotic figures, the *muqaddam* and the *naib*, there are other very modern and globalised figures who fill similar roles in many structures characteristic of the neoliberal era, particularly those operating according to externalisation. For example, police and security roles in international organisations or embassies but also university departments, hospitals, grand hotels, congress centres or airports are all filled by subaltern figures with no particular status, who work as subcontractors in these regalian positions. What political signification do they have, particularly in understanding the formation of public order and the spread of domina-

WEAVING POLITICAL TIME IN MOROCCO

tion? Based on taxation, Prasenjit Duara has subtly shown how the Chinese state was constructed by a simultaneous expansion of formal structures and informal procedures, particularly through local intermediaries and thus a certain form of indirect government.[51] These are all things that we have seen with our two Moroccan figures and their neoliberal avatars. However, in the desire to avoid the dangerous ground around the distinction between formal and informal and the debate on disorder, disintegration and anarchy, it is more fruitful to turn to the concepts of "consensus" (*Einverständnis*) and consensual action (*Einverständnishandeln*).[52] Weber defined this concept like this:

> By "consensus" (*Einverständnis*) we shall understand: that an action oriented according to expectations concerning the behaviour of other persons has an empirically "valid" chance of seeing those expectations realised, because there is an objective probability that these other persons will in practice treat those expectations as being, in terms of meaning, "valid" for their behaviour, even though no agreement to this effect exists. ... If, and to the extent that, the course of communal action is determined by the orientation in accordance with such chances of "consensus" (*Einverständnis*), it shall be called "consensual action" (*Einverständnishandeln*).[53]

This action through "consensus" therefore refers to an action that relies on implicit meaning, "as if" an order existed but without a specific agreement, because it does not rely on harmony and consent but involves the permanence of struggles and conflicts. Government by "consensus" therefore reflects multiple ways of governing based on a shared imaginary, implicit norms, that are drawn on a plurality of modes of action from the most interventionist and direct to the least constraining, from the most explicit to the most implicit, from the state affirmation to its effacement, from affinity and convergence of interests, to compromise in a context of struggle. The question of how actors themselves interpret the meaning of their action and how they anticipate its results are fundamental. The possibility or even the necessity of an interpretation suggests that there is no univocally meaningful relationship between actors who impose and actors who submit; it also

ADMINISTRATING BY CONSENSUS (*EINVERSTÄNDNIS*)

reflects the existence of conflicts, oppositions, the lack of harmony, in any case the diversity of positions, interests and logics of action.

We have mentioned the role played by interpretation in relation to the chain of informal delegations on which the work of these two figures of everyday administration is based. There are at least two kinds of interpretation here.

On the one hand there is the definition of danger, of that which breaks with public order or threatens peace and stability, which must be interpreted at the local level. This is the case for the *muqaddam*, with Salafism and the fight against radicalisation. Given the extent to which external markers of Islamisation have become commonplace (long beards, clothing and lifestyles) and that he follows "his" people from an early age, he does not act in the instant but seeks to detect unprecedented activities or events within a life cycle—group meetings, types of prayers, particularly in relation to age (for example, dawn prayer is normal for an elderly person but not for a young person and therefore becomes an indicator of the "prevalence of a switch"), dress codes, social circles and so forth. All these appreciations are open to interpretation and intuition, unlike the control of sermons, which must respond to strict criteria set out by the Regional Council of Ulema. Evaluations of order and disorder are also the responsibility of the *naib* who is responsible for defining what is arable land and what is not in an area destined for pastoral farming.

On the other hand, the question of anticipation, or the "expectation of expectation" in Weberian terms, must be taken into account. The *muqaddam* must "decode" possible directives, appropriate them when he is on the ground and concretely and locally interpret general slogans that may be unclear. He must not only understand, apply and interpret but also anticipate what the *caid* (or the "power", the King) wants. This is also true for all the "courtiers" and intermediaries with whom he works, who in order to maintain good relations with the *muqaddam* and benefit from the advantages or promotions he can procure them, must anticipate and interpret what he wants and defines as important, such as *hania* and so forth. This is even more explicit in the case of the *naib*, because he is constantly in conflict with the actors with whom he interacts, whether that is the state when the interests of the group are threatened or the beneficiaries when the governor exerts pressure on him in the case of general interest operations.

As we can see in our fieldwork and in these two subaltern administrative figures, security and public order appear to be the results of a constellation of interests, logics and behaviour operating as "consensual action", in the sense that they converge because they conform to what is usual, because they share a habitus (or an imaginary), because they are constantly adjusting—not spontaneously and harmoniously but through conflict and asymmetrical relations—because they are part of the same universe of meaning. In other words, this encounter, this convergence, accounts for the everyday functioning of legitimacy and allows us to very concretely understand the multiple modalities of domination, if we understand that, as Weber writes "'domination' does not mean that a stronger force of nature somehow prevails but that the action ('command') of [certain] people is related in terms of its meaning to the action ('obedience') of [certain] other people, and vice versa, so that one *may*, on the average, count on the realisation of the expectations according to which the action of both sides is oriented."[54]

Thus, security and public order are not only the results of actions of the state, which exerts its power in more or less formalised and direct terms but also—in this vein of least-cost government inherited from the Sharifian empire and rationalised by the Protectorate—of the actions of those who govern and are governed, which converge because they share the same universe of meaning, the same orientation and because they conform to an order, whether that is effective and institutionalised or not.

PART THREE

THE NEOLIBERAL ART OF GOVERNING
AFFINITIES WITH IMPERIALISM

Studying contemporary Morocco means studying neoliberalism in a particular context. How can we reconcile the claim of a globalised, connected, modern Morocco with the constant reinvention of tradition that has been held up in recent decades as a veritable ideology? How can we take into account the coexistence of two different worldviews, without falling prey to either exoticism or the pitfalls of the instrumental, developmentalist and historicist analyses we have criticised above? In other words, how does the hegemonic and global nature of the neoliberal moment interact with repertoires of action that are inherited from a sometimes-distant past to permeate Moroccan society? These questions are of course not specific to Morocco. Neoliberalism is not immutable, established or unchanging, it is always dependent on context. In all contexts, questions to do with how it takes shape but also its essence are raised. To use Weber's metaphor about all ideologies, the precepts of neoliberalism "do not blossom like a flower"[1] but are necessarily filtered by practical, material and ideal interests[2] which must be explored for the case of Morocco, as in any other concrete situation.

However, one of the most striking things to note is that in Morocco, neoliberalism is not named as such and yet it has never-

165

WEAVING POLITICAL TIME IN MOROCCO

theless spread in various ways. Firstly, by "extraversion"[3] and osmosis with the international ideological context but also by very concrete external constraints (market norms, demands from Europe or the West more generally and particularly from lenders and financiers), by mimicry and a desire for Europe and globalisation, for international recognition and so forth. This leads to the hypothesis that, if the concept of neoliberalism has failed to take root in Morocco, perhaps this might be because the practices associated with it are understood and interpreted differently from the ethereal, discursive vision it aims to convey? This avenue for research brings us to consider the intermediaries of Moroccan neoliberalism and more particularly its "bearers"[4] and the processes that tend to shape it within social relations.

Moreover, the fact that the semantic fields—between English, Arabic and French (and not just Moroccan French but also international French, between francophone Moroccans and Arabist Moroccans)—do not perfectly overlap encourages us to explore the deeper meaning of neoliberalism in a specific historical and cultural situation. It provides the opportunity to explore the specific meanings of global practices and to reflect on what makes society, in the social configurations specific to contemporary Morocco, including the imaginary, habits of thought and/or shared understandings. One of the hypotheses we explore here is that the "hold" of neoliberalism has been made possible by the elective affinity between these practices and certain characteristics of Empire that permeate all layers of Moroccan society, through the ways of conceiving and understanding power but also the ways it is exerted and legitimated. Indeed, neoliberal practices are understood and interpreted through the prism of history and the shared imaginary in which imperial elements valorise the use of intermediaries, rituals, rules and norms established beyond the law and do not consider nomadism, itinerancy or the intermittence of the state as a threat.

Unlike in other contexts, for example in Tunisia or in France where we have also worked, the government configurations specific to neoliberalism in Morocco are not considered as breaking away from government traditions, understandings of public action

PART THREE: THE NEOLIBERAL ART OF GOVERNING

or the general interest, or indeed the imaginary of the state. On the contrary, the neoliberal artforms but also more diffuse mechanisms or even practices, are experienced as being familiar, commonplace or banal. This is true of delegation, the multiplication of sites of power, the multiplicity of mediations through which domination operates, or government by advisory bodies or a conception of low-cost government. All these techniques, all these processes, which appear to be symbols of a new era, are successfully integrated into Moroccan state imaginary, to the point where they are not identified with any particular political belief but rather as new reinventions of tradition. This process of naturalisation can be glimpsed in the interviews with the senior state actors and also in the observation of everyday practices. They are simply self-evident and never questioned.

The idea that there might be an "elective affinity" between neoliberalism and imperial government should not be misinterpreted, however. This affinity cannot be seen as the reactivation of older practices or the expression of the permanence and role played by the concept of the *Makhzen*.[5] Rather, affinity must be understood here as the existing "relationship of compatibility" between specific forms of government stemming from the intellectual hegemony and global politics known as neoliberalism and from the shared ways of understanding power in a historically situated context. In Morocco, this compatibility has given rise to the acceptance, support, reinforcement and acceleration of neoliberalism, rather than to the rejection, mistrust or suspicion of this ideology. This compatibility meant that these modalities of action seemed familiar, natural and self-evident, when they were in fact new and to a certain extent in tension with previous practices (particularly the interventionism and developmentalism of the 1960s and 1970s). The affinity between imperial government and neoliberalism is in no case synonymous with the uniform acceptance of neoliberal reforms. The use of certain intermediaries required for the ideal of the "frugal government"[6]—which favours the valorisation of the market, of the private sector, businesses and civil society—by no means threatens power. It seems self-evident that community associations, businesses, institutionalised professionals or sector-wide structures,

167

WEAVING POLITICAL TIME IN MOROCCO

communities, groups or even individuals who may or may not represent a group, operate as essential links in the chain of government. And what are generally considered deep transformations or breakdowns in forms of government are not perceived as such. Similarly, the interconnection between contradictory logics overseeing the state's actions is not considered problematic in Morocco. The naturalness of this stems precisely from the historicity of these practices of "government at a distance",[7] which involve mediation and intervention and a specific understanding of politics that emphasises the ability to adapt and be resilient. In other words, it comes from an impression that there is a certain continuity between imperial practices and contemporary practices. Of course, this is not the case; we have constantly reiterated the differences between experiences under the Sharifian empire or the Protectorate and today's experiences. However, the sense of "déjà vu" explains the extent of the naturalisation process.

5

INDIRECT GOVERNMENT

Indirect forms of government are often presented as being a specificity of neoliberalism. Foucault, for example, talks about "government at a distance" to characterise this very specific moment in which the state is subject to a critical gaze that leads to radical change in forms of domination and subjectivation.[1] However, these ways of governing are entirely banal from a historical perspective,[2] as we have seen for the Moroccan case since the beginning of this book. Indirect government is a characteristic of the pre-colonial Sharifian empire, of which the Protectorate broadly continued certain modalities. Moreover, in contemporary Morocco, the imperial reference has enabled government through absence and intermittence, even in moments of nation-building, and has lent its strength to symbolic power and to the different forms of redistribution specific to indirect government.

Of course, indirect forms of government do not reflect the full extent of the neoliberal art of governing. The state continues to intervene directly through investments, norms and procedures. Morocco is no exception to this, spreading New Public Management within all institutions,[3] investing massively in free trade zones or industrial zones,[4] adopting a strategy of risk management that is structured around norms of prevention or precaution,[5] or enforcing a certain type of planning.[6] However, indirect govern-

169

ment remains particularly salient. Identifying its specific dynamics sheds light on a range of logics of action, behaviour and ways of understanding the art of governing and being governed. Among them, there are four that appear particularly representative of the current modalities of government. They are by no means specific to Morocco in principle and can be found to various degrees in any society. They simply take on the colours of the political imaginary that has been historically constructed in the Moroccan context.

Formal delegations

Delegation may contribute to public policy in the traditional sense. It is based on a desire to reduce direct intervention in the economy through privatisation programmes and the introduction of contract-based approaches such as public-private partnerships. Although this is not specific to the current era, neoliberalism shapes delegations in ways that are ever more formalised, establishing new rules and procedures that are adapted to new "markets." These are the result of a rationalisation strategy and are institutionalised, bureaucratised, technocratised and follow the "government by contract" model that is typical of the neoliberal state.[7] Neoliberalism confers another meaning to the different forms of delegation in affirming the superiority of the market and the delegate over the state and the delegatee and by transforming the user into a client.

The historicity of formal delegation

The Moroccan authority's acceptance and generalisation of public service concessions demonstrates the ease with which a framework that is often considered a loss of sovereignty was adopted in the country. As a result, Morocco has had more experience with the concessionary regime than with direct public management.[8] Delegation was a normal mode of government under the Sharifian empire and although it was often implicit, tacit or non-formalised, it could also be explicit and institutionalised. The concessionary regime was dominant, particularly in sectors relating to tax and foreign trade. The work of Daniel Schroeter draws us into the

INDIRECT GOVERNMENT

detail of how the leases were formalised for the port of Essaouira. With only a touch of anachronism, we can consider that eighteenth-century Essaouira was like the TMSA today—a special territory. The state invested there by creating and funding warehouses and providing advance payments to merchants. In certain ports, such as Essaouira (Mogador) but also Agadir, trade was in the hands of "the king's merchants", both Jews and Muslims, according to written agreements for amounts that were set by contract in advance and periodically renegotiated.[9] Tax on foreign trade was entrusted by concession contract to local notables or others originally from major cities in the empire.[10] All these procedures were subject to negotiations, proposals and auctions, as the correspondence between the concession companies and the *Makhzen* demonstrates. Although the imperial government was reticent to award concessions to foreigners, as can be seen in the history of mining or customs concessions, delegation to Moroccan actors was often normal and even the most obvious modality for the government.

From the mid-nineteenth century, delegations progressively shifted to being exclusively for the benefit of European actors. They took on new forms, which were just as formalised and institutionalised but now had a different meaning. The first and the most violent was the capitulary regime, specifically the fact that certain subjects were excluded from state sovereignty and their protection delegated to European powers.[11] Delegation was later extended to equipment, major public works and production (at the time essentially mining). But during the Sharifian imperial era, delegations (including those conducted under pressure from overseas) did not follow the ideology of public service but rather that of government at least cost. Delegations extorted by Europeans followed the ideology of capitalism in order to facilitate access to economic resources or simply financial logic in order to control sites where tax is levied and to have Moroccan debt reimbursed as directly as possible. In this era, public service was not an aspect of state thought. It was incorporated by communities based on the concept of the *maslaha* (general interest). The *waqf*, tribe or corporations were the only actors involved in public service, which was then understood as community service.[12] Conceptualised in this

171

WEAVING POLITICAL TIME IN MOROCCO

way, public service was born as a form of concession during colonisation. During the Sharifian empire there was no mention of "public service" and still less "public service concessions".

Under the Protectorate, delegation expanded to what would today be called public services, such as infrastructure, equipment, access to water and electricity.[13] During that period, the dominant approach was based on liberal ideology, directly influenced by Saint-Simonianism. According to this view, the state must not directly intervene in these services but rather delegate management of them to "forces of progress" in the form of colonial, industrial and agricultural interests.[14]

Ideologically speaking, independence was the critical moment when delegation and concession were abandoned and direct state intervention in public services and economic development in general were promoted. In practice, however, it is not clear that this intervention was particularly substantial, and there were many breaches. This was particularly the case for urban and inter-urban transport. Although at independence, most public services were grouped together under the form of state-owned companies, offices or public bodies, transport was initially organised around private companies for buses[15] and taxi licences.

Nor was the rural world exempt from such breaches. In 1967, for example, as structuration into offices and other public organisms was in full swing, the Ministry for Agriculture created Aeropesam, the association for breeders of purebred selected sheep in Morocco,[16] according to a cooperative model following the logic of delegation and concession to private actors. The state granted the association technical staff and funding, and in return, it subcontracted activities for breeder members, such as controlling reproduction, selection and sales. The association itself delegated certain tasks to veterinarians who worked for it. It ensured redistribution to co-opted individuals and particularly to the most important breeders. This system is still in place. The only thing that has changed is that these are no longer called concessions but public-private partnerships, which means delegation can be depoliticised. Subcontractors are no longer "co-opted," but are seen as partners in a "win-win" process.

INDIRECT GOVERNMENT

The rediscovery of public-private partnerships: emphasising the state's solicitude through distinction

With neoliberalism, this tendency toward delegation spread to new areas. It was not the practices that changed but rather the underlying ideology. Neoliberalism makes use of private actors (including associations, corporate groups and market actors), but above all, it legitimises these actors in other ways; the ideology of public service was no longer associated with that of progress, as it had been during colonisation for the benefit of foreign economic interests alone. Nor was it based on communities and orders as it was under the Sharifian empire according to the principle of government at a distance. The logic of the best public service—in the sense of the most efficient, effective and profitable—now reflects the supposed superiority of the private sector in management (including of public goods) and the extension of private sector techniques. The philosophical foundation for these practices is therefore new, as is the language used to describe it. However, these practices are not experienced as radical shifts and even less so because they are produced by the same actors or their successors. This impression of familiarity or "déjà vu" does not prevent there being conflicts or resistance, as we can see in the tensions within the administration and even parliament, or between competing economic actors and their repercussions in social movements, both before and after the February 20 Movement.[17] The fact is that this form of government appears desirable to some and problematic to others, but it is familiar to all. Moreover, it appears controllable because it echoes two of the traditional foundations of government in Morocco: the intervention of appointed intermediaries, now justified by internationally recognised skill and expertise; and the use of human and technical resources from overseas as a factor in internal legitimacy, which Jean-François Bayart called "extraversion strategies."[18]

Formalised through conventions, with clauses and written specifications, the management of public services is generally conceded to major international companies such as Suez (formerly Lyonnaise des Eaux) or Veolia (formerly Compagnie Générale des Eaux) for water and sanitation and Pizzorno, Tecmed, Suez or Derichebourg for waste management, or Veolia again or the RATP for trans-

WEAVING POLITICAL TIME IN MOROCCO

port.[19] These foreign actors are supposed to provide expertise and technical skills, investment capacity, rapid reactions, monitoring and professionalism and improved services through close attention to clients. But this logic of rationalisation and profitability does not prevent the incursion of politics into these practices of delegation, nor political influence on contracts and partnerships.[20]

Public-private partnerships can also be established between state entities and foundations, some of which are subsidiaries of industrial groups or banks.[21] Even though they have the pompous and prestigious title of 'foundation', they do not have that legal status because Moroccan law only recognises associations governed by the *dahir* of 1958, which is considered very liberal in terms of public freedoms. There are few genuine foundations, and they fall under a specific regime. The most prestigious of them were created by a *dahir* establishing law or by a decree-law in the wake of royal solicitude. Most of these foundations, regardless of what sphere they operate in, are named after a King—Mohammed V, Hassan II or for the more recent, Mohammed VI. Their activities are no different from the social organisations that emerged after independence, following an agreement between the state and the only union that existed at the time, the UMT, so that unionists who were considered guarantors of social harmony could receive annuities. The primary tools of this alliance were the public enterprise councils (*Conseil des œuvres sociales* or COS). For example, the ONE council was funded by a levy per kWh sold and over time has become extremely wealthy. The electricians' COS (as well as the social security organism in the private sector, CNSS) benefited from the real estate boom in the 1980s and has become the main real estate developer in Casablanca and the main tourism promoter in the country. The CEO, Mohammed Abderrazak was one of the most powerful figures in the country, occasionally even more powerful than the omnipotent secretary general of the union Mahjoub Benseddik.[22]

Foundations created by law are the expression of the King's concern for a particular social category. Each foundation was associated with a shift in political life and reveals royal attention and solicitude to a particular group. For example, in the 1980s, author-

174

INDIRECT GOVERNMENT

ity agents attracted this attention when the question of security and territorial management by loyal, devoted state representatives was particularly salient. The Ministry for the Interior was then granted the status of the "mother of ministries", and Driss Basri was given the position of Viceroy, combining the portfolios of the interior, communication and information, urbanism and territorial planning.[23] In the 1990s, it was Moroccans living overseas who benefited from this solicitude, which says much about the importance of remittances paid in foreign currency to Moroccan banks and the materialisation of the perpetual allegiance between the King and the expanding overseas community.[24] Then, in the 2000s, the Foundation Mohammed VI for Social Actions on Education, which symbolises the reformist movements of the new reign, inaugurated the reconciliation with the teaching body after the crisis of the late 1970s.[25] Finally in the 2010s, the reorganisation of religion showed the importance of low-level clerics (imams in mosques, *khatib*, Qur'an readers) in promoting state Islam, and the Foundation Mohammed VI for the Promotion of Social Actions of Religious Agents was created to materialise the link between the Commander of the Faithful and religious leaders.[26] These foundations were born out of two government logics—the imperial logic of an ordered society that operates according to the granting of distinctions; and the nation-state logic that delegates part of the state's prerogatives in the management of communities and the social sphere, which allows it to mobilise and manage substantial financial resources while also breaking away from the constraints imposed by the laws of finance.

All these forms of indirect government rely on interfaces that are structured and sometimes very formalised, responsible for implementing one of these aspects of government, involving either citizen-users (now clients) or particular bodies selected by the highest authority in the land, citizens distinguished for their loyal service. Governing and administrating change according to different contexts, just as the prerogatives and rules of the state and its extensions change according to the goals pursued, the results expected, the benefits obtained and populations targeted. By extension, these forms of government convey a conception of pub-

WEAVING POLITICAL TIME IN MOROCCO

lic order, of good and bad government and of the general interest. Formalised delegation appears to be a particularly well adapted and effective mode of government. It allows the division, diversification and pluralisation of points of intervention, and it increases possibilities and dilutes responsibilities. And when the explicit delegation is personalised, it perpetuates a kind of orderly society that values certain figures and segments of society according to various priorities.

Implicit delegation

The delegation process may also be implicit and stem from the appropriation of concepts promoted by those in power or policies implemented by it. In this case, there are no formal contracts but rather a tacit agreement between parties and roles that are genuinely shared. This agreement does not prevent power relations, tensions and sometimes conflict, but it is nevertheless the result of shared desires.

Action without the means for action: betting on the ingenuity of the disadvantaged

The programmes updating basic equipment in rural areas, launched by the state in the 1990s, reveal several aspects of these public policies based on various forms of delegation enabling the government to act at least cost.

Officially inaugurated in 1995, the programme to bring electricity to rural areas (*Programme d'électrification rurale globale* (PERG)) was, along with large-scale hydraulic power, one of the most ambitious territorial planning actions undertaken by the nation-state since independence, and its modus operandi has often been praised.[27] The plurality of technical and institutional norms and the importance of informality with formalisation after the event was characteristic, as was its implementation of cascading delegations. The delegation first concerned the work to be carried out itself. The operator laid out a register of eligibility for the companies that wished to submit tenders for work on different sites. Given that the criteria for eligibility required substantial financial backing and

INDIRECT GOVERNMENT

high levels of technical ability, only major companies could compete for the market. However, they delegated this to local tradesmen, who were often notables themselves and who then subcontracted to pieceworkers, who were also clients to be recruited for elections.[28] The delegation also concerned users, who had to be organised into associations to be able to call on collateral surety and above all recuperate the *douar*'s contribution to the provision of electricity. This whole framework was to the benefit of local notables, but it also marginalised them as elected officials. It also means that some of the poorest rural households had to shoulder some of the funding burden, running the risk of over-indebtedness.

Also launched in 1995, was the rural water supply programme (*Programme d'approvisionnement groupé en eau potable des populations rurales*, PAGER), which aimed to bring water close to the *douar* in some 31,000 localities. This is based on a partnership, which is formalised but without a legal framework, between the Ministry for the Interior and the Ministry for Equipment, local authorities and users' associations—which did not exist when the programme was initially launched. During the first years it was implemented, technicians called on an army of experts "in participation" who, with the help of a "kit", created communities from scratch and organised them into "users' associations" capable of signing a convention with the programme.

These two programmes demonstrate a certain ingenuity. This can be seen in the increasing number of forms of delegation and in the choice of informality in adapting to the context. It also appears in the ability to create complicity between delegate actors and those delegating in order to increase the possibilities for effective participation, particularly by reinterpreting local usage and drawing on the mediation of notables who had been promoted to administrate users' associations. It can also be seen in the mobilisation of a familiar vocabulary (*jma'a, touiza, 'amazal*).[29] The polysemous nature of these terms makes it possible to satisfy actors with opposing interests—such as technicians, users, funding providers, elected representatives and authorities. Moreover, these programmes tend to minimise costs for the state, which can offload a whole series of prerogatives in service management in this way.

The vagaries of implicit delegation: the impact of power relations

Implicit delegation can take another equally banal form, in the encounter between the strategies and interests of state and non-state actors. This form of government may be extremely efficient, but it may also become weaker over time and in different contexts, depending on the transformations of interests and logics of actions or the intrusion of new protagonists that destabilise former arrangements. This is the case for maintaining social harmony, for example. For many years there was a tacit delegation of the state toward the UMT—the first and for a long time the only union both in administration and private enterprise—and toward the SNESUP—which is still largely responsible for education policy, hand in hand with the state.

In Morocco, unionism emerged from within the nationalist movement. The UMT was born with the resistance, channelling workers' action in their struggles for independence. In the period between 1955 and 1956, it was thought of as "managing the masses",[30] in an alliance with the monarchy. The offices, funding and staff were all provided by the state in the name of King Mohammed V, who thus rewarded the union's commitment to struggles for independence.[31] The UMT supported the social and economic transformations of the country in keeping with the then hegemonic ideas of voluntaristic modernisation and socialism. In 1960, Mahjoub Benseddik talked about a "common understanding", to describe the connection forged between the government and the union movement.[32] Although oppositions and power relations were expressed from these first years, there was a tacit "non-aggression pact" strategy between the UMT and central power. Unionism implicitly contributed to defining public and social order by overseeing workers.[33] In this sense, it also defined the strategy that was characteristic of its golden age—serve power while serving yourself.

As a result, the UMT very quickly turned away from social struggle and toward what Abdelatif Manouni called "integrative management"[34] associated with the political strategy of central

INDIRECT GOVERNMENT

authority taking control at the expense of nationalist parties. This was part of a tacit agreement that ensured privileged treatment and the continuation of its union activities.[35] Managers were invited to encourage animation and integration actions within mixed organisations. They contributed to the Moroccanisation of institutions and heritage handed down from colonial unionism incarnated and modelled by the French CGT union, particularly social projects and insurances that play a fundamental role in the foundation of the UMT. This union contributed to the debate around questions of "social security" and "collective conventions". For this, it had the advantage of work allocations, public servants on secondment, subsidies and recruitment positions. The union pluralism imposed by the Istiqlal, which created its own central branch, the UGTM, did little to change the situation. This was a genuine alliance; it was no accident that union policy coincided with state public policy, it was the result of a "compromise for the survival of the organisation"[36] which made "unionism an instrument of official policy" in a sort of general "ambiguity."[37]

With hindsight, it seems that, more than ambiguity, this was a question of implicit delegation. Within the tension and struggle, tacit and sometimes unexpected arrangements were found, effectively contributing to maintaining the social peace, or in any case, stability. This situation of "consensus" (*Einverständnis*) was not solely the result of a strategy that was decided by the palace or the government alone but was born of power relations between them and the union movement, between different sections within the UMT and between that union and the other union organisations that progressively emerged. It was also the result of relations between workers and the union and of course between workers and business leaders.

This implicit delegation of the management of social peace showed its limits, however, at the end of the 1970s and especially the 1980s, with the end of the UMT's monopoly and the increasing power of other central branches.[38] It was also affected by the loss of union influence over social organisation in Morocco, as was the case elsewhere around the world after the 1990s.

WEAVING POLITICAL TIME IN MOROCCO

Accommodating actors' strategies

Indirect government may also be driven by non-state actors who deliberately act to appropriate functions considered regalian or coming under the responsibility of the state, without the latter necessarily objecting, and perhaps even encouraging this. The two forms of delegation analysed above were the fruit of conscious and strategic choices by the state, even where they were in practice sometimes vague and/or improvised. The configurations we will look at now are not the result of the state's intentions, although it accepts the arrangements, sometimes very happily. Rather, they come from the encounter between the goals of public authorities—which are sometimes clearly identifiable, sometimes only intuitively so—and the strategies of economic, political or social actors pursuing their own interests. Social housing policies in urban areas are a paradigmatic example of this.

The dominance of informality, or state-negotiated agreements to local strategies

Social housing policy developed in the late 1970s during the period of administrative centralisation. Under colonisation, housing programmes for the local population were extremely limited even though certain experiments in this area had real resonance. With independence, the primary concern of the authorities was to develop the middle class, particularly via access to housing. This policy was conceptualised very formally, as a source of complementary income, particularly for public servants, with the idea that it was necessary to make up for the shortfalls in their retirement funds. It essentially focused on the distribution of building lots for construction and housing was knowingly abandoned in favour of owner-building. It was only in the late 1970s that increased urbanisation and demographic growth and the increasing number of public servants with low salaries, meant that the public authorities felt the need to develop another social housing policy. In keeping with a French-inspired approach to territorial planning, the state was alone at the helm, acting through regional public bodies (*Établissements régionaux d'aménagement et de construction* (ERAC)) but also the

180

INDIRECT GOVERNMENT

Tacharouk (an institution dedicated to absorbing slums in major cities such as Rabat, Salé and Casablanca), the ANHI (an agency fighting against insalubrious housing and repurposing houses constructed illegally) and the Sonadac SONADAC (*Société nationale d'aménagement communal*). But this system produced very few houses for low-income people. In the mid-1990s, only 100,000 houses had been constructed (all kinds combined). For the period between 1990 and 2000, industry specialists estimate there were around 55% owner-builders, 15% building by property developers and 15% constructions that did not meet regulations. The portion of social housing paid for by public institutions only constituted 15% over this period, even though the needs of this portion of the population were substantial.[39]

This initial historical sequence sheds light on the extent of informality and how much it was tolerated, with arrangements by the public authorities conducted almost openly and in any case accepted without constraint. "Spontaneous" housing that does not meet regulations and self-building on authorised plans can thus be seen as laissez-faire. But "informal" means little in this respect, and it is important to understand what lies hidden behind this often-convenient term.

Informal does not mean the absence of the state. There are many actors involved in this process—the president of the Municipal Council, the elites and local administrations, the governor, the pasha or the *caid*, the elected representatives, the central state through the question of social order, security and the arbitration between different local interests[40]—and they are not all private. Illegality is tolerated socially if it occurs within networks that are connected to each other.[41] The regularisation of informal neighbourhoods that do not meet regulations,[42] for example, supposes the convergence of very different logics and interests in which "public" and "private" are perpetually intertwined. These include demands by the public for recognition of their housing, a desire among notables and political elites to preserve their role as intermediaries and their local legitimacy, the interests of local authorities in maintaining a certain social harmony or at least public order and major landowners who want to make the most of their

181

WEAVING POLITICAL TIME IN MOROCCO

resources and so on.[43] It is not unusual for these actors to be in conflict with each other, which explains the delays and difficulties in regularisations but also the accelerations once a blockage or obstacle is overcome. It also explains the limitations of this mode of government.

Searching for the Moroccan Bouygues:[44] how to benefit from the dynamism of the private sector

At the end of his reign, Hassan II decided to focus on what would later be seen as his "reign-long project" (*chantier de règne*). In 1995, he launched the policy known as "200,000 dwellings" designed to address the historical deficit in social housing and create homes for "new arrivals". The goal was to double production capacity. This policy intensified under the *alternance* government and especially the technocratic governments of the early years of Mohammed VI's reign, particularly that of Driss Jettou. It took the surprising form of support for "national champions" in real estate, via detours that are interesting to explore because they reveal convergences in interest that generate public policies different from those of the laissez-faire approach analysed for the years 1970 to 1990.

It was the *alternance* government led by the socialists that announced, argued and rationalised the "problem with accessing housing for the most disadvantaged". They made the paradoxical decision that the public sector was not equipped to carry out this policy and decided to call on the private sector as part of a "win-win" policy, according to the current jargon. The financial solvency of the purchasers was supported by the state which guaranteed their bank loans. Above all, a partnership was implemented between the government and its arm for the management of property, El Omrane[45] on the one hand and on the other between the government and private operators who benefited from favourable conditions to access it. The crucial question was land. This was both a source of profit for private actors and also a source of power for those who, because of their public position, could redistribute these potential profits. Thus, accessing it required connivance between public and private. Although it has adopted a private logic of profitability, performance and efficiency, El Omrane is now the

182

INDIRECT GOVERNMENT

only public institution with access to collective land, the main source of property reserves, as part of a programme and contract with the state. Once the land has been acquired, El Omrane must equip it and make it available for private property developers via calls for interest. These developers then put forward propositions for social housing, and when a project is selected and accepted, the land is sold at cost price to the highest bidder. It is important to bear in mind that the total property value must not exceed 200,000 dirhams per dwelling. In compensation for this cap on prices, the developer benefits from authorisations to build up-market housing and shops on part of this land acquired at very low cost.

After 2006 in particular there was a sudden increase in the sale of public land to the private sector, consolidating traditional real estate actors and favouring the emergence of new ones, like Addoha (run by Anas Sefrioui) and Alliances (by Mohammed Alami Lazrak). To a certain extent there was a convergence of interests between social policy, state voluntarism and a reorganisation of capitalism associated with the emergence of new actors and characterised by non-transparent handovers of public contracts, a lack of systematic calls for tender, a clear preference for private arrangements and the development of partnership conventions between El Omrane and certain private actors without public calls for expression of interest and so forth. But these practices, which are commonly known as corruption, dispensations and favouritism, can only be understood in the context of the social policy that has become the priority, the "reign-long project". This is a social policy that is informally delegated to national private actors, based on the observation of their essential role and the power of the logics from "below".

These abuses, often decried as a symbol of corruption and archaic practices, are only meaningful when considered as part of the encounter between a strategy legitimating the state—involving the rapid and effective implementation of social policy through clear economic voluntarism and support for "national champions"—and the dominant ideology of the time, which highlights the efficiency of the private sector, budgetary restraint and the logic of public-private partnerships. The modalities of this indirect government

WEAVING POLITICAL TIME IN MOROCCO

have the supreme advantage of benefiting everyone or nearly everyone. In housing, and in the social sphere more generally, the state's adaptation to non-state logics appears to be the principal modality of public policy and also the main modality for the exercise of power. It creates a community of interest between these different actors and in so doing reflects the traits of our Empire ideal type: including government at least cost, the role of intermediaries, the creation of notabilities and "people of status." Today these figures are private businessmen lauded as "national champions."

Shared visions

The fourth configuration that we would like to analyse is that in which private actors find themselves doing things that are the state's responsibility, sometimes intentionally and sometimes without having planned or designed it. The state adapts to this situation, sometimes with ease (even later provoking it) sometimes with more difficulty, after struggles or disputes. These private actors then become auxiliaries of the state even though they present and promote themselves as distinct from public entities, maintaining a distance from or even an opposition to them. Yet this modality of indirect government may only come about if all actors, public and private, share the same understanding of life in society. Although this might be the case for other forms of indirect government, the implicit sharing of the same understanding of order, sometimes in situations of tension or even conflict, appears more clearly here because of the denial of proximity. We will try and explain this through two variants.

The first of these reveals actors who consider themselves private and independent and proclaim their autonomy but in fact find themselves doing things that are generally the responsibility of the state—even though they may do so in their own way and according to their own vision. This is the case for the major private enterprises that take charge of training for the populations of the territories in which they operate but also concessionary companies around the world. The second variant concerns actors who consider themselves critical or dissident, even opposed to the state,

INDIRECT GOVERNMENT

but who find themselves serving as its intermediary, whether they wish to or not. This is the case for development or activist associations whose expertise engages with propositions from government. These two variants are not merely neoliberal originalities. For example, up until the eighteenth century, racing was run by independent actors, but the sultans nevertheless profited and sometimes enabled or facilitated the activity, until it became counterproductive for the authorities and was prohibited, as was the case under Moulay Abderrahmane.[46] The same is true of the role of tribes in controlling borders.[47] It is also true for the contemporary period and all the intermediaries, official or not, that eventually act as agents of public order, contributing to the definition of social and sometimes even legal norms, becoming de facto auxiliaries of the police.[48]

Autonomy and delegation—the private definition of public interest

The most emblematic illustration of the first of these two configurations is the OCP, which has consistently stated its societal responsibility since 2008. This responsibility is no longer merely social but also global, part of a discourse based on the rationalisation of objective data linked to it holding three quarters of global phosphate reserves and its unexpected potential for inventiveness and the development of industrial tools its managers believe in.[49]

This optimistic narrative was tested in 2011, during the Arab Spring when demonstrators at Khouribga—the oldest phosphate mining site—set fire to education buildings and organised a sit-in on the railway tracks that transported cargos of phosphate, momentarily halting the activity. Damage to the company was minimal, but the trauma was deep nonetheless. The OCP felt "abandoned" by the local authorities, left "alone" to face demonstrators.[50] The directors of the company felt the need to adopt a more hard-line discourse on the company's social responsibility and follow a more ambitious project, described at the time by the CEO himself as "an environmental policy" and as the "company's societal responsibility". This project would take into account not only the question of pollution but also human issues.[51]

185

WEAVING POLITICAL TIME IN MOROCCO

In 2011, the OCP decided to recruit 5,800 workers "in advance,"[52] and established a training programme for 15,000 job-seekers living in its zone of operation. Under the name "OCP Skills",[53] this was a pioneer in employability programmes.[54] The goal was to train young job seekers, not to recruit them directly, but to "adapt" them to the demands of the local labour market and have them employed by subcontractors or other companies set up in Morocco. To run this programme in a style closer to that of an association, the OCP reorganised its management, hired new people from civil society and drew massively on social networks.[55] When it launched in September 2011, the point of access dealing specifically with requests from people under 35 recorded some 90,000 candidates.

The involvement of the OCP in social issues could be interpreted in two ways. Some see it as a fully thought-out policy of delegation, an intentional policy by the state or the *Makhzen* aiming to address social tensions, particularly since the February 20 Movement. For others it is proof of the weakening of the state; given the withdrawal or even the absence of public authorities, the OCP was obliged to fill the gap. These two interpretations share the same representation of an omnipresent *Makhzen*, an all-powerful monarch and a centralising state managing affairs directly. However, based on the numerous interviews we conducted, particularly between 2011 and 2013, we wanted to propose an alternative interpretation, which was suggested by the forceful denial of OCP leaders. In response to a question on the meaning of the "OCP Skills" programme, the latter constantly replied "no, no, this is not delegation"[56] and that "nobody asks anything of us."[57] Their very negative view of the state and its policy could be considered proof of this. For them, it is merely out of an ethic of responsibility that the OCP decided to address an issue that was previously the responsibility of public authorities, given that it was faced with the economic difficulties of the region, rising social tensions, the "malfunctioning of the state", or more specifically the "hesitations of different public entities" and their "inability to deal with these issues."

This conclusive discourse on the state and its components encourages us to think about cultural hegemony, political imagi-

INDIRECT GOVERNMENT

nary and power. It invites us to think about people with unusual trajectories, different ideologies or positions, who constantly seek to distinguish themselves from others and who nevertheless contribute to the possibility of governing by delegation. "OCP Skills" can be seen as a response to constraint, the reality of having to deal with miners' children but also with the rest of the local population. However, the choice that it implements illustrates the vision of the company's leadership, a vision that goes beyond the company and its immediate environment to include the idea of the general interest. This is an interest based on rationality and efficiency, adhering in every way to neoliberal doctrine. For the OCP, this is what differentiates it from public policies and gives it the legitimacy to define the general interest in a sort of inversion, which is ultimately quite typical in capitalism:[58] what is good for the company is good for Morocco. This aspiration to incarnate the general interest is associated with a general disdain for politicians—who are seen as self-interested, lacking competence, unable to manage the administration—as well as a denial of politics itself. It obscures the eminently political nature of any intervention in society. But it also operates as though the decision-making and operation of the company (and its foundation) were perfectly transparent, as though the "black box" period was over, and the shadow of the royal parasol did not cover top management. It operates as though the definition of the general interest were technical, neutral and uncontroversial if the actors are "in good faith".

Marginality and opposition used for the art of governing

To illustrate the second configuration, that of actors who consider themselves critical or dissident but find themselves serving as intermediaries for the state, we have chosen to use the example of the Targa association.[59]

Targa emerged in the continuation of the Moroccan sociologist Paul Pascon's activities with his team in the High Atlas Mountains. The association initially worked there on behalf of the IFAD and the UN FAO—including on actions to provide clean water supply, electricity networks and renewable energy, developing beekeeping and fish farming or building and running women's refuges.[60]

WEAVING POLITICAL TIME IN MOROCCO

The first partnership between Targa and a state institution took place through the intermediary of the Agency for the North, which at the time was managed by Driss Benhima. The agency was involved with the Geopolitical Observatory on Drugs (OGD) and wished to take back control of the observatory's report writing by obtaining credible scientific expertise, and Targa was already operating in the region on traditional projects such as the supply of drinking water and the establishment of watchdogs funded by international donors. Its teams did not consider cannabis a problem, even though it took up a significant portion of the territory. This position piqued the interest of the agency, and inversely, the possibility of accessing fieldwork that was otherwise closed to researchers pushed the association to accept the proposition. Between 2004 and 2007, Targa conducted several studies on the sociology[61] and economy of cannabis.[62] In spite of the team's reservations about converting this scientific research into an operational document for a state agency, the association eventually—in response to the insistence of the agency—provided a series of recommendations. These recommendations divided the territory into three zones: a "historical" zone where the state was advised to give up any attempt to eradicate cannabis and to content itself with educating and assisting populations and even buying production for medical or industrial (hemp textile) use; a second zone where the state was advised to negotiate with the population in order to substitute cannabis for an alternative and provide the necessary funding for progressive eradication; and finally, a third zone where it was advised to act immediately and with its full force in order to definitively eradicate cannabis production that had become quasi-industrial.

The success of this experience led Targa far from its initial concerns. This trajectory was facilitated by the adoption of a conceptual arsenal and a "kit for planning and operating" designed for the Larache province by the Ministry of the Interior that was then in full transformation since the arrival of a new team. The year 2008 brought another milestone, the signature of the triangular convention between the association, the Agency for the North and the Ministry of the Interior, for the conception and realisation of 250

INDIRECT GOVERNMENT

development plans for the whole northern region, in collaboration with the population and municipalities.

The case of Targa suggests that indirect government can also lead to the Moroccan political system gaining resources from the integration of dissidence[63] and the, sometimes implicit, predisposition of associative actors to think of development, social order and the general interest from the perspective of change for the common good. The state and associations ultimately "walk the road together", with the state benefiting from exploratory experiments conducted by associations, without accepting responsibility or risk, which are transferred to the new "partners". The associations adopt an "entryist" perspective and console themselves with the fact they have a certain influence, although limited, and attempt to change the major political orientations of the system, if only on the fringes. Thus, a critical and lucid perspective is no obstacle to participation in government.

* * *

The reference to the imperial register that is found in indirect government, a specific trait of the art of governing, sheds light on other traits as well. These include an investment in people that depends on the strategic value accorded to information, and frugality and minimisation of costs, which become all the more strategic when resources are rare and their allocation must be deferred. Yet in the name of pragmatism and efficiency, rapidity and rationalisation, one of the principles of neoliberalism is specifically this deferral of treatment, which illustrates the value of poles of excellence or the legitimacy of exceptions and derogations. Frugality and the minimisation of costs are therefore not symptoms of weakness, lack of initiative or a loss of sovereignty but the sign of another reorganisation around the state, based on a conception of sovereignty that does not rely on a purely material definition or on direct control. Under Empire, sovereignty is not a daily test of power, nor is it incarnated in a continuous presence. It is on the contrary, precisely the ability to "have things done" (*faire faire*),[64] or to master the consequences of what is "done by others".

This understanding of sovereignty and power is not dissimilar from the neoliberal moment of the nation-state, which involves the

189

redeployment of similar forms of government by regulation and the production of norms. Of course, the situation is different, and indirect government does not necessarily have the same content, the same signification or the same consequences. The fundamental difference is the degree of uncertainty. In the Sharifian empire, uncertainty was deep and widespread, a source of constant negotiation and arrangements. Today, this uncertainty has been reduced through a complex process of institutionalisation, formalisation and bureaucratisation.

The neoliberal moment, as we have seen, combines both direct and indirect government. In direct government, relations between actors must be legible, immediately decodable; discourses must have clear meaning and follow unambiguous rules. In indirect government, by contrast, clarity is relative—intrigues and concealment of the prince's desires are commonplace. This lack of clarity is part of the art of government, relations are high-risk, and actors always (try to) occupy a middle ground that increases the range of possibilities. The system allows itself the possibility to broaden the spectrum of actors who define the social order but also the public order. It also allows itself the possibility to act without necessarily having the means to do so or by making the choice to not grant the means to these causes. This dual reference explains how two apparently contradictory evolutions can coexist so easily. On one hand, neoliberal government at a distance is accepted in spite of the conflicts and struggles it provokes. It is not perceived as being the expression of a loss of sovereignty, nor as a challenge to social order; in fact, quite the contrary, because it merely reinforces the place and role of intermediaries and notabilities. On the other hand, it is striking to note the recurrence of discourses and feelings on the "weakness" and insufficient presence of the state and its loss of authority. This combination suggests that in spite of the widespread existence of indirect government, naturalised by the implicit salience of the imperial register, these techniques and frameworks play out in a context in which the Nation-state, including in its new neoliberal form, remains the explicit governmental reference.

6

THE BEARERS OF NEOLIBERALISM

As is the case with any ideology, neoliberalism relies on groups that defend it and whose practical, material, immaterial and ideal interests operate as filters, guiding the interpretations and significations of the processes underway. In order to create a typology of these groups in Morocco that is as exhaustive as possible, we decided to set out not from their perspective on neoliberalism but from their vision of society, social justice, economics and reform and their understanding of responsibility. To do that we have taken into account their conscious discourses and strategies but also and perhaps even more their practices and behaviour. The latter, which are often unconscious or at least unconceptualised and removed from petitions based on principle, in fact contribute as much, if not more, to what can be perceived from the outside as their participation in neoliberalism and power relations.

The idea that all these actors "bear" neoliberalism does not mean that they cooperate to define a new neoliberal order. It is the congruence between these different actors that shapes the face of neoliberalism in Morocco. This congruence is born from the context in which these actors operate but also, and above all, from the shared imaginary that we have discussed over the course of this book, and which defines the scope of what can be conceptualised. Emphasising the diversity of these bearers of neoliberalism is a way of underlin-

191

WEAVING POLITICAL TIME IN MOROCCO

ing the fact that this ideology does not exist as such; it is not the result of a grand scheme and cannot be easily grasped, or only in terms of techniques, modes of government and certain ways of reasoning or principles of behaviour. From the perspective of economic theory, neoliberalism is nebulous, a constellation of varied and sometimes contradictory currents that all tend toward a shared goal: the reconfiguration of markets and a self-limiting state.

The same is true from the perspective of political economics, or more specifically the actors involved in these so-called "neoliberal" reforms. Interests and logics of action differ from one actor to the next, as do ways of implementing them, interpreting them and understanding them, and even within each actor they vary according to circumstances and power relations. They also evolve over time, particularly between the moment in which neoliberalism began to emerge as a new ideological orthodoxy, when it spread within the government (from the mid-2000s), and the moment when it was vulgarised, adopting forms that were both broader and more consensual but also more insidious and invisible, under the effect of naturalisation that works through the imaginary. These different moments of neoliberalism involve different bearers.

The engineer-technocrats of economics and finance

These engineer-technocrats were undoubtedly the first bearers of neoliberalism. Their role in its spread operated essentially through the promotion of technical frameworks targeting the efficiency of the state, in which they are important civil servants but also through their ways of understanding public action and their "engineering mindset."[1] Developing practices directed towards interventionism, promoting a "business friendly" environment, conformity with business and the market, they effectively promoted the first version of the neoliberal art of governing.[2] There were several variants of these engineer-technocrats in economics and finance. Firstly, there were senior public servants who—as part of a purely French tradition— moved between the public and private sectors depending on circumstances and the most propitious sites for public action—Morocco is no exception in this respect. However, in the Sharifian empire they

THE BEARERS OF NEOLIBERALISM

adopted the role of the new janissaries, providing the administration with a touch of modernity, skill and efficiency. Particularly present during the rise of neoliberalism, this figure is embodied by people like Mohammed Hassad[3] or Mustapha Bakkoury.[4]

Alongside these senior public servants, there are private actors who find themselves involved in public action in various ways (such as by moving into the circles of power through the royal holdings) and who lend the authorities their image as "winners" of neoliberalism. Khalid Oudrighi[5] is one of them. They project the same economic and social vision as their senior public servant peers, frequent the same social spaces and are cast from the same mould. They participate in defining the shape of government of the economy and society through the role devolved to the private institutions they manage. Even more importantly, because of their scope, and more importantly the scope of these institutions—in which the key stakeholder is none other than the King—they are central players in the transmission of an understanding of what constitutes "good government." These technocrats are not always flamboyant and visible in the public sphere, but they are no less important. Like Ahmed Rahhou,[6] they share the belief that they are contributing to the modernisation of the state, but their careers are discreet and follow the logic of hard work well done. Even though they may have their own perspective on the system, they remain quiet about it, and it does not impact on their involvement. They serve the state because of their skills and their ethic of responsibility. Their discretion does not prevent them from playing a central role in spreading neoliberalism through their technical expertise, their inclination for public service or at least the collective and their basic commitment to serving the general interest.

More recently, the profile and training of these actors has become more diverse as new opportunities for higher education have emerged in Morocco and abroad, both in public and private institutions. Some of these actors are graduates from the most prestigious engineering schools in Morocco—the Mohammedia and Hassanyia schools—or from foreign engineering schools. The former are represented by Anas Alami, of the Supervisory Board of the Casablanca Stock Exchange,[7] the latter by Moulay Hafid Elalamy.[8] Often the products of meritocracy, they have adopted the major principles of neoliberalism (good governance, homothety between the public and private, competition, transparency, financial performance, etc.) as well as its major techniques (management, data-based government, benchmarking, certification etc.). Consequently, they become promoters of the most standard neoliberal frameworks, such as new public management, public-private partnerships, independent agencies, international norms, delegation contracts and the most sophisticated financial projects. In this respect, they are the Moroccan equivalents of neoliberal public servants anywhere in the world. Indeed, the pioneers among them are often graduates from the same prestigious Parisian schools that train their French peers. In the name of skills, excellence and managerial rationality, they set out to break down traditional sociabilities linked to family ties, marital alliances, regionalism but also the nationalist movement and its shifting forms. However, they are also fully implanted in Moroccan society and participate in the local texture of neoliberalism and its rapid spread through shared references and certain types of behaviour. Thus, the importance of the revived community—former *"taupins"*[9] or graduates from elite schools[10]—they reinvented this belonging and shared experience according to the traditional model of a status society. Behind the discourse of modernity and technicality, they embed their understanding of reforms in the depths of Moroccan history.[11] In spite of their appreciation of competition and transparency, they are the first to advocate for mediation, recalling how this practice is rooted in traditional culture.[12] In spite of their desire to appear to be the main promotors of a changing society, they justify their actions in reference to concepts, arguments or behaviour from another time. It is difficult to fully depict these understandings and their impact on the neoliberal art of governing, because they take shape in styles, attitudes, positions and uses of a lexicon that are the only way to give meaning to the events. But there is one particularly symbolic example, the case of a housing development in Rabat, which was then made available to senior public servants of the state. During the summer of 2016, the case came out in the media and began to provoke debate in public opinion. Surprisingly, the argument used to justify the purchase of land

THE BEARERS OF NEOLIBERALISM

at subsidised prices was not that of social peace (which any administration could envisage for the benefit of its public servants, like anywhere in the world) but rather the argument of personalised and exceptional "reparation" for these servants of the state (or in this case the prince) as payment for "services rendered."[13] In other words, the "archaic" logic of the *khadim* sometimes remains the reflex of defending the most "sophisticated" of senior civil servants. The use of this imperial reference can be seen as a way of dealing with the fatality of low points of professional and social life. However, it is impossible to generalise from this, as some are more likely to mobilise this reference and others more sensitive to the idea of state service.

By affirming their allegiance to the palace rather than to the elected government, engineer-technocrats in finance and economics share the same anti-political understanding of politics. They fully accept their connexion to the palace but not as a link to a political body, rather as a link to a body that recognises expertise and ensures "independence" from party political forces, as a link with a body that is de-bureaucratised and efficient. These engineer-technocrats are those with power in the state apparatus, in its public and "privatised" dimensions. Through the primacy that they confer on managerial and financial techniques, they contribute to a managerialisation and financialisation of legitimacy and legitimate skill. Managerial and financial legitimacy thus came to dominate in the appreciation of government performance. Through the pre-eminent role the engineer-technocrats play in public administration they have progressively economised, financialised and technocratised political legitimacy. However, this does not prevent them from taking on the role of the new *khadim*, as we have seen. Those involved probably do not recognise themselves in this portrayal; they do not consider themselves neoliberal but rather modern and apolitical. They aim for efficiency, promote the modernisation of the economy and even of social relations, they intend to increase the performances of the state framework, etc. They do not consider themselves imperial or close to the *Makhzen* and do not see themselves as political actors but rather as a segment of the enlightened elite: essentially the technocratic elite.

WEAVING POLITICAL TIME IN MOROCCO

In recent years, the stage for these actors has evolved or at least become more diverse under the impact of a new vision of politics. On one hand, taking into account the increased importance of elections in accessing positions of power, particularly since 2011, they began to use their skills to serve a political party—for example, Ahmed Reda Chami[14] (for the USFP), even though some of them may already have had a partisan connection, such as Karim Ghellab[15] with the Istiqlal. On the other hand, the institutionalisation of royal anger, the violence of royal curses, in the name of the search for responsibility by the Court of Accounts on behalf of the palace, have challenged the omnipotence of the technocrats and the figure of the untouchable *khadim*. In recent years, many engineer-technocrats have been struck down by the *Makhzen*'s power: Mohammed Boussaïd, Mohammed Hassad and Ali Ghannam, for the senior civil servants, Khalid Oudrighi, Saâd Bendidi and Karim Zaz for technocrats at the service of the *Makhzen*. As for Saïd El Hadi or Mustapha Bakkoury, they were also painfully side-lined.

Former left-wing figures turned economic actors

Former left-wing figures who became central actors in the denationalised Moroccan economy have become significant bearers of neoliberalism, even more so than traditional economic actors, who often became fervent partisans of the protected economy and sometimes the rentier economy. In fact, these left-wing figures see neoliberalism as a way of getting around the state which, despite their conversion, they continue to distrust. Contrary to appearances, their role in the spread of neoliberalism is not paradoxical. They mobilise an important aspect of this spread, which is different to that of the senior civil servants but no less intricately connected to the neoliberal philosophy of the state—they reject a state that is all the more illegitimate because its power is authoritarian and its modes of government rely on exploitation and distribution of rents, against a backdrop of generalised corruption. In this respect, they are the perfect examples of bearers who convey the second dimension of the neoliberal art of governing, which is based on the criticism of state administration and government practices.[16] They

THE BEARERS OF NEOLIBERALISM

have generally been previously active in the fight against corruption—particularly with the association Transparency Maroc[17]—which provided these former activists (who have often spent time in prison) a space in which to continue their struggles in an economic and political context other than that of the Years of Lead. Some, like Bachir Rachdi,[18] promote ethics and transparency through their economic and militant activities. Others, such as Fouad Abdelmoumni,[19] Mostafa Meftah[20] or Mouhcine Ayouche[21] contribute to the respectability of entrepreneurship, promoting private initiatives and even enterprise as a way of life.

Although they still defend an anti-liberal, and for some anti-capitalist, worldview, they are in fact vectors for neoliberalism in at least two complementary ways. On the one hand, they defend the need for a smaller state and legitimate the rise of private actors in the art of governing. This ideological position is not in contradiction with the senior public servants' understanding of neoliberalism, analysed above, but tends to broaden the understanding of it to aspects other than new public management and the search for an "efficient" state. On the other hand, and above all, they spread the techniques, frameworks and practices of neoliberalism in different ways. They value participation in civil society, promote entrepreneurship (through their own activities directly or indirectly via the dynamic of entrepreneurship or self-entrepreneurship) or contribute actively to the legitimisation of transparency frameworks. Although this position may seem schizophrenic it is not; instead it is the result of the interconnection between at least four different rationales. The first of these is an extremely detailed political strategy (reform from the inside via entryism, to use political language), the second involves an emphasis on ethics and a moral dimension justifying neoliberal reform (emphasis on equality of treatment and justice, meritocracy and upward social mobility, which symbolise the fight against rentier capitalists). The third rationale, more prosaically, involves the need to adapt to a world of material contingencies; and last but not least, the fourth involves the desire to continue to maintain a space for dissidence in which they can speak out freely or pursue their activist activities.

Their trajectory and their activities reveal an important foundation for the spread of neoliberalism—through critical discussion of it.[22] This is another element that sheds a particular light on this general process, a critique that allows neoliberalism to renew itself, and which is associated with this "anti-system discourse" shoring up the system. Indeed, many of these former left-wing figures have maintained a hostility toward the *Makhzen* from their prior (sometimes current) political positions, but they draw on the same frame of reference in their opposition. By granting the *Makhzen* all explanatory powers and attributing blockages in the "system" to its manipulation, the supposed expectations of the palace or the intentions of the King, they remain prisoners of an omnipresent and omniscient vision of power that defines what is politically conceivable. In so doing, not only are they unable to extract themselves from the political imaginary and representations that are at the heart of practices of domination, but they consolidate and reproduce them. Indeed, this reading constitutes a powerful form of the spread of neoliberal ideology and practices. Transparency is perceived as a way of fighting against the impenetrability of the *Makhzen* and its corrupt, nepotistic, clientelist, "tribal" and thus authoritarian forms of government. The market is seen as the way of overcoming incestuous relations between economic and political elites, and self-management is seen as a way of sublimating the collective constraints of the system. This critical participation in neoliberalism and simultaneously in the system perpetuates practices that are historically embedded, specifically the acceptance of dissidence and the regeneration of the state through the integration of this dissidence.

These former figures of the left, who have become the enemies of corruption, do not recognise themselves in this depiction any more than senior public servants do. They do not feel like neoliberals but like anti-neoliberals, as they are anti-rentier and opposed to conflicts of interest; they defend transparency, independence, responsibility. They do not consider themselves imperial, still less *Makhzenian* but as "knights" of good governance and as a model of anti-capitalist economics. However, as realistic political actors, they nevertheless invest in new arenas of power and positions of accumulation. Unlike senior civil servants, however, they take full responsibility for the political nature of their trajectory. This is not

THE BEARERS OF NEOLIBERALISM

a sign of denial, as a moral condemnation might suppose; it reflects a change in perspective and context that brings these actors, driven by their convictions, to continue their work by other means.

Modernised traditional elites

Modernised traditional elites are represented by their "heirs"; like their fathers, this elite group plays on their position at the intersection of economics and politics, which explains their influence and how they are able to profit from it. Like senior public servants, these "heirs" are neoliberal because they above all seek to modernise the state, making it more efficient through the rationalisation of its techniques. But, unlike those discussed above, they also accept their proximity with the central power and even the palace. In other words, they very naturally combine neoliberal understandings and imperial visions of the art of governing. They shed light on a fundamental characteristic of neoliberalism that is rarely emphasised because it does not really conform to the anti-political canons of this doctrine, but which is nevertheless widespread: the overlap between the positions of power and positions of accumulation that are fed by the logics behind public-private partnerships, public service concessions and privatisation. This elite is diverse because of its origins (*Makhzen* families, provincial notables, major religious families, Istiqlal families) and because of the kind of links it has with the *Makhzen* (belonging to *dar-al Makhzen*, local notabilities serving the *Makhzen*, old *Makhzen* or nationalist families). However, members of this elite share the same trajectory, they are graduates from elite schools in France or the USA, serve the state and proclaim not only their genealogy but also their political position. Several well-known figures in Morocco are representative of this group, such as Mostafa Terrab[23] but also Driss Benhima,[24] whose father was minister and even Prime Minister in the 1960s and whose ancestors worked in the public service for the sultan well before the Protectorate. Benhima combines service for the *Makhzen* with the fact he himself is a notable, and this allows him to pose as a reformer of the state.

Although there are not many of them, the members of these modernised traditional elites play an important role in the naturali-

WEAVING POLITICAL TIME IN MOROCCO

sation of neoliberalism. Like the engineer-technocrats mentioned above, with whom they share elements of their education, they have adopted the neoliberal "toolkit" as part of their everyday practices. But they are different in at least two respects. On one hand, they openly accept their connection to the palace—they are "heirs", situating themselves explicitly in this dual relationship to power, based on legality and allegiance and even proclaiming the primacy of the latter. On the other hand, their skills are also the fruit of their socio-political knowledge, their social backgrounds and their place in (the upper echelons of) society. What makes them modern is that unlike the old elite, they incorporate political reality into neoliberal doxa. Those who survive are those who manage to combine different registers, different forms of knowledge, different logics of action. Not only do they accept the proximity between neoliberal doctrine and the imperial register, but they make the neoliberal aspect of the *Makhzenian* ethos natural by associating traditional behaviour and neoliberal understandings of the art of governing. They cultivate a certain elegance and benefit from interpersonal knowledge and an etiquette that—through their actions, the words they use, the behaviour they adopt[25]—allows them to confer nobility on neoliberalism and thus normalise and legitimate it.

Unlike senior civil servants and former left-wing figures, the members of this modernised traditional elite do feel neoliberal, or in any case liberal, and also consider themselves imperial, or at least *Makhzenian*. However, like senior public servants and unlike former left-wing figures, most consider themselves apolitical, out of a desire to distance themselves from political parties and partisan and government politics in search of efficiency, modernity and performance. However, they recognise the political side of the *Makhzen*, a politics independent of the temporalities and tumults of society.

Bourgeois civil society

Neoliberalism also spreads through bourgeois civil society. But contrary to what might be assumed, this spread is not linked to the understanding these actors have of economic transformations or

THE BEARERS OF NEOLIBERALISM

changes in their professional activities, which are often part of a protected, interventionist and sometimes rentier economy. This neoliberalism flourishes elsewhere, in the social and cultural spheres. These bourgeois actors generally inherited or created their wealth in the spheres of commerce or industry and represent an updated form of secular piety reflecting a "charitable" understanding of the social and a reticence to, or at least a distance from, the state. Like for the previous groups, they may vary in the type of relation they have with the state but come together in their attention to social issues and a feeling of responsibility toward the bodies and classes behind their privilege. This explains the fact that they created charitable associations, a neoliberal form of social action. They may build partnerships with the state for example, such as Nourredine Ayouch's Zakoura Fondation,[26] or have a more distant, even hostile attitude to it, such as the Touria and Abdelaziz Tazi Foundation,[27] which demonstrated alternative cultural commitments, of which the Banque alimentaire stands out in its help for victims of natural disasters, to the point where it was seen as being in competition with the royal foundations. Finally, these bourgeois figures may also operate "ordinary" corporate sponsorship, albeit coloured by Muslim charity, focused on the poor, on orphanages or disabilities (rather than on the arts, which is the favoured beneficiary of charity for banks[28] and the corporate sector), like the Fondation Sekkat,[29] which built four orphanages in Casablanca, a hospital in Aïn Chock and renovated a wing of the youth prison in Oukacha.

From a position that is different to that of modernised traditional elites and more in keeping with the neoliberal doxa than that of the senior civil servants, these bourgeois figures convey another fundamental characteristic of neoliberalism, their aversion toward intermediary political bodies, which is another aspect of anti-statism and the valorisation of civil society. With no reservations about their paternalistic liberalism or their anti-parliamentarism, they contribute in their own way to the spread of a very specific understanding of neoliberalism—one based on social and political practices inherited from history—which values the intermediation of notabilities and not unionism for example. Thus, charity is understood as being

201

the expression of social and cultural action delegated to civil society, which is in turn understood as the enlightened bourgeois elite. Foundations and patronage operate as the intermediaries of power but not of the state, even though they benefit from major state projects and cultivate good relations with the administration. In certain cases, this intermediation is considered a cog in the machine of power, and the position of Noureddine Ayouch is the best example of this.[30] In other cases, it tends to oppose authority in an attempt to promote greater justice, like Karim Tazi.[31] Whatever the case, their activities do not challenge the established order.[32] On the contrary, not only do they act as a "social safety net" alongside those put in place by the state, allowing the latter to "offload" actions beyond its abilities or roles it could not take on, but they extend certain neoliberal principles, such as performance, excellence, efficiency, objectivity in procedures and so forth, to society as a whole. We might say that these bourgeois figures were the incarnation of "neoliberalism with a human face"; they promote the idea of a state that supervises but is not interventionist, deregulated minimum wages and decreased taxation, emphasising the virtues of the market and enterprise, proclaiming the superiority of the private sector and yet are no less benefactors for all that. They spread an understanding of life in society that is fairer and more attentive to needs, but which still respects the established order.

Like most of the other groups studied, these actors do not feel neoliberal. Through their social and charitable actions, they consider themselves humanists, concerned with reconciling efficiency, modernity, performance, dominant economic logics of competition and competitivity, with genuine social action. As they are mistrustful of central power and its perceived negative incursions, they clearly do not see themselves as imperial or close to the *Makhzen*. Yet their ethos, their charitable practices and their understanding of the social all draw on the pastoral aspect of the imperial frame of reference.

Multipositioned local notables

Local notables must be able to act as mediators between the state and society in keeping with the amount of overlap between their

THE BEARERS OF NEOLIBERALISM

positions of power and accumulation. As a result, they are important in the spread of neoliberalism at the deepest levels of society. Of course, there are differences between these notabilities; they are not all equally successful in their neoliberal "conversion". Those who manage this shift well are generally those who also play on the government fashions at the time. In other words, they are able to associate their multiple positions with a dynamic of entrepreneurship and involvement in associative or participatory logics.

These local notables, whether they are animal breeders,[33] farmers,[34] agricultural companies[35] or small entrepreneurs,[36] seized the opportunities that came with the privatisation of land, the development of outsourcing and the promotion of income-generating activities. But they also took advantage of the mobilisation of local populations around participatory projects that always required intermediaries, mediators and entrepreneurs. As part of the policy of intensifying agricultural production, they were able to access long-term leases on irrigated areas or become "aggregators"[37] in the policy to modernise agriculture as part of the *Plan Maroc Vert* (Green Morocco Plan). In the name of entrepreneurial efficiency, held up as a universal principle, their economic success enables them to consolidate their political hold by presenting themselves as new actors and thus diversifying their power relations—in spite of their previous role in now-stigmatised traditional practices, particularly in the depletion of groundwater. In this respect, they are the ones who gave the *Plan Maroc Vert* its credentials and status, as they are among the tenderers of land privatisation. Set up as ethno-familial cooperatives, they promoted social advancement cloaked in the language of participation and the transformation of tribes into efficient economic actors. They became the virtuosos of this framework, which combines the struggle against the degradation of pastures, the organisation of peoples, crop rotations and participation, reasoning by sectors and labelling with projects like automated abattoirs. Yet at the same time, over a decade, small breeders have all but disappeared, and livestock breeding has become ever more concentrated in the hands of these "aggregators".[38]

The local notables' ways of operating reveals a dimension of neoliberalism that the groups analysed above only express implic-

WEAVING POLITICAL TIME IN MOROCCO

itly. This is the mobilisation of practical knowledge, pragmatism and an ability to take advantage of entrepreneurial resources. Their relationship with neoliberalism is very indirect, it is even less pre-conceptualised than for the groups discussed above, even in its various vulgarised dimensions. It is above all guided by interests, specifically material interests and by the contingency between interests, behaviour, entrepreneurial ethos and neoliberal logic. However, these notables only spread neoliberalism to the extent that, beyond their personal interests, they represent the "new figures of success"[39] and are considered examples. Their role as bearers of this ideology is therefore directly linked to the conditions now necessary for success. The turn of the 1990s was marked by agricultural economics and rural expertise being removed from the clutches of the state administration. Since then, the mood has been for programmes and projects that cannot be reduced to rhetorical strategies and speeches, but which translate into a variety of frameworks for rationalising interventions. These take shape within the context of the demise of public companies and the privatisation of their land through long-term lease contracts and the dismantling of collective property by the separation and leasing of the most fertile lands. Henceforth, to maintain their positions of power, notables must often be multipositioned. As actors and bearers of this transformation, they contribute to the accentuation of the process by which the state withdraws from certain development functions to the point where, for example, the OCE (Board for Commercialising Exports) finds itself obsolete. Alongside this, the programmes and projects become more participative and are now only conceived in connection with local associations—in which these notables are often the leaders. Their position in local society is reinforced in situations where the principles of delegation, public service concessions, public-private partnerships or participation demand forms of intermediation they alone can provide.[40]

Like most of the other groups, these multi-positioned local notables do not consider themselves neoliberal. Neoliberalism probably does not mean much to them. Through their work as mediators and facilitators, their interpersonal skills and relations, their position in the hierarchy of local companies and their involve-

THE BEARERS OF NEOLIBERALISM

ment in the local economy, they feel they are locally invested in a "political" role, because they occupy positions of power that they promote and benefit from. And yet, their role in the spread of neoliberal practices is just as important because they naturalise these practices by passing them through the filter of historically constructed political notions. For example, delegation, public service concessions, participation or public-private partnerships are not considered new frameworks but rather forms of government that enable intermediation, create new positions and feed the process of notabilisation. Some may become frontline actors; Haj Ali Qayouh,[41] for example, went from being a local notable in the Sous region, to the figurehead for the Istiqlal, placing two of his children in parliament and ensuring his business in agriculture and livestock thrived. The Derham family[42] by contrast, who were active in agriculture, fishing, oil and real estate, moved into politics under a range of colours (RNI, PPS, USFP, MP). The most emblematic examples are undoubtedly Aziz Akhannouch,[43] current president of the RNI and Prime Minister and formerly Minister for Agriculture, Fishing, Rural Development and Forests and Waterways, former president of the Souss-Massa-Draâ region and CEO of the Akwa group, and Mohammed Sajid, president of the Constitutional Union, appointed in 2019 as Minister for Tourism and former Mayor of Casablanca in the 2000s.[44] They represent two of the most exemplary trajectories of upward mobility for men of the fringes.

Experts

Typically, ideology is spread via experts, anywhere around the world, at any time. In the case of neoliberalism, experts have had all the more impact because their technical, scientific and objective skills are echoed by a claim to apoliticism and universality. This grants them greater legitimacy in reforms than political actors, of course, but also more legitimacy than the engineer-technocrats who are civil servants.[45] In the case of Morocco it is important to distinguish between two periods of neoliberal expertise—the era of pioneers and that of institutionalised experts.

WEAVING POLITICAL TIME IN MOROCCO

The first period begins in the mid-1980s with the analyses by contributors to the dissident journal *Lamalif*. This journal published work by academic experts (most of whom were involved in politics) who enthusiastically supported IMF injunctions while criticising the social impact of structural adjustment plans, a position that they did not consider an endorsement but rather as justified by the need to shake up a rentier state that has fallen into bureaucracy and corruption.[46] Here the implication was both professional and political; more specifically it was brought about by the fact that scientific knowledge was made available for political involvement based on Saint-Simonianism, in reaction against "archaisms" and "totalitarian excesses". Much like the former left-wing figures who moved into economics and who sometimes shared their commitment, these activist experts embraced this new world view and helped to make it hegemonic, as a way of getting around the authoritarian state. Political commitment takes on the form of shrewd expertise, fed by terms of reference that aspire to universality, developed in the offices of the investment centre in the FAO in Rome or the World Bank in Washington. It is precisely this distance and universality that are seen as vectors of objectivity and transparency but also efficiency, side-lining political constraints that are liable to alter the course of development objectives.

In the mid-1990s this expertise was unquestioningly set to serve major public-private partnership projects, with the firm belief that this was "to do good". The private sector here was all the more accepted by these experts because these projects were run by NGOs and local companies that were in fact conducting the first outsourcing actions to implement the PERG, the PAGER or the PNRR.[47] The work of these experts—despite their militancy—followed specific sequences in the projects' time scales, which made it difficult to engage in prior reflection. And when that prior reflection did exist, it was outside their field of expertise and lacked their tools of conceptual analysis and ultimately had little consequence for the recommended actions. Its only use was to enable a sort of redemption, which did not prevent another round of expertise, in the hope of impacting the course of history. Like former left-wing figures, and despite their lucidity about the limits or even negative

THE BEARERS OF NEOLIBERALISM

side effects of their actions, these experts believe in a possible transformation from within because of their knowledge (and not their political legitimacy). But they too find themselves to be the best agents for the spread and vulgarisation of neoliberalism.[48]

The second period of neoliberal expertise began with the generalisation of procedural guides and the opening up of the community of experts beyond ex-academic experts who saw this as a militant action and a source of complementary income. This has been the period of institutionalisation of expertise that has seen local consultancy firms flourish. These firms are generally one of two kinds. The oldest, which emerged during the welfare-state era, were associated with public institutions such as the SCET, the consultancy office of the CDG that worked to prepare major projects, as well as engineering companies, such as that of Anis Balafrej,[49] which although private were close to the public sector due to personal contacts. With liberalisation and privatisation, a second wave of consultancy firms has emerged, along the lines of AgroConcept, run by Hassan Ben Abderrazik, a former G14 member and by Omar Aloui.[50] More recently, experts with international experience created their own consultancy firms, such as the Minister for African Affairs, Mohcine Jazouli, who had formerly worked at Ernst & Young and who founded Valyans, which became very active in urban planning.[51] These men often situate themselves in the continuity of the pioneers analysed above, but they made the choice to specialise in consultancy and expertise. Like their peers in major international consulting firms, their experience extends beyond the national context, but they remain linked to Morocco. To a certain degree they are close to the local notables juggling multiple positions, combining knowledge of local society, practical skills and a clear sense of economic opportunity.

The institutionalisation of expertise ultimately increased and deepened with the development of franchises such as Vigéo-Eiris, specialised in corporate social responsibility and locally managed by Fouad Benseddik, nephew of the eternal manager of UMT Mahjoub Benseddik. It was also influenced by the establishment of major international groups such as the ever-present McKinsey, Boston Consulting Group (in which Hamid Maher was appointed

WEAVING POLITICAL TIME IN MOROCCO

Partner and Managing Director in 2018) or Roland Berger (directed in Morocco by Younès Zrikem,[52] who has now "moved" to the Boston Consulting Group). These consultancy experts circulate indifferently between the public and private sectors. They are graduates of elite French schools (HEC, Sciences Po, Dauphine) or Ivy-League or Oxbridge universities in the anglophone world and are part of a professional and market logic that obscures politics. They do not question the ready-made tools they use and are adepts of "PowerPoint government". They are not disconnected from Moroccan society, however, on the contrary they often have an intimate understanding of power relations and "those who matter," through their family connections. They describe themselves as apolitical but are embedded in sociabilities of power, close in this respect to the traditional modernised elites analysed above. The forms of Morrocanisation of these franchises or these major companies have not involved social breakdowns or the creation of a new local elite. They have occurred through the investment of the children of the traditional elite. The latter, having completed prestigious degrees overseas, return to Morocco with international experience that allows them to believe (or encourage others to believe) that they are exempt from local political contingencies, unquestioningly mobilising what they see as "neutral" and "objective" language, with no qualms or hesitations.

This categorisation is clearly based on ideal types. In reality, these profiles and experiences are intertwined. The expert activists who emerged early on have also pursued their own "egotistical" self-interest, and equally, the now dominant understanding of consultancy as a profession and as a market does not prevent other forms of political engagement and a desire to change things from within. What differs between these two kinds of experts are ethos and social origin on the one hand and attitudes towards politics on the other. The first kind of experts are often children of the working classes or middle classes who tackle the political question head-on, as part of the process of upward social mobility through knowledge, based on their actions or reflections on power relations. The second group, the most visible of them are the children of the elite, who mobilise their social relations to successfully obtain tenders

THE BEARERS OF NEOLIBERALISM

and influence not the orientation but the actors of neoliberal normalisation, with total disdain for politics.

Islamists, outsiders *who became* insiders

Contrary to what is often stated, it is not only Islamist ideology that has an elective affinity with neoliberalism.[53] The "pedagogical" aspect of the Islamists in power, their ability to inculcate and spread shared meaning has also made them vectors of the naturalisation of neoliberalism by enabling the popularisation of certain traits that are characteristic of the current ideational hegemony.

There are many different kinds of Islamists, and they do not all have the same foundations. Some are even hostile to neoliberalism—such as the Al Adl wal Ihsane movement, which refuses these new rules—and which would fit better into the category of former left-wing figures who paradoxically reinforce neoliberal hegemony through their critique of capitalism and the global economic order.[54] Sufis clearly engage with the entrepreneurial spirit, however. For example, Boutchichiyya[55] is both an enterprise brotherhood of faith and an enterprise anchored in the modern economy. Bouchichi's grandson, Moulay Mounir Elkadiri is the president of the Independent Committee for Islamic Finance in Europe (CIFIE), which specialises in marketing and strategic monitoring and has shown itself to be very active in introducing decrees on participative finance.[56] With a doctorate in Islamic law, a master's in strategic management and an undergraduate degree in economics, Elkadiri has become a prophet of green economics and for a social and solidarity economy.[57] The brotherhood promotes the ethos of entrepreneurship, effort and the individual. To a certain extent, it is a symbol of the neoliberal miracle, both conservative and modern, in its capacity to organise and take part in globalisation. For example, during the *moussem*, it provides a stage for moderate Moroccan Islam, which is technological and sophisticated, green, bohemian and globalised.[58]

The PJD operates on a slightly different register, particularly because it works in a governmental perspective. Although it values entrepreneurship, private property and an attachment to

WEAVING POLITICAL TIME IN MOROCCO

market rules from a traditional perspective, it puts more emphasis on two other fundamental aspects of neoliberalism than the Sufis do. These other aspects are competition and the critique of administration. Thus, before being appointed Prime Minister, Abdelilah Benkirane had been head of a bleach company, a printmaker and a private primary school in Salé. He was also explicitly involved in the privatisation of education, being one of the promoters of this policy within the COSEF (Special Commission on Education and Training). Once he was Prime Minister, he continued to express his strong opinions about the administration, even though he was at its head. Although ideological belief was undeniably an important element in the promotion of these principles, contingency nevertheless played a role. The criticism of the rentier economy and acquired positions and the call to lift obstacles for new actors entering the economy intersect with more prosaic interests associated with the position of Islamist actors in Moroccan society. In fact, the electoral base of the PJD is largely made up of new provincial actors looking for ways to take hold, grow and ultimately dominate.

These different groups not only share an entrepreneurial ethos and the valorisation of enterprise as a symbol of economic success, social mobility and prosperity. Their attachment to charity as a central concept in the reallocation of resources, the search for social peace and the salvation of souls rather than taxes (with which they have a problematic relationship) have contributed to their desire to not challenge the social and economic order, which they are in any case unable to do. Once again, here they appear consistent with the neoliberal image of social policy that emphasises philanthropy and social safety nets rather than systems that generalise systematic redistribution. More recently, the extent of these affinities has increased further with the increasing power of engineers within the party, to the detriment of traditional figures, lawyers, teachers, preachers and theologians. These new actors have made space for themselves in management positions as well as in the heart of the production of religious doctrine. Those in management positions were represented as engineer ministers, such as Aziz Rebbah,[59] at the Ministry for Energy, Mining and

THE BEARERS OF NEOLIBERALISM

Sustainable Development, or by MPs such as Abdessamad Sekkal,[60] president of the region. Those involved with producing religious doctrine were represented by the last two presidents of the MUR (Movement for Unity and Reform), Abderrahim Chikhi or Mohammed Hamdaoui, both of whom were also engineers.

The neoliberalism of the Islamists is one of common sense. It is the neoliberalism of economic rigour, balanced budgets and sensible macroeconomics, good "breadwinner" policies, where, to pursue the analogy, the head of the household must not "live beyond his means." That policy does not change the order of things, still less an order that is well-established. This explains why Islamists are the best agents for the naturalisation of neoliberalism, its most salient vectors in the society. By reflecting common sense habits, they complete the construction of this political hegemony by making it potentially accessible to the population as a whole. But the neoliberalism of the Islamists is the same as that of international donors. This is a genuine change, both in terms of relations with other political parties and in terms of the Islamists themselves. Islamists have not only made neoliberal precepts natural, indispensable and beneficial for the people, including or beginning with the poorest among them, they have transformed relations with international donors by making them natural too. The Islamist government's "tag-along" approach to international recommendations—particularly those of the OECD—was openly proclaimed and even made explicit by Abdelilah Benkirane.[61] This position was partly ideological and partly contingent. Even as the Koutla parties were careful to distance themselves from international donors, the rapprochement with the latter was quickly seen by the Islamists as a principle of differentiation and a way of obtaining technical and managerial legitimacy, particularly on an international level.

It is now commonplace to note the lack of texts in political Islam, which focus on economics and social justice.[62] In this respect, it is reasonable to say that Islamist neoliberalism is merely the expression of their adaptation to the times. Islamists are undoubtedly the only group among the bearers of neoliberalism who genuinely feel neoliberal, within a movement of piety that is openly expressed, even though it is not formulated in these terms. But

211

WEAVING POLITICAL TIME IN MOROCCO

although this explanation is not incorrect, it does not allow us to understand the ease with which Islamists adopted the garb of neo-liberal reformism. Equally, it does not account for the virtuosity that they have demonstrated in ensuring that reforms appear both natural and the expression of significant political courage (for example, the Compensation Fund or the retirement reforms), nor the ease with which they have managed to make these orientations understandable and acceptable for both their militants and for potential voters.

Although the explanation for this does not lie in religious deter-minism, given that subscribing to a particular ethic is only one element among many others guiding government action, focusing on doctrine helps to delimit the field of possibilities. Yet the understanding of economics and good government is undeniably fundamental. If we consider the principle of inequality to be natu-ral and not open to discussion, people have no other choice than to accept the unequal order created by God. This vision of society that is differentiated and naturally stratified but without class struggle echoes the neoliberal doctrine of "good governance" that depoliticises inequality. Within this field of possibilities there are at least three characteristic elements of the Islamists' position in power, which naturalises neoliberalism or at least some of its essential traits.

The first of these elements is pragmatism. The PJD subscribes to the position of the monarchy that considers that Moroccans prefer a rite that can be interpreted based on experience of society and prioritises the *maqassid* (finalities) over the *oussoul* (foundations) and the *amal* (law in action) over the *fiqh* (jurisprudence).[63] In so doing, the PJD situates the issue of economics in the context of a moral economy that is itself based on elements of the foundation of Islamic jurisprudence, *oussoul al-fikh*, reformulated to constitute a paradigm for the adjustment and construction of compromise.

The second of these elements is the legitimacy of reform. Neoliberalism is understood in terms of Muslim reformism, which has historically structured government practices and power rela-tions by bringing together conservatism and a need to adapt through compromise—between diverging forces, different posi-

212

THE BEARERS OF NEOLIBERALISM

tions and discordant voices.[64] The idea of reform also allowed the Islamists to declare their place in the continuity of the national trajectory and the spaces left free in the cracks between older political parties. The PJD's experience in government should be read as part of a long process of pluralisation and competition between political actors with different historical and social foundations. It should also be resituated within a historic move to resolve conflicts through constitutionalisation and legal and political compromise—in other words by a certain kind of reformism—rather than through open confrontation. This serves to "defuse" the political field.

Finally, the third element is the moral aspect of public action. The Islamists in power place the respect of norms and rules above the definition and direction of public intervention. That is why the fight against corruption takes such a central place and is depicted as both immoral and unjust, because it is above all a burden on the poor and the weak. This also has the advantage of allowing the Islamists to distinguish themselves from the Istiqlal, the main competitor of the PJD, and which has always based its political hold on redistributive policies as part of an openly clientelist tradition. In reality, actions to combat corruption have been limited, even token. What remains are the moralising speeches and criticism of the administration. The demands for equal opportunity and transparency, the fight against unearned income and unfairly acquired rights, demands for rigour (*maakoul*) and the fight against corruption (*fassad*) all echo the idea of "good governance" with its populist and moralising overtones.

* * *

This overview of the bearers of neoliberalism in Morocco (and not of political actors as a whole) sketches the outline of a typology, which naturally tends to put people in boxes. Yet this cannot exhaustively account for their singularity, the range of their behaviour and their ways of considering their role in the economy, politics and power relations. A rapid reading runs the risk of reification, as if each had a stable and even conscious definition of the order they promote or the values that pushed them to action, as

WEAVING POLITICAL TIME IN MOROCCO

though there were not, running alongside this, other alternative dynamics and repertoires of action, or as though action in society was not carried out in the in-between, in ambivalent places. Not only are these categories extremely varied—and of course no one corresponds entirely to the characteristics described for each of them—but they also overlap. Certain actors from the modernised traditional elites could have been included in the category of engineer-technocrats of economy and finance, and some pioneer experts could have been put in the category of left-wing figures turned economic actors. Moreover, this typology cannot comprehensively cover all of the bearers of neoliberalism in Morocco, such as certain CEOs of national companies or expatriates in foreign corporations or international organisations. It focuses on those figures who appear most influential as a group. Much like the ideal-type approach adopted throughout the book, this typology must be understood for what it is: an intellectual exercise that allows us to observe distinctive characteristics, ways of reasoning and understanding and, through their multiplicity and simultaneity, to grasp different ways of governing.

Analysis through typologies such as this one faces an additional risk, however, that the staging and construction of these types might be interpreted as an indictment. We hope that the portraits we have sketched here express all our empathy for these figures, whom we frequented for a long time. We have never interpreted the changes and evolutions of their trajectories as being backflips, renunciations or abandonments, or even as a sign of incoherence. On the contrary, these transformations encourage us to see—without moral or political judgement—the full role of contingency and context, the "mood of the time", without assuming the right to judge beliefs and gauge convictions. This typology is also the result of a broader reflection, including on ourselves. It aims to reveal the diversity of actors and channels by which neoliberalism is spread and to account for the complexity of the process of its naturalisation, while paying close attention to the unexpected or paradoxical, to the unconscious or unintended, and to what happens unbeknownst to the actors, as powerful or lucid as they may be. Our approach, examining the groups that bear and promote neoliberal-

214

THE BEARERS OF NEOLIBERALISM

ism, deconstructs this ideology as a new coherent order, the expression of a configuration that is breaking away from the past. By shedding light on so many kinds of figures, understandings and forms of diffusion, we want to show that not only is neoliberalism not born of a grand project, nor does it express a clear line or a single signification but also that it is achieved through a diversity of mediums, positions and logics of actions—which are numerous and sometimes contradictory—and thus essentially through oppositions, tensions and conflicts.

* * *

These developments regarding indirect forms of government and bearers of neoliberalism have enabled us to ultimately identify what is shared, what leads to the definition of a community that occurs and is perpetuated without any intentional action, without there being harmony or consensus and without shared values, conceptions or significations. Seen in this light, neoliberalism does not seem to be the result of actions induced by a naturally superior force (the state, along with international organisations) that could exert its power in various ways (more or less formalised, more or less bureaucratised, more or less coercive). It is the result of actions by those who govern and those who are governed, who, through conflicts and adjustments, end up coming together at a given moment in time, for a specific length of time and temporarily sharing a direction, a sense of meaning and following an order of things, whether actual and institutionalised or not.

This is also why the analysis here has not incorporated the King and the Palace in our analysis of bearers of neoliberalism or what journalists in Morocco refer to as the "economic *Makhzen*".[65] There are three primary reasons for this.

First and foremost, for us, the notion of the economic *Makhzen* leads to a confusion between different economic actors—the king-entrepreneur, the king-head of state, the king-guarantor, the royal advisors, the royal family, the royal entourage and friends. It also tends to confuse different kinds of intervention: the ability to alter the principle of competition; interventions of complacency; the influence of the palace circles in public policy; the seizing of oppor-

215

WEAVING POLITICAL TIME IN MOROCCO

tunities; the desire to guide the national economy and protect it, etc.[66] It is in this respect that we consider that the economic *Makhzen* does not exist and that the notion is a smokescreen that prevents us understanding modes of government. Seeking to grasp it means renouncing an understanding of how these different elements interact in the economy and in power relations. It traps them into a black box that cannot be explored. On the contrary, our approach seeks precisely to go beyond global analysis on the eminently political aspect of the economy or the compatibility of neoliberalism with authoritarianism—an observation that the case of Morocco can only support,[67] as elsewhere.[68] Obviously the cronyism of the Palace is a reality that has always existed, but which is probably more visible and normalised today because there is a greater understanding of the workings and the importance of the economy and processes of economisation of power relations.[69] It is precisely this importance, normalisation and increased visibility that make it more difficult to circumscribe. To move beyond merely condemning, to understand the logics that define connections between business, economics and politics and how they are embedded in society, it seemed essential to rid ourselves of notions of the economic *Makhzen* and venal opportunism and to shed light on the myriad forms of domination that take place through unexpected logics, unforeseen actors or opportunities that are "seized".

Moreover, the structure of the rentier economy and the search for niches, collusion and the impact of interest groups, the quasi-monopoly of royal holding interests in certain sectors, the effects of the proximity of the palace on the access to exemptions or privileges, are all realities that are by no means specifically neoliberal. This behaviour is driven by logics and rationalities that are not particularly suited to the principles of this ideology. The overlaps, positions of power and accumulation did not suddenly appear in the last two decades.[70] Indeed, one of the strengths of neoliberalism and its legitimacy in society, is to seek to challenge these overlaps that distort competition and aggravate inequalities.

This is also why we have not included entrepreneurs and management in our analysis of the bearers of neoliberalism. Of course, these bearers are often the first to condemn the cronyism of the

216

THE BEARERS OF NEOLIBERALISM

Palace, which threatens the development of their own interests and empowerment,[71] and the neoliberal moment, in addition to its economic rationale, provides ample opportunities to do business, particularly in public-private partnerships and indirect government. But these are also the first people to seek to profit from it, to obtain exemptions and special allowances and to share the same business ethos.

Finally, and this is a fundamental point, the focus on the "powerful" (the King, the palace, the royal holding and its subsidiaries, royal advisors, whether official or secret)[72] leads to an under-estimation of the social and historic depth of modes of government and of domination at work. If neoliberalism is naturalised, and we might even say "Moroccanised", it is because it is inscribed in the deepest aspects of social relations. If delegation and the laissez-faire approach are so widespread and so anchored in ways of governing, it is because the "logics from below" penetrate into power relations. The analysis of indirect government and mediators in the economy, the interconnectedness of interests, actors and networks, suggests that power is neither indivisible nor unconditional. It also suggests that resistance, latent or explicit tensions and frictions are common and contribute to the hegemonic construction of neoliberalism.[73] Focusing the analysis on the sovereign and his pre-eminence in the economy and his power of derogation prevents us taking into account the mutual dependences, relations of domination, power plays and social relations without which power cannot operate in society.[74]

CONCLUSION

In this book, we have sought to propose a renewed way of understanding the state and the relations between state and society in the neoliberal era based on a conceptualisation of the plurality of registers and time frames that we have called "woven time". Morocco has provided the case study from which to conceptualise the state, the modes of government and the processes of subjectivation, in the specificity of its historical trajectory, taking into account the materiality of the imaginary, but it is clear that other configurations have also contributed to this reflection. The comparativism that we have applied here is not one of situation, nor is it "assigned" by area studies, which is why we have not drawn on North African or Arab situations more broadly. The comparativism that we have applied here compares questions rather than situations or solutions; it is based on problematisation, which constantly enriched and refined our questioning, in ways that were both subtle yet fundamental. There is a significant difference between anglophone "comparative politics" and francophone "comparative political sociology".[1] We can only hope that one of the book's strengths is to share an alternative intellectual tradition with anglophone readers. The comparatist backdrop of the book led us to sort the banal from the specific and provide an "inventory of differences",[2] while avoiding the reification of singularities and—especially—the exoticism transmitted by vernacular concepts and the staging they are associated with. In other words, this comparativism, because it is implicit, does not work through borrowing or transferring con-

219

cepts but rather through suggestions or "paradigmatic traces",[3] which encourage autonomous reflection based on heterogenous scientific works.

Thus the idea of Empire, stripped here of many of the traits generally associated with this form of the state, but which, based on the contrast between Moroccan history and other imperial experiences, has helped us forge an ideal-type allowing us to move forward, ideally in a more detailed understanding of certain aspects of the art of governing in Morocco today. We also hope that, in return, this book contributes to enriching the academic debate on ways of governing, on attitudes to the state and on the exercise of domination, thanks in particular to the approach and methodology we have adopted here. Notably, the idea of "woven time" appears to us to be helpful in understanding a number of situations. This idea, which aims to express the fact that a plurality of repertoires, representations, staging, action, rationality and understanding refer to different periods, durations and sometimes even to the very long term, is not specific to Morocco by any means. In any situation, the state, its modes of government, its engineering, its imaginaries, can only be understood by taking into account this embeddedness, this superposition and interconnections between different durations.

What might be considered contradiction, confusion or schizo- phrenia, is read here as the interlocking of different registers of meaning from different temporalities, an interconnectedness that allows a very broad interpretative scope. The Moroccan case is interesting because, in all their gestures, the Moroccan people tend to evoke this discourse on historicity. This discourse is of course ideological, presenting Morocco as different from other countries because it has a longer historicity. It is striking for example to see the number of sites dedicated to the Sharifian empire and its cur- rent affairs, particularly in the controversies that oppose web users from Morocco and Algeria. In reality, this historicity is found everywhere. The case of Morocco is simply interesting for its open and explicit reference to the past, which provided fascinating mate- rial through which to theorise our "woven time". But this is by no means specific to Morocco.

220

CONCLUSION

Each country weaves time differently, but political time is woven everywhere. And it seems that the conceptualisation in terms of weaving or interconnectedness of temporalities allows us to conceptualise invisibilities. For the French case, this would apply to territorial discontinuity (French overseas territories), legal pluralism (specific religious laws, such as canon law in the Alsace Loraine region or state Islam in Mayotte), which according to the Jacobin ideology of the French nation-state can only be understood as anomalies or exceptions. Yet these examples express other ways of exercising power, when alternative state registers or references are introduced. We can also evoke the French fascination with the monarchy, even feudalism, not to mention the French Revolution. Thus, without these repertoires we cannot understand the importance of presidential tours around the country, the very regal pomp of republican ceremony, the centrality of the figure of Napoleon in politicians' discourses as well as in the furniture of the Republic, in the French legal arsenal (in terms of the organisation of the state and the governing of religions) or the continuity in the production of statutes by the president of the Republic, for example. France has a different weaving of time, a different tapestry.

Similarly, the analysis of the elective affinities between neoliberalism and the imperial register is not specific to Morocco. By highlighting the salience of indirect government and more generally other characteristics of power, such as investing in people rather than territory, the centrality of information and mobility, it is broadly generalisable to other situations such as former empires like China (and its famous model, "one country, multiple regimes") or Turkey (and its neo-Ottoman vision). But our analysis of neoliberalism is interesting beyond the case of former empires, because it shows that neoliberalism does not mean anything in itself, it is merely an ideal-type, and in order to understand its dynamics and practices in terms of their significations and meanings in context, it is important to take into account the political imaginary and the woven time specific to each state. Those who bear neoliberalism always have a specific history and act according to historically constituted foundations. They understand situations and events according to historically constructed representations and give

WEAVING POLITICAL TIME IN MOROCCO

meaning to their actions according to the imaginary of the state forged in its own history.

Problematisation in terms of woven time and recourse to registers of Empire and Nation-state, may have been interpreted as a depoliticised understanding of mechanisms and practices of repression.[4] Yet it seems to us that this reading results from a confusion that sees the repertoire of the Empire solely as imaginary, understood as non-real, symbolic or based on representations of the past and an ideological or traditionalist process. On the contrary we have constantly shown that the repertoire of the Empire does not stem from the past but is inscribed in the present-day reality and everyday materiality; that today political decisions may be made according to "imperial" understandings of social situations or relations. The chapters on representation and violence have shown this concretely. Since this register is part of the actual foundation of power, the logics of domination are diverse, even the most powerful among them. Although they have been made banal and promoted by the principle of participative democracy and the critique of electoral representation, cooperation and integration of dissent are highly political processes that can feed either political openness or closure, and which allow for tactical and strategic room to manoeuvre. Similarly, imperial violence is absolutely not symbolic and does not act only in the order of representations. It is particularly brutal but sporadic and intermittent and targeted on specific actors who are close to power. But it also has a continuous effect on the population as a whole, feeding the understanding of power that plays on uncertainty and surprise, on the concealment of intentions and on fear.

This depoliticised understanding of our analysis in terms of woven time and this critique of a minimisation of the logics of authoritarian control also result from close attention to the mechanisms of repression and pure violence in Morocco, for example against certain social movements or against investigative journalists—an attention that neglects the "insidious leniencies"[5] of domination. Yet in an intellectual tradition initiated by Etienne de La Boétie[6] and pursued by Max Weber[7] and then Michel Foucault,[8] we have sought to understand the painless everyday experience of

222

CONCLUSION

domination specifically because its forms are less well known, less analysed and "difficult to glimpse or to attribute."[9] The use of ideal-types or woven political time, therefore helped us shed light on the plurality of modes of everyday domination, to denaturalise these practices, by situating them in a historical trajectory, perceiving these modalities of domination within the most banal of social relations. The *muqaddam* is not a subaltern person from another time who now helps state agents to provide documents, he participates in domination by defining the public and social order in neighbourhoods and in the countryside. Similarly, the *semsar*, valued by the urban middle class, removed from even informal circles of power, a clandestine realtor, or recruiter of servants, plays practically the same role as the *muqaddam*. He is often the guardian to whom social and public order are subcontracted.[10] Ultimately mobilising this plurality of interconnecting times, has allowed us to show that the most banal everyday practices are imbued with power relations, with struggles and conflicts, tensions that sketch the outlines of domination.

Finally, studying everyday life in all its banality does not mean minimising domination; describing government by consensus (*Einverständnis*) does not mean neglecting conflicts and tensions. Analysing the processes of integration of dissidence does not mean it is neutralised. On the contrary, from a very Foucauldian approach, that does not oppose state and society, the mobilisation of ideal times, repertoires of Empire and Nation-state and woven time allow us to highlight this subtlety in power relations. Most often, there is not power on one side and resistance on the other or repression on one side and contestation on the other. That is why we do not follow James Scott's analyses on resistance.[11] As Foucault said, power "circulates"[12] and it is made of relations that are more or less tense and conflictual. Highlighting the rationality of accepting domination should not be understood as a minimisation of aspirations of dissidence, contestation or challenges to domination. Situations of dominance and submission are never definite. There are situations of acceptance and situations of challenge that may be coincident over time. Dissidence always lies beneath acceptance. Our approach has been precisely to highlight situations perceived

WEAVING POLITICAL TIME IN MOROCCO

as anecdotal and marginal, even though they in fact reflect practices that are at the heart of domination because they are widespread throughout society. The examples of the dancer Zinoun under Hassan II or the earthquake under Mohammed VI are reminders of this.[13] The Moroccan trajectory has proved to be a rich case through which to deconstruct and reformulate those binary pairs that simplify political analysis: politicisation/depoliticisation, domination/resistance, regulated/spectacular violence, rupture/continuity, transition/authoritarian restoration and so forth. We have explored it from the angle of the state rather than the political regime and through subaltern actors as well as through elites. The two ideal types constructed for this purpose, Empire and Nation-state, have allowed us to grasp the specificity of modes of government and conceptions of power while avoiding the pitfalls of exoticism and particularism. Above all, they have allowed us to describe the processes of the changes that are underway. We have not considered these changes as a radical break, as the arrival of a new order or as the emergence of radically different power relations and modes of government.

The analysis presented in this book is situated beyond the theme of (dis)continuity, in an approach inspired by the Weberian tradition, which sees historical sociology as interpretative sociology (*Verstehende Soziologie*). By emphasising this shift in perspective, meaning and perception, as much as in institutional alterations (whether publicised or not), we have aligned ourselves more with someone like Peter Brown, who criticises the "rhetoric of change" that focuses on paroxysmic moments with the idea of a before and after.[14] Our descriptions of the transformations underway have not revealed any dramatic moments that could have shaken the foundations of the *Makhzen*. The February 20 Movement or the *hirak* of 2017–18 were not precursors to the downfall of the regime but the expression of tensions provoked by ongoing changes. Similarly, this research has not led us to consider the "major events" in contemporary Morocco (such as the emergence of a new regime, the implementation of the IER or the 2011 constitution) as tipping points that ought to be analysed with notions like "revolution", "transition" or "unavoidable chain-reactions" decided by the actors

224

CONCLUSION

who control time (but especially power relations and the course of history) or through the idea of the "resilience" of individuals able to adapt to any kind of context.

For us, change is permanent and must be understood as the effect of a long transformation of social relations, taking into account the "thickness" of social facts and not merely the facts of power.[15] This understanding of change is the direct result of our approach to historical sociology and an understanding of politics that—not content with observing the "traditional" sites and actors of politics—pushes us to increase the vantage points from which to observe the different modalities of action and levels of government. The attention we pay to the banality of everyday social relations and attitudes to politics rather than royal speeches, legal texts, the constitution or partisan games explains why we chose to conduct an ethnography of sites, actors and moments that are often considered ordinary or marginal, even outside the political field. By revealing the multiplicity of understandings and points of shifting meaning, these "scenes" have helped us perceive change as a series of infinitesimally small transformations, almost invisible in their consequences for the modalities of the exercise of domination and power relations. They also led us to refrain from describing the direction that these changes may take, given that depends both on the objective conditions of their actualisation and the ways increasing numbers of actors understand them.

We have observed marginal changes that have occurred in the ways of understanding the state and the foundations of power but also administration and territorialisation and the shifting relations between social organisations and authority. We have seen progressive evolutions in ways of accommodating the population, representing and conceiving continual adjustments in forms of political subjectification that define the contours of responsibility of power and of challenges to it. What is considered possible or not depends on subjectivity shaped by social experience and context.

This methodological position does not mean that we have failed to take into account the major morphological shifts in society as seen by geographers and sociologists. It is the macro level changes, visible or concealed, which make marginal changes, shifts and

225

transformations of meaning possible and bring new subjectivities to light. Our observations of them are nourished by our previous research and fieldwork both in rural and urban environments. This allows us to take into account changes in landscapes, the morphology of individuals, dress codes, culinary arts, modes and forms of communication but also social links, relations between town and country and even less visible things such as the foundations of leadership and the circulation of women, now marked by a propensity for ethnic exogamy combined with homogamy in profession and status.

The most significant morphological change concerns the territory where politics is played out, in other words the space of government outlined by the planning and projects undertaken by the state—the freeways, railways, subsidised airline routes—which all now neutralise the geographical constraints imposed by the Atlas Mountains and make the differentiated administration between plains and mountains somewhat obsolete. Inversely, government through the control of mountain peaks and passes has not entirely disappeared, but it has shifted to other places—souks, universities, town entrances, bus stations, taxi stations, rest areas and so forth.

Investing in people and mediations has also become more and more difficult in this configuration, demographic change even makes it impossible. Government of people rather than territories was based on genealogical knowledge of major families and tribes and on stratification according to prescribed statuses (*chorfa*, *igourramen*, *haratin*). This close knowledge of groups and networks of loyalty meant a knowledge of individuals was not essential. In 1936, Morocco's population was 7,244,136—European colonisers included. Some 258,567 of them lived in Casablanca, which laid the foundation for its future as a metropolis. By comparison, imperial cities like Marrakech or Fez had no more than 200,000 inhabitants, and Rabat had fewer than 100,000. In 1960, there were already 11,625,000 Moroccans. By 2019, Morocco had 35,481,848 residents, of which nearly one third were under 15 years old and more than 60% lived in towns. This number also excluded Moroccans living overseas. This change in dimension calls for the use of biometrics and the generalisation of national identity cards and makes

CONCLUSION

it almost impossible to rely on management by interpersonal knowledge and relations, even though the principle of family lines has not disappeared. The latter remains relevant due to the persistence of important families in Fez, Rabat, Salé and Tétouan, the updating of genealogies with cohorts from preparatory school classes and other elite institutions or the use of the *nisba*.

Finally, a third important change has redefined and enlarged Moroccan territory, restoring its imperial dimension somewhat—the invention of the administrative category "Moroccans of the world" and the revival of the strategic interest in Africa and the way it is staged. The reactivation—via the CGEM—of old nineteenth-century networks in West Africa, in the form of spiritual kinship or fraternity, provides the King's very personal ambition with imperial overtones and marks his wanderings with the yellow of the traditional babouche shoes and the millions of Mohammadian Qur'ans distributed along the way.[16] The same is true of the launch of the "thirteenth region", also by the CGEM,[17] in the form of a digital platform to bring together the various Moroccan diasporas scattered around the world. More than merely a communication gadget, this platform illustrates the power of the imaginary that incorporates the colours of the past into a technologically sophisticated framework and puts long-established artforms of government to the test.[18] In return, this population of nearly four million people—nearly one Moroccan in ten—makes it possible to reshape the codes that constitute social and political links, accelerating shifts in the moods of government and in living standards. Their online presence, combined with a physical presence in summer (more than a million cross the Strait of Gibraltar every season), their contribution to social movements and their dual allegiance (most are binationals) have already helped to change mentalities.

This book has explored several kinds of changes, which have been approached through the idea of shifting meanings, the emergence of new values and behaviour marked with the seal of ambivalence. Institutional changes, presented in the public debate as innovations, regressions or breaking points, may in fact prove to be less important, even ambiguous and paradoxical. Not because they suffer from insincerity of those in government, the hyper-

227

WEAVING POLITICAL TIME IN MOROCCO

power of the *Makhzen* or the immaturity of society, as has been often argued, with claims of "blockages" or "regressions". On the contrary, we consider that these actors operate in good faith and take them at their word. This assumption, which may seem naive and recklessly optimistic, has the advantage of revealing the understandings that are shared and those that are in competition, compromises based on misunderstandings and conflicts that the power relations in society fail to change or in fact push into stalemate situations.

This is the case, for example, for the independence of the justice system and the emancipation of the prosecutor's office from the tutelage of the government, a principle that is now inscribed in the constitution. These reforms, demanded by the most progressive actors in the political field according to international standards, are the result of the work of the IER and a broader dialogue with civil society and are rightly presented as being revolutionary. The concrete implementation of the reform, stemming from a framework engineered by the most advanced democracies, along with the irreproachable composition of a senior council for the magistrature, nevertheless provoke scepticism and uneasiness. Indeed, these institutional shifts are driven by conservative and sometimes incompetent judges who accept autonomy but refuse independence. Their understanding of the latter makes them mistrustful of politics and politicians (in other words of elected representatives and the government they constitute), preferring the Sharifian parasol that shades and protects them from any accountability on judicial policy. They are autonomous but not fully independent and are convinced that they are the heirs to a judiciary delegated by the Caliph. As a result, it is impossible for them to develop a self-awareness that would protect them from the temptation of serving the prince rather than the rule of law. The ultimate paradox is that their legal culture, which is in principle distinct from religion, disconnects them from the ethos of the *cadi* who is responsible before God, yet without inculcating in them the ethos of the judge whose conscience is framed by a corporation that shares a universal understanding of justice. The shade of the imperial parasol frees them of any responsibility towards those under their jurisdiction

CONCLUSION

and leads them, at best, to a positivism marked with the brutality of the security laws of the present day, and at worst, to an anticipation of the unfathomable will of the prince and a desire to be more royalist than the King.

Other examples suggest changes that are not really changes, particularly because of an imaginary that weaves time, reducing distances between remote time scales. This is the case of the 2011 constitution, which both increases the importance of elections and promotes the principles of "third generation constitutions", explicitly recording social and economic rights and above all questions of governance, participation and accountability. The constitutionalisation of a dozen regulatory councils and agencies has resulted in an increasing number of co-optations that favour political bargaining and the consolidation of patronage. Above all, political actors have proved themselves unable to use the leverage available because they are so imbued with the principle, a legacy of Moroccan history, that only a strong King—a *deus ex machina*—is able to overcome problems and resolve political tensions. The archetypal illustration of this is the spread of demands for royal pardons, special derogations and interventions by the King through both the population and the political class.

Inversely, institutional changes presented as minor, technical or sometimes simple adjustments may in fact prove to be decisive. This is the case for the emblematic issue of women's access to professions in the legal system, particularly that of the *'adel*.[19] In spite of the fact that it was presented and appeared as a mere technicality, the controversy provoked by this top-down change suggests it was a major transformation. Religious conservatives intuitively understood this, including those working within the state apparatus who organised the rebellion. Although granting women access to the professions of judges and lawyers had provoked little debate, opposition to women becoming *'adel* went beyond the country's borders, with the most ferocious opponents coming from the Middle East. The conservative position is understandable—even though there are only a few dozen women *'adel*, the access to this profession is a head-on "threat" to male hegemony in a society that continues to give precedence to male testimony in

WEAVING POLITICAL TIME IN MOROCCO

material facts, proof of paternity, marriage or property, for example. The same is true for another important change that went unnoticed—transmission of nationality by women, firstly to their children and probably soon to their husbands. This reform was implicitly announced and defended by a minority of female activists. Nevertheless it constitutes a revolution in a country that is based on patrilineal transmission because it challenges the foundation of patriarchal society. In a completely different domain, that of taxation, which is almost entirely absent from public debate, a technical measure like the digitalisation of tax declarations and payments, associated with the possibility of tracing banking movements, also raises unprecedented questions about the link between the citizen and the state, well beyond issues of tax evasion.

The examples mentioned here, and above all the demonstration presented over the course of this book, show that changes presented as major may in reality be inconsequential, not produce the effects hoped for, have the opposite effects or even change meaning entirely due to misunderstandings. Inversely, changes that may seem to be minor may in reality have a deep impact on the anthropological foundations of society and result in shifting concepts and meanings. Because these changes take different directions and occur through heterogenous mediations, it is difficult to rank them on a continuum that would go from modernisation and democratic development at one extreme, to tensions and the restoration of authoritarianism at the other. Moreover, because these changes depend on power relations that are necessarily specific, shifting and particular to a given context, they are "indeterminate."[20] This means it is impossible to describe them according to their contributions to a pre-conceived idea of progress.

Over the course of these Moroccan wanderings, we have sought to capture the multiple ways in which the "compulsory" nature of order—whatever emotions it might provoke—are maintained, altered, transformed or even dissolved. As we reach the end of this book, it has become clear that these changes are not the result of external action but of the interplay between ambivalences, understandings and the subjective idea of the legality of that order or its legitimate necessity and particularly around the transformations of

CONCLUSION

the signification of social relations themselves. It is through the mediation of "meaning" (even though this is constantly elusive) that it is possible to grasp these tipping points in which traditional formulations are erased and replaced by new, emerging ones.

As we have shown over the course of these pages, actions have multiple significations. Reforms, decisions and social actions more generally may be subject to plural interpretations and initial logics or intentions may be overturned and reinterpreted in a sense completely opposite from their original purpose. Consequently, we can only hypothesise as to the decisive or inconsequential nature of a given action, on whether a particular shift in mentality is significant or not in terms of domination or emancipation. This is particularly true given that we forbade ourselves from considering facts—whether thought to be central or anodyne—as part of a chain of known and predetermined causality. The same is also true for responsibility. Shifts in the meaning of responsibility are difficult to understand in the context of their processes and effects, even though there can be no doubt that the question of responsibility and accountability must now take into consideration the importance of public opinion. In this respect, the case of the Spanish paedophile pardoned in August 2003 in the context of a visit from the Spanish King Juan Carlos to Morocco clearly constituted one of the tipping points in the meaning of political responsibility—the shift from the sovereign responsible "for" the people, to a sovereign responsible "towards" the people.[21] This was in fact the first time that the King's responsibility was challenged on a social issue, when historically it had only ever been so over questions to do with religion or the state.[22] It was more of a tipping point than the 2011 constitution in which article 58 simply formalises the emotion expressed when this criminal was pardoned, with no guarantees of implementation. The temporary compromise as it stands today does not draw all the conclusions from the King's responsibility, but cracks have appeared that challenge the shared belief that he is a victim of his entourage.

Another series of seemingly trivial facts also seem indicative of these new paradoxical processes, and above all the unexpected moments of transformation that may begin in private and intimate

WEAVING POLITICAL TIME IN MOROCCO

spheres, even when these spheres concern the *dar-al-Makhzen*. Mohammed VI's arrival on the throne was associated with several decisions ostentatiously staged to affirm a desire for transformation. These decisions were perceived as private decisions full of political intent; they concerned court matters, such as the simplification of protocol, abandonment of hand-kissing, royal cars stopping at red lights and at the King's personal request for the separation of work and leisure time, the dissolution of the harem and even the publicisation and media coverage of the sovereign's wife. The progressive reversal of these changes, and the equally ostentatious return of court protocol, were only possible for the formal apparatus. The minor changes in the private sphere that fed the chronicles of the court continued to take place, and it is our view that they constituted moments of tension between two ages or even two vectors of a shift in meaning. For example, the publicity surrounding the separation between the King and his wife and the exile of the latter, or the remarriage of the King's mother after the death of Hassan II, and the rumour of her divorce, did not provoke much surprise. These events are not merely court gossip or even just changes in the mores of the court—they reflect much deeper change. Henceforth, it is the broader society that produces hegemonic culture. We would be tempted to say that in this particular case, *dar-al-Makhzen*, which previously drew on the expertise of the urban bourgeoisie and the energies of dissident tribes—in the form of horses or women given as gifts or captured during *harka*—to validate and spread norms through different channels in society, has lost the prerogative of the transmission of knowledge, values and lifestyles.

This impression of a loss of control over the production of symbolic values of cohesion is reinforced by many things. Our overview of the artforms of government described in the Prolegomenon encourages us to note a loss of competency, which is linked as much to the personality of the King and his style and to the transformations of society and forms of communication, as it is to the degradation of socialising mechanisms within the court, including in its bureaucratised intermediaries (the royal cabinet, the authority agent entities of the Ministry of the Interior or the Ulema of the

CONCLUSION

Senior Council and Regional Councils). Over the course of this book, we have seen competencies such as the close knowledge of elites and genealogies, the science behind intrigues and arbitrations, the artforms of casting and appointments, the virtuosity of letter writing, the production of statuses, the art of comparing sources of information, the cultivation of diverse networks of intermediaries and the broadening of interactions with all kinds of social groups. All this knowledge is now the exclusive domain of a minor group of "prelates" who are in danger of becoming extinct.

GLOSSARY

LIST OF ARABIC AND BERBER TERMS USED*

'Amal (Al-Amal)	law in action
Ahl	people
Adoul (sing. *'adel*)	traditional notary
Amane	(guarantee of) security
Amazal (Amazigh/Berber)	official responsible for the distribution of water (especially for irrigation)
Amghar (Amazigh/Berber)	title of an eminent figure in the community
Awbach (Moroccan Arabic)	worse than nothing, dregs of society
Bay'ah	allegiance (allegiance ceremony)
Baraka	blessings; to be blessed
Bour (Moroccan Arabic)	zone of pluvial (or rain-fed) agriculture
Bled (Moroccan Arabic)	country; region
Bled siba	break-away region; dissent region
Bled makhzen	submitted region

---

* Most of the terms in the glossary are in classical Arabic. In the inverse case (Berber or dialectal Arabic), the language is mentioned.

GLOSSARY

Cadi	judge, jurisconsult
Caid	authority figures; tribe chief
Chfa'a	right of pre-emption in favour of an owner in joint ownership
Sharia	Muslim law
Chechia (Moroccan Arabic)	traditional red hat
Chorfa	descendant of the Prophet; eminent figure
Chikaya	claim, grievances of the people
Dahir	Sultanic edict, royal law or decree
Dahir de tawqir wa al-ihtiram	edict on respectability
Darija	Moroccan Arabic
Dar-al-makhzen	palace, enclosures, palace outbuildings
Dhimmi	protected people in the Empire (Jewish or Christian)
Drari (sing. *derri*) (Moroccan Arabic)	street children
Fann	art
Foqaha	scholars, ulema
Fassad	corruption
Fiqh	jurisprudence, Islamic law
Fatwa	religious opinion, response to a consultation on the basis of Islamic law and tradition
Fitna	anarchy, rebellion
Guich	army, tribe mobilised as an army; land of mobilised tribes
Habous	religious foundation/charity
Haiba	reverential fear
Haj	pilgrimage to Mecca

GLOSSARY

Hajeb	chamberlain
Handassa	engineering expertise
Hania (Moroccan Arabic)	peaceful
Haratin (sing. *hartani*)	Black people
Harka	military campaigns
Hdya	the presentation of blessings and gifts during religious celebrations
Hijab	veil
Hirak	in revolt, in motion; protest movement
Hôrm	sacred enclosure within a mosque, zawiya or marabout; holy space
Igourramen (sing. *agourram*)	man of good omen
Isnad	the chain of those who vouch for information connected to the Prophet
Istiqlal	Independence
Jihad	holy war
Jma'a	deliberative assembly of heads of household
Khadim	servant of the prince
Khalifa	Viceroy
Khatib	preacher, the person who delivers the Friday prayer sermon
Khettara (Moroccan Arabic)	traditional irrigation system
Koutla	coalition, league
Kulfa	trials
Lamalif	letter of the alphabet; here the title of the journal *Lamalif*
Maqassid	finalities
Maakoul (Moroccan Arabic)	rigour

237

GLOSSARY

Malik	King
Mohatassib ou mohtasseb	a public servant responsible for controls and accounting, weights and measurement and quality control and possibly good morality
Makhzen	literally warehouse; here administration, Moroccan state
Moussem	festive pilgrimage celebrating a saint
Mourabit	Holy man
Maslaha	service (public service), general interest
Mehalla	movements of the court
Moucharit	contractual man
Moudawana	personal status code
Mechouar	square in front of the palace
Muqaddam	authority auxiliaries at neighbourhood or *douar* level; brotherhood leader
Naib (pl. *nouab*)	representative of populations belonging to an ethnic community for the management of collective lands
Nisba	descendance, genealogical belonging
Ulema	theologian
Ummah	community of the faithful but also national community
Oussoul	foundations
Oussoul al-fikh	foundation of Islamic jurisprudence and law
Qaida	traditions; rules of conduct, know-how and interpersonal skills; etiquette
Siba	dissent, rebellion, disorder
Silslat	chain of transmission
Sira	prophetic practice
Syassa	politics, government

GLOSSARY

Semsar	informal courtier
Taghr	towns or barracks-towns (ribat) vulnerable to invasion
Taleb (pl. *tolba*)	master of a Qur'anic school
Targa (Amazigh/Berber)	water channel
Tacharouk	participation; association
Touiza (Moroccan Arabic)	collective mutual assistance
Wali	equivalent of a prefect
Waqf	*see* Habous
Watan	nation
Ztata (Moroccan Arabic)	passers

pp. [xv–5]

NOTES

PREFACE TO THE ENGLISH EDITION

1. See in particular chapters 2, 4 and 7 of the French edition (Hibou and Tozy 2020).
2. Grossein 2016b: 16–20.
3. Geertz 1973; Warnier 1999; Bayart and Warnier 2004.
4. This approach is particularly inspired by Ginzburg (1980a; 1980b;1990); Levi (1988); Colonna and Le Pape (2010). It was above all nourished by our close association with colleague and friend Irene Bono, whose work on the national in Morocco is specifically articulated around the notion of traces and clues. See Bono (2024).

INTRODUCTION

1. This definition by Max Weber (1904) is quoted here from the translation by Hans Henrik Bruun (2012: 130), Weber's emphasis. It is worth quoting in full as it clearly justifies our approach. It also resonates with the world of Michel Foucault and his concept of "governmentality" (Foucault 2004a), Jean-François Bayart and his concept of the "rhizome-state" (Bayart 1989), or "politics from below" (Bayart 1981), or John Lonsdale and his distinction between the "building" and "formation" of the state (Lonsdale 1989; Berman and Lonsdale 1992).
2. Hibou 2011.
3. Breuer reminds us that for Weber, democracy is a way of finding compromise, however uncomfortable, and not a philosophy lecture or moral education for the purposes of the true, the good and the beautiful (Breuer 2010: 8).
4. Brown 1978.
5. To use the expression proposed by Al-'Azm 1981.
6. Sharabi 1988.
7. In Morocco, the term "tribe" does not have the same colonial connotation as in

pp. [5–11] NOTES

sub-Saharan Africa, for example. It is still used in everyday language as well as politics. The tribe is even a legal entity with rights over 15 million hectares of collective land.

8. Hammoudi 1997.

9. Gardet 1956.

10. All these expressions come from Weber 2001 [1910]: 106.

11. An ideal type "is a mental image that is not historical reality ... still less is meant to serve as a schema into which it would be possible to fit reality as a specimen." Weber 2012 [1904]: 126.

12. For Weber it is just as possible to construct ideal types of brothels as well as of religions. Weber 2012 [1904]: 130.

13. On the Maghreb region, including Morocco see: Hermassi 1972; Leca and Schemeil 1983; Saaf 1991; Sharabi 1988.

14. Weber 1978 [1922]: 212–302; Linz and Stepan 1996; Linz 2000.

15. This observation, which is very true, was made by Irene Bono, who remarked that the Italian nation-state model did not place unity at the centre (most likely true for the German and Swiss models also).

16. Foucault 2004a; 2004b.

17. Weber 1978 [1922]: 20–1.

18. Grossein 2016a: 60–3.

19. In this book, Empire (with a capital E) refers to this register of the state, a figure constructed for conceptual purposes, an ideal type therefore, whereas empire (lower case) refers to a concrete historical experience, and here, for the most part, the Sharifian empire. The same applies to the nation-state. Nation-state (with a capital N) refers to the ideal type whereas nation-state (with lower case) refers to a concrete historical experience. Although it does not reflect common usage, this choice was made to better support and clarify our demonstration.

20. Formerly an edict from the sultan, the *dahir* is now a law or a royal decree.

21. This is generally translated as interpretative sociology even though it is more about *understanding* than interpretation. See Grossein 2016b.

22. Bezzaz 1992; Rosenberger and Triki 1973; 1974; Rosenberger 1977.

23. Hibou 1999.

24. Up until the Protectorate, the *Makhzen* referred to the royal house and then to the state apparatus of the Sharifian empire. Today, the term refers to a "form of government of the people" (Claisse 1992: 286) but also, and above all, to a "way of being and doing, which resides in words, spices up meals, celebrates weddings, weaves the fabric of circumstance and establishes the key rituals determining the form and content of the relationship between those who govern and those who are governed." (Tozy 1991a: 158). See also Cherifi 1988.

25. "*Dar-al-Makhzen* is a particular area in the royal palaces and their outbuildings. It is the site of reverential fear (*haiba*) which constitutes the foundation of power" (Tozy 1999: 43). "*Dar-al-Makhzen* is the central place where the culture of power is constructed. It is here that the codes of obedience and commandment

NOTES

pp. [11–14]

are conveyed" (*ibid*: 40). It is also the place of construction for the marks (*qaida*) and knowledge of good conduct in the halls of power, whether in court or other institutions: *Makhzen*, parliament, political parties, families, etc. This is what the nineteenth-century correspondence called *Makhzenyia*.

26. The most influential reference text in recent years is undoubtedly that by Burbank and Cooper (2010). See also: Eisenstadt 1963; Barkey and von Hagen 1997; Tilly 1997; Veinstein 2017.

27. At least those of the majority that take a linear vision of the transformations of the state, considering empire as an obsolete form, characteristic of a particular moment in history, prior to the advent of the nation-state. There are of course exceptions to this, for example, Bayly (2004), particularly the third part, or Kumar (2017), who does not consider empire and the nation as two successive and antithetical forms of the state. However, unlike us, these authors study past situations, and although they note the relevance of research on empire, as historians they do not concretely analyse contemporary situations from this perspective.

28. Certain studies on colonial empires have been attentive to this cohabitation and particularly to the fact that the nation state was shaped by empire and by globalisation more generally. See, for example, Cooper and Stoler 1997; Cooper 2005; Steinmetz 2013; Sawyer 2014; Kumar 2017; Fradera 2018. Wilder 2005 and Lignereux 2012 talk about an "imperial nation state" for example.

29. When we refer to the "art of governing" in this book we are specifically thinking of an art as something that is both technical and creative but is above all a set of expertise and a form of mastery. This notion will be presented in more detail in the Prolegomenon.

30. In the Foucauldian sense of *dispositif*.

31. This is not unrelated to what Clifford Geertz had to say about culture (Geertz 1973) or Jacques Berque about collective identity (Berque 1978/2001: 327–333), but it has the advantage of avoiding the pitfalls of those two notions.

32. Veyne 1988.

33. Deleuze 1990: 65.

34. Castoriadis 1975: 170.

35. Debarbieux who, taking issue with Benedict Anderson (1991), added that, "what specifies imagination is not that it fills an absence. It is the vector by which an individual connects his/her direct experience to very varied things .... Only some arise from absence." (2015: 9)

36. Bayart 1996: 137.

37. *Ibid.*, also Geertz 1973.

38. As shown by Marc Bloch, who talks about the "twofold act" of instrumentalisation and adhesion, quoted by Bayart 1996: 163.

39. Weber 2012 [1907]: 209.

40. Grossein 2016b: 8.

41. Meeker 2002.

243

pp. [14–21] NOTES

42. Levi 1988.
43. These different modes of production, in opposition to the capitalist mode, are the feudalist mode (Benali 1969) or the "composite mode" (Pascon 1971).
44. Green 2000; Chesnaux 2004.
45. In the Sharifian empire the "*caid* of the stables" (the *caid rwa* in Arabic) was responsible for the Sultan's horses and stables. He accompanied him in all his movements.
46. These are different Moroccan dynasties. The Almoravids reigned from 1060 to 1147, the Almohads from 1145 to 1248, the Marinids from 1244 to 1465 and the Saadians from 1564 to 1659.
47. A Senegalese national dish.
48. Tozy 1991a. This expression (deactivated—*désamorcé* in French) has become popular among specialists of Morocco and the Arab world more broadly, but it has often been misunderstood. It was interpreted as the expression of depoliticisation and neutralisation of politics, but for Tozy it refers to a phenomenon that is much more complex and ambivalent, in which politics is expressed differently and indirectly in order to address the constraints of domination but is no less affirmative in other spaces and forms of expression. From this perspective there is no Power but only power relations that are constantly shifting. The stakes are therefore not in accessing or taking power but in having enough power to impact decisions and influence them and to change power relations. This is undeniably a way of being political or conducting politics.
49. Gluckman (1968) states that each institution or cultural system has its own type of timescale, a specific temporality for its effectiveness. This is what he calls "structural duration".
50. As Hartog 2003 developed it.
51. For a good overview, see Dubar 2008.
52. Bloch 1992 [1941].
53. Husserl 1964 [1928]; Bergson 1999 [1922].
54. Hobsbawm and Ranger 1983.
55. Bayart 2022.
56. Bergson 2002 [1908]; 1998 [1907].
57. Chesnaux 2004 talks about the domination of "technico-economic, constrained, dominating, imperialist time", over "personal, free, autonomous and democratic time". This conception reflects that defended by Hannah Arendt (1958).
58. Certeau 2000 [1987].
59. Tozy (1999: 266*ff*) explains how this functions in the everyday lives of the followers of the Tabligh movement. On the concept of *sira*, see Hussein (2007).
60. Grossein 2016a.

PROLEGOMENON: THE MOROCCAN STATE OVER TIME

1. ICJ 1975: 34/42.

NOTES

pp. [22–25]

2. *Ibid.*: 34/42.
3. *Ibid.*: 36/44.
4. *Ibid.*: 36/44.
5. The advisory opinion of 1975 concludes: "The materials and information presented to the Court show the existence, at the time of Spanish colonization, of legal ties of allegiance between the Sultan of Morocco and some of the tribes living in the territory of Western Sahara. They equally show the existence of rights, including some rights relating to the land, which constituted legal ties between the Mauritanian entity, as understood by the Court, and the territory of Western Sahara. On the other hand, the Court's conclusion is that the materials and information presented to it do not establish any tie of territorial sovereignty between the territory of Western Sahara and the Kingdom of Morocco or the Mauritanian entity. Thus, the Court has not found legal ties of such a nature as might affect the application of resolution 1514 (XV) in the decolonization of Western Sahara and, in particular, of the principle of self-determination through the free and genuine expression of the will of the peoples of the Territory."
6. *Cahiers du Sahara* 2015.
7. On the reformist paradigm, see *Hespéris-Tamuda* 2001 and more specifically Roussillon 2001a; 2001b; Baida 2001 and Kaddouri 2001. See also: Ahmida 2002; El Mansour 1990; Simou 1995; Tuzani 1979.
8. *Taghr* towns, or barracks-towns, like Tangiers, Larache or Safi, are not only barracks (*ribat*). They are towns that are vulnerable to invasion, which has a series of consequences ranging from political organisation and the skills required of leaders, to the conditions for religious practice. A frequent Muslim tradition, referring to verse 69 of Surat 29 (known as The Spider) is the basis for this particularity, linked to the status of soldiers, which residents in these cities mostly are. In Mohammed Abdel-Haleem's translation of the *Qur'an*, this verse reads, "We shall be sure to guide to Our ways those who strive hard for Our cause: God is with those who do good."
9. The example of Tétouan's administration cannot be generalised to other cities, however. Fez, for example, demonstrated co-management with notables and deep municipal power during the Tanners' Revolt in 1873–4. See Sebti 1991.
10. This is proposed by Léopold Victor Justinard and repeated in many texts: Justinard (1925; 1926; 1954).
11. This interpretation is shared by Mohammed Mokhtar Soussi (Al-Susi 1966) and by Mohammed Ennaji and Paul Pascon (Ennaji and Pascon 1988).
12. El Mohammadi 2010; 2014.
13. The Madrid conference served to open the doors of the Sharifian empire to European powers, particularly by allowing their citizens to own land and assets in Morocco. For many, it marked the beginning of the internationalisation of the "Moroccan affair".
14. Ahmida 2002.

245

pp. [25–30]   NOTES

15. In Arabic literature, the term means "training" in the context of breeding and training horses and implies domination without violence. See Moudden (2018: 92–93). In the Amazigh language, the word *assayss*, which is probably not connected to the etymology of *syassa*, evokes, in the context of the Ahwash dance, the dance space, the village square, an agora where a kind of joust between poets is performed. In Amazigh, politics is termed *tasrtit*, which reflects the Arabic meaning of *syassa* or *tanbat*, which means government.

16. Strictly speaking a *taleb* is the master of a Qur'anic school, but more generally, he is a figure who acts as an imam and teaches the Qur'an to young children. As a local notable, he may also act as an intermediary of the state, as is the case here.

17. Ennaji and Pascon 1988: 13.

18. See Lakhsassi and Tozy 2000: 183–214.

19. Ennaji and Pascon 1988: 15.

20. In the long biography that his grandson Soussi wrote on him, the latter noted that his grandfather did not die wealthy although he lived in abundance. His notoriety and virtuosity allowed him to become a respected Ulema, required for the decisions and rulings involving successions, in addition to his role as *taleb moucharit* of a Madrasa of some one hundred young *tolba* (plural of *taleb*). Writing acts of succession brought him between 3% and 5% of whatever the inheritance in question was estimated at, and the edict of respectability from the sultan exempted him from certain tasks and taxes owing to the state, protected him from exactions from local potentates and allowed him to claim for himself the dues owed by the people of Maader. Soussi recounts that "one day the *taleb* had received so much butter in donations that he had no more jars to keep it in. He had to empty a bedroom, where he washed the floor to store the butter" (Al-Susi 1966: t. 5, 179).

21. On the importance of these documents and archives from "adouls", see Bussellam 1994.

22. Daoud 1966.

23. Abdelkader Aachaach had previously been governor of the city under the Sultan Abderrahman, between 1844 and 1850, before the Spanish took the city in 1860.

24. Letter of 14 April 1862.

25. Letter of 20 May 1862.

26. Letter of 25 April 1862.

27. Letter of 6 May 1862.

28. Letter of 20 August 1862.

29. Letter of 10 May 1862.

30. A public servant responsible for controls and accounting, weights and measurement and quality control.

31. This is the Benhima family from Safi. One of its descendants, Driss, an engineer who graduated from the prestigious French school, *Ponts et Chaussées*, will figure in chapters 3 and 6.

NOTES

pp. [30–36]

32. This is the Azziman family from Tétouan, whose descendent, Omar, was also a lawyer and features in chapters 2 and 6.
33. Letter of 13 September 1862.
34. Letter of 1 January 1863.
35. Cf. the title of the book by Louis Arnaud (1952).
36. Abitbol 2009; Mouline 2009.
37. Ibn Zaidane 1962: 4.
38. On the importance of writing and written regulations, see also Pascon 1978; Lydon 2009; Warsheid 2017.
39. Expressions used by Boutier, Landi and Rouchon (2009: 13) in reference to fourteenth—eighteenth century Italy.
40. Ennaji 1992.
41. Boutier, Landi and Rouchon 2009: 11.
42. This is clearly not limited to the Sharifian empire but can be seen in many other polycentric situations governed at a distance. For the case of Italy in the fourteenth—eighteenth centuries, see Boutier, Dewerpe and Nordman 1984 and Boutier, Landi and Rouchon 2009.
43. Fumey 1903; Pascon 1975–77: 165*ff.*
44. Pascon and Ennaji (1988) distinguish letters *in themselves* (content) and letters *for themselves* (utilitarian, orders, notes, tickets, quasi-vulgar).
45. From a comparative perspective, see Brown 1992 or Chartier 1991.
46. Ibn Zaidane 1962: 40.
47. Moudden 1995.
48. In addition to Moudden 1995, see Aafif 1980–81; Nordman 1980–81; 1986; Dakhlia 1988; Benhima 2016; Jamous 2017.
49. This is one of the most common characteristics of the imperial state and not only in far-off times when nomadic lifestyles were important, such as for the Mongols (see Lefèvre 2007; Burbank and Cooper 2010). It can be seen in more recent political formations, such as the Angevin empire (see Madeline 2014) or in the Germanic kingdoms. Weber reminds us (1978 [1922]: 1042) that the German monarchs of the Middle Ages "moved about almost constantly" because it was only their constantly renewed presence that sustained their authority over their subjects. In France, it was not until the reign of Louis XIV that the court ceased to move around. Weber (ibid.) speaks of this constant travelling as a form of government that renews and updates the reality of the ruler's authority by their personal presence.
50. Ibn Zaidane 1962: vol. 1, 189–270.
51. The nomadic backdrop explains this connection in Moroccan society between mobility and the impression of improvisation. It is not only shepherds who are mobile; people in general move around easily, for example in very small towns around the saints during the *mawsim*. And the caterer, as a person who provides food for others, is the embodiment of this, both for their much-appreciated culinary skills but also because they are essential to socialisation, particularly in towns. See Hibou and Tozy 2015b.

247

pp. [37–42]   NOTES

52. For the letter in which the sultan instructs the governor of Tétouan to place his servants (slaves) with bourgeois families in the town so they can learn culinary skills, see Daoud 1966: vol. 6, 284.
53. *Ibid.*: 426.
54. Lakhsassi and Sebti 1999.
55. Ibn Zaidane 1962: vol. 1, 127–131 and 175.
56. Ennaji and Tozy 1987b: 72.
57. Gellner 1969b.
58. As Hassan I himself put it. See Nasiri 1997 [1907]: vol. 9, 175.
59. This servitude to religious time has not disappeared, as we can see in the fact that Mohammed VI is obliged to return to Morocco for Ramadan and religious celebrations.
60. See, among others, Rivet 1988; Hoisington 1995; Jobin 2014.
61. A multitude of sensibilities were represented within the colonial Protectorate. This opposition in fact began well before the Protectorate. It began with an opposition between the producers of the "scientific mission" run by Le Chatelier and the Algiers group and later another between the mission and those behind Moroccan colonial policy, the reform of the *Makhzen*, direct administration and tribal policy (see Burke III 1979; Rivet 1988: vol. 1, 20–37). It then continued into the implementation of colonial policy. The balance between the various factions that can be seen in the unfinished legal texts resulted in numerous ambiguities, such as the 1919 *dahir* on collective land (see Chapter 4). This can also be seen in the actions conducted in the name of an avant-gardist idea of progress, such as the urban developments in Casablanca by architects Prost and Ecochard (see Ecochard 1955; Frey 2004) or the late modernisation of the rural environment (Berque 1958b; 1963).
62. Rivet 1988: vol. 1, 40–47; Guillen 1967.
63. The most emblematic text of this period is a kind of summary of the first ten years of the Protectorate, written by Lyautey's team while he was at his height, see *La Renaissance du Maroc: dix ans de protectorat, 1912–1922*, Rabat, Résidence générale de la République française au Maroc, 1922.
64. Indirect rule and government by traditionalisation are typical of Victorian colonialism, for example with the Maharajas in the Raj (see Cohn 1996; Bayly 2004; Markovits 2017). British historiography recognises Lyautey's proximity to indirect rule (for example Sebe 2015, Chapter 4). Recent studies are more nuanced however regarding this influence. They show that Lyautey did not meet Lord Lugard until later, in the 1920s, and emphasised the influence of Victorian engineer Charles Hartley, whom he met in 1893 (see Finch 2018).
65. Burke III 2014.
66. Rivet 1988: vol. 1, 158–63.
67. "The Sultan Moulay Youssef recently re-established a traditional role within the court: the officer with the bag (*moul ach-chkara*), whose place in the parade is among those charged with ablutions. On his back he carries a leather backpack

NOTES

pp. [42–47]

full of coins, attached to his chest with silk straps. He hands out alms to the poor when the sultan gives him the order to." *Ibid.*: 111.

68. On indirect government by the grand *caids*, see Justinard 1951; Pascon 1978: vol. 1, 293–369; Julien 1978: 109–11.

69. Baita 1987; Burke III 2014.

70. "I would not hesitate to express my preference for the regime of the grand chief, it is more in keeping with the methods of the Protectorate. It is more flexible, less costly, requires less staff, demands less time and ensures greater respect for customs and traditions." Quoted, in French, by Rivet 1988: vol. 1, 190.

71. Pascon 1978.

72. Taoufiq 1983: 493. The author is referring here to the different counter-powers that limited arbitrariness by *caids* appointed by the *Makhzen*. In addition to the right to dissidence, which underpinned the empire, he mentions the existence of deliberative assemblies, the autonomy of the *cadis*, the control of the central Makhzen by local informers in direct contact with the sultan, as well as the fuelling of internal oppositions and a dynamic of contenders for power.

73. Tozy 1981.

74. Inspiration from socialism had a strong presence as far back as the 1930s, as we can see in the connections to the *Front Populaire* but fully blossomed in the 1950s. This context encouraged a demand for reforms, the experience of the journal *Maghreb* (run by the socialist lawyer, Robert-Jean Longuet, with the collaboration of, among others, Balafrej, Ouazzani, Ben Abdeljalil, Lyazidi, etc.) and the condemnation by certain French socialists of dealings between the Residence and Catholic spheres, which would lead them to support the nationalists in the condemnation of "Berber" policy. See Julien 1978: 180.

75. Under the stewardship of Edgar Faure, the discussions—and not negotiations—involved three groups: the traditionalists, the "assumed collaborators" of the Protectorate authorities such as the Grand Vizier, Al-Muqri, the Pashas of Agadir, Meknes and Casablanca, the *caids* of Zaër and Ait Ayach; moderate nationalists such as the former Pasha of Fez Fatmi Benslimane and the Pasha of Rabat Abbass Tazi, who were not insisting on the sultan's return from exile; then there were the supporters of Istiqlal and the Shura parties, the former represented by Mohammed Lyazidi, Mehdi Ben Barka, Omar Ben Abdeljlil, Abderrahim Bouabid and Mhammed Boucetta and the latter by Mohammed Cherkaoui and Abdelhadi Boutaleb. They were defending the idea of an abrogation of the Treaty of Fez and an immediate return of the sultan. See Faure 1984.

76. The first Bekkay government included ten ministers from the Istiqlal, six from Ouzzani's Democratic Independence Party (PDI), four independents not counting Ahmed Reda Guedira, who represented the Moroccan Liberal Party. In the second Bekkay government, the Istiqlal gained an additional minister, and Rachid Mouline from the Liberal Party joined the government. The independents close to the King, whose status had been previously recognised by the former Protectorate authorities, took up key positions, such as Council President

pp. [47–50] NOTES

(Bekkay) and his deputy, Mohammed Zeghari, as well as Minister of the Interior (Lahcen Lyoussi) and Health Minister (Faraj).

77. On 8 November 1955, Thami El Glaoui left Marrakech for Paris where the sultan, having returned from exile in Madagascar, was finalising his affairs before returning to Morocco as the figurehead of independence, newly won from the French. The sultan agreed to receive Thami El Glaoui but humiliated him as punishment for his support for the French during the deposition of Mohammed V in 1953 (Maxwell 1968: 314). In November 1955, the Pasha was pardoned and his house saved following this audience with Mohammed V. However, the investigative commission established by the *dahir* of 27 March 1958, once again included him in the list of figures condemned to national degradation and the confiscation of assets (16 August 1958). Thami Glaoui was later pardoned again, along with others, by the *dahir* of 8 November 1963. He died on 23 January 1956.

78. See below.

79. See among others, Mounjib 1992; Buttin 2010; Mouline 2016.

80. Which Moroccan historiography has tended to ignore until recently. For a critical review see Bono 2024.

81. The Sous, which was loyalist to the point of providing the core of the liberation army, also rebelled against what it considered the control of the Istiqlal. During this episode, the Majjat ransacked the residence of the Istiqlal *caid* Jmaat Tighirt. See Tozy 1988.

82. Gellner 1969a; 1962.

83. Hassan II 1976: 68.

84. In his interview with Eric Laurent, Hassan II—who pleaded amnesia over these early years of confrontation—did not hesitate to hand down his opinion as a kind of ruling on this question, saying "Listen Mr Laurent, I will give you some advice, or rather a very important recipe. If you wish to really know Morocco and not waste any time, never position the opposition or oppositions within this country as you would classify them elsewhere." Hassan II 1993: 49.

85. Collective 1976.

86. The documents published by the Centre Ben Saïd Aït Idder shed new light on this historic episode. See Slimani, Mansouri and Zakaria 2018.

87. The Koutla, literally "bloc", is a coalition of parties born out of the national movement in 1970, from an agreement between the Istiqlal party and the National Union of Popular Forces (UNFP), who came together to oppose the constitutional revision of July 1970. But the Koutla was suspended from 1972. Five years later a split within the UNFP led to the formation of the USFP, the Socialist Union of Popular Forces, which suspended the alliance for over a decade. The term Koutla then disappeared from political vocabulary until the early 1990s. Then, on 17 May 1992, a founding charter for the "Koutla addimoqratiya" was signed by the leaders of five parties. In addition to Abderrahmane Youssoufi, from the USFP and M'hamed Boucetta from Istiqlal, this "historic

NOTES

pp. [50–53]

alliance" also included Ali Yata, from the PPS ex-PCM, Mohammed Bensaïd Aït Idder, from the Organization of Democratic Popular Action (OADP, ancestor of the PSU) and Abdellah Ibrahim of the UNFP. Along with Hassan II, the Koutla embarked upon a long process of negotiation that led to what can be called a "consensual alternation" and the Youssoufi government, led by the USFP in 1998. See Bouaziz 1998 and Lahbabi 2009. See also http://www.jeuneafrique.com/mag/371715/politique/maroc-etait-koutla/

88. Laroui 2005.
89. Rollinde 2003: 133.
90. For details on the logistics and organisation of the Green March, see Bardonnet et al. 1989.
91. This was how Hassan II himself described it some years later. See Hassan II 1976.
92. Essoulami has been discussed in detail in another text. See Hibou and Tozy 2015b. In this context, the caterer is not merely responsible for meals. His job is to create the royal miracle of an encampment *ex nihilo* anywhere in the territory or outside it, that is to create what are today essentially cities that host royal festivities.
93. These measures led to bread riots in 1981, known as the "Casablanca riots" in Morocco, which were met with bloody repression leading to more than on 100 deaths (see chapter 2). For more on these riots, see the articles from the era in the journal *Lamalif* (Daoud 1981; Jibril 1981); Clément 1992; Le Saout and Rollinde 1999; Daoud 2007.
94. This was the case particularly around the negotiations on subcontracted management, for Lydec in Casablanca and Redal in Rabat, with its "fake-real" public debates. Interviews conducted in Casablanca and Rabat, November 1997, January 2000, February 2011 and March 2012. See also Catusse 2008.
95. This was of course not the case for institutions, but this reasoning was real for actors, particularly those from the left, "integrated" into public institutions over the course of the regime's liberalisation and the co-optation processes. See chapter 6 for examples.
96. For example, the OECD and later the BNDE (2005, https://www.lavieeco.com/news/economie/le-demantelement-de-la-bnde-coutera-2-milliards-de-dh-935.html).
97. This was typically the case of certain ministries, such as the Ministry of Finance, or bodies such as engineers or experts. Interviews in Casablanca and Rabat May 1997, June 2002, April 2013, May 2015. This dynamic can be seen in many countries on the continent, see Samuel 2013.
98. This speech, which was broadcast widely, was provoked by World Bank reports that criticised Morocco for its delay in reforms, for its breech of the state of law and for its flagrant shortcomings on social measures. Hassan II had himself asked that these reports be made public and incited public debate on the subject. See the media coverage of the time and the report itself: World Bank 1994.

251

pp. [55–64]   NOTES

99. See chapters 5 and 6.
100. The "*haras caid*" was the royal intendent who looked after the stables in the Sharifian empire. Interview, Casablanca, May 2011.
101. Even a figure as important as the *wali* (the equivalent of a prefect) is the fruit of this kind of process, both contingent and rationalised after the event, see Hachimi Alaoui 2016; 2019.
102. Ibn Khaldun 2014.

PART ONE: THE FOUNDATIONS OF POWER

1. While Minister for General Affairs and Governance, he had publicly come out in support of the Danone workers by participating in a sit-in organised on 5 June 2018 outside the company (see the news reports of 6 June and the following days).
2. To use the suggestive expressions employed by Jacques Berque in his discussion on collective identity (1978/2001: 327).

1. REPRESENTATION

1. In a long interview conducted in February 2017, Benkirane told Mohamed Tozy that the King had called the night of the vote as soon as the provisional results were in showing the PDJ was ahead. The mandate given to the PJD leader to form a government was announced the following day, just after the results were announced by the Minister of the Interior.
2. In 2011, during his nomination as head of government, the magazine *L'Express* wrote: "Another essential aspect in understanding Abdelilah Benkirane: he presents himself as deeply monarchist. 'We fully support the sultan' he proclaimed in 2008, and more recently 'I am a deep believer in the monarchy', adding that 'a Prime Minister who stands off against a king is not likely to succeed'." Addressing his successor on 19 November 2018, he said: "Your nomination is a pact between you and His Majesty … the party is important, but the State is more important." (https://www.yabiladi.com/articles/details/61570/abdelilah-benkirane-nous-sommes-monarchistes.html)
3. Nasiri 1907: 51; 1997: 134–8.
4. Nasiri 1907 86–95; 1997: 161–4.
5. This idea of sainthood and hagiographic legitimacy are found throughout the twentieth and twenty-first centuries, from Michaux-Bellaire (1925), Gellner (1969b), Waterbury (1970), Geertz (1971) Eickelman (1976), Munson (1993), Hammoudi (1997) and Bazzaz (2010) to Jamous (2017).
6. Michaux-Bellaire 1908.
7. Jamous 2017.
8. Since the sixteenth century onward, two Sharifian sovereign dynasties have dominated in Morocco. The first, the Saadis, reigned for nearly a century. They were

NOTES

pp. [64–67]

replaced in the seventeenth century by the Alawite dynasty who have reigned now for 400 years and whose longevity is unparalleled in the history of the country. The Sharifian sovereign does not come from a tribal group or a city but from a lineage descended from the Prophet. He is therefore external to both the tribe and the city. His authority is based on religious legitimacy as the 'Commander of the Faithful'" (Jamous 2017: 15).

9. Among others, Waterbury 1970; Geertz 1971; Gellner 1969b; Simenel 2010.

10. Ibn Khaldun reminds us that he who is absent is not represented, nor is God, who is everywhere. See Ibn Khaldun 2014.

11. Laoust 1970.

12. Such as Ali Abderraziq (1925) who inaugurated a tradition according to which God refrained from managing the affairs of the city, which was a matter for men.

13. "Derived sovereignty" (derived from the religious status of the King) is a concept used by a Moroccan constitutionalist (the "King's jurist") to justify Hassan II's abusive use of Article19 of the old constitution, which gave the King the right to legislate in all areas. See Tozy 1999: 92–3.

14. Article 19 also says that "the man and the woman enjoy, in equality, the rights and freedoms of civil, political, economic, social, cultural and environmental character, enunciated in this Title and in the other provisions of the Constitution, as well as in the international conventions and pacts duly ratified by Morocco and this, *with respect for the* provisions of the Constitution, of the *constants [constantes]* of the *Kingdom* and of its laws" (our emphasis).

15. "An induced amnesia enables the new regime to be made into the direct heir of a mythical *Makhzen* presented as the political expression of an eternal Morocco" (Laroui 2005: 41).

16. Only the Senior Council for Education had its organic law promulgated as early as 2014 (dahir n°1.14.100 of 16 May 2014 promulgating law n°105.12 relating to the Senior Council for Education, Training and Research). However, other older instances, are a perfect illustration of this practice. For example, the Royal Consultative Council on Saharan Affairs (Corcas), whose official presentation is very explicit in this respect, "The council, composed of Chioukh tribes, elected representatives and civil society personalities, is a framework of consultation and proposition that assists the king in all the issue related to defend the kingdom's territorial integrity and national unity, promote economic and social development of the southern provinces and preserve their cultural identity." The French version of the appointment speech states that the council draws on all spheres of society, promotes tribal balance and political and regional representativity, open society and participation of women, young people and social and economic actors. The new council is made up of elected officials for more than 50% of its members, as well as members of civil society working in social and human rights, who represent 15% of the Council members. Women make up 10% of members. There are also Moroccan Sahrawis and representatives of economic spheres. See http://www.corcas.com/Default.aspx?tabid=662 (in French).

253

pp. [68–75]   NOTES

17. These are the instances for the protection and promotion of the Rights of Man: Article 161 (human rights), Article 162 (mediator), Article 163 (Moroccans abroad), Article 164 (parity and struggle against discrimination); Instances of Good Governance: Article 165 (communication and broadcasting), Article 166 (competition), Article 167 (probity and anti-corruption); Instances for the Promotion of Human and Lasting Development and Participative Democracy: Article 168 (education), Article 169 (family and childhood) and Article 170 (youth and associative action).

18. Around eighty-five councils or commissions were requested in total. Fieldnotes of Mohamed Tozy, during his participation in the Commission revising the constitution.

19. There are a plethora of studies covering this crisis of representation and democracy. See, among many others, Przeworski, Stokes and Manin 1999; Bevir 2010; Rosanvallon 2006; 2015. For a critical analysis of these different positions, see Cuono 2013a.

20. See Hassan II 1993: 51.

21. From the Consultative National Assembly presided over by Ben Barka under Mohammed V (1959), to revisions of COSEF (the Royal Commission responsible for reforms to national education, created in March 1999, which functioned until 2004) and Commissions 1 and 2 of the reform of the Moudawana (the personal status code that was reformed firstly by Hassan II in 1993 and a second time by Mohammed VI in 2004).

22. The biographies of the nineteen figures who made up the Menouni commission illustrate this art of casting. It included constitutionalists, human rights activists, feminist activists, representatives of the Amazigh, Jewish and Sahrawi communities as well as representatives from the Ulema, the constitutionalists, political scientists and legal scholars.

23. Descendance, genealogical belonging; see Rosen 1979; Geertz 1979: 341*ff* as well as Cefaï 2003: 28*ff*.

24. Marin 1981.

25. In 1845, Eugène Delacroix immortalised Moroccan power through a monumental painting depicting the sultan Moulay Abderrhamane leaving his palace in Meknes.

26. Bourqia 1993.

27. This expression is often used in the *fiqh* treaties and history books. It refers to the elite made up of the Ulema, the war chiefs and the tribes who acted on behalf of the Muslim community, particularly when new sultans were invested.

28. The Idrisids are the descendants of Idriss I, great grandson of the Prophet, who is believed to have founded the Moroccan state in 789.

29. The town of Tlemcen, which is now in the west of Algeria, was always disputed territory between Morocco and the Ottoman empire.

30. The preamble is as follows: "A sovereign Muslim state, attached to its national unity and to its territorial integrity, the Kingdom of Morocco intends to pre-

254

NOTES

pp. [76–91]

serve, in its plenitude and diversity its one and indivisible national identity. Its unity is forged by the convergence of its Arab-Islamic, Berber and Saharan-Hassanic components, nourished and enriched by its African, Andalusian, Hebraic, and Mediterranean influences."

31. On these forms of theatralisation, see Geertz 1980.
32. The example of Islamic State in the Maghreb (IS or Daesh) is something to think about in this respect.
33. In reference to Revault d'Allonnes 2016.
34. Riderless horses are a symbol of prestige and an anticipation of risk, in the form of a substitute horse that ensures one's power.
35. Tozy 1991a.
36. Tozy 2009; Tamim and Tozy 2010.
37. In keeping with the now-cliched quote from Lampedusa's book *The Leopard*, "Everything must change for everything to remain the same."
38. Interview with Mostafa El Khalfi after his successful campaign in the Doukkala region, Rabat, February 2017.

2. VIOLENCE

1. Published in French and Arabic in 2011 by the Royal Institute for Research on the History of Morocco and coordinated by Mohammed Kably, a specialist on the Middle Ages in North Africa, it involved more than fifty researchers, most of whom are historians. A synthesis and update was translated into English in 2015.
2. This was most likely due to the fashion of the time and to a generation effect, but it was also a result of the fact that he studied law in France, and his teacher was Maurice Duverger in Bordeaux, and his thesis supervisor, Rémy Leveau, was also a former student of Duverger.
3. Hassan II 1993: 68.
4. Tozy 1999: 75–102.
5. Jebli 2015: 150*ff*.
6. Kably 2011: 653.
7. The Black Crescent is an armed resistance movement that emerged in Casablanca at the end of the protectorate and carried out a number of executions of "collaborators."
8. Slyomovics 2005.
9. The IER received 20,046 requests for information concerning 16,861 individuals. Based on these demands, it conducted its investigation, organising visits to the regions to interview those concerned, as well as meetings at the IER offices for additional interviews, reports and studies on controversial historical events, and visits to detention centres, in particular those that were kept secret.
10. Based on the sites of graves and visits to secret detention centres, the IER was able to identify victims of what can be called a "civil war" of independence, par-

pp. [91–95]   NOTES

ticularly during armed clashes between members opposed to the national movement.

11. 109 deaths revealed by the IER.
12. The IER investigations have determined that 325 people, some of whom were considered missing, were in fact killed during these riots (50 in Casablanca in 1965 and 114 in 1981; 112 in Fez in 1990; 49 in the north in 1984).
13. On the "events of March 1973" see Bennouna 2002.
14. The IER investigations on the "conflict in the Southern provinces" provided clarification on the fate of 211 people who were reported disappeared, of whom 114 died during or following armed confrontations and 67 were taken to Tindouf by the International Red Cross (ICRC) in October 1996.
15. Julien 1978: 43–4.
16. Ayache (1979) is one of the first historians of the contemporary era to analyse these terms, in direct opposition to Waterbury (1970).
17. Michel Foucault (1994) developed this expression, literally the "strategy of the perimeter", in response to the violent repression of demonstrators during the strike at the metalwork factory at Longwy in 1979. Unlike the striking workers themselves, university and high school students and young unemployed people who had come to support them were severely sanctioned by the justice system. This strategy aims to scare, to make examples of people, to intimidate in the pursuit of security and order rather than justice.
18. See, among many others, Taoufiq 1983; Sebti 1991; Moudden 1995; Nasiri 1997. All these narratives reveal extreme violence that did not lead to eradication, whether under the reign of Moulay Slimane, for the tribes of Chaouia (Nasiri 1997 [1907]: vol. 9, 2–3), Zemmour (Nasiri 1997 [1907]: vol. 9, 4), under that of Moulay Abdelaziz for the Beni Hassan tribes (Ibn Zaidane 1962: vol. 1, 260–1) or under Moulay Hassan for the Rhamma tribes. See also Ayache 1979.
19. This can be seen in the correspondence of Hassan I: see Al-Susi 1973, vol. 5. See also the Prolegomenon.
20. See L. Gardet, "Fitna" in *Encyclopédie de l'Islam. Fitna* is considered supreme evil. Most Sunni *foqaha* agree that they prefer impious power to anarchy because without order there can be no religion.
21. Ayache 1979.
22. The *hajeb* or chamberlain is the person who prevents subjects seeing the monarch. He protects the Sultan and protects the subjects from him. He also controls access to the Sultan. In many respects, he operates like a *hijab*, that is, a veil.
23. "Know too that God is severe in punishment yet forgiving and merciful" and "your Lord's punishment is truly stern—it is he who brings people to life and will restore them to life again." (*Qur'an*, translation by Abdel Haleem, 5: 98, and 85: 12–13)
24. On the concept of *hôrm* spaces, see Tozy 1991.

NOTES

pp. [95–101]

25. These are the sacred months—1 (moharam), 7 (rajab), 11 (doualqida) and 12 (douhiga)—of the Muslim calendar, quoted in the Qur'an (9:36). This is a pre-Islamic practice also found in Judaism. The Ulema adopted it and extended it to the point that the blood debt must be increased for murders committed during these months.

26. Sebti (1991) shows the moment when the *hôrm* of the mausoleum of Moulay Idriss in Fez functioned and its efficacy in decreasing social tension in the Idrisid capital.

27. https://www.youtube.com/watch?v=sCsp43C-8AA

28. He is referring to a 1935 *dahir* known as the "troubles to public order", which was used by Hassan II after independence to repress different protests and demonstrations. It was only revoked in 1994.

29. Hassan II 1993: 68.

30. Oufkir M and Fitoussi 1999; Oufkir F 2000; Oufkir R 2003; Oufkir M 2006.

31. On the prisoner as a community rather than an individual, see Ennaji and Tozy 1987a.

32. Lahcen Zinoun is a star dancer, trained in Belgium, who returned to Morocco in the 1980s with the aim of creating a troupe to revisit the choreography of traditional dances.

33. See https://www.youtube.com/watch?v=sCsp43C-8AA, put online by H24info on 14 January 2018 during an inauguration ceremony for the restoration of one of the doors to the Medina in Fez, organised by the Minister for National Territorial Planning and the National Order of Architects, during which Mohammed VI made the date of his father's speech (14 January 1986) the national "Day of the Architect". The ceremony, presided over by the Minister, coincided with the commemoration of the thirty-second anniversary of Hassan II's speech before the architects and the 12th anniversary of the Royal Letter sent by HRH Mohammed VI to the architects on 18 January 2006.

34. The *mokhazni* is a lower-level police officer belonging to a traditional service, formerly soldiers of the *Makhzen* institutionalised under the Protectorate.

35. *Le Monde*, 11 September 1981 (article by Paul Balta).

36. Mohammed Mansour (1922–2015) was a former resistance member. A member of the "secret organisation", he is famous for having participated in the so-called *Carrières centrales* attack. He was also an active member of the Istiqlal, where he was involved in preparations for the Sultan Sidi Mohammed Ben Youssef's historic visit to Casablanca, directly after the Throne Festival celebrations. In 1975, he participated in the first Ittihadi Congress, alongside Omar Benjelloun and Mohammed Abed Al-Jabri. Since then, he was an influential member in the socialist party: https://www.h24info.ma/maroc/Mohammed-mansour-icone-de-la-resistance-armee-au-maroc-nest-plus/

37. Quoted by Yabiladi.com of 26 June 2017.

38. Zayani served three Alaouite sultans during the late eighteenth and early nineteenth centuries, but he was also a historian. His book (Zayani 1967) is a key reference for this period.

257

pp. [101–109] NOTES

39. Berque 1958a; 1958b; 1982.
40. Zayani 1967: 13.
41. For Mohammed Jaïdi's account of this episode, see *La Dépêche*, 31 October 2017.
42. With this metaphor Hassan II reminds his subjects that he is all powerful and can make them disappear or be reborn absolved from their sins. Their re-birth is his decision because he has the power to control their life and death in political terms.
43. For the period between 1960–80, see Bono 2024.
44. One of the newspaper articles that transmitted the royal statement was revealing—"Political earthquake: the ruling is banishment."
45. This is the case for the article published in *L'Observateur*, on 9 January 2018, by Naïm Kamal, previously close to the Istiqlal and former manager of *L'Opinion*, famous for his acerbic pen.
46. The article in the *Reporter* "Political earthquake: the King and the two forgotten powers", by Bahia Amrani, published 7 November 2017, thus mentions "decisive sanctions" and, to justify that, mentions the first article of the constitution that associates responsibility and accountability.
47. Nasser Zefzafi is the main leader of the protest movement (*hirak*) in the Rif, which began in 2016. As of 2024 he was still imprisoned.
48. Mohammed Amrani Boukhoubza, interviewed in *L'Économiste*, 11 June 2018.
49. See "Limogeage royal, les questions qui se posent", *La Dépêche*, 25 October 2017.
50. Summary note of the Court of Accounts report on the Development project, dated 2017, available at http://www.courdescomptes.ma/fr/Page-27/publications/rapport-particulier/synthese-du-rapport-devaluation-du-programme-de-developpement-de-la-province-dal-hoceima-manarat-al-moutaouassit/3–196/
51. Statement from the royal cabinet on 24 October 2017, available at: http://www.mapexpress.ma/actualite/activites-royales/communique-du-cabinet-royal-2/
52. This case was widely covered in the media. For an exhaustive presentation see *Tel Quel*, 21 December 2018.
53. It is worth noting that the Court of Accounts, which is today systematically involved in this kind of case, was not yet functional at the time.
54. For a summary of the first day of the trial and the exchange of arguments, see Younes Saâd Alami "Affaire CGI: le procès sera long et passionnant", *L'Économiste*, 5 April 2018.
55. Because Article 23 of law 69–00 on the financial control of the state excludes the CDG and the BAM from the control of the IGF.
56. "Affaire CGI: le procès sera long et passionnant", op. cit.
57. *Ibid.*
58. There are other "incidents" that have functioned according to the exact same logic. Taoufiq Ibrahimi, former PDG of Comanav and former president of the board of managers of Tangiers Med, was accused of "forming a criminal group

NOTES
pp. [109–115]

and revealing professional secrets" and "sabotaging public establishments and infringing on freedom of work." In 2013, he was imprisoned and sentenced to five years detention; for a few months he faced the death penalty when his initial accusations mentioned "a threat to state security". He was eventually released from prison in 2014. Karim Zaz on the other hand was only released when he had completed his sentence (in May 2019). In 2015, he had been sentenced to five years in prison for "constituting a criminal group", "forgery and falsification" in a case involving the redirection of international calls.

59. Eventually the appeals court pronounced its verdict on 4 February 2020: the two business leaders were sentenced to one year in prison and a fine of 5,000 dirhams each, and the twenty-four other accused were acquitted.

60. "Affaire CGI: le procès sera long et passionnante", op. cit.

61. Since the period of *alternance*, the Ministries of Sovereignty have been those the King considers to be the most important and strategic, in which ministers are appointed by the King rather than the Parliament. This traditionally concerned above all the Ministry of the Interior and the Ministry of Religious Affairs but also the Ministry for Justice for a long while. The latter is no longer considered a Ministry of Sovereignty, because the Senior Magistrate's Council, presided over by the King, now manages judges' careers. The Minister for Justice is now a party man rather than a *Makhzen* man.

62. "The feeling of insecurity and unpredictability that limits initiatives is due to the gap between social reality and certain laws that include 'grey zones'. It is also to do with a justice system that suffers from a lack of trust, punctilious bureaucracy and dysfunctional appeals, which limits both entrepreneurial dynamic and the participation of civil society actors, or the ability to attract and preserve Moroccan skills from overseas" (NDM report, p. 38) (https://www.csmd.ma/rapport-fr)

63. Hibou 2012a.

64. Ginzburg 1991.

65. Levi 1988.

66. Such as the use of life insurance or bequests, wills and civil society real estate. Interviews, Casablanca, January 2002, February 2015, May 2016.

67. This is the position of the PJD but also conservative sectors of power who call for "social confrontation" on everything related to values.

PART TWO: GOVERNING THE NATION

1. See, among many others, Brignon et al. 1967; Pascon 1978; Brown 1976; Abitbol 2009.

2. Ayache 1956; Lahbabi 1957; Laroui 1977; Ayache 1981.

3. Under the Ottoman empire and up until French colonisation in 1830, the Regency of Algiers was made up of three beyliks, under the control of the Dey of Algiers who governed in the name of the Sublime Porte (the Ottoman sultan).

pp. [116–122]   NOTES

4. An article by the historian Mohammed Hajji (1968) provides a surprising overview of the "Moroccan nation" (talking about the "Moroccan race"), tracing its territorial embeddedness back to the Saadi era.

5. For a different approach that emphasises the compatibility of the nation and empire, see Bayly 2004 and above all Kumar 2017.

3. SHIFTING SPACES OF TERRITORIALISATION

1. This literature is extremely broad. Among the works that most inspired us, see Chartier 1980; Bertho 1980; Alliès 1980. From a Foucauldian perspective, see Elden 2007; Elden and Crampton 2007. On Morocco, see Saigh 1986; Correale 1994–95; Nordman 1997.

2. On the imaginary aspect of territory, see Debarbieux 2015.

3. This process is of course not specific to Morocco. As Paul Alliès (1980) has shown for France, the idea of territory itself involves the shift from limits to borders, that is from a given space to a dominated territory in the sense of a legal, normed, unified and mapped sense of the nation.

4. For the Mackenzie case, see Schroeter 1988: 190–5; above all Ben Srhir 2011: 179–286.

5. A letter from Hassan I to the Izerquiyine tribe, before his first *harka* as sultan, warned the peoples of the coast against trading with foreigners. See Ben Srhir 2009: 513–14.

6. Following Ben Srhir 2013.

7. Considering a whole range of arguments, including the nomination of *cadis* by the sultan who acted as a guarantor for their rulings, the involvement of the latter in the resolution of disputes, particularly over land and between rival lineages, to the sending rewards to religious elites and assistance from magistrates in the oases to *Makhezn* public servants during tax collection. See Warsheid 2017.

8. Ben Srhir 2013: 270.

9. The concept of "nomadic territory" comes from Edmond Bernus (1982), Denis Retaillé (1998) and Laurent Gagnol (2011): beyond the territorialisation of nomadic tribes, this expression reflects the existence of a different form of territorialisation, in which the limits are mobile and fluid and respond to a plurality of logics (economic, environmental, social, political). In these territories, control is indirect and operates through people and animals.

10. Moudden 1991.

11. On the disputes and tensions, see Ben Srhir 2013: 270*ff*.

12. *Ibid.*: 272.

13. Foucauld 1888: Aubin 1904; Doutté 1914.

14. Hoffman 1967; Burke III 1976.

15. Taoufiq 1983; Moudden 1995; Sebti 2009; Bourqia 1991.

16. In addition to the recent works in Moroccan historiography that we used in the

260

NOTES
pp. [123–130]

Prolegomenon (Ibn Zaidane 1962; Daoud 1966; Zaiyani 1967; Nasiri 1997) which use the full text of correspondence with the *Makhzen*, see Fumey 1903; Ben Srhir 2009: 513–14; Tazi 1979; Nehlil 2013 [1915].

17. Warsheid 2017.
18. Chartier 1980: 29.
19. Veyne 1976b.
20. The synthesis coordinated by Kably 2011 is therefore a first in this respect. See Sebti 2015.
21. Ibn Zaidane 1962; 2008: vol. 2; Aafif 1980–81; Nordman 1980–81; 1986; Dakhlia 1988; Benhima 2016; Jamous 2017.
22. On the *harka*, see Moudden 1983; Aafif 1980–81; Nordman 1980–81.
23. Benhima 2016.
24. Nordman 1980–81.
25. Benhima 2016 identifies three; our reading of Ibn Khaldun (2014) leads us to add a fourth.
26. The symbolic aspect of itinerance has often been emphasised: Dakhlia 1988; Ghouirgate 2014; Bennison 2014.
27. Ibn Khaldun 2014.
28. This is not specific to the Sharifian empire. As Madeline (2014) showed for the Plantagenet dynasty, there was no capital but rather a royal road that remained important even when the different royal residences were established and power was conceived as having multiple centres.
29. Sebti 2009.
30. *Ibid.*: 64–65.
31. *Ibid.*: 68*ff*
32. Moudden 1983.
33. Sebti 2009: 43*ff*.
34. For a very close analysis of the multiple functions of the *harka*, see Moudden 1995: 307–60.
35. Elden 2007. See also Foucault 2004a. This is now a position that is broadly shared among geographers.
36. Rivet 2012. See also the third part of the Prolegomenon.
37. Bidwell 1973: 164.
38. Baida 2012.
39. Dahir of 21 November 1916 published in the BO of 18 December 1916, p. 1170.
40. Dieste and Villanova 2013.
41. Leveau 1985: 29*ff*.
42. Chambergeat 1961; 1965; Marais 1963; Leveau 1985.
43. This is Dahir 1–15–83 of 20 Ramadan 1436 (7 July 2015) promulgating the organic law 111/14 concerning regions.
44. Speeches of 3 January 2010; 20 August 2010; 6 November 2008; 30 July 2009.
45. The Datar (Delegation for Territorial Planning and Regional Action, *Délégation*

pp. [131–135]   NOTES

à l'aménagement du territoire et à l'action régionale) is an inter-ministerial entity created in 1963 and destined to prepare, drive and coordinate territorial planning policies conducted by the French state.

46. Planel 2009: 8.
47. Bennafla 2013.
48. Chartier 1980: 30.
49. The MASEN is the Moroccan Agency for Sustainable Energy, responsible for overseeing renewable energies in Morocco.
50. The full name of which is the Agency for the Promotion and Economic and Social Development of Prefectures and Provinces in the North of the Kingdom, *Agence pour la promotion et le développement économique et social des préfectures et provinces du nord du royaume* (APDN).
51. "Driss Benhima à cœur ouvert: l'Agence du Nord se veut le miroir de la bonne gouvernance", *Le Matin du Sahara*, 28 December 2003.
52. "Driss Benhima, cap au Nord", *Jeune Afrique*, 2 April 2003.
53. Targa 2003; 2005.
54. "Bab Sebta: mise en échec d'une tentative de trafic de 15.000 euros", *Le 360*, 7 September 2016.
55. "Sebta: moins de contrebandiers pour faciliter le passage des RME", *Bladi.net*, 23 July 2017.
56. Interviews in Issaguen and Ketama in 2005 during the sociological investigation into cannabis.
57. Note from the Geopolitical Observatory on Drugs on Morocco in September 1997.
58. Hibou 2011: Chapter 5, inspired by Michel Foucault (2004a: lessons of 11, 18 and 25 January 1978) on *laissez faire* as a self-regulating mechanism when total domination is impossible.
59. A return that was made possible through the "merciful nation" programme to assist the integration of Sahrawis who wanted to become Moroccan.
60. Cherkaoui 2007.
61. Joumani 2009; Naïmi 1990; 2004; Boubrik 1998.
62. Particularly through the Royal Consultative Council for Saharan Affairs (CORCAS) created by dahir, by Mohammed VI in 2006. Made up of 141 members it brings together major notables (such as the Joumani and Derham, Ouled Er-Rachid families) and representatives of all the tribes and factions (Rguibat, Tekna, Ouled Dlim, Aroussine, Ouled Bousbaa, etc).
63. This was very visible in representations of both politics and the population as can be seen in Allal El Fassi's idea of "Greater Morocco", developed in the late 1940s and massively taken up by the nationalist movement and even by the newly independent Moroccan government at the turn of the 1950s and 1960s.
64. "Morocco is a tree whose roots stretch down into Africa, and which breathes in Europe through its leaves", Hassan II had affirmed on 3 March 1986. This phrase became emblematic and can be found in the speeches of politicians as well as in

NOTES

pp. [135–141]

discussions among ordinary citizens to justify Morocco's African policy, the legitimacy of its claims to the Sahara and its proximity with Europe. This discourse does not override the pledge of the Green March, which is now inscribed in all the school curriculum and parade grounds: "I swear before God the all-powerful to remain faithful to the spirit of the Green March fighting for the unity of my homeland from the delta to the Sahara. I swear before all-powerful God on high to teach this pledge to my family and my descendants and to make it a profession of faith. God the Almighty is witness to the sincerity of my feelings and my intentions."

65. Hassani culture refers firstly to the Hassani language (a composite language in which Amazigh and Arabic are combined) but also, and above all, to the nomadic culture that concerns both the tribes of Western Sahara and Morocco. It is a culture in which women have a much higher status and importance than in the rest of the Muslim world and in which poetry and art are important.

66. Berque 1951.

67. This was also the argument of Fariba Adelkhah (2012) in her demonstration that the state is shaped by its borders.

68. *Ibid.* for an analysis, see Bennafla 2013.

69. For specific figures and concrete information, see CESE 2013; the April 2009 issue of *Tel Quel* is based on the work of Fouad Abdelmoumni, an activist and economist who provides the most detailed data (http://www.telquel-online.com/368/couverture_368.shtml) as well as the Dierckx de Casterlé (2008) report. See Also Mohsen-Finan 1997; Troin 2002; Bennafla 2013.

70. The National Promotion is a programme created in 1961, during a drought that particularly affected the rural areas. It has been continued and aims to provide work for underemployed peasants.

71. CESE 2013: 41; Veguilla 2009; 2011.

72. F. Iraqi, "Cher, Très cher Sahara", *Tel Quel*, 15 April 2009.

73. See in particular "Les barons du désert", *La Gazette du Maroc*, 17 April 2006.

4. ADMINISTRATING BY CONSENSUS (*EINVERSTÄNDNIS*)

1. In Amazigh, *amghar* is the title of an eminent figure in the community, also attributed to the *muqaddam* and the Sheikh; he can be a war chief or a simple mediator (Tozy 2000).

2. Lipsky 1980; Vinzant and Crothers 1998; Dubois 2003; Siblot 2006; Spire 2008; Dubois 2010.

3. Weber 2012: 480. Jean-Pierre Grossein particularly emphasises this point in the French translation (2005).

4. The official number of *muqaddam* is very difficult to find if not nonexistent. These figures appeared in the media in 2011 in the context of the rights movements they launched (see below).

5. Here the *khalifa* is a figure of authority who is below the *caid* and above the *muqaddam*.

263

pp. [141–149]   NOTES

6. In 2011, the *muqaddam* took a stand against the Ministry of the Interior to obtain the status of "auxiliary of authority," and have had some victories since 2017, but which have remained largely unformalised.

7. Interviews, Ouneine, June 1990, March 1995, May 2003, March 2017.

8. Interviews Casablanca, January–February 2016, March 2017.

9. The Ramed (Medical Assistance Regime) was established in 2002 for disadvantaged people based on solidarity (https://www.ramed.ma).

10. This refers to the rehousing policy for residents of the slums.

11. As there are no legislative or administrative texts—see below—this list of the roles and functions of the *muqaddam* has been established based on the only two scientific texts that cover this figure, and which are in fact the work of a single person because Chambergeat is a pseudonym for Leveau (Chambergeat 1965; Leveau 1985: 26–33 and 44–50), author of the only thesis found on the subject (Harit 2010). It also draws on the national media, during the "Arab spring" and the February 20 Movement and numerous articles relaying the demands of the *muqaddam*.

12. Circular n° 3165 DGSN of 17 May 2003, quoted by Diallo 2017.

13. In addition to articles in the media, this overview of his roles was possible from reading studies on local life, particularly Iraki 2003; Zaki 2005; 2010; Baron and Belarbi 2010.

14. The *touiza* is solidarity-based participation in collective projects in the countryside.

15. For example, around the AUEA (water management associations) in rural areas: Kadiri, Tozy and Errahj 2010.

16. Bono 2010.

17. Rousset 1968; Leveau 1985.

18. Daadaoui 2011: 67.

19. For urban areas, see, for example, Anglade (2015: 279) for whom the *muqaddam* is "more the eyes and ears of the repressive authorities than the intermediary supposed to facilitate access to administrative requests", and for rural areas, see Pascon and Bentahar 1970.

20. Iraki 2003; Tamim 2005; Diallo 2017.

21. Ambivalence concerns corruption among the *muqaddam*. Like other authority agents, he is seen as "eating on the back" of those under his administration and, at the same time, in the extent to which he comes from the local community and is one of its emanations and is not destined to leave it; he can only eat "with restraint" and defend the community. See Couleau 1968: 83sq.; Leveau 1985; 30sq.

22. http://www.lopinion.ma/def.asp?codelangue=23&id_info=19906&date_ar=2011-4-20

23. Often, in the media the *muqaddam* are mentioned as receiving salaries, which is incorrect. Up until today, they have simply received allowances as demonstrated in the texts that lay out the pay increases in 2016. Decree n° 2–16–166 modi-

264

NOTES

pp. [150–155]

fying decree n° 2–86–586 of 24 Muharram 1407 (29 September 1986), relating to the creation of an *allowance* for the *chioukh*, *muqaddam* and *arifate* in urban areas, and decree n° 2–16–167 modifying decree n° 2–11–141 of 27 ioumada II 1432 (31 May 2011) setting the *allowances* granted to the *chioukh* and *muqaddam* in rural areas (our emphasis). Mohammed Hassad's argument for justifying this increase is precisely that it concerns allowances not wages, and that as a rule, these fundamental cogs in security policy had not benefited from the substantial increases of 2011.

24. https://www.youtube.com/watch?v=jVTD73vOoqo
25. According to a special issue dedicated to them in the journal *Assabah* in 2017, 23 October 2017: https://assabah.ma/258394.html
26. Dahir n° 1–60–120 of 8 kaada 1379 (5 May 1960) completing article 15 of dahir n° 1–59–161 of 27 Safar 1379 (1 September 1959) relating to the election of communal councils.
27. Dahir n° 1–63–273 of 22 rebia II 1383 (12 September 1963) relating to the organisation of prefectures, provinces and their assemblies.
28. Quoted by Leveau 1985.
29. For the 1960s, see Chambergeat 1965; Leveau 1985.
30. Iraki 2016; Zaki 2005.
31. http://www.maghress.com/fr/aujourdhui/68273
32. Schehl 2016.
33. Bouasria 2016.
34. We could have studied the role played by the people of the High Atlas following the events of Imlil in 2018, in which two hikers were murdered. Public authorities, unable to send the *gendarmerie* into the mountains, now use guides as guarantees of security in these areas. The decision was a straightforward one; ensure all hikers are obliged to take a guide as they leave Imlil, increase the daily rates of the guides from 300 to 400 dirhams, broaden their role to include people without formal training but who belong to the region and have technical and geographical knowledge that can be accredited by the *muqaddam* or the sheik of Imlil. Observation, Imlil, July 2019.
35. Rhassoul, is a natural volcanic clay collected in the Middle Atlas region, which is used for washing and particularly as a shampoo. It is a central element in hammam rituals. The main quarry is near Missour and has made the fortune of the Sefrioui family and led to the creation of one of the largest real estate groups, Addoha, in the early twenty-first century.
36. These tribes were part of the sultan's armies and were moved around according to need, for the protection and defence of imperial cities.
37. Vivification is de facto usage that entails property rights after ten years of continued, peaceful and unchallenged use.
38. Milliot 1922; 1953: 515.
39. The OCP is one of the major purchasers of land for the extension of mines in the phosphate plateau region, where the collective is the region that is legally

pp. [155–161] NOTES

dominant. Since 2008, when the OCP changed its status as a public body for that of an independent company with the state as its (almost) single shareholder, it lost its privilege of drawing directly on this heritage through its tutelary council. Normally it must engage with the property market like any other private actor, but this is not the case, as the governors and walis, even those who are reticent, continue to facilitate the task in the name of the general interest. However, they can no longer act against certain *nouab* who may prove tough in business, despite pressure put on them.

40. Bendella 2016.

41. As a minimum estimate provided by a World Bank report of 12 million hectares, whereas the tutelary ministry numbers 15 million hectares and the Ministry of Agriculture gives estimates between 21 million and 50 million hectares. This figure is the result of a subtraction of land regimes from the area of national territory: the public domain managed by the Ministry for Infrastructure (1%), the forestry land managed by the High Commission for water, forests and desertification (29%), the private domain of the state (3.4%), managed by the ministry for Finances, Habou land (0.3%) managed by the Ministry for Islamic Affairs, and Melk private property (26%), belonging to either individuals or private companies. These figures are from the World Bank report 2007.

42. Article 12 and 13 of the 1919 dahir.

43. *Bour* is the term used in Morocco to describe a zone of agriculture. Under the Abdallah Ibrahim government, "operation labour" was a programme to mechanise the labouring of rain fed arable land, according to the soviet model of valorisation of agriculture.

44. Bendella 2016.

45. Berriane 2015; 2017; Aït Mous and Berriane 2016.

46. In other words, the shares in housing developments that are due to beneficiaries in the instance of a transfer of ownership to a public or private developer who acquires the collective land following an agreement with local authorities and agrees to house them.

47. The association set itself the objective of "defending the population's right to land and wealth", both in connection with the Amazigh movement, the movement of defence of indigenous rights and Association for Environmental Protection. See http://albayane.press.ma/Casablanca-la-politique-du-paturage-suscite-la-colere-des-soussi.html

48. This information was made public in the context of Parliamentary Question Time of 10 June 2014. See the media reports on that date.

49. See for example ouledboubker.blogspot.com; alkanounia.com; the website of the Moroccan association for social justice and reform created on 3 October 2011, which is home to the national commission for the defence of collective land in Morocco.

50. Two examples of this, chosen at random: on 3 November 2017 three *nouab* were arrested in Kenitra for having obtained 400,000 dirhams from an inves-

NOTES

pp. [162–169]

tor to whom they had promised the sale of collective land for the construction of a tourist complex on the outskirts of Mahdia; on 31 July 2017 a *gendarme* and four *nouab* from the Aït Chgagag ethnic group were brought before the court in Sefrou having been caught in the act of falsifying a document enabling the transfer of collective land.

51. Duara 1987; 1988.
52. Weber 2012. This is the analysis suggested by Jean-Pierre Grossein (2005), which made its relevance for our research clear. See also *Economy and Society* (Weber 1978: 1378).
53. Weber 2012: 291.
54. Weber 2012: 290.

PART THREE: THE NEOLIBERAL ART OF GOVERNING AFFINITIES WITH IMPERIALISM

1. Weber 2002 [1904–05]: 88.
2. Grossein (2006: 67*ff*) emphasises the importance of these "bearers" and "mediations" in Weber's analysis by which ideas necessarily transit.
3. The concept of extraversion was developed by Jean-François Bayart in his work *The State in Africa* (1989). This term refers to a common political strategy involving the actors in a given society mobilising external material or immaterial resources, of which the meaning, interpretation and enunciation is subject to processes specific to that society, whether as part of a more or less conscious strategy or in the realm of imagination. See also Bayart 2000.
4. This is the standard translation of Weber's concept (*träger*), used to refer to those who carry and disseminate the concept. We will return to this in chapter 6, see Weber 1993 [1920] and 2002 [1904–05]. See also Weber 2012.
5. This is one of the reasons we have consciously chosen to not analyse what journalists have called the "economic *Makhzen*", and which some academics consider "connivence capitalism". For further discussion see the conclusion of Part 3.
6. To use Foucault's expression (2004b: 28).
7. Particularly developed in governmentality studies: Barry, Osborne and Rose 1996; Rose 1999.

5. INDIRECT GOVERNMENT

1. Foucault 2004b.
2. Examples here are legion, but the Ancien Regime in France (Dessert 1984) or the Ottoman empire (Salzmann 1993; Barkey 1994) are two obvious ones. See also Hibou 1999.
3. Hibou and Tozy 2020.
4. One indication of this is the range of institutions and frameworks involved in supporting the industrial zones (MedZ, subsidiary of the CDG; the Hassan II

267

NOTES

Foundation for Economic and Social Development; *le Fonds d'équipement communal*) or directly involved in investment (Regional Centres for Investment, Investment Promotion Fund, Industrial Development Fund; Moroccan Agency for Development of Investments).

5. OECD Review of Risk Management Policies in Morocco, OCDE 2016; *Strategic Plan for Disaster Risk Management*, Rabat, working paper for the Ministry of the Interior, March 2018.

6. Hibou and Tozy 2020.

7. Gaudin 1999. For a historical perspective see Mastropaolo 2011.

8. Miras and Godard 2006.

9. Miège 1961; Schroeter 1988: 155*ff*.

10. *Ibid.*: 153–4. See the Prolegomenon also.

11. Kenbib 1996.

12. Belmqadem 1993: t. 1, 15–94; Ben'alla 2007.

13. Saul 2002.

14. One of the most interesting experiences in this respect is the delegation of irrigation management to colonisers organised into agricultural unions (*association syndicale agricole privilégiée, ASAP*) in the Haouz region. Pascon 1975–77; Jolly 2000: 35.

15. Buses have always been organised into companies that were initially private but later managed by municipalities and then concessions.

16. A remanent of colonial projects, from the late rural development inspired by Jacques Berque and the agronomist Julien Couleau. See Berque and Couleau 1977, as well as the Julien Couleau collection as the library of the MMSH in Aix-en-Provence.

17. The "February 20 Movement" is the Moroccan version of the "Arab Spring". Its main demands were the transformation of the political system into a constitutional monarchy, greater accountability and a genuine fight against inequality and privilege.

18. Bayart 1989; 2000.

19. The choice of concessions is not widespread, however. Major towns such as Casablanca, Rabat, Tanger and Tétouan have adopted it but not Marrakech, Fez, El Jadida or Agadir, which remain under public management.

20. For public service concessions, see Guerraoui 2000; Haoues-Jouve 2004; Miras, Le Tellier and Saloui 2005; Miras and Godard 2006; Miras 2010. For a broader perspective on the transformations of meaning of the notion of public service in Morocco, see Hachimi Alaoui 2017a.

21. Among the most important we could mention, the Foundation BMCE, which manages the Medersat.com program for public schools, run by alternative private management, or the OCP Foundation, which manages professional training centres at the University Mohammed VI Polytechnic in partnership with the state.

NOTES

pp. [174–181]

22. Bazwi 1993.
23. The Foundation Hassan II for the Social Actions of Authority Agents was created by the decree-law n° 2–80–520 of 28 Kaâda 1400 (8 October 1980), signed by Maati Bouabid, who was then Prime Minister.
24. The Foundation Hassan II for Moroccans living overseas, created by law n° 19–89 promulgated by dahir n° 1–90–79 of 20 Hija 1410 (1 July 1990), is funded by part of the interests from the money collected. Among others, its objectives are teaching Arabic, religious training and funding funeral services.
25. The Foundation Mohammed VI for Social Actions on Education, whose president is appointed by the King (who is himself honorary president) manages a substantial amount of revenue automatically deducted from the wages of its 250,000 members. This royal solicitude is also material. The foundation operates like a powerful union, able to force economic actors liable to propose products to this creditworthy middle class to fall into line, because it negotiates directly on behalf of all its members with real estate promoters, banks, companies, travel agencies and hotels.
26. Created on 23 February 2012, the Foundation Mohammed VI for the Promotion of Social Actions by Religious Agents is responsible for complementary insurance, leisure activities and home ownership for religious employees. It also finances access to houses and the purchasing of mutton for the Eid festival. In 2017, according to the Minister of Islamic Affairs, more than 67,000 religious workers were members, and there were over 243,000 beneficiaries (women and children included).
27. There are many articles presenting the successes of the PERG, see for example: http://www.ondh.ma/sites/default/files/perg.pdf and http://www.mem. gov.ma/SitePages/GrandsChantiers/DEERElectrificationRurale.aspx. Scientific articles are almost non-existent, however, with the exception of Planel 2009.
28. Michelon et al. 2010: 17.
29. *'amazal* (in the Berber language, Amazigh) is an official responsible for the distribution of water, particularly for irrigation.
30. Palazzoli 1974: 366.
31. *Ibid.*: 372*ff.*
32. Menouni 1979: 67.
33. Palazzoli 1974: 377*ff.*
34. Menouni 1979: 467.
35. *Ibid.*: 387*ff.*
36. *Ibid.*: 393.
37. *Ibid.*: 404.
38. The UNTM was created in 1976, close to the Islamists and the CDT was created in 1978, close to the USFP. Today, there are around twenty union organisations.
39. Information from the Real Estate Federation. Sources: interviews, Casablanca, October 2011.

NOTES

40. Iraki 2003.
41. Abouhani 2013.
42. These neighbourhoods are never described as illegal—in Arabic they are described as *'achoua'i*, as anarchic.
43. Iraki 2003.
44. Bouyges is one of the biggest French construction groups.
45. El Omrane is a state-owned holding company born in 2004 from the fusion between several public entities to incarnate the new housing policy as part of a public-private partnership. For more details on its functions, scope and results, see www.alomrane.ma
46. Zaim 1990 and Mansour 1990.
47. Ben Srhir 2013: 106, 122–3, 231–2.
48. As we saw for the *naib* of collective lands and for the *muqaddam* in Chapter 4. We can also add the example of the car watchmen and the *semsar*. See Bendella 2011 and Bouasria 2016.
49. For a presentation of RSE policies within OCP, see Labaronne 2012.
50. Interviews, Khouribga, March 2012; Marrakech, April 2012; Casablanca, March and December 2012, June 2013.
51. Interviews, Casablanca, December 2011.
52. These workers were to be incorporated into the company once the planned investments were carried out.
53. See www.ocpskills.org
54. On employability policy in Morocco see Aoufi and Hanchane 2011. For a critical perspective on this approach and its political signification see Bono 2013 and 2015.
55. One of the most famous bloggers at the time was hired to work as a manager on the project.
56. Mostafa Terrab, interview, Casablanca, 20 December 2011.
57. Amar Drissi, interview, Casablanca, 9 January 2012.
58. Reflecting the expression coined by Charles Wilson, the CEO of General Motors in the 1950s, who famously said: "What is good for General Motors is good for America."
59. *Targa* means water channel, *séguia* in Amazigh.
60. See the Targa website: http://www.targa-aide.org/
61. Targa 2006 explores the effects of this crop on other agricultural activities, on social structures, on access to the state and the weakening of social and political ties.
62. Targa 2007 monitors operations whose main activity is growing cannabis.
63. Moudden 1995; Tozy 1999; Sebti 2009.
64. The French expression *faire faire* should be understood in opposition to the notion of *laissez faire*, with the former emphasising an incentive to action rather than the absence of incentives to action.

NOTES

pp. [192–193]

6. THE BEARERS OF NEOLIBERALISM

1. On this engineering mindset, see Vatin 2008.

2. If we accept the Foucauldian analysis that distinguishes two inseparable aspects of the neoliberal art of governing: the critique of state administration and government practices on the one hand, and on the other the development of practices tending towards an interventionism concerned with frameworks, market conformity and business. See Foucault 2004b.

3. A graduate of *Polytechnique et des Ponts et Chaussées* in France, Mohammed Hassad was the director of the *Office national d'exploitation des ports* (ODEP) before being appointed minister, firstly of Public Works and Professional Training and Managerial Training and then of the Interior and finally of National Education. He was also the CEO of RAM and regional *wali and* president of TMSA.

4. A graduate of the French elite school *Ponts et Chaussées*, holding a master's in banking and finance, Mustapha Bakkoury worked in banking (BNP Paribas, BMCI) and at SONADAC (limited holding company responsible for major urban planning projects in Casablanca) before being appointed by Mohammed VI as director general of the CDG (2001–09) then president of the Masen (Moroccan Agency for Sustainable Energy, responsible for piloting sustainable energy in Morocco) since 2009. He came late to politics, in 2007, with the creation of the PAM and it was under this banner than he was elected in Mohammedia and became the president of the region of Casablanca-Settat.

5. A graduate of the *École centrale* in Paris, Khalid Oudrighi initially worked in the oil industry before moving into finance: Indosuez (1987–92), then BNP Paris, where he ended up eventually directing the Moroccan branch of this bank, the BMCI and being the BNP representative for North Africa and the Middle East (1992–2002). In 2002, he was appointed CEO of the Banque Commerciale de Maroc that the following year became Attijariwafabank after merging with Wafa. He was brutally dismissed from his position for fraud and counterfeiting in 2011 but pardoned in 2012 and totally cleared of any wrongdoing the following year. He was appointed executive president of the Saudi Islamic bank Aljazira Bank (2008–09) and has since been active in investment funds in the Maghreb and in Luxemburg.

6. Rahhou was a graduate of France's elite *Polytechnique* and the *École nationale supérieure des télécommunications* in Paris. He initially worked for RAM (1982–85) before joining Crédit du Maroc (1994–2003). He was CEO of Lesieur Maroc (subsidiary of ONA, 2003–09) before being CEO of the CIH (2009–19). He was appointed Ambassador of the Realm to the European Union in November 2019 and in 2021 was appointed president of the Competition Council.

7. A graduate of the Mohammadia Engineering school in Rabat, with an American MBA, Anas Alami worked in finance (Upline Securities) before being appointed head of the supervisory board for the company on the Casablanca stock exchange (2005) then he was director general of Barid al-Maghrib (*La Poste*, in 2006) and

271

pp. [193–195] NOTES

director general of the CDG (in 2009). He was brutally removed from his positions in 2014 following the CGI-Madinat Badis case (see chapter 2).

8. An IT graduate from Sherbrooke University in Canada, Moulay Hafid Elalamy primarily worked in insurance, with the ONA group, then the Agma company, before creating his own group, Saham. He was the president of the employers' representatives between 2006 and 2009 and since 2013 he has been Minister for Commerce, Industry, Investment and the Digital Economy.

9. On 30 July 2007, during the ceremony for the Throne Festival, the King bestowed the status of Commander of the Order of Ouissame Alaouite on professor Bernard André Spenlehauer, former coordinator of the preparatory class programme in elite schools and teacher training for physics and sciences teachers in Morocco. A former communist, he was responsible for opening a scientific preparatory class in the lycée Lyautey in Casablanca. Due to him, a community of "*taupins*" (a word used to refer to students at elite preparatory schools) would emerge during the 1960s and 1970s (among whom were such figures as Rachid Belmokhtar, Mostafa Terrab, Fouad Laroui, Mohammed Fikrat, Abdelaziz Abarro, Ahmed Rahou, Mohammed Soual and so forth). The elite that would govern Morocco between the end of Hassan II's reign and the beginning of Mohammed VI, was born out of this milieu and a thick web of complicity spanning the (invisible) borders between students from good families and *affaquis* from provincial Morocco or the suburbs of Casablanca. In 1985 a newspaper article from *Le Matin* noted: "Thanks to two key figures, Mohammed Kabbaj and Rachid Belmokhtar, there are preparatory classes in the public system. The man behind this project is none other than the professor *agrégé*, Bernard Spenlehaue who was the professor of physics in the Belmokhtar Ministry for Education between 1995 and 1998 then between 2013 and 2017". https:// lematin.ma/journal/2005/Garantie-d-embauche--Les-grandes-ecoles-sont-tres-prisees/54601.html).

10. Particularly graduates from the elite *Ponts et Chaussées*, in Paris, who have a reputation for excellence and not only in Morocco. For France, see Brunot and Coquand 1982; Picon 1992; Vatin 2008.

11. During interviews with some of them, it was striking to see them refer to the precolonial reformist tradition and the understanding of reform in Islam.

12. An example of this is the unbridled competition in telecommunications at the turn of the 2000s. In spite of tensions, Saâd Bendidi, who was president of Méditel did not want to sue Maroc Telecom (under Abdelslam Ahizoune) for false advertising and always promoted the path of mediation (Hibou and Tozy 2002).

13. Given the outcry, the Ministry of the Interior (then under Mohammed Hassad) who oversaw the *wali* and the Ministry of Finances (under Mohammed Boussaïd) published an official statement justifying the attribution of these particular allotments as part of a normal development operation for the benefit of "*khadims dawala*" (servants of the state) planned under Hassan II and decreed by the then

NOTES pp. [196–197]

Prime Minister Abderrahmane Youssoufi back in December 1995. See the debates in the Arabic speaking media, relayed by the francophone press: https://fr.le360.ma/politique/affaire-laftit-ces-serviteurs-de-letat-qui-auraient-beneficie-des-lots-de-terrain-a-des-prix-81085.fr

14. A graduate of the *École centrale* in Paris, Ahmed Réda Chami also has an MBA from the USA; he worked in the private sector in Morocco and in America before being appointed to the Ministry for Industry, Trade and New Technologies, under the label of the USFP (2007–12). He has been an MP since 2011, and from 2017 to the end of 2019, he was Morocco's Ambassador to the European Union; in December 2018 he was appointed to the head of the Social, Economic and Environmental Council.

15. A graduate of *Ponts et Chaussées*, he joined the Ministry for Social Infrastructure after working in consulting. A member of Istiqlal, he has been an MP since 2002, he was Minister for Transport and Infrastructure (2002–11) and President of the House of Representatives (2011, 2014).

16. Foucault 2004b.

17. Transparency Maroc is an anti-corruption association created by former left-wing activists and political prisoners including Sion Assidon and Abdeslam Aboudrar; in 1996 it joined Transparency International and became Transparency Maroc.

18. As a student at Mohammadia Engineering school, he was a member of UNEM and was forbidden from defending his final thesis. After working at Promoconsult, he was then recruited by the CIH bank. He returned to one of the other subsidiaries, Batisoft, and with two other colleagues created Involys (a local management company) in 1986, of which he is still the CEO. A member of Transparency Maroc and president of the Ethics and Good Governance Commission of the CGEM, he represents technological modernity for the benefit of transparency and ethics. In December 2018, he was appointed head of the ICPC (anti-corruption body) by Mohammed VI.

19. A left-wing activist, imprisoned twice, he was trained as an economist and initially worked in banking (CDG and Maghreb Développement Investissement). He founded and ran Al Amana, the largest Moroccan microcredit association, and was a member of the AMDH and Transparency Maroc, where he has been general secretary since 2016.

20. A left-wing activist who was imprisoned for ten years (1974–84), he continued his studies in economics while in prison. When he was released, he was hired as director of the national building and public works foundation in 1984 and after a year in the Chaabi group (1990–97) he returned there. He was the Mr Clean of the construction industry, a member of Transparency Maroc and the ICPC.

21. After graduating in political science and international relations, he was an activist in the "March 23" group and was imprisoned in the 1970s–80s. After working in the Federation for building in public works he joined the Tazi group and

273

pp. [198–202]   NOTES

became the cabinet director for the employers' representative association and secretary general of the CGEM from 1995 to 2006. He then created his own company and specialised in coaching, cleverly capitalising on the new mine of Sufi values. He published the books, *Paroles de coachs du Maroc* and *Soufisme et coachisme*.

22. The current CEO of the all-powerful OCP, Mostafa Terrab claims to belong to the *Makhzen* through his mother, a relative of the king and daughter of the famous ulama Moulay Mohamed Ben Larbi Alaoui. After graduating from the *Ponts et Chaussées* engineering school in Paris, he was awarded a scholarship from the palace and sent to Harvard and MIT. He was also head of the telecommunications regulatory agency (ANRT) and worked at the World Bank before heading the OCP.

23. Born into a Safi family serving the *Makhzen*, Driss Benhima graduated from both *Polytechnique* and the *École des mines* in Paris. In his own words, he describes himself as a "servant of the Prince", like his ancestors. After working at the OCP, he was appointed head of the ONE. He was also Minister for Transport, Tourism, Energy and Mining (1997–98), before being one of the first "technowalis" (he was appointed *wali* of Greater Casablanca in 2001). He was then director of the Agency for the North (2004–06) then CEO of RAM (2006–16). See also Hachimi Alaoui 2019.

24. Weber 1978 [1922]; Marcuse 1982 [1941].

25. It is particularly the *nakhoua* (noble elegance, bearing) and the *taaouil* (know-how) that constitute urbaneness and sophistication in social relations in this milieu.

26. An advertising executive, Nourredine Ayouch created Shem's agency after working for Havas and PR, communication and design companies. In addition to his work as an activist (2007 Daba, Democracy and Modernisation Commission), he was involved in associations through the Zakoura foundation, which specialised in microcredit and education.

27. This foundation was created in 2013 to promote culture and creation through sponsorship and through a site, Uzine, in the spirit of openness to the world. As for the Food Bank, it was founded in 2002. Abdelatif Tazi was a self-made man who created the Richbond group, while also a member and financial supporter of the Moroccan Communist Party (which later became the PPS). His son Karim took over the company and made it a Moroccan leader in the furnishings textile industry. In addition to these associations, Tazi was also a fervent promoter of a network that brings together companies and neighbourhood associations, and which supports the *L'Boulevard* festival.

28. Such as the AttijariWafabank foundation for art and literature; the ONA Foundation that funded the Arts Villa in Casablanca and in Rabat; or the Alliance Foundation, with its museum of contemporary African Art Al Maaden.

29. The Sekkat group is active in steel, cables and electrical equipment, plastics, household items and real estate. The Sekkat Fondation was created in 2005.

30. Noureddine Ayouch boasts of being a friend of the King, which is probably

274

NOTES

pp. [202–203]

somewhat true in that he is on several administrative councils under the patronage of the royal family. The May 2006 edition of *Jeune Afrique* presents this unusual mediator as follows: "During the private party given by Mohammed VI, in mid-April, the guests, some seventy people noticed that the King spent two hours alone with Noureddine Ayouch. A star of civil society, this advertising executive had not concealed his sympathy for the PJD in recent times and was not unhappy to see the Islamists arrive in power after the 2007 elections. No one knows what these two men said to each other. But the day after the reception Ayouch announced the creation of an association called '2007 Daba' [*daba* means 'right now' in Arabic]. The goal was to mobilise citizens to ensure widespread participation in the 2007 elections. In spite of appearances, the operation was not in the interests of the PJD. This party was banking on voting discipline to achieve their victory but also on depoliticisation and demobilisation of public opinion. Failing that, any mobilisation of Moroccans had to be of disservice to the Islamists." See https://www.jeuneafrique.com/56468/archives-thematique/quoi-sert-noureddine-ayouche/

31. Karim Tazi, who moved away from the left-wing PSU, was very active in the February 20 movement.

32. This has been demonstrated by a whole series of studies, among which Magat 1989; Guilhot 2004; Damon and Verducci 2006; Seghers 2007; *Problèmes économiques* 2008; Zunz 2012; Lambelet 2014.

33. For example, Bachir Labyad, a breeder in the Oriental region, who was a central figure in the documentary by the anthropologist Mohammed Mahdi, dedicated to the nomads in this region, See "Nomad Itineraries" www.youtube.com/watch?v=9Fw3Oc3HkPo

34. The most emblematic of these is undoubtedly Abdessamad Qayouh, born in the Sous region. He was one of the sons of Haj Ali Qayouh, a notable who had an extensive network covering the towns in the Sous plains and in the mountains. He was said to be the "owner" of 780 community advisors and ten parliamentarians distributed across the two houses". He was the "champion of parliamentary longevity", with six successive mandates as an MP and continued presence in the lower house since 1977, firstly under the label of the National Democrat Party, then under that of the Istiqlal. In 2011, he was invited to join Abdelilah Benkirane's government. He left government in 2013 when the party withdrew from the coalition led by the PJD. He is currently the vice-president of the House of Councillors.

35. For example, Soussi Tarek Kabbaj. Former Mayor of Agadir (2009–15), he was a distinguished and liberal member of the USFP. After completing his studies in France, he returned to his father's farm on the Sous plain. He was responsible for substantial property in Oulad Taima and Sebt El Guerdane and more recently in Dakhla and in the Gharb. His agriculture is very modern and focused on export.

36. The most interesting case is that of Abdenbi Biioui, who became president of

pp. [203–206]   NOTES

the Oriental region for the PAM. As a small independent construction entrepreneur, he was able to benefit from outsourcing and subcontracting of major projects in order to grow.

37. Aggregators are private actors or professional organisations "with good management capacity" around whom smaller farmers are organised, particularly for the purposes of industrialisation and the commercialisations of their products (storage, conditioning, transformation); they constitute a pillar of the *Plan Maroc Vert*. See http://www.agriculture.gov.ma/pages/le-modele-de-lagregation

38. Thus, in the Oriental, one of Morocco's border zones, the PDPEO project on livestock and pasture (*Projet de développement des parcours et de l'élevage dans l'Oriental*) was conducted within a technical and ecological framework, without consideration for the general interest or the interest of smaller farmers. See FIDA 2002.

39. Banégas and Warnier 2001.

40. Tozy 2009; Mahdi 2010.

41. He was the manager of a dairy cooperative in the Sous, before becoming president of the regional Chamber of Agriculture in the Sous.

42. Sahrawi of the Ait Ba'Amran. Hassan Derham was at the head of the largest oil company in the Sahara, Atlas Sahara, and was elected to parliament for the USFP. His father, Ahmed, was a founding member of the UNFP; his brother, Slimane, was also an MP running under different tickets and his sister Rkia Derham was appointed Secretary of State for Foreign Trade.

43. Aziz Akhannouch was born in Tafraout in 1961. His father, Haj Hmad Oulaj Akhannouch, an important Berber nationalist made his fortune selling crude oil and then in packaging butane gas. He was one of those rare self-made men who managed to be successful in trade but was also involved in politics. Having participated at a young age in the last battle between the people of Tafraout (Aït Abdallah) and the French army in 1933, he settled in Casablanca and then Agadir, where he was appointed coordinator for the Istiqlal in the Sous region. In 1974, he created the progressive Liberal Party, with an Amazigh connotation (see Amarir 2014: 143*ff*). Aziz obtained an MBA in Canada at Sherbrooke. As the CEO of Akwa, he led the group to prosperity, in the distribution of fuel and lubricants, gas and fluids, media, mobile phones, tourism and real estate.

44. Mohammed Sajid was born in Settat in 1948. A graduate of the *École supérieure de commerce de Lille* in France, he was Mayor of Casablanca between 2003 and 2011 after being previously elected in the region of Ounein (Tozy 2010; Hachimi Alaoui 2019). His father, Abdallah Sajjid, had followed the same trajectory as Akhnouch. Originally from a little *douar* called Ougog in the Anti-Atlas mountains, he firstly settled in Settat in 1925. After marrying the niece of his employer, Madani Diouri, he settled in Casablanca where he moved into trading fabrics for the textile industry (Amarir 2014: 385*ff*).

45. Pierru 2012; Saint-Martin 2006.

46. During the 1980s (and specifically issues number 130 and 200, in 1981 and 1988

NOTES pp. [206–209]

respectively) *Lamalif* was a valuable space for observing this paradoxical movement of ideas. It was a space in which economists, political scientists and sociologists (whether party members or not) expressed their views—people such as Habib El Malki, Khalid Alioua, Abdelali Doumou, Nadir Yata, Najb Benabdeljali, Mohammed Salaheddine, Driss Gerraoui, Najib Akesbi, Mohammed Tozy and Mohammed Ennaji, along with the editors Zakia Daoud, Mohammed Jibril and expert engineers Zakia Daoud, Mohammed Jibril. With three decades of hindsight, we can say that these now-dated texts express the seeds of reformism already dominated by nascent neoliberal thought—although it appeared under or through a firm stance against the authority of religion, patriarchy and the power of the state. Issues 136, 145, 146, 149, 152, 153, 154, 156 and 159 are particularly edifying in this respect.

47. PERG: Global Rural Electrification Programme (*Programme d'électrification rurale global*); PAGER: Collective Rural Drinking Water Supply Programme (*Programme d'approvisionnement groupé en eau potable pour les populations rurales*); PNCRR: National Programme for Rural Roads (*Programme national de construction des routes rurales*).

48. The list is long here and includes Mohamed Tozy alongside Abdesslam Dahman Saïdi, Mohamed Mahdi, Mohamed Tamim, Aziz Iraki, Khalid Alioua, Ahmed Herzeni, Rabia Naciri, Larabi Jaïdi, Hayat Zirar, Larbi Zagdoun and so on. For a concrete example, see the development on the Targa association in chapter 5.

49. At the head of Team Maroc, a Moroccan engineering firm, the son of Ahmed Balafrej, important nationalist and one of the authors of the Declaration of Independence, Anis Balafrej became Minister for Foreign Affairs and President of the Council during the early years of independence.

50. Created in 1985, AgroConcept provides consultancy for Moroccan and international corporations and sometimes also the administration, on the privatisation of agriculture, pastoral actions and the dismantling of national public agricultural entities. It is run by Hassan Ben Abderrazak (economist and statistician who constantly moved between the public and private sectors his whole career) and Omar Aloui (former member of the PPS and still politically engaged, he could have been classed in the category of the former left-wing figures).

51. An engineering graduate from Paris Dauphine, Jazouli was director of a consultancy firm in Morocco and associated with the conception and implementation of numerous strategic plans. On the role of Valyans in the urban planning of Casablanca, see Hachimi Alaoui 2017b.

52. Born into an Istiqlal family, he studied in Paris (at the prestigious *École normale supérieure* and Sciences Po) before becoming director of Azura, a major agribusiness group in Morocco, and then moving into specialist consultancy in agribusiness, international negotiation and free trade agreements.

53. Haenni 2005; Achcar 2013.

54. Merieme Yafout (2017) demonstrates this well for education.

55. The Boutchichiyya Sufi order, which was founded in Berkane in north-east

277

pp. [209–217] NOTES

Morocco, is a brotherhood derived from the Qadiriyya order. See Ben Driss 2002 and Tozy 1984: 267–80.

56. According to law 103–12 on Islamic finance, promulgated in January 2015, a decision made early 2016, by the Bank-al-Maghrib and the circulars published in the official administrative journal of January 2017.

57. http://www.cifie.fr/biographie-des-membres/

58. For example, a famous French pastry chef came to make crêpes during the *moussem* of Mouloud in December 2016. Observations in the field, Madagh, 13 December 2016.

59. A graduate of INSEA in Paris, with a Master's in software engineering obtained in Quebec, Aziz Rebbah is a founding member of Sigma 2, an information technology association that played an important role in the Islamists' investment in the economy. He was Minister for Transport between 2012 and 2017 and has been Minister for Energy and Mining since 2017.

60. Trained in architecture in Morocco, Abdessamad Sekkal was the director of the Agadir Urbanism Agency and of the Centre for Study and Research in Urban Planning and then director of urbanism at the Planning Agency of the Bouregreg Valley. He is now president of the Rabat-Salé-Kénitra region.

61. http://www.medias24.com/ECONOMIE/ECONOMIE/151807-Maroc.-Le-FMI-explique-par-Abdelilah-Benkirane-video.html

62. Ayubi 1991; Roy 1992 (Chapter 8); 2002; Richards and Waterbury 1996; Warde 2010.

63. See, for example, the throne speech of 2003.

64. Hibou 2006.

65. Some of these studies are purely denunciatory on principle. Others are concerned with the competition of economic interests. Others shed light on actual practices between venality and connivance and politics, and still others emphasise the extent of privileges without necessarily engaging in an understanding of their socio-political foundations, which would require research in political sociology and a mastery of social sciences methods.

66. This is a critique that can be levelled at studies like Benhaddou 2010; Zeroual 2014; Oubenal and Zeroual 2017; 2021.

67. Hibou and Tozy 2002; 2015b; Bogaert 2018.

68. Bayart 2004; 2017; Hibou 2012b; Hanieh 2013; Brown 2015; Tansel 2017; Chamayou 2018; Amable 2021; Ibrahim 2022.

69. Hachimi-Alaoui and Hibou 2023.

70. On the pre-colonial period: Kenbib 1996. On the colonial period: Rivet 1988; Cherifi 1988. On the first decades of independent Morocco, see: Waterbury 1970; Saïd Saadi 1989; Berrada and Saïd Saadi 1992; Tangeaoui 1993; Bono 2023.

71. Hibou 2023: It should be noted that most often it is not for them a question of principle but beyond that of the denunciation of an *excess* of privileges.

72. Catusse 2008; Benhaddou 2010; Zeroual 2014; Oubenal and Zeroual 2017; 2021.

NOTES   pp. [217–227]

73. Hibou and Bono 2016; Bono and Hibou 2017.
74. Foucault 2004a. It also runs the risk of "institutionalised egotism" that Peter Brown (1992, Chapter 1) criticises.

CONCLUSION

1. This is now quite banal in the French tradition of political sociology. See Bayart 2010; 2022; Hibou 2011.
2. Veyne 1976b.
3. Passeron 2006: 562.
4. This critique was voiced in various debates on the presentation of our book, particularly by Abdelahad Sebti, published as "A new reading of *Tisser le temps politique au Maroc*" (in Arabic) in the journal *Ribat al Koutoub*, June 2021 (https://ribatalkoutoub.com/?p=3798), in addition to remarks from reviewers.
5. Hibou 2006a; 2011 based on a reading of Foucault 1975.
6. In his famous text *Discourse on Voluntary Servitude*, la Boétie reconceptualises the practice of domination and obedience in a more complex and ambivalent way, revealing a fundamental element. The foundation of servitude is not primordial fear; power is not imposed from above but finds its power in its often painless and "venomous" integration into the mechanisms of everyday life and the interaction of multiple dependencies.
7. Based on the concept of the "constellation of interests", Weber (1978 [1922]) shows that domination operates most likely through the duo "command/obedience" or that of "action/repression" but that it occurs above all by transiting through situations in which heterogenous interests meet.
8. Foucault 1975 speaks of a power that is everywhere.
9. But most often it "is difficult to glimpse or attribute to social actors" in the extent that it "moves the situations of heterogenous interests". See Dobry, "Légitimité et calcul rationnel ... ", op.cit, pp. 130, 131.
10. Bouasria 2016.
11. Scott 2008.
12. Foucault 1997: 14.
13. See Chapter 2.
14. See Brown 1978, and particularly his preface to the French edition that explains his approach.
15. Inspired by both Starobinski 2002 and Bergson 1998 [1907] who talks about transitory continuous transition and the non-existence of discrete states.
16. Cohen 2016; 2017.
17. http://aujourdhui.ma/economie/une-13eme-region-marocaine-lancee-par-la-cgem-et-le-ministere-charge-des-mre
18. The national football team that participated in the World Cup in Russia, only had two resident-Moroccan subs who played in the national championships. Working languages on the team—other than football—were Rifian, German,

279

NOTES

English, Arabic, French and Spanish. Arabic-speaking journalists for the BEIN channel who covered the team were scandalised and ended up hiring translators to interview these young players, who brandished the Moroccan flag and played enthusiastically for the King, even though they did not bring him victory. See H. Aïdi, "The (African) Arab Cup", 13 December /2022 (https://africasacountry.com/2022/12/the-afro-arab-cup 2022).

19. An *'adel* is a traditional notary who still plays a fundamental role in everyday life. See Hibou and Tozy 2020, Chapter 6.

20. This is one of the important arguments Max Weber puts forward in his analysis of democracy analysed by Breuer 1995.

21. Daniel Valgan Viña, a Spanish national aged around sixty, had been sentenced to thirty years prison in Morocco for paedophilia. When the King of Spain visited Morocco, King Mohammed VI had given this man a royal pardon, before going back on his decision following an unprecedented protest movement. For an exhaustive analysis, see Hibou and Tozy 2020, Chapter 2.

22. As illustrated by the case of Sultan Moulay Abdelaziz (Algeciras Treaty) or the Sultan Moulay Hafid (Protectorate Treaty).

REFERENCES*

Aafif, M. (1980–81), "Les harka hassaniennes d'après l'œuvre d'Ibn Zaidane", *Hespéris-Tamuda*, 19, pp. 153–68.

Abdel-Haleem, M. (2005), *The Qur'an: A New Translation*, Oxford, Oxford University Press.

Abderraziq, A. (1925), *Al-islam wa oussoul al-houkm*, Cairo, Dar al-Hilal. Translated into French by Abdou Filali Ansari as *L'Islam et les fondements du pouvoir*, Paris, La Découverte, 1994.

Abitbol, M. (2009), *Histoire du Maroc*, Paris, Perrin.

Abouhani, A. (2013), *Gouverner les périphéries urbaines: De la gestion notabiliaire à la gouvernance urbaine au Maroc*, Paris, L'Harmattan and Rabat, INAU.

Achcar, G. (2013), *The People Want: A Radical Exploration of the Arab Uprising*, Berkeley, University of California Press.

Adelkhah, F. (2012), *Les Mille et une frontières de l'Iran: Quand les voyages forment la nation*, Paris, Karthala. Translated as *The Thousand and One Borders of Iran*, London, Routledge, 2019.

Ahmida, M. (2002), *Al-kitabat al-islahiya bi al Maghrib khilala al qarn al-tassi' 'achar, qadaayaha wa khassa'ssiha al fanniya* (Reformist Writings in Nineteenth-Century Morocco: Technical Themes and Particularities), Rabat, Imprimerie Dar al-Manahil.

Aït Mous, F. and Berriane, Y. (2016), "Droit à la terre et lutte pour l'égalité au Maroc: Le mouvement des soulaliyates", in H. Rachik (ed.), *Contester le droit: Communautés, familles et héritage au Maroc*, Casablanca, La Croisée des chemins, pp. 87–173.

Al-'Azm S. J. (1981), "Orientalism and orientalism in reverse", *Khamsin: Journal of Revolutionary Socialists of the Middle East*, 8, pp. 5–26. Translated into French as *Ces interdits qui nous hantent*, Marseilles, Parenthèses, MMSH-IFPO, 2008.

---

* Where French books are translated into English, we have cited the original French editions in the chapter endnotes. We have added available English translations here.

REFERENCES

Alliès, P. (1980), *L'Invention du territoire*, Grenoble, Presses universitaires de Grenoble.

Al-Susi, M. (1966), *Al-Mukhtar, Illigh qadiman wa haditan*, Rabat, Imprimerie royale.

———— (1973), *Al Ma'sul*, 20 volumes, Casablanca, Imprimerie Najah al-Jadida.

Amable, B. (2021), *La résistible ascension du néolibéralisme: Modernisation capitaliste et crise politique en France*, Paris, La Découverte.

Amarir, O. (2014), *Al issamiyoune assoussiyoune* (Soussis Autodidacts), Casablanca.

Anderson B. (1991), *Imagined Communities: Reflections on the Origin and Spread of Nationalism*, London, Verso.

Anglade, M.-P. (2015), *Casablanca, une "ville à l'envers": Urbanités métropolitaines au prisme de la marginalité sociale au Maroc*, PhD thesis in geography, University François-Rabelais, Tours.

Aoufi, N. and Hanchane, S. (eds) (2011), *Employabilité des jeunes: Les voies et les moyens. Agir sur le chômage et s'engager pour l'emploi qualifié*, Social and Economic Council, Senior Council for Education, Morocco.

Arendt, H. (1958), *The Human Condition*, Chicago, University of Chicago Press.

Arnaud, L. (1952), *Au temps des "mehallas" ou le Maroc de 1860 à 1912*, Casablanca, Éditions Atlantides.

Aubin, E. (1904), *Le Maroc d'aujourd'hui*, Paris, Armand Colin.

Ayache, G. (1956), *Le Bilan d'une colonisation*, Paris, Éditions sociales.

———— (1979), "La fonction d'arbitrage du makhzen", *Bulletin économique et social du Maroc*, 138–139, pp. 5–21.

———— (1981), *Les Origines de la guerre du Rif*, Paris, Publications la Sorbonne and Rabat, SMER.

Ayubi, N. (1991), *Political Islam: Religion and Politics in the Arab World*, London, Routledge.

Baida, J. (2001), "La pensée réformiste au Maroc à la veille du Protectorat", *Hespéris-Tamuda*, 39 (2), pp. 49–70.

Baida, J. (2012), "Les officiers des affaires indigènes et les contrôleurs civils au Maroc, quelles connaissances du pays et des habitants?", in M. Kenbib and J. Adnani (eds), *Le Local et le global dans l'écriture de l'histoire sociale, travaux offerts à Larbi Mezzine/Al mahalli wa al-choumouli fi kitabat at-tarikh al-ijitima'i, a'amal muhdat ila al-arabi Mezzine*, Publications of the Humanities Department, Mohammed V University, Rabat, pp. 115–18.

Baita, A. (1987), "La 'retraditionalisation' des structures étatiques dans le Maroc colonial", in K. Alioua and A. Doumou (eds), *L'État marocain dans la durée, 1850–1985*, Rabat, Edino, Codesria, pp. 35–64.

Bardonnet, D. et al. (eds) (1989), *Hassan II présente la Marche verte*, Paris, Plon.

Barkey, K. (1994), *Bandits and Bureaucrats: The Ottoman Route to State Centralisation*, Ithaca, Cornell University Press.

Barkey, K. and Hagen von, M. (eds) (1997), *After Empire: Multi-ethnic Societies and Nation-Building—The Soviet Union, and the Russian, Ottoman, and Habsburg Empires*, Boulder, Westview Press.

REFERENCES

Baron, C. and Belarbi, W. (2010), "Gouvernance participative et rôle des associations pour l'accès à l'eau dans la périphérie de Casablanca (Maroc)", in G. Schneier-Madanes (ed.), *L'Eau mondialisée*, Paris, La Découverte, pp. 381–401.

Barry A., Osborne, T. and Rose, N. (eds) (1996), *Foucault and Political Reason: Liberalism, Neo-liberalism and Rationalities of Government*, Chicago, University of Chicago Press.

Bayart, J.-F. (1981), "Le politique par le bas: Question de méthode", *Politique africaine*, 1, pp. 53–82.

——— (1989), *L'État en Afrique: La politique du ventre*, Paris, Fayard (second edition with new preface published in 2006). Translated by Mary Harper et al. as *The State in Africa: The Politics of the Belly*, London, Longman, 1993.

——— (1996), *L'Illusion identitaire*, Paris, Fayard. Translated by Steven Rendall as *The Illusion of Cultural Identity*, Chicago, University of Chicago Press, 2005.

——— (2000) "Africa in the world: A history of extraversion", *African Affairs*, (99), pp. 217–67.

——— (2004) *Le gouvernement du monde: Une critique politique de la globalisation*, Paris, Fayard. Translated by Andrew Brown as *Global Subjects: A Political Critique of Globalization*, Cambridge, Polity Press, 2007.

——— (2008), "Comparing from below", *Sociétés politiques comparées*, 1, http://fasopo.org/sites/default/files/papier1_eng_n1.pdf

——— (2010), *L'Islam républicain: Istanbul, Téhéran, Dakar*, Paris, Albin Michel.

——— (2017), *L'Impasse national-libérale: Globalisation et repli identitaire*, Paris, La Découverte.

——— (2022), *L'énergie de l'État: Pour une sociologie historique et comparée du politique*, Paris, La Découverte.

Bayart, J.-F. and Warnier, J.-P. (eds) (2004), *Matière à politique: Le pouvoir, le corps et les choses*, Paris, Karthala.

Bayly, C. (2004), *The Birth of the Modern World, 1780–1914: Global Connections and Comparisons*, Oxford, Basic Blackwell.

Bazwi, H. (1993), *L'UMT: Le rêve et la réalité*, Casablanca, Imprimerie Najah al-Jadida.

Bazzaz, S. (2010), *Forgotten Saints: History, Power, and Politics in the Making of Modern Morocco*, Cambridge, Cambridge University Press.

Belmqadem, R. (1993), *Awaqaf Maknass fi 'ahdi Moulay Ismail* (The Waqf in Meknes at the Time of Moulay Ismail, 1672–1727), Rabat, Ministry for Habous and Islamic Affairs, 2 volumes.

Ben'alla, M. (2007), *Tarikh al-awqaf al-islamiya fi al-Maghrib fi 'asri as-sa'diyines min khilali hawalaat Taroudante wa fas* (History of Islamic Waqf in Morocco Era: Based on Texts from Taroudant and Fez), Rabat, Ministry for Habous and Islamic Affairs, 2 volumes.

Bendella, A. (2011), "Artiste de rue", in M. Péraldi and M. Tozy (eds), *Casablanca: Figures et scènes métropolitaines*, Paris, Karthala, pp. 137–40.

——— (2016), "Une catégorie juridique pour gouverner la question du social", in

REFERENCES

B. Hibou and I. Bono (eds), *Le Gouvernement du social au Maroc*, Paris, Karthala, pp. 275–320.

Ben Driss, K. (2002), *Sidi Hamza al-Qadiri, Boudchichi: Le renouveau du soufisme au Maroc*, Rabat, Al Bouraq.

Benhaddou, A. (2010), *L'empire des sultans: Anthropologie politique au Maroc*, Paris, Riveneuve.

Benhima, Y. (2016), "Gouverner en movement: Le pouvoir itinérant dans le Maghreb mérinide (milieu du xive siècle)", in *Gouverner les hommes, gouverner les âmes*, Paris, Publications de la Sorbonne, pp. 241–53.

Benjamin, W. (1996), "Critique of Violence", in *Walter Benjamin: Selected Writings*, Cambridge Mass., Belknap Press.

Bennafla, K. (2013), "Illusion cartographique au Nord, barrière de sable à l'Est: les frontières mouvantes du Sahara occidental", *L'Espace politique*, 20 (2).

Bennison, A. K. (2014), "Drums, Banners, and Baraka: The Symbols of Authority During the First Century of Marinid Rule, 1250–1350", in A. K. Bennison (ed.), *The Articulation of Power in Medieval Iberia and the Maghrib*, Oxford, Oxford University Press, pp. 195–216.

Bennouna, M. (2002), *Héros sans gloire: Échec d'une révolution, 1963–1973*, Casablanca, Tarik Éditions.

Ben Srhir, K. (2009), *Morocco in British Archives: The Correspondence of J.D Hay with the Makhzen (1846–1886)*, Rabat, Dar Aby Raqraq (2nd edition).

———— (2011), *Britania wa ichkalyatou al-Islah fi al-Maghrib, 1904–1886* (Great Britain and the Question of Reform in Morocco), Publications of the Humanities Department, Mohammed V University, Rabat.

———— (2013), *Waahaat at-toukhoum wa houdoud al-Maghrib ac-charquiya: wata'iq wa khara'it moukhtara* (also published in 2013 in English as *Moroccan Confines Oases and Eastern Borders in the British Archives, 1882–1903*), Rabat, Publications de l'Institut royal de la recherche sur l'histoire du Maroc.

Bergson, H. (1907), *L'évolution créatrice*, Paris, Presses universitaires de France. Translated by Arthur Mitchell as *Creative Evolution*, New York, Dover, 1998.

———— (1922), *Durée et simultanéité*, Paris, Presses universitaires de France. Translated as *Duration and Simultaneity: Bergson and the Einsteinian Universe*, London, Clinamen Press Ltd, 1999.

———— (1908), *Le souvenir du présent et la fausse reconnaissance*, Paris, Presses universitaires de France. Translated as "Time and Free Will", in *Bergson: Key Writings*, edited by Keith Ansell Pearson and John Mullarkey, London, Continuum, 2002.

Berman, B. and Lonsdale, J. (1992), *Unhappy Valley: Conflict in Kenya and Africa*, London, James Currey, 2 volumes.

Bernus, E. (1982), "Territoires nomades: approche d'un géographe", *Production pastorale et société: Bulletin de l'équipe écologie et anthropologie des sociétés pastorales*, 11, pp. 84–90.

Berque, J. (1939), "Deux ans d'action artisanale à Fès", *Questions nord-africaines*, 15, pp. 3–28 (reprinted in *Opera Minora*, vol. 3, pp. 7–24).

REFERENCES

———— (1951), "Terroirs et seigneurs du Haut Atlas occidental", *Annales HSS*, 4, pp. 474–84.

———— (1958a), *Al-Yousî: Problèmes de la culture marocaine au xviiie siècle*, Paris, La Haye, Mouton.

———— (1958b), "Droit des terres et intégration sociale au Maghreb", *Cahiers internationaux de sociologie*, 25, pp. 38–74.

———— (1963), "Le système agraire au Maghreb", in J. Dresch, R. Dumont et al., *Réforme agraire au Maghreb*, Paris, Maspero, pp. 51–68.

———— (1967), *French North Africa: Maghrib Between Two World Wars*, New York, Praeger. Translation by Jean Stewart.

———— (1978/2001), "Identité collective et sujet de l'histoire", in *Opera minora*, Paris, Bouchène, vol. 3, pp. 327–33.

———— (1982), *Ulémas, fondateurs, insurgés du Maghreb (xviie siècle)*, Paris, Sindbad.

———— (1983), *Arab Rebirth: Pain and Ecstasy*, London, Al Saqi Books.

Berque, J. and J. Couleau, (1977), *Nous partons pour le Maroc*, Paris, PUF.

Berrada, A. and Saïd Saadi, M. (1992), "Le grand capital privé marocain", in J.-C. Santucci (ed.), *Le Maroc actuel: Une modernisation au miroir de la transition?* Paris, CNRS Éditions, pp. 325–91.

Berriane, Y. (2015), "Inclure les 'n'ayants pas droit': Terres collectives et inégalités de genre au Maroc", *L'Année du Maghreb*, 13, pp. 61–78.

———— (2017), "Development and countermovement: Reflections on the conflicts arising from the commodification of collective lands in Morocco", *International Development Policy*, 8.

Bertho, C. (1980), "L'invention de la Bretagne: Genèse sociale d'un stereotype", *Actes de la recherche en sciences sociales*, 35, pp. 45–62.

Bevir, M. (2010), *Democratic Governance*, Princeton, Princeton University Press.

Bezzaz, M. A. (1992), *Tarikh al-awbi'a wa al-maja'at bi al-Maghrib fi al qarnayn attamine wa al-attassi' 'achar (History of Epidemics and Famines in Morocco 18–19th centuries)*, Publications of the Humanities Department, Mohammed V University, Rabat.

Bidwell, R. (1973), *Morocco Under Colonial Rule: French Administration of Tribal Areas, 1912–1956*, London, Frank Cass.

Bloch, M. (1941), *Apologie de l'histoire, ou le métier d'historien*, Paris, Armand Colin. Translated by Peter Burke as *The Historian's Craft*, Manchester, Manchester University Press, 1992.

Bogaert, K. (2018), *Globalized Authoritarianism: Megaprojects, Slums, and Class Relations in Urban Morocco*, Minneapolis, University of Minnesota Press.

Bono, I. (2010), *In nome della società civile: Un caso di sviluppo participato in Marocco*, Milan, Guerini e Associati.

———— (2013), "Comment devenir employable? Certifier l'exclusion, l'indifférence et la stigmatisation sur le marché du travail au Maroc", in B. Hibou (ed.), *La Bureaucratisation néolibérale*, Paris, La Découverte, pp. 49–76.

———— (2015), "L'emploi comme revendication sectorielle. La naturalisation de la

REFERENCES

question sociale", in I. Bono, B. Hibou, H. Meddeb and M. Tozy, *L'État d'injustice au Maghreb: Maroc et Tunisie*, Paris, Karthala, pp. 261–304.

——— (2019), "Rescuing Biography from the Nation: Discrete Perspectives on Political Change in Morocco", in Y. Berriane, A. Derks, A. Kreil and D. Lüddeckens (eds), *Snapshots of Change: Methodological Approaches to the Study of Transforming Societies*, Basingstoke, New York, Palgrave Macmillan.

——— (2023), "Souveraineté économique et capitalisme de dissidence au Maroc: Jouer les conflits politiques dans la discretion", *Politique africaine*, numéro spécial "Souveraineté économique, lieu du politique au Maroc" coordinated by Béatrice Hibou and Nadia Hachimi-Alaouî, 171, October.

——— (2024), *Un entrepreneur du national au Maroc: Ahmed Benkirane, traces et discrétion*, Paris, Karthala.

Bono, I. and Hibou, B. (2017), "Development as a battlefield", *International Development Policy*, 8, pp. 3–36.

Bouasria, L. (2016), "La main invisible du service domestique: *Tsemsir* et production de l'ordre social à Casablanca", in B. Hibou and I. Bono (eds), *Le Gouvernement du social au Maroc*, Paris, Karthala, pp. 321–61.

Bouaziz, M. (1998), *Aux origines de la Koutla démocratique*, Casablanca, Publications of the Humanities Department, Aïn Chok, University Hassan II, Casablanca.

Boubrik, R. (1998), "Hommes de Dieu, hommes d'épée: Stratification sociale dans la société bidan", *Journal des africanistes*, 68 (1–2), pp. 261–71.

Bourqia, R. (1991), *Ad-dawla wa as-sulta wa al-mujtama', dirasa si at-tabit wa al-moutahaouil fi 'alaqat ad-dawla bi al qaba'il fi al maghrib* (The State, Power, and the Tribe: Permanence and Change in Relations Between the State and the Tribes), Beirut, Dar at-Tali'a.

——— (1993), "Don et théâtralité. Réflexion sur le rituel du don (*hadiyya*) offert au sultan au xixe siècle", *Hespéris-Tamuda*, 31, pp. 61–76.

Boutier, J., Dewerpe, A. and Nordman, D. (1984), "Le gouvernement épistolaire", in J. Boutier, A. Dewerpe and D. Nordman, *Un tour de France royal: Le voyage de Charles IX, 1564–1566*, Paris, Aubier, pp. 213–35.

Boutier, J., Landi, S. and Rouchon, O. (eds) (2009), *La Politique par correspondence: Les usages politiques de la lettre en Italie (xive xviiie siècle)*, Rennes, Presses universitaires de Rennes.

Breuer, S. (1995), "Max Weber et les formes de démocratie", *Revue européenne des sciences sociales*, 33 (1–01), pp. 39–50. Translated as "The concept of democracy in Weber's political sociology", in Schroeder R. (ed.), *Max Weber, Democracy and Modernisation*, London, Palgrave, 2020, pp. 1–13.

Breuer, S. (2010), "La domination rationnelle: À propos d'une catégorie de Max Weber", http://trivium.revues.org/3758.

Brignon, J. Abdelaziz, A., Boutaleb, B., Martinet, G. and Rosenberger, B. (1967), *Histoire du Maroc*, Paris, Hatier and Casablanca, Librairie nationale.

Brown, K. (1976), *The People of Sale*, Cambridge Mass., Harvard University Press.

Brown, P. (1978), *The Making of Late Antiquity*, Cambridge Mass., Harvard University Press.

REFERENCES

———— (1992), *Power and Persuasion in Late Antiquity: Towards a Christian Empire*, Madison, Wisconsin University Press.

Brown, W. (2015), *Undoing the Demos: Neoliberalism's Stealth Revolution*, New York, Zone Books.

Brunot, A. and Coquand, R. (1982), *Le Corps des Ponts et Chaussées*, Paris, CNRS Éditions.

Burbank, J. and Cooper, F. (2010), *Empires in the World History: Power and the Politics of Difference*, Princeton, Princeton University Press.

Burke III, E. (1976), *Prelude to Protectorate in Morocco: Precolonial Protest and Resistance, 1860–1912*, Chicago, University of Chicago Press.

———— (1979), "La mission scientifique au Maroc: Science sociale et politique dans l'âge de l'impérialisme", *Bulletin économique et social du Maroc*, 138–139, pp. 37–56.

———— (2014), *The Ethnographic State: France and the Invention of Moroccan Islam*, Berkeley, University of California Press.

Bussellam, M. (1994), "Musàhamat al-wathà 'iq aladliya fi Kitabati ba 'di a/jawànib min tarikh al-bàdiya: namüdaj tadla fi al qarn at-tàsi'ashar" (Adoul Documents to Describe Rural History: The Case of Nineteenth Century Tadla), *Hespéris-Tamuda*, 32, pp. 7–25.

Buttin, M. (2010), *Hassan II, de Gaulle, Ben Barka: Ce que je sais d'eux*, Paris, Karthala.

Cahiers du Sahara (2015), "Sahara: Aspects historiques, juridiques et économiques", *Les Cahiers du Sahara*, 16, Rabat, Ministry of Communication.

Castoriadis, C. (1975), *L'Institution imaginaire de la société*, Paris, Seuil. Translated by Kathleen Blamey as *The Imaginary Institution of Society*, Cambridge, Polity, 1987.

Catusse, M. (2008), *Le Temps des entrepreneurs? Politique et transformations du capitalisme au Maroc*, Paris, Maisonneuve & Larose.

Cefaï, D. (2003), "Introduction à Clifford Geertz", in C. Geertz, *Le Souk de Séfrou: Sur l'économie de bazar*, Paris, Bouchène, pp. 1–58.

Certeau (de), M. (1987), *La Faiblesse de croire*, Paris, Seuil. Translated by Saskia Brown, "The Weakness of Believing", in Graham Ward, *The Certeau Reader*, Oxford, Oxford University Press, 2000.

CESE (2013), *Nouveau Modèle de développement pour les provinces du Sud*, Rabat, Economic, Social and Environmental Council, October, http://www.ces.ma/Documents/PDF/Web-Rapport-NMDPSR-FR.pdf

Chamayou, G. (2018), *La Société ingouvernable: Une généalogie du libéralisme autoritaire*, Paris, La Fabrique. Translated as *The Ungovernable Society: A Genealogy of Authoritarian Liberalism*, Cambridge, Polity Press, 2021.

Chambergeat, P. (1961), "Les élections communales marocaines du 29 mai 1960", *Revue française de science politique*, 11 (1), pp. 89–117.

———— (1965), "L'administration et le douar", *Revue de géographie du Maroc*, 8, pp. 83–7.

Chartier, R. (1980), "Sciences sociales et découpage regional: Note sur deux débats, 1820–1920", *Actes de la recherche en sciences sociales*, 35, pp. 27–37.

REFERENCES

Chartier, R. (ed.) (1991), *La Correspondance: Les usages de la lettre au xixe siècle*, Paris, Fayard, 1991.

Chesnaux J. (2004), "Cinq propositions pour appréhender le temps", *Temporalités*, 1.

Cherifi, R. (1988), *Le Makhzen politique au Maroc: Hier et aujourd'hui*, Casablanca, Afrique-Orient.

Cherkaoui, M. (2007), *Morocco and the Sahara: Social Bonds and Geopolitical Issues*, Oxford, Bardwell Press.

Claisse, A. (1992), "Le makhzen aujourd'hui", in J.-C. Santucci (ed.), *Le Maroc actuel: Une modernisation au miroir de la transition?*, Paris, CNRS Éditions, pp. 285–310.

Clément, J.-F. (1992), "Les révoltes urbaines" in J.-C. Santucci (ed.), *Le Maroc actuel: Une modernisation au miroir de la transition?*, Paris, CNRS Éditions., pp. 393–406.

Cohen, A. (2016), "Le Coran dans le Maroc contemporain", *Genèses*, 105 (4), pp. 57–75.

———— (2017), "Voir et entendre le Livre: Une édition marocaine du Coran", *Gradhiva*, 26, pp. 72–99.

Cohn, B. (1996), *Colonialism and Its Forms of Knowledge: The British in India*, Princeton, Princeton University Press.

Colonna, F. and Le Pape, L. (2010), *Traces, désir de savoir et volonté d'être: L'après-colonie au Maghreb*, Paris, Sinbad, Actes Sud.

Collective (1976), *Abd el-Krim et la République du Rif: Actes du colloque international d'études historiques et sociologiques*, 18–20, January 1973, Paris, Maspero.

Cooper, F. (2005), *Colonialism in Question: Theory, Knowledge, History*, Berkeley, University of California Press.

Cooper, F. and Stoler, A. L. (eds) (1997), *Tensions of Empire: Colonial Cultures in a Bourgeois World*, Berkeley, University of California Press.

Correale, F. (1994–1995), *Frontières et territorialisation au Maroc: La naissance et l'évolution de la frontière méridionale—éléments pour une étude*, Master's thesis, Université d'Aix-Marseille.

Couleau, J. (1968), *La Paysannerie marocaine*, Paris, CNRS Éditions.

Cuono, M. (2013), "La rappresentanza democratica alla prova di governabilità e governance", *Fenomenologia e Società*, 34 (1), pp. 53–66.

Daadaoui, M. (2011), *Moroccan Monarchy and the Islamist Challenge: Maintaining Makhzen Power*, Basingstoke, New York, Palgrave MacMillan.

Daoud, M. (1966), *Tarikh Tetouan*, Tetouan, Imprimerie Mahdiya, vol. 6.

Daoud, Z. (1981) "Le cri de Casablanca et la situation explosive de Casablanca", *Lamalif*, 127, pp. 20–6.

———— (2007), *Les Années Lamalif, 1958–1988: Trente ans de journalisme au Maroc*, Casablanca, Tarik Éditions.

Dakhlia, J. (1988), "Dans la mouvance du prince: La symbolique du pouvoir itinérant au Maghreb", *Annales HSS*, 43 (3), pp. 735–60.

Damon, W and Verducci, S. (2006), *Taking Philanthropy Seriously: Beyond Noble Intentions to Responsible Giving*, Bloomington, Indiana University Press.

REFERENCES

Debarbieux, B. (1995), "Le lieu, le territoire et trois figures de rhétorique", *Espace géographique*, 24 (2), pp. 97–112.

———— (2015), *L'Espace de l'imaginaire: Essais et détours*, Paris, CNRS Éditions. Translated by Sheila Malovany Chevallier as *Social Imaginaries of Space*, Cheltenham, Edward Elgard Publishing, 2019.

Deleuze, G. (1990), *Pourparlers: 1972–1990*, Paris, Minuit. Translated by Martin Joughin as *Negotiations: 1972–1990*, New York, Columbia University Press, 1995.

Dessert, D. (1984), *Argent, pouvoir et société au Grand Siècle*, Paris, Fayard.

Diallo, A. (2017), *Le Gouvernement des itinérants par l'itinérance: Une sociologie historique des démarches d'immatriculation des migrants au Maroc*, research report Fasopo for the AFD.

Dieste, J. L. M and Villanova, J. L. (2013), "Les *interventores* du protectorat espagnol au Maroc: Contextes de production d'une connaissance politique des *cabilas*", *Cahier d'études africaines*, 211, pp. 595–624.

Duara, P. (1987), "State involution: A study of local finances in north China, 1911–1935", *Comparative Studies in Society and History*, 19 (1), pp. 132–61.

———— (1988), *Culture, Power and the State: Rural North China, 1900–1942*, Stanford, Stanford University Press.

Dubar C. (2008), "Temporalité, temporalités: Philosophie et sciences sociales", *Temporalités*, 8.

Dubois, V. (2003), *La Vie au guichet: Relation administrative et traitement de la misère*, Paris, Economica.

———— (2010), "Politiques au guichet, politique du guichet", in O. Borraz and V. Guiraudon (eds), *Politiques publiques 2: Changer la société*, Paris, Presses de Sciences Po, pp. 265–86.

Ecochard, M. (1955), *Casablanca: Le roman d'une ville*, Paris, Éditions de Paris.

Eickelman, D. F. (1976), *Moroccan Islam: Tradition and Society in a Pilgrimage Center*, Austin, University of Texas Press.

Eisenstadt, S. (1963), *The Political Systems of Empires*, New York, Free Press of Glencoe.

Elden, S. (2007), "Governmentality, calculation, territory", *Environment and Planning D: Society and Space*, 25, pp. 562–80.

Elden, S. and Crampton, J.W. (eds) (2007), *Space, Knowledge and Power. Foucault and Geography*, London, New York, Routledge.

El Mansour, M. (1990), *Morocco in the Reign of Mawlay Sulayman*, Wisbech, Middle East and North African Studies Press.

El Mohammadi, A. (2010), *Annasaq al-makhzani wa mas'alat al-istimrar* (The Makhzen System and the Question of Continuity), Publications of the Humanities Department, Mohammed V University, Rabat.

———— (2014), *As-sulta wa al mûjtama' fi al-Maghrib, namoudaj Ait Baamrane* (Power and Society in Morocco: The Case of Aït Baâmran), Publications of the Humanities Department, Mohammed V University, Rabat.

REFERENCES

El Moudden, A. (1983), "État et société rurale à travers la harka au Maroc du xixe siècle", *The Maghreb Review*, 8 (5–6), pp. 141–45.

————— (1991), "The Sharif and the Padishah: Three letters from Murad III to Abd al-Malik", *Hespéris-Tamuda*, 29 (1), pp. 113–26.

————— (1995), *Al Bawadi al-maghribiya qabla al isti'mar: qaba'il Inawen wa al-Makhzan bayna al qarn As-asadis 'achar wa at-atamin 'achar* (Moroccan Countryside Before Colonisation: The Inanouen Tribes and the Makhzen Between the Sixteenth and the Eighteenth centuries), Humanities Department, Mohammed V University, Rabat.

————— (2018), "Pouvoir makhzénien et vie locale entre harka et siyassa", in A. El Moudden, A. Bouhsane and Bouchentouf, L. (eds), *Confluences: Histoire, anthropologie et études littéraires*, Rabat, Éditions Bouregreg.

Ennaji, M. (1992), "Note sur le document makhzénien", *Hespéris-Tamuda*, 31 (2), pp. 69–74.

Ennaji, M. and Pascon, P. (1988), *Le Makhzen et le Sous al-aqsa: La correspondance politique de la Maison d'Illigh, 1821–1894*, Paris, CNRS Éditions and Casablanca, Éditions Toubkal.

Ennaji, M. and Tozy, M. (1987a), "La prison marocaine au xixe siècle", *Lamalif*, 186, pp. 38–40.

————— (1987b), "Visite d'un caïd rural à la cour de Hassan Ier", *Lamalif*, 188, pp. 70–2.

Faure, E. (1984), *Mémoires: Si tel doit être mon destin ce soir*, Paris, Plon.

Finch, M. P. M. (2018), "Imperial connections: Frederick Lugard, Charles Hartley, and Hubert Lyautey's English influences", *Journal of Imperial and Commonwealth History*, 46 (6), pp. 1044–66.

Foucauld, C. de (1888), *Reconnaissance au Maroc, 1883–1884*, Paris, Challamel.

Foucault, M. (1975), *Surveiller et punir. Naissance de la prison*, Paris, Gallimard. Translated by Alan Sheridan as *Discipline and Punish*, London, Vintage Books, 1977.

————— (1994), "La stratégie du pourtour", in *Dits et Écrits III, 1976–1979*, Paris, Gallimard.

————— (1997), *Il faut défendre la société: Cours au Collège de France, 1975–1976*, Paris, Gallimard. Translated by David Macey as *Society Must be Defended: Lectures at the College de France, 1975–1976*, New York, Picador, 2003.

————— (2004a), *Sécurité, territoire et population: Cours au Collège de France 1977–1978*, Paris, Gallimard, Le Seuil, Collection Hautes Études. Translated by Graham Burchell as *Security, Territory, Population: Lectures at the College de France, 1977–1978*, Basingstoke, Palgrave Macmillan, 2008.

————— (2004b), *Naissance de la biopolitique: Cours au Collège de France, 1978–1979*, Paris, Gallimard-Seuil. Translation by Graham Burchell, *The Birth of Biopolitics: Lectures at the Collège de France, 1978–1979*, New York, Palgrave Macmillan, 2008.

Fradera, J. M. (2018), *The Imperial Nation: Citizens and Subjects in the British, French, Spanish and American Empires*, Princeton, Princeton University Press.

REFERENCES

Frey, J.-P. (2004), "Henri Prost (1874–1959), parcours d'un urbaniste discret", *Urbanisme*, 336, pp. 79–87.

Fumey, E. (1903), *L'Art de la correspondance marocaine pour servir à l'étude du style épistolaire administratif employé au Maroc*, Paris, Librairie orientale et américaine.

Gagnol, L. (2011), "Le territoire peut-il être nomade? Espace et pouvoir au sein des sociétés fluides et mobiles", *L'Information géographique*, 75, 1, pp. 86–97.

Gardet, L. (1956), *La Cité musulmane: Vie sociale et politique*, Paris, Vrin.

Gaudin, J.-P. (1999), *Gouverner par contrat: L'action publique en question*, Paris, Presses de Science Po.

Geertz, C. (1971), *Islam Observed: Religious Development in Morocco and Indonesia*, Chicago, Phoenix Edition.

———— (1973), *The Interpretation of Cultures*, London, Hutchinson of London.

———— (1980), *Negara: The Theatre Stade in Nineteenth-Century Bali*, Princeton, Princeton University Press.

Geertz, H. (1979), "Patronyms in Action", in C. Geertz, H. Geertz and L. Rosen, *Meaning and Order in Moroccan Society: Three Essays in Cultural Analysis*, Cambridge, Cambridge University Press, pp. 315–91.

Gellner, E. (1962), "Patterns of rural rebellion in Morocco during the early years of independence", in *European Journal of Sociology*, 3(2), pp. 297–311, Cambridge, Cambridge University Press.

———— (1969a), "The great patron: A reinterpretation of tribal rebellions", *Archives européennes de sociologie*, 10 (1), pp. 61–9.

———— (1969b), *Saints of the Atlas*, London, Weidenfeld & Nicolson.

Ghouirgate, M. (2014), *L'Ordre almohade (1120–1269): Une nouvelle lecture anthropologique*, Toulouse, Presses universitaires du Mirail.

Ginzburg, C. (1980a), *The Cheese and the Worms: Cosmos of a Sixteenth-Century Miller*, translated by J. and A. Tedeschi, Baltimore, Johns Hopkins University Press.

———— (1980b), "Morelli, Freud, and Sherlock Holmes: Clues and the scientific method", translated by Anna Davies, *History Workshop*, 5–32.

———— (1990), *Myths, Emblems, Clues*, translated by John Tedeschi, London, Hutchinson Radius.

———— (1991), *Ecstasies: Deciphering the Witches Sabbath*, translated by Raymond Rosenthal, Chicago, University of Chicago Press.

Green A. (2000), *Le temps éclaté*, Paris, Les Éditions de Minuit.

Grossein, J.-P. (1996), "Présentation", in M. Weber, *Sociologie des religions* (French translation and presentation by J.-P. Grossein), Paris, Gallimard, pp. 51–129.

———— (2005), "De l'interprétation de quelques concepts wébériens", *Revue française de sociologie*, 46 (4), pp. 685–721.

———— (2006), "Présentation", in M. Weber, *l'Éthique protestante et l'esprit du capitalisme* (French translation and introduction by J.-P. Grossein), Paris, Gallimard, pp. 5–65.

———— (2016a), "Leçon de méthode wébérienne", in M. Weber, *Concepts fondamentaux de sociologie*, (texts chosen, translated and presented by J.-P. Grossein), Paris, Gallimard, pp. 9–90.

REFERENCES

———— (2016b), "Théorie et pratique de l'interprétation dans la sociologie de Max Weber", *Sociétés politiques comparées*, 39, http://www.fasopo.org/sites/default/files/varia1_n39.pdf

Guerraoui, D. (2000), "Le système des concessions: Une alternative pour la rénovation des services publics", *Critique économique*, 3, pp. 81–5.

Guillen, P. (1967), *L'Allemagne au Maroc de 1870 à 1905*, Paris, PUF.

Guilhot, N. (2004), *Financiers, philanthropes*, Paris, Raison d'agir.

Hachimi Alaoui, N. (2016), "Gouvernement par moment: Le wali dans les transports urbains à Casablanca", in B. Hibou and I. Bono (eds), *Le Gouvernement du social au Maroc*, Paris, Karthala, pp. 83–120.

———— (2017a), "Les enjeux et les impensés du service public au Maroc: Le cas du service public des transports à Casablanca", in G. Gallenga and L. Verdon (eds), *Penser le service public en Méditerranée*, Paris, Karthala-MMSH, pp. 143–68.

———— (2017b), "A 'time' to act: The 2015–20 Development Plan for Greater Casablanca", *International Development Policy*, 8, pp. 189–219.

———— (2019), *Gouverner l'incertitude: Les walis de Casablanca (2001–2015)*, PhD thesis in political science, Institut d'études politiques d'Aix-en-Provence.

Hachimi Alaoui, N. and Hibou, B. (2023), "Souveraineté économique et fondements du pouvoir. Réflexions à partir du Maroc contemporain", *Politique africaine*, special issue "Souveraineté économique, lieu du politique au Maroc" coordinated by Béatrice Hibou and Nadia Hachimi-Alaoui, n° 171, October.

Haenni, P. (2005), *L'Islam de marché: L'autre révolution conservatrice*, Paris, Seuil.

Hajji, M. (1968), "L'idée de nation au Maroc au xvie et xviie siècle", *Hespéris-Tamuda*, 9, pp. 109–22.

Hammoudi, A. (1997), *Master and Disciple: The Cultural Foundations of the Moroccan Authoritarianism*, Chicago, University of Chicago Press.

Hanieh, Adam (2013), *Lineages of Revolt: Issues of Contemporary Capitalism in the Middle East*, Chicago, Haymarket Books.

Haoues-Jouve, S. (2004), "La gestion déléguée des services d'eau et d'assainissement à Casablanca: entre ruptures et continuités", in C. Baron, J.-L. Coll, J.-J. Guibert, S. Haoues-Jouve et al., *Les Services urbains liés à l'environnement entre mondialisation et participation: Regards croisés Maroc-Sénégal*, researche report for the Urban Development Research program, project n° 82, pp. 231–62.

Harit, B. (2010), *Le Makhzen et ses auxiliaires d'autorité: Chioukhs, Mokademines et Arifates: histoire d'un corps d'agents publics en quête de reconnaissance*, PhD thesis in law, University of Perpignan.

Hartog F. (2003), *Régimes d'historicité: Présentisme et expérience du temps*, Paris, Le Seuil. Translated as *Regimes of Historicity: Presentism and Experiences of Time*, New York, Columbia University Press, 2015.

Hassan II (1976), *Le Défi: Mémoires*, Paris, Albin Michel.

———— (1993), *La Mémoire d'un roi: Entretiens avec Éric Laurent*, Paris, Plon.

Hermassi, E. (1972), *Leadership and National Development in North Africa*, Berkeley, University of California Press.

REFERENCES

Hespéris-Tamuda (2001), "Conference proceedings 'La réforme et ses usages', Bordeaux 1–3 December 1999", *Hespéris-Tamuda*, 39.

Hibou, B. (1999), *La Privatisation de l'État*, Paris, Karthala. Translated by Jonathan Derrick as *Privatizing the State*, London, Hurst, 2004.

———— (2006a), *La Force de l'obéissance: Économie politique de la répression en Tunisie*, Paris, La Découverte. Translated by Andrew Brown as *The Force of Obedience*, London, Polity, 2011.

———— (2006), "Maroc: d'un conservatisme à l'autre", in J.-F. Bayart, R. Banégas, R. Bertrand, B. Hibou and F. Mengin, *Legs colonial et gouvernance contemporaine*, vol. 2, Paris, Fasopo, pp. 123–186, http://www.fasopo.org/sites/default/files/legscolonial2_bh_1206.pdf

———— (2011), *Anatomie politique de la domination*, Paris, La Découverte. Translated by Andrew Brown as *The Political Anatomy of Domination*, New York, Palgrave Macmillan, 2017.

———— (2012a), "Economic crime and neoliberal modes of government", *Journal of Social History*, 45 (3), pp. 642–60.

———— (2012b), *La Bureaucratisation du monde à l'ère néolibérale*, Paris, La Découverte. Translated by Andrew Brown as *The Bureaucratisation of the World in the Neoliberal Era*, New York, Palgrave Macmillan, 2015.

———— (2023), "L'impossible politique des champions nationaux au Maroc: Souveraineté, imaginaire politique et modes de gouvernement ", *Politique africaine*, special issue "Souveraineté économique, lieu du politique au Maroc" coordinated by Béatrice Hibou and Nadia Hachimi-Alaoui, 171, October.

Hibou, B. and Bono, I. (2016), "Introduction: Gouverner le vivre ensemble", in B. Hibou and I. Bono (eds) *Le Gouvernement du social au Maroc*, Paris, Karthala, pp. 5–43.

Hibou, B. and Tozy, M. (2002), "De la friture sur la ligne des réformes: La libéralisation des télécommunications au Maroc", *Critique internationale*, 14, pp. 91–118.

———— (2015a), "Gouvernement personnel et gouvernement institutionnalisé de la charité: L'INDH au Maroc", in I. Bono, B. Hibou, H. Meddeb and M. Tozy, *L'État d'injustice au Maghreb. Maroc et Tunisie*, Paris, Karthala, pp. 383–432.

———— (2015b), "Une lecture wébérienne de la trajectoire de l'État au Maroc", *Sociétés politiques comparées*, 37, http://www.fasopo.org/sites/default/files/varia1_n37.pdf

———— (2020), *Tisser le temps politique au Maroc: Imaginaire d'Etat à l'ère néolibérale*, Paris, Karthala.

Hobsbawm, E. and Ranger, T. (eds) (1983), *The Invention of Tradition*, Cambridge, Cambridge University Press.

Hoffman, B. (1967), *The Structure of Traditional Moroccan Rural Society*, The Hague, Paris, Mouton.

Hoisington, W. A. (1995), *Lyautey and the French Conquest of Morocco*, Basingstoke, New York, Palgrave Macmillan.

Hussein, M. (2007), *Al-Sira, le prophète de l'islam raconté par ses compagnons*, Paris, Hachette.

293

REFERENCES

Husserl, E. (1928), *Vorlesungen zur Phänomenologie des inneren Zeitbewusstseins*, Max Niermeyer Verlag. Translated by J. Churchill as *The Phenomenology of Internal Consciousness*, Bloomington, Indiana University Press, 1964.

Ibn Khaldun, A. (2014), *Al Muqqadimah: Prolegomena*, Milton Keynes, Jiahu Books.

Ibn Mansour, A. (1962), "Introduction", in A. Ibn Zaidane, *Al-'Iz wa as-sawla fi Maalimi nodhomi ad-dawla* (Presitge and Authority in the Organisation of the State), vol. 1, Rabat, Imprimerie royale, pp. A-I.

Ibn Zaidane, A. (1962), *Al-'Iz wa as-sawla fi Maalimi nodhomi ad-dawla* (Prestige and Authority in the Organisation of the State), Rabat, Imprimerie royale, 2 volumes.

————— (2008), *Ithaf a'lam an-nass bi akhbari Hadirati Maknas* (Celebrating Illustrious Figures Through the History of the Town of Meknes), Cairo, Maktabat at-taqafa ad-diniya, 5 volumes.

Ibrahim, A. (2022), *Authoritarian Century: Omens of a Post-Liberal Future*, London, Hurst.

ICJ, International Court of Justice (1975), "Sahara occidental, avis consultatif du 16 octobre 1975", *Recueil des arrêts, avis consultatifs et ordonnances*, The Hague, International Court of Justice/ "Western Sahara: Advisory Opinion of 16 October 1975", *Reports of judgments, advisory opinions and order*, International Court of Justice, The Hague.

Iraki, A. (2003), *Les Notables du makhzen à l'épreuve de la gouvernance: Élites locales, gestion urbaine et développement au Maroc*, Paris, L'Harmattan and Rabat, INAU.

————— (ed.) (2016), *Mobilisations collectives, mouvement associatif et procédures de mise en œuvre de l'INDH dans les quartiers cibles*, research project INAU-ONDH, summary, 2 June 2021.

Jamous, R. (2017), *Le Sultan des frontières: Essai d'ethnologie historique du Maroc*, Nanterre, Société d'ethnologie.

Jebli, A. (2015), *Awraq min sahat al-mouqawama al-maghribiya* (Notes on the National Resistance Movement), Rabat, Dar al-maarif al-jadida.

Jibril, M. (1981), "Les événements et les problèmes de fond", *Lamalif*, 127, August, pp. 28–31.

Jobin, G. (2014), *Lyautey, le Résident: Le Maroc n'est qu'une province de mon cœur*, Casablanca, Express and Paris, Magellan & Cie.

Jolly, G. (2000), *Gestion de l'eau dans le N'fis Haouz de Marrakech et mise en place des Associations des utilisateurs des eaux d'irrigation*, summary report, Centre nationale des études agronomiques des régions chaudes, http://www.isiimm.agropolis.org/OSIRIS/report/moHaNfis_Jolly03102000_Synthese.pdf

Joumani, A. (2009), *L'Oasis d'Asrir: Éléments d'histoire sociale de l'oued Noun*, Casablanca, La Croisée des chemins.

Julien, C.A. (1978), *Le Maroc face aux impérialismes*, Paris, Éditions Jeune Afrique.

Justinard, L. (1925), "Notes sur l'histoire du Sous au xixe siècle. 1", *Hésperis-Tamuda*, 5, pp. 265–76.

————— (1926), "Notes sur l'histoire du Sous au xixe siècle. 2", *Hésperis-Tamuda*, 6, pp. 351–64.

————— (1951), *Un grand chef berbère: Le caïd Goundafi*, Paris, Atlantides.

294

REFERENCES

———— (1954), *Un petit royaume berbère: Le Tazeroualt—Un saint berbère, Sidi Ahmed ou Moussa*, Paris, Maisonneuve.

Kably, M. (ed.) (2011), *Histoire du Maroc: Réactualisation et synthèse*, Rabat, Institut royal pour la recherche sur l'histoire du Maroc.

Kaddouri, A. (2001), "Les réformes au Maroc: Usages politiques, usages sociaux", *Hespéris-Tamuda*, 39 (2), pp. 39–47.

Kadiri, Z., Tozy, M. and Errahj, M. (2010), "L'eau d'irrigation et les élections communales au Moyen Sebou: L'association des irrigants (AUEA) comme espace de compétition politique", in M. Tozy (ed.), *Élections au Maroc: Entre partis et notables (2007–2009)*, Casablanca, Imprimerie Najah al-Jadida, pp. 199–227.

Kenbib, M. (1996), *Les Protégés. Contribution à l'histoire contemporaine du Maroc*, Publications of the Humanities Department, Mohammed V University, Rabat.

Kumar, K. (2017), *How Five Imperial Regimes Shaped the World*, Princeton, Princeton University Press.

La Boétie, E. (de) (2015), *De la servitude volontaire*, Paris, Éditions Bouchène, annotated, commented and translated by A. Mahé with M. Safouane, H. Berrada, M. Naoui, A. Hamdi-Chérif and A. Kezzar). Translated as *Discourse on Voluntary Servitude*, Indiapolis, Hackett Publishing, 2012.

Labaronne, D. (ed.) (2012), *RSE, culture d'entreprise et développement territorial: Analyse monographique d'une entreprise publique marocaine, l'OCP*, Casablanca, final research report, Université de Bordeaux-OCP research convention (2011–2012).

Lahbabi, M. (1957), *Le Gouvernement marocain à l'aube du xxᵉ siècle*, Rabat, Éditions techniques nord-africaines (republished in 1958 with a preface by Mehdi Ben Barka).

———— (2009), *L'Union socialiste des forces populaires, un demi-siècle d'école de patriotisme et de citoyenneté: Al Koutla El Watania, l'agonie d'une grande espérance*, Rabat, Top Press.

Lakhsassi, A. and Sebti, A. (1999), *Mina achay ila athai, al 'ada wa at-tarikh* (From Chai to Tea, uses and history), Publications of the Humanities Department, Mohammed V University, Rabat.

Lakhsassi, A. and Tozy, M. (2000), "Segmentarité et théorie des leff-s: Tahuggwat et Taguzult dans le Sud-Ouest marocain", *Hespéris-Tamuda*, 38, pp. 183–214.

Lambelet, A. (2014), *La Philanthropie*, Paris, Presses de Sciences Po.

Laoust, H. (1970), *Politique de Ghazali*, Paris, Paul Geuthner.

Laroui, A. (1977), *Les Origines sociales et culturelles du nationalisme marocain, 1830–1912*, Paris, Maspero.

———— (1977b), *The History of the Maghrib: An Interpretive Essay*, Princeton, Princeton University Press.

———— (2005), *Le Maroc et Hassan II: Un témoignage*, Québec, Presses Inter Universitaires and Casablanca, Centre culturel arabe.

Le Saout, D. and Rollinde, M. (eds) (1999), *Émeutes et mouvements sociaux au Maghreb*, Paris, Karthala.

Leca, J. and Schemeil, Y. (1983), "Clientélisme et patrimonialisme dans le monde

REFERENCES

arabe", *International Political Science Review / Revue internationale de science politique*, 4 (4), pp. 455–94.

Leveau, R. (1985), *Le Fellah marocain défenseur du trône*, Paris, Presses de Sciences Po.

Levi, G. (1988). *L'eredità immateriale. Carriera di un esorcista nel Piemonte del Seicent*, Translated by Lydia Cochrane as *Inheriting power, the story of an exorcist*, Chicago, Chicago University Press.

Lignereux, A. (2012), *L'Empire des Français, 1799–1815*, Paris, Seuil.

Linz, J. (2000), *Totalitarian and Authoritarian Regimes*, Boulder, London, Lynne Rienner.

Linz, J. and Stepan, A. (1996), *Problems of Democratic Transition and Consolidation: Southern Europe, South America and Post-Communist Europe*, Baltimore, London, Johns Hopkins University Press.

Lipsky, M. (1980), *Street-Level Bureaucracy: Dilemmas of the Individual in Public Services*, New York, Russel Sage Foundation.

Lonsdale, J. (1986), "Political Accountability in African History", in P. Chabal (ed.), *Political Domination in Africa: Reflections on the Limits of Power*, Cambridge, Cambridge University Press, pp. 126–57.

———— (1989), "The Conquest State of Kenya, 1895–1905", in J. A. de Moor and H. L. Wesseling (eds), *Imperialism and War: Essays on Colonial Wars in Asia and Africa*, Leiden, Brill.

Lydon, G. (2009), *On Trans-Saharan Trails: Islamic Law, Trade Networks and Cross-Cultural Exchange in Western Africa*, Cambridge, Cambridge University Press.

Madeline, F. (2014), *Les Plantagenêts et leur empire: Construire un territoire politique*, Rennes, Presses universitaires de Rennes.

Magat, R. (1989), *Philanthropic Giving: Studies in Varieties and Goals*, New York, Oxford University Press.

Mahdi, M. (2010), "La tribu au secours du développement pastoral", *Études rurales*, 184 (2), pp. 133–48.

Marais, O. (1963), "L'élection de la Chambre des représentants du Maroc", *Annuaire d'Afrique du Nord*, 2, pp. 85–106.

———— (1964), "La classe dirigeante au Maroc", *Revue française de science politique*, 14 (4), pp. 709–37.

Marcuse, H. (1941), "Some Social Implications of Modern Technology" in A. Arato and E. Gebhardt (eds), *The Essential Frankfurt School Reader*, London, Continuum, 1982, pp. 138–62.

Marin, L. (1981), *Le Portrait du roi*, Paris, Minuit.

Markovits, C. (2017), "Le monde indien", in P. Singaravélou and S. Venaire (eds), *Histoire du monde au xixe siècle*, Paris, Fayard, pp. 663–75.

Mastropaolo, A. (2011), *La democrazia è une causa persa? Paradossi di un'invenzione imperfetta*, Turin, Bollati Boringhieri. Translated as *Is Democracy a Lost Cause? Paradoxes of an Imperfect Invention*, Colchester, ECPR Press, 2012.

Maxwell, G. (1968), *El-Glaoui, dernier seigneur de l'Atlas, 1893–1956* (translated by J. Papy), Paris, Fayard.

REFERENCES

Meeker, M. (2002), *A Nation of Empire: The Ottoman Legacy in Turkish Modernity*, Berkeley, University of California Press.

Menouni, A. (1979), *Le Syndicalisme ouvrier au Maroc*, Casablanca, Les Éditions maghrébines.

Michaux-Bellaire, E. (1908), "Proclamation de la déchéance de Moulay Abdelaziz et de la reconnaissance de Moulay Abdelhafid par les ouléma de Fès: Une tentative de restauration idrisside à Fès", *Revue du monde musulman*, 5 (7), pp. 424–435.

———— (1925) "La souveraineté et le Califat au Maroc", *Revue du Monde Musulman*, Vol LIX, pp. 117–45.

Michelon, B., DosGhali, J. Boulay, J.-C., Saidi Dahman, A., Nejmi, A., Tamim, M., Tozy, M., Yghir, M. and Simond, J.-J. (2010), *Électrification rurale décentralisée: Les leçons de la vallée de l'Ouneine*, Cahier de la coopération, 7, Lausanne, École polytechnique fédérale de Lausanne.

Miège, J.-L. (1961), *Le Maroc et l'Europe (1830–1894)*, vol. 1, Paris, PUF.

Milliot, L. (1922), *Les Terres collectives*, Paris, Leroux.

———— (1953), *Introduction à l'étude du droit musulman*, Paris, Sirey.

Miras, C. (de) (2010), "Les services urbains de distribution d'eau potable et d'assainissement au Maroc, ou les exigences de l'émergence", *Géocarrefour*, 85 (2), pp. 119–27.

Miras, C. (de) and Godard, X. (2006), "Les firmes concessionnaires de service public au Maroc: Eau potable, assainissement et transports collectifs", *Méditerranée*, 106, pp. 113–24.

Miras, C. (de) and Le Tellier, J. (avec Saloui, A.) (2005), *Gouvernance urbaine et accès à l'eau potable au Maroc: Partenariat public-privé à Casablanca et Tanger-Tétouan*, Paris, L'Harmattan.

Mohsen-Finan, K. (1997), *Sahara occidental: Les enjeux d'un conflit régional*, Paris, CNRS Éditions.

Mouline, N. (2009), *Le Califat imaginaire d'Ahmad al-Mansûr: Pouvoir et diplomatie au Maroc au xvie siècle*, Paris, PUF.

———— (2016), "Qui sera l'État? Le soulèvement du Rif reconsidéré (1958–1959)", *Le Carnet du Centre Jacques Berque*, https://cjb.hypotheses.org/186

Mounjib, M. (1992), *La Monarchie marocaine et la lutte pour le pouvoir: Hassan II face à l'opposition nationale*, Paris, l'Harmattan.

Munson, H. Jr. (1993), *Religion and Power in Morocco*, New Haven, Conn., Yale University Press.

Naïmi, M. (1990), *As-sahra min khilali bilad Takna* (The Sahara Through the Tekna Country), Rabat, Éditions Okad, pp. 121–83.

———— (2004), *La Dynamique des alliances ouest-sahariennes*, Paris, Éditions de la Maison des sciences de l'homme.

Nasiri (alias Ahmed Bin Khâlid al-Nâsiri Esslâoui) (1907), *Al istiqsaa li akhbar dowali al Maghrib al aqsaa*, vol. 9, Rabat, Dar Al Kitab. Translated into French by Eugène Fumey as *Chronique de la dynastie alaouite du Maroc, 1631–1894*, Paris, Ernest Leroux, 2nd edition 1997.

REFERENCES

Nehlil, M. (1915/2013), *Rassa'il Charifa* (Sharifian Letters), prepared and presented by J. Adnani and A. Benhadda, Publications of the Humanities Department, Mohammed V University, Rabat.

Nordman, D. (1980–81), "Les expéditions de Moulay Hassan", *Hespéris-Tamuda*, 19, pp. 23–152.

———— (1986), "La mémoire d'un captif", *Annales ESC*, 41 (6), pp. 1397–418.

———— (1997), "De quelques catégories de la science géographique: Frontière, région et hinterland en Afrique du Nord", *Annales HSS*, 52 (5), pp. 969–86.

OCDE (2016), *Étude de l'OCDE sur la gestion des risques au Maroc*, Paris, Éditions de l'OCDE. Translated into English: *OECD Review of Risk Management in Morocco*, Paris, OECD, 2017.

Oubenal, M. and Zeroual, A. (2017), "Gouverner par la gouvernance: Les nouvelles modalités de contrôle des élites économiques au Maroc", *Critique internationale*, 74, pp. 9–32.

———— (2021), "État actionnaire et capitalisme de connivence: Le cas de la Caisse de dépôt et gestion (CDG)", *Revue de la régulation*, n° 30.

Oufkir, F. (2000), *Les Jardins du roi: Oufkir, Hassan II et nous*, Paris, Michel Lafon.

Oufkir, M. (2006), *L'Étrangère*, Paris, Grasset.

Oufkir, M. and Fitoussi, M. (1999), *La Prisonnière*, Paris, Grasset.

Oufkir, R. (2003), *Les Invités: Vingt ans dans les prisons du roi*, Paris, Flammarion.

Palazzoli, C. (ed.) (1974), *Le Maroc politique*, compiled and presented by C. Palazzoli, Paris, Sindbad.

Pascon, P. (1971), "La formation de la société marocaine", *Bulletin économique et social du Maroc*, vol. 33, pp. 1–25.

———— (1975–1977), "Sigillographie marocaine. 1. Empreintes de validation des souverains 'alawites", *Hesperis-Tamuda*, 17, pp. 165–214.

———— (1978), *Le Haouz de Marrakech*, Paris, Maisonneuve Larose, 2 volumes.

Pascon, P. and Bentahar, M. (1970), *Ce que disent 296 jeunes ruraux*, Rabat, Société d'études économiques, sociales et statistiques du Maroc.

Passeron, J.-C. (1996), "Introduction", in M. Weber (1996), *Sociologie des religions*, translated and presented by J.-P. Grossein, Paris, Gallimard, pp. 1–49.

———— (2006), *Le raisonnement sociologique*, Paris, Albin Michel. Translated by Rachel Gomme as *Sociological Reasoning: A non-Popperian Space of Argumentation*. Oxford, Bardwell Press, 2013.

Picon, A. (1992), *L'Invention de l'ingénieur modern: L'École des Ponts et Chaussées (1747–1851)*, Paris, Presses de l'École nationale des Ponts et Chaussées.

Pierru, F. (2012), "Le mandarin, le gestionnaire et le consultant: Le tournant néo-libéral de la politique hospitalière", *Actes de la recherche en sciences sociales*, 94 (4), pp. 32–51.

Planel, S. (2009), "Transformations de l'État et politiques territoriales dans le Maroc contemporain", *L'Espace politique*, 7 (1).

Problèmes économiques (2008), issue "Le capitalisme saisi par la philanthropie", 2957, pp. 3–25.

REFERENCES

Przeworski, A., Stokes, S. C. and Manin, B. (1999), *Democracy, Accountability and Representation*, Cambridge, Cambridge University Press.

Rabinow, P. (1989), *French Modern: Norms and Forms of the Social Environment, 1800–1950*, Chicago, University of Chicago Press.

Retaillé, D. (1998), "Concepts du nomadisme et nomadisation des concepts", in R. Knafou (ed.), *La Planète 'nomade': Les mobilités géographiques d'aujourd'hui*, Paris, Belin, pp. 37–58.

Revault d'Allonnes, M. (2016), *Le Miroir et la scène: Ce que peut la représentation politique*, Paris, Seuil.

Richards, A. and Waterbury, J. (1996), *A Political Economy of the Middle East*, Boulder, Oxford, Westview Press.

Rivet, D. (1988), *Lyautey et l'institution du protectorat français au Maroc, 1912–1925*, Paris, L'Harmattan, 3 volumes.

———— (2012), *Histoire du Maroc*, Paris, Fayard.

Rollinde, M. (2003), "La Marche verte: Un nationalisme royal aux couleurs de l'islam", *Le Mouvement social*, 202, pp. 133–51.

Rosa, H. (2015), *Social Acceleration: A New Theory of Modernity*, New York, Columbia University Press.

Rosanvallon, P. (2006), *La Contre-démocratie: La politique à l'âge de la défiance*, Paris, Seuil. Translated as *Counter-democracy: Politics in an Age of Distrust*, New York, Cambridge University Press, 2008.

———— (2015), *Le Bon Gouvernement*, Paris, Seuil.

Rose, N. (1999), *Powers of Freedom: Reframing Political Thought*, Cambridge, Cambridge University Press.

Rosen, L. (1979), "Social Identity and Points of Attachment: Approaches to Social Organization", in C. Geertz, H. Geertz et L. Rosen (eds), *Meaning and Order in Moroccan Society: Three Essays in Cultural Analysis*, Cambridge, Cambridge University Press, pp. 19–122.

Rosenberger, B. (1977), "Population et crise au Maroc aux vie et xviie siècles: Famines et épidémies", *Cahiers de la Méditerranée*, hors-série 2, pp. 137–49.

Rosenberger, B. et Triki, H. (1973), "Famines et épidémies au Maroc aux xvie et xviie siècles", *Hespéris-Tamuda*, 14, pp. 109–75.

———— (1974), "Famines et épidémies au Maroc aux xvie et xviie siècles (suite)", *Hespéris-Tamuda*, 15, pp. 5–103.

Rousset, M. (1968), "Le rôle du ministère de l'Intérieur et sa place au sein de l'administration marocaine", *Annuaire de l'Afrique du Nord*, 7, pp. 91–106.

Roussillon, A. (2001a), "La réforme et ses usages: Perspectives marocaines", *Hespéris-Tamuda*, 39 (2), pp. 7–14.

———— (2001b), "Salafisme, réformisme, nationalisme: Essai de clarification", *Hespéris-Tamuda*, 39 (2), pp. 15–37.

Roy, O. (1992), *L'Échec de l'islam politique*, Paris, Seuil. Translated by Carol Volk as *The Failure of Political Islam*, Cambridge, Mass., Harvard University Press, 1994.

Saïd Saadi, M. (1989), *Les groupes financiers au Maroc*, Rabat, Éditions Okad.

REFERENCES

Saaf, A. (1991), "Vers la décrépitude de l'État néopatrimonial", in M. Camau (ed.), *Changements politiques au Maghreb*, Paris, CNRS Éditions, pp. 73–107.

Saigh, S. (1986), *La France et les frontières maroco-algériennes, 1873–1902*, Paris, CNRS Éditions.

Saint-Martin, D. (2006), "Le consulting et l'État: Une analyse comparé de l'offre et de la demande", *Revue française d'administration publique*, 120, pp. 743–56.

Salzmann, A. (1993), "An Ancient Regime Revisited: Privatization and Political Economy in the Eighteenth-Century Ottoman Empire", *Politics and Society*, 21 (4), December, pp. 393–423.

Samuel, B. (2013), *La Production macroéconomique du reel: Formalités et pouvoir au Burkina Faso, en Mauritanie et en Guadeloupe*, PhD thesis in political science, Institut d'études politiques de Paris.

Saul, S. (2002), "L'électrification du Maroc à l'époque du protectorat", *Outre-Mers*, 89 (334), pp. 491–512.

Sawyer, S. W. (2014), "Ces nations façonnées par les empires et la globalisation: Réécrire le récit national du xixᵉ siècle aujourd'hui", *Annales. Histoire, sciences sociales*, pp. 117–37.

Schehl, V. (2016), "Du blé au pain, que régule-t-on? L'ambiguïté comme mode de gouvernement", in B. Hibou and I. Bono (eds), *Le Gouvernement du social au Maroc*, Paris, Karthala, pp. 121–58.

Schroeter, D. (1988), *Merchants of Essaouira: Urban Society and Imperialism in Southwestern Morocco, 1844–1886*, Cambridge, Cambridge University Press.

Scott, J. (2008), *Domination and the Arts of Resistance: Hidden Transcripts*, New Haven, Conn., Yale University Press.

Sebe, B. (2015), *Heroic Imperialists in Africa: The Promotion of British and French Colonial Heroes*, Manchester, Manchester University Press.

Sebti, A. (1991), "Chroniques de la contestation citadine: Fès et la révolte des tanneurs (1873–1874)", *Hespéris-Tamuda*, 29 (2), pp. 283–312.

——— (2009), *Bayna az-zattat wa qati' at-tariq, amnou at-torouqfi maghribi qabla al-ist'mar* (Facilitating or Blocking the Road, the Security of Roads in Precolonial Morocco) Casablanca, Éditions Toubkal.

——— (2015), *At-tarikh al-mûta'did, qira'at wa mûhawarat taarikhiya* (Multiple Pasts: Historical Readings and Discussions), Casablanca, Éditions Toubkal.

Seghers, V. (2007), *Ce qui motive les entreprises mécène:. Philanthropie, investissement, responsabilité sociale?*, Paris, Autrement.

Sharabi, H. (1988), *Neopatriarchy: A Theory of Distorted Change in Arab Society*, New York, Oxford University Press.

Siblot, Y. (2006), *Faire valoir ses droits au quotidien: Les services publics dans les quartiers populaires*, Paris, Presses de Sciences Po.

Simenel, R. (2010), *L'origine est aux frontières: Les Aït Ba'amran, un exil en terre d'arganiers (Sud Maroc)*, Paris, CNRS Éditions, Éditions de la Maison des sciences de l'homme.

Simou, B. (1995), *Les Réformes militaires au Maroc de 1844 à 1912*, Publication of the Humanities Department, Mohammed V University, Rabat.

REFERENCES

Slimani, A., Mansouri, O and Zakaria, A. (2018), *L'Instance rifaine*, Rabat, publications du Centre d'études et de recherches Ben Saïd Aït Idder.

Slyomovics, S. (2005), *The Performance of Human Rights in Morocco*, Philadelphia, University of Pensylvania Press.

Spire, A. (2008), *Accueillir ou reconduire: Enquête sur les guichets de l'immigration*, Paris, Raison d'agir.

Starobinski, J. (2002), *Montaigne en mouvement*, Paris, Gallimard.

Steinmetz, G. (ed.) (2013), *Sociology & Empire: The Imperial Entanglements of a Discipline*, Durham, London, Duke University Press.

Tamim, M. (2005), *Reproduction sociale, territorialité des populations et pouvoir local. Cas de la vallée d'Ouneine dans le Haut-Atlas*, PhD in geography, Publication of the Humanities Department, Mohammed V University, Rabat.

Tamim, M. and Tozy, M. (2010), "Politique des marges et marges du politique: Les logiques du vote collectif à Ouneine (Haut-Atlas, Maroc)", in M. Tozy (ed.), *Élections au Maroc, entre partis et notables (2007–2009)*, Casablanca, Centre marocain des sciences sociales, pp. 107–60.

Tangeaoui, S. (1993), *Les entrepreneurs marocains: Pouvoir, société et modernité*, Paris, Karthala.

Tansel, C. B. (ed.) (2017) *State of Discipline: Authoritarian Neoliberalism and the Constested Reproduction of Capitalist Order*, Lanham, Maryland, Rowman & Littlefield Publishers.

Taoufiq, A. (1983), *Al Mujtama' al maghribi fi al-qarn al-tassi' 'ashar. Inultan, 1850–1912* (Moroccan Society in the 19th Century), Publications of the Humanities Department, Mohammed V University, Rabat.

Targa (2003), *Étude sur la sociologie de la culture du cannabis dans le Rif central*, http://www.targa-aide.org/index.php/12-projets/projets-realises/25-etude-sur-la-sociologie-de-la-culture-du-cannabis-dans-le-rif-central

———— (2005), *Études complémentaires sur la transformation, la production et la sociologie de la culture du cannabis dans le Rif central*, http://www.targa-aide.org/index.php/12-projets/projets-realises/22-etudes-complementaires-sur-le-cannabis

———— (2006), *Sociologie du cannabis*, miméo, Rabat, Targa.

———— (2007), *Économie du cannabis*, miméo, Rabat, Targa.

Tazi, A. (1979), *Correspondance officielle relative aux règnes des deux souverains, Mawlay al-Hassan et Mawlay Abdelaziz*, Rabat, Publications de l'IURS, Imprimerie Agdal.

Tilly, C. (1997), "How Empires End", in K. Barkey and M. von Hagen (eds), *After Empire: Multi-ethnic Societies and Nation-Building—The Soviet Union, and the Russian, Ottoman, and Habsburg empires*, Boulder, Westview Press.

Tozy, M. (1981), "Monopolisation de la production symbolique et hiérarchisation du champ politico-religieux", in C. Souriau (ed.), *Le Maghreb musulman en 1979*, Paris, CNRS Éditions, pp. 219–34.

———— (1984), *Champ et contrechamp politico-religieux au Maroc*, PhD thesis in political science, Université d'Aix-Marseille.

———— (1988), "De quelques lieux de la compétition politique au Tazeroualt", *Bulletin économique et social du Maroc*, 159 (60–61), pp. 155–81.

REFERENCES

———— (1991a) "Représentation/intercession: les enjeux de pouvoir dans les champs politiques désamorcés au Maroc", in M. Camau (ed.), *Changements politiques au Maghreb*, Paris, CNRS Éditions, pp. 153–68.

———— (1999), *Monarchie et islam politique au Maroc*, Paris, Presses de Science Po.

———— (2000), "L'Amghar, variacions entorn de les modalitats de producció del lideratge al Gran Atles", *Revista d'etnologia de Catalunya*, 16, pp. 62–73.

———— (2008), "Morocco's elections. Islamists, technocrats, and the palace", *Journal of Democracy*, 19 (1), pp. 34–41.

———— (2009), "Leaders et leadership: configurations complexes, ressources politiques et influence potentielle des leaders dans le cas de l'Oriental marocain", in P. Bonte, M. Elloumi, H. Guillaume and M. Mahdi (eds), *Développement rural, environnement et enjeux territoriaux: Regards croisés Oriental marocain et Sud-Est tunisien*, Tunis, Cérès Éditions, pp. 363–78.

———— (ed.) (2010), *Élections au Maroc: Entre partis et notables (2007–2009)*, Casablanca, Centre marocain des sciences sociales, Imprimerie Najah al-Jadida.

Tozy, M., with the collaboration of Bendella, A., Ouazzani, A. and Rachik, H. (2013), *Pour une mise en œuvre des droits de pétition populaire et d'initiative législative: Étude comparative*, Casablanca, Forum des alternatives Maroc.

Troin, J.-F. (2002), *Maroc: Régions, pays, territoires*, Paris, Maisonneuve & Larose.

Tuzani, N. (1979), *Al oumana fi al-Maghrib fi 'ahd Mawlay al- Hassan al-awwal* (Moroccan intendants in the time of Moulay Hassan Ier), Publications of the Humanities Department, Mohammed V University, Rabat.

Vatin, F. (2008), "L'esprit ingénieur. Pensée calculatoire et éthique économique", *Revue française de socio-économie*, 1, pp. 131–52.

Veguilla, V. (2009), "Conflits et actions collectives autour de l'exploitation du poulpe au Maroc", *Politique africaine*, 116, pp. 43–51.

———— (2011), "La gestion localisée de 'conflits invisibles': Les mobilisations économiques de jeunes Sahraouis à Dakhla", *Maghreb et sciences sociales 2011*, Paris, L'Harmattan, pp. 105–115.

Veinstein, G. (2017), *Les Ottomans: Variations sur une société d'Empire*, Paris, Éditions de l'EHESS.

Veyne, P. (1976 a), *Le Pain et le cirque: Sociologie historique d'un pluralisme politique*, Paris, Seuil. Partially translated as *Bread and Circuses: Historical Sociology and Political Pluralism*, London, Penguin Books, 1992.

———— (1976 b), *L'Inventaire des différences*, Paris, Seuil.

———— (1992), *Les Grecs ont-ils cru à leurs mythes? Essai sur l'imagination constituante*, Paris, Seuil. Translated by Paula Wissing as *Did the Greeks Believe their Myths?*, Chicago, University of Chicago Press, 1988.

Vinzant, J.-C. and Crothers, L. (1998), *Street-Level Leadership. Discretion and Legitimacy in Front-Line Public Service*, Washington D.C., Georgetown University.

Warde, I. (2010), *Islamic Finance in the Global Economy*, Edinburgh, Edinburgh University Press.

Warnier, J.-P. (1999), *Construire la culture matérielle: L'homme qui pensait avec ses doigts*, Paris, PUF.

REFERENCES

Warsheid, I. (2017), *Droit musulman et société au Sahara prémoderne: La justice islamique dans les oasis du Grand Touat aux xvii-xixe siècles*, Leiden, Brill.

Waterbury, J. (1970), *The Commander of the Faithful: The Moroccan Political Elite, a Study in Segmented Politics*, New York, Columbia University Press.

Weber, M. (1904) "The Objectivity of Knowledge in Social Sciences and Social Policy", in Hans Henrik Bruun et al., *Max Weber: Collective Methodological Writing*, Oxford, Routledge, translated by Hans Henrik Bruun, 2012.

———— (1904–1905), *The Protestant Ethic and the "Spirit" of Capitalism and Other Writings*, edited and translated by Baehr P. and Wells G., New York, Penguin, 2002.

———— (1907) "Stammler's 'Overcoming' of the Materialist Conception of History" in Hans Henrik Bruun et al., *Max Weber: Collective Methodological Writing*, Oxford, Routledge, translated by Hans Henrik Bruun, 2012.

———— (1910), "Weber's Second Reply to Rachfal, 1910", in David J. Chalcraft and Austin Harrington, and Mary Shields, *The Protestant Ethic Debate: Max Weber's Replies to His Critics, 1907–1910*, Liverpool, University of Liverpool Press, 2001.

———— (1920), *The Sociology of Religion*, translated by Ephraim Fischoff, Boston, Beacon Press, 1993.

———— (1922), *Economy and Society: An Outline of Interpretative Sociology*, Berkeley, University of California Press, 1978.

———— (1994), *Political Writings*, Lassman P. and Speirs R. (eds). Cambridge, Cambridge University Press.

———— (2004), *The Vocation Lectures: Science as a Vocation, Politics as a Vocation*, translated into English by Rodney Livingstone, Cambridge, Mass., Hackett Publishing

———— (2012), *Max Weber: Collective Methodological Writing*, translated by Hans Henrik Bruun et al., Oxford, Routledge.

Wilder, G. (2005), *The French Imperial Nation-State: Negritude and Colonial Humanism Between the Two World Wars*, Chicago, University of Chicago Press.

World Bank (1994), *Kingdom of Morocco: Preparing for 21st Century. Strengthening the Private Sector in Morocco*, Report 11894-MOR, Washington D.C., World Bank.

———— (1995), *Morocco—Country Economic Memorandum: Toward Higher Growth and Employment.*, vol. 1, report 14155-MOR, Washington D.C., World Bank.

———— (2007), *Marchés fonciers pour la croissance économique au Maroc*, Washington D.C., World Bank.

Yafout, M. (2017), "The activities of Adl Wal Ihsane in the neighbourhoods: How to build a 'non-legal' consensus from a 'tolerated' conflict", *International Development Policy*, 8, pp. 109–33.

Zaim, F. (1990), *Le Maroc et son espace méditerranéen: Histoire économique et sociale*, Rabat, Confluences.

Zaki, L. (2005), *Pratiques politiques au bidonville: Casablanca (2000–2005)*, PhD in political science, Institut d'études politiques de Paris.

———— (2010), "L'électrification temporaire des bidonvilles casablancais: Aspects et limites d'une transformation 'par le bas' de l'action publique", *Politique africaine*, 120, pp. 45–66.

REFERENCES

Zayani, A. (1967), *Al wajiz mina Attorjoumana al koubra al-lati jama'at akhbar al Maamour barran wa bahran* (Extracts from the Great Biography that Brought News of the Universe by Land and Sea), edited and with an introduction by M. El Mansour, Rabat, Ketabcom.

Zeroual, A. (2014), "Modernisation néolibérale et transformation du profil des dirigeants des entreprises publiques au Maroc: Cas de la Caisse de dépôt et de gestion (CDG): 1959–2009", *Afrika Focus*, 27 (2), pp. 23–47.

Zunz, O. (2012), *Philanthropy in America: A History*, Princeton, Princeton University Press.

INDEX

Adel, 27–28, 31, 149, 229–230
administration, 3, 10, 31, 34, 36,
  41, 50, 51, 54, 100, 117, 127
  139–164, 173, 181, 193, 196,
  202, 204, 210, 213, 225, 226
  direct, 28, 41, 123
  everyday, 9
  French, 41, 43–44
  indirect, 41
  itinerancy as a mode of, 35–36,
    123–124
  least cost, 37–38
  territorial, 9, 29, 49, 120, 128–
    130, 131–138
Akal ("land" in Amazigh), 160
allegiance, 8, 16, 22–23, 50–51,
  71, 121, 134, 138, 175, 195,
  200, 227
  Ceremony of, 9, 45, 51, 71
artform, 32–33, 35, 37, 39, 40,
  45, 47, 56, 84, 130, 141, 167,
  227, 232, 233

Bled Siba/Bled Makhzen, 22, 64
bureaucratisation, 9, 112, 190

charity politics, 11, 84, 201, 210
clientelism, 8, 80, 134, 198, 213

comparative political sociology,
  219
comparative politics, 219
comparativism, 219
consensus (*Einverständnis*), 139–
  140
  administration or government
    by consensus, 161–164, 223
  consensual action, 162–164
  Weber definition, 162
consensus, 89, 100, 113–114,
  215
  consensual, 82, 87, 88, 113,
    190
  consensus model, 113
  production of consensus, 113
  ideology of consensus, 113
Constitution, 61–62, 65–69, 70,
  78, 80, 82, 103–104, 110–113,
  129, 157, 224, 229, 231
co-optation, 60, 65, 67, 78, 127,
  134, 229
  spread of, 78–85

domination, 5–6, 12, 18, 41, 55,
  81, 95, 103, 118 153, 164,
  167, 169, 198, 216–217, 220,
  222–225, 231

INDEX

douar, 142, 149, 177

election, 5, 49, 61, 62, 65–70,
  78–85, 104, 111, 113, 127,
  128, 133, 141, 145, 148, 150,
  158, 177, 229
extraversion, 166, 173, 267

fitna (rebellion), 95

government, 7, 10, 39, 52, 66,
  79, 81, 105, 109, 115, 122,
  152, 166, 178, 217
  "alternance", 110, 182
  art of, 10, 190, 232
  at a distance, 24–28, 34, 96,
    138, 168, 190
  by contract, 170
  by mobility, 123–125
  direct, 28–31, 190
  diversity (plurality) of modes
    of, 6–9, 11, 23–24, 31, 55–
    56, 126, 138, 175, 224
  frugal or at least cost or low
    cost, 38–39, 42, 95, 151,
    155, 167, 171, 184
  governmental practices, 11,
    14, 17
  good, 193, 212
  head of, 61–70, 104
  imperial (modes of), xvii, 12,
    31–33, 38, 53, 55, 95, 137,
    167, 171
  indirect, 11, 24–28, 38, 51,
    84, 120, 123–126, 130,
    136, 138, 162, 169–190,
    215, 217, 221
  laissez-faire as a mode of, 133
  levels of or scale of, 48, 94
  mobile, 124
  of the fringes, 130–138
  of people, 226
  of territories, 123

powerpoint, 208
  technocratic, 182
Green March, 50–51, 102, 134

haiba (reverential fear), 95, 98,
  99–100
hajeb (chamberlain), 89, 95
"hania" ("peaceful"), 144, 145,
  152, 163
harka (action and movement),
  25, 26, 36, 38, 39, 75, 120,
  121, 232
  mobility of, 126
  roles of, 123–5
hijab (veil), 95, 96
hirak (2017–18), 224

ideal type
  Weberian definition, 6–8, 242
  thinking with, 6–11, 224
  empire ideal type, 7, 77, 138,
    184
  Nation-state ideal type, 7, 8, 9,
    12, 77–78
ideology, 7, 12–13, 55, 62, 77,
  112, 116, 139, 165, 171, 187,
  205, 215–216, 220, 221, 223
  ideology of change, 5
  colonial ideology, 41–42
  ideology of traditionalisation,
    45
  nationalist ideology, 46
  neoliberal ideology, 52, 165–
    167, 172, 183, 191, 192,
    197, 198, 204
  ideology of consensus, 113
  liberal ideology, 156, 172
  islamist ideology, 209, 211
imaginary, 2, 6, 12–14, 21, 32,
  54–55, 66, 78, 84, 96, 103,
  105, 115, 117, 119, 141, 162,
  166–167, 170, 191, 192, 198,
  219, 221–222, 227, 229

306

INDEX

definition of, 13
indirect rule, 41, 248
intermediation, 7, 75, 95–96, 134, 138, 151, 152, 201–202, 204–205
    intermediaries, 11, 24, 25, 42, 53, 83, 96, 98, 139–140, 152, 155, 162, 163, 166, 167, 173, 181, 184, 185, 187, 190, 202, 203, 232–333
intercession, 75, 79, 84, 151

khadim (servant of the prince), 15, 55, 108, 195–196

legitimacy, 7, 9, 11, 25, 48, 52, 53, 55, 66, 67, 70, 83, 85, 89, 94, 104–105, 164, 173, 181, 187, 189, 195, 205, 207, 211, 212, 216
    legitimisation process, 6, 16, 23, 32, 34, 59, 106–107, 166, 173, 183, 197, 200
    legitimate, 4, 55, 62, 70, 79, 82, 92, 95, 106, 197, 230

Moroccanisation, 52, 179
Makhzen (governing institution), 10, 23, 26, 27, 28, 30, 34, 35, 39, 40, 41, 42, 43, 68, 96, 98, 101, 116, 117, 120, 121, 122, 123, 125, 126, 134, 151, 171, 186, 195, 196, 198, 199, 200, 202, 224, 228
    concept of, 11, 167
    dar al Makhzen, 11, 37, 100, 199, 232
    makhzen route, 123–126
    economic *makhzen*, 215–217
malik (king), 89, 98, 108, 112
maqassid (finalities), 212
maslaha (general interest), 171

mediation, 49, 54, 56, 59, 81, 122, 151, 153, 167–168, 177, 194, 226, 230
mobility, 125–126, 151, 221
    art of mobility, 51, 151
    logistics of mobility, 35–36
    governing by mobility, 123–125
    social mobility, 157–158, 208, 210
muqaddam, 2–4, 9, 128, 139, 140, 141–158, 159, 161, 163, 223

naib (representative of authority), 139, 140, 141, 153–161, 163
naturalisation, 42, 69, 75, 105, 106, 115, 167–168, 192
    of co-optation, 85
    of the curse, 103
    of imperial traits, 52–55
    of neoliberalism, 211
    of violence, 102–112
negotiation
    dissidence as, 10
    harka as, 25
    in the empire, 34, 49, 94–95, 120, 126, 171, 180–182, 190
    in the colony (Protectorate), 41
    for Independence, 46
    in the Nation-state, 61, 79, 151, 154, 188
neoliberalism, 46, 53, 165, 169, 170, 173, 189, 191–217
    elective affinity, 55, 116, 166–167, 209, 221
nisba (descendance), 69, 80, 227
normalisation, 105–106, 216

orientalism, 5, 41, 43
    in reverse, 5

INDEX

participation, 5, 54, 59, 66–67, 69, 80, 82, 84, 88, 106, 177, 189, 191, 197, 198, 203–204, 205, 229
participative democracy, 67, 84, 132, 222
pragmatism, 189, 204, 212

radicalism, 144
rationalisation, 103
 of archaisms, 43, 155, 157
 of co-optation, 79
 nation-state form of, 104
reform
 reformism, 10, 23, 69, 175, 212–213
 in the Sharifian empire, 25, 27, 42, 120
 in the independent Morocco, 10, 15, 52, 53, 68, 103, 112–113, 149, 160, 161, 228, 230–231
 neoliberal, 167, 191, 192, 194, 197, 205, 212–213
responsibility, xvii, 9, 11, 53, 58–60, 98, 176, 189, 191, 196, 198, 201, 225, 228, 231
 ethic of, 187, 193
 of the government, 2, 113
 of the King or the Sultan, 25, 39, 42, 90, 106, 110–113, 125, 231
 of the muqaddam, 2, 141, 142, 146–148, 150
 of the naïb, 163
 political, 11, 231
 of the state, 10–11, 32, 180, 184
 social or societal, 185, 207

Saint-Simonianism, 41, 172, 206
semsar (courtiers), 152, 163, 223
Sharifian empire, 2, 9, 21, 64

and its regions, 23–24
modes of government
nomadic territories, 121
violence in, 94–95
sovereignty, 8, 9, 22–23, 25, 32, 42, 50, 64–65, 69, 75, 76, 78, 87, 101, 110, 117, 119, 123, 124, 138, 170, 171, 189, 190
staging, 7, 9, 17, 36, 51, 60, 70–76, 77, 79, 100–102, 120, 214, 219, 220
style, 41, 99, 100, 133, 186, 232
syassa, 25, 27, 246

tribes
 in controlling borders, 185
 history, 157
 Maader, 25
 vs. Makhzen, 10, 122
 mountain, 27
 Saharan, 22, 134
 of Tétouan region, 29
 weakness, 158

violence, xvii, 6, 7, 10, 25, 46, 49, 55, 56, 58–60, 65, 75, 87, 109, 119, 171, 196, 222
 avoiding violence, 59, 95–96
 imperial violence, 93
 of the Moroccan nation-state, 87–93, 97–112
 open and pervasive, 88
 in the Sharifian empire, 94–95, 222
 and the struggle for power, 89
violent struggle for power, 90

weaving of register, 19
weaving of a rug, 19
weaving of time (or woven time), 15, 18, 19, 23, 44–46, 219–223